HOWARD HAWKS
AMERICAN ARTIST

Edited by
Jim Hillier and Peter Wollen

BRITISH FILM INSTITUTE

bfi

BFI PUBLISHING

First published in 1996 by the
BRITISH FILM INSTITUTE
21 Stephen Street, London W1P 2LN

The British Film Institute exists to promote appreciation, enjoyment, protection and development of moving image culture in and throughout the whole of the United Kingdom. Its activities include the National Film and Television Archive; the National Film Theatre; the Museum of the Moving Image; the London Film Festival; the production and distribution of film and video; funding and support for regional activities; Library and Information Services; Stills, Posters and Designs; Research; Publishing and Education; and the monthly *Sight and Sound* magazine.

British Library Cataloguing-in-Publication Data.
A catalogue record for this book is available from the British Library.

ISBN 0-85170-592-8
     0-85170-593-6 pbk

Cover designed by Mark Goddard.
Title logo designed by Dewynters Plc.

Typeset by Fakenham Photosetting, Norfolk.
Printed and bound in Great Britain.

CONTENTS

Introduction

PETER WOLLEN

Individual films by Howard Hawks were noted by intelligent critics from the late 1920s onwards. Yet it was not until Jacques Rivette wrote his 1953 article on *The Genius of Howard Hawks* (reprinted in this volume) that he was considered to be a major artist. Rivette was one of the central core of critics who wrote for the *Cahiers du Cinéma* and revolutionized film criticism by launching the *politique des auteurs*, the controversial and programmatic idea that great film artists existed even within Hollywood itself. Hawks, together with Hitchcock, was put forward as the prime example of an auteur director – one who could be discussed in the same way that any other kind of artist could be discussed. Previously the Hollywood director, whatever his talent, had been automatically demeaned as little more than a competent functionary of the studio system.

Hawks's new status as auteur was endorsed both in England and North America from the early 1960s on. In 1961 a full Hawks retrospective, organized by Richard Roud, gave critics their first opportunity to survey his career as a whole and, besides solidifying his reputation in France, this led to serious consideration of his work by Andrew Sarris in New York and, in England, by the critics gathered around *Movie* magazine, including Victor Perkins and Robin Wood, as well as by Lee Russell, writing for *New Left Review*. In 1968 Robin Wood wrote his magisterial book on Hawks for the BFI's *Cinema One* series and the following year I myself submitted Hawks's *œuvre* to an elaborate structuralist analysis in my book *Signs and Meaning in the Cinema*, which aimed to place Hawks, along with John Ford, at the centre of serious film studies.

For the next twenty years there was a vigorous expansion of writing about Hawks, particularly in America, with many fine discussions of individual films, looked at from a wide variety of angles – feminist appraisals, production studies, ideological critiques, and so on. Looking back in this changed context at my own earlier work, I am struck by how the structuralist methodology of the 60s still seems appropriate for writing about Hawks. Today, of course, structuralism is widely supposed to have been superseded by post-structuralism, which itself might be seen as dissolving into the miasma of cultural studies. Structuralist analysis, I would still

1

maintain, had the merit of providing a way of looking systematically at a director's career, observing first a primary armature of repeated motifs – both semantemes and stylemes, as the jargon of the time would have it – and then, running counter to that framework of repetition, a set of differences and variations which were themselves structured.

Structuralism in fact posited two structures – a structure of sameness and generality and a counter-structure of difference and singularity. My own argument, in *Signs and Meaning*, was that Hawks's work was structured synchronically by a contrast between his adventure dramas (which always had a comic subtext) and his comedies (which always parodied his dramas). Consider fishing, for instance, first in *Tiger Shark* and *To Have and Have Not* and then in *Man's Favorite Sport*. Even anomalous films like *Scarface* fell within this pattern, as Hawks himself recognized when, in Joseph McBride's interview book, *Hawks on Hawks*, he accepted that *Scarface* was essentially a comedy. At the same time, within each series, drama and comedy, Hawks built up a diachronic structure over time by repetition and variation film by film.

This structuralist approach, I was later delighted to discover, received some confirmation from an unexpected source. In June 1955, speaking to a journalist about Hawks's recently released film *Land of the Pharaohs*, William Faulkner noted that 'It's *Red River* all over again. The Pharaoh is the cattle baron, his jewels are the cattle, and the Nile is the Red River. But the thing about Howard is, he knows it's the same movie, and he knows how to make it.' In effect, Faulkner was outlining the classic auteurist case for Hawks, the realization that, in film after film, Hawks repeated himself, albeit giving each repetition a new twist, a new flavour. Hawks worked in almost all the genres but, in each one, he would find a way to make a quintessentially Hawksian film. In the terms which Hawks himself repeatedly used, 'I stole from myself'. But he did it differently each time.

William Faulkner had a long and fruitful relationship with Howard Hawks, lasting for over thirty years. He worked on the scripts of six Hawks films, as well as a number of unrealized projects. Modestly, he described himself as 'a patcher-upper' for Hawks. His job was to find a new way of writing an old scene, so that it fitted with a new group of characters in a different type of story, at a different place in a different narrative. Soon after Hawks had first met Faulkner, he described to him what he wanted from his writers: 'The first thing I want is a story. The next thing I want is a character. Then I jump to anything I think is interesting.' He frequently emphasized the importance of creating individual scenes round interesting situations and it was Faulkner's job, rather than story construction, to make situations interesting.

When John Wayne started working with Hawks he was told, 'Duke, if you can make three good scenes in this picture and don't annoy the audience, the rest of the time, you'll be good.' For further emphasis, he insisted, 'Yeah. If I make five good scenes in this picture, and don't annoy the audience, I think I'll be good.' Talking about cameramen, he elaborated: 'I tell them, "If you make two good scenes for me, you can make two mediocre ones and one bad one." All I'm interested in is the good one. So they go ahead and take chances, and their work shows it. Because you people [critics, audiences] pass up the bad scenes, but you really appreciate the good one.' Another scriptwriter, A. I. Bezzerides, observed that, in each film, Hawks wanted to achieve 'one good scene, the moment that makes the picture work or not, the one good scene that spills over to the others'.

Hawks took a lot of trouble to make sure he had these memorable scenes in every picture. He would slow down the whole production while everybody stood around, encouraging his collaborators to throw out ideas until he got a scene exactly the way he wanted it. He rarely stuck strictly to his script while shooting, always looking for ways of introducing a new element into familiar material, trying to improve material which had already passed the test of time. Of course, he stole not only from himself, but from other directors too. He prized Jules Furthman as a writer because he had a fantastic memory for scenes in other pictures, all the ways in which somebody else had done a scene, which Hawks could then steal, re-frame and give new life to. Hawks often acknowledged his debt to Ford and Lubitsch, but I think that perhaps he owed most of all to Sternberg. Furthman, of course, had been Sternberg's preferred scriptwriter – he helped write *Underworld*, which Hawks also worked on, a crucial film which influenced Hawks films as far apart as *A Girl in Every Port* and *Rio Bravo*.

Jules Furthman also wrote *Morocco* for Sternberg, with the Marlene Dietrich role which Hawks later recycled to give added lustre to Bacall's image in *To Have and Have Not*. Furthman worked on this Hawks film too, inventing cigarette gags, finding (with Faulkner) new lines for Lauren Bacall – creating the scenes in which Hawks defined what later came to be known as the Hawksian woman. Hawks took the cover-girl created for *Harper's Bazaar* by Diana Vreeland and her photographer Louise Dahl-Wolfe, made her take exercises to deepen her voice and then melded her image with Marlene Dietrich and with his own wife, 'Slim' Hawks (and perhaps an early noir-ish touch of Veronica Lake?). The Hawksian woman turned out to be not simply a fashion plate or a projection of Hawks's fantasies (which, as Bacall and Slim both note, were basically Svengali fantasies) but also a palimpsest of movie lore about girls-with-a-past.

Hawks described Furthman as contributing 'a kind of cynicism, an idea of doing different things'. It is the appeal of the cynicism which is especially interesting. Andrew Sarris puts it well when he writes of 'Hawks's distinctively bitter view of life'. Raymond Chandler spotted it when he noted that Hawks brought 'the gift of atmosphere and the requisite touch of hidden sadism' to *The Big Sleep*. He also liked Bogart's performance (in effect the new Bogart lastingly created by Hawks) for his 'sense of humour that contains the grating undertone of contempt' – again Furthman's contribution, on Hawks's behalf. Jacques Rivette comments on laughter that 'sticks in your throat'.

In effect, Hawks's screenwriters were his group of buddies, just like the groups of airmen or cowboys in his adventure films – the brilliant drunk, the hard-bitten professional, the crabby old man. Leigh Brackett, of course,

3

was a woman, but, as Hawks put it, she wrote 'like a man. She writes good.' Faulkner was a man's man, like Hawks – obsessed with flying and with the danger of death. They would go hunting and fishing together (they caught the fish, Slim gutted and cleaned them). When he hired Leigh Brackett, sight unseen, Hawks expected her to be a man. She turned out to be a woman, but she was 'good', she was professional. She had fun. Hawks, of course, was the sheriff, the commander – slow, deliberate, undemonstrative. He showed in *Red River* how not to behave as a leader if you wanted to get the job done. He got his own way with the crew and the cast and even within the studio.

Using *Bringing Up Baby* as a detailed test case, Richard B. Jewell has demonstrated that Hollywood studios were not just film factories, assembly lines for movies. In fact, they both were and they weren't. Hawks had as much power as any director – according to his biographer, Todd McCarthy, as much as Hitchcock, perhaps more than Ford – but this degree of autonomy was still unusual. Hawks was able to deploy his WASP background, his family money, his Ivy League education at Cornell, his tough-guy image, his immaculate suits, his flying and hunting and motor-racing stories, his Hemingwayesque myth, in order to intimidate executives. He would stop working when an executive came on the set. On top of that he was also a Hollywood insider – he began as a producer before he became a director, back in the silent days.

Hawks's first wife, Athole, was the sister of Norma Shearer – a relationship that made Hawks into Irving Thalberg's brother-in-law. His own brother was a powerful agent. Hawks cultivated influential people. He had a support network of writers. He became friends with his stars. He gathered actors and directors into his informal Moraga Drive motorcycle club. He entertained on a lavish scale. He hosted croquet tournaments. He knew exactly what he wanted from the studios and he was uncompromising in getting it. And he was literate. As John Ford curtly remarked, in a reply to a Hollywood executive who wondered why Hawks knew so much about stories, 'He reads books.' Finally, most important of all, his films made money.

Shortly before *Land of the Pharaohs* was released, in May 1955, André Bazin was writing his famous essay 'How Could You Possibly Be a Hitchcocko-Hawksian?' which appeared in the February number of *Cahiers du Cinéma*. Bazin took considerable care to keep his distance from the militant auteurism of his younger colleagues while giving them full credit for redirecting their readers to the formal and technical qualities of film-making, rather than simply to its subject matter. A director like Hawks, Bazin conceded, brought a moral dimension and a quality of intelligence even to films whose scripts and subject matter were frankly petty and fatuous. These scripts, of course, so obviously 'idiotic' to Bazin, had often been written by William Faulkner – a man who had won the Nobel Prize for Literature just a few years before. A strange paradox!

Since Bazin's day, the pendulum has swung the other way. The critical emphasis has shifted away from Hawks's approach to film-making and his no-nonsense style – no flashbacks, no screwed-up camera angles, no unnecessary camera movements, no unnecessary close-ups, nothing to annoy the audience. It has turned instead to his stories, his world-view, his vision of human relationships. At the same time the spotlight has fallen on the issue of gender and sexual politics in Hawks's films – the homosocial world of the male group, the pros and cons of the Hawksian woman, active and assertive, but also afflicted by an irrecuperable lack. Attention has shifted away from the action dramas (albeit conversation pieces in disguise) to the screwball comedies, in which the man in a negligée or losing his trousers provides a strange counterpoint to the woman with a husky voice and professional skills.

There are other recurrent tropes in Hawks's stories, of which the two most significant are probably the triangle of two male friends in love with the same woman and the near-suicidal death of one of the group, acutely described by Andrew Sarris as situations which 'have quasi-suicidal climaxes, but the moral arithmetic balances out because in each instance the martyr is a replacement in an obligatory situation'. This last category is strongly represented in Hawks's 30s films but seems to fade away again with the onset of World War II. The martyr's death in *Air Force*, written by Faulkner, is handled differently – as a check-through of pilot's procedures for take-off, experienced by the dying man in a delirium. It is almost as if there are two separate paths which threaten male friendship – the path of martyrdom and the path of marriage.

The screwball comedies present the same dilemma but from a different angle. As Stanley Cavell points out, they are set in the latency period, their heroes and heroines are immature, even infantile, in their behaviour, and they arrive at maturity only reluctantly and through a series of mishaps. The relationships between men and women are portrayed as parodic versions of the relationships between predator and prey, full of outrageous innuendo and double entendre. *Bringing Up Baby* starts with a hero (Cary Grant) who is meant to get married the very next day, before his life is brusquely and uncontrollably thrown into a downward spiral of humiliation by a chance encounter with a madcap young woman (Katharine Hepburn). In the end, he realizes that she is the one he is fated to marry, the one who has seen him at his most abject but also brought him the most fun.

Bringing Up Baby, like *Hatari!* or *Man's Favorite Sport*, is a comedy about hunting, about pursuit and the chase, about facing danger and being lured, about capture and entrapment. The two leopard hunters end up being captured and caged themselves, by a psychiatrist and a sheriff. In the end Grant tames and cages the leopard (a wild leopard rather than the tame leopard which is Susan's pet) and, his mission as hunter and rescuer accomplished, swoons into his inamorata's strong arms. These endless reversals – man/woman, predator/prey, adult/infant, in control/out of control – structure all of Hawks's comedies. In Hawks's dramas, the nurturing male group takes the place of the supportive mother, while in the comedies the dizzy dominatrix provokes his regression and loss of equilibrium. In

5

considering them, Cavell uses standard psychoanalytic categories to discuss the way in which the characters negotiate the transition to mature adulthood and break out of their infantile states of masculine entrancement and feminine automatism. I would prefer to approach the Hawksian world down a rather different psychoanalytic path, through Michael Balint's concepts of 'philobatism' and 'ocnophilia'.

In his book *Thrills and Regression*, a psychoanalytic study of the attraction of fun and thrills – the staples of Hawks's comedies and adventure films – Balint traces the origins of two polarized tendencies, the urge to seek out danger and the urge to clutch at security, to the moment when the child first learns to walk, either venturing out into the open space of a room or feeling its way cautiously around the edge of the space, from piece of furniture to piece of furniture. Like weaning, this phase represents a process of detachment from the mother, from the tactile and the secure, to the visual and the unsafe, until full motor co-ordination is finally achieved. Thrills come from seeking to relive this primal process, encountering danger with confidence that everything is going to be all right – the car will not fly off the roller-coaster, the plane will not crash, the savage beast can safely be subdued. Comedy ensues when the ocnophil is forced, uncomfortably, to play the philobat or when the philobat, humiliatingly, loses motor control and is brought down to earth. Tragedy ensues when the philobat's confidence and security are shattered permanently – breakdown, death.

For Hawks fun comes from the humiliation of the hero by a dominant woman, who is master of the social and motor skills he lacks. In *Hawks on Hawks*, Joseph McBride asks him whether dressing Cary Grant up in woman's clothing is done 'to humiliate the character to the utmost possible degree'. Hawks accepts the term 'humiliation' and goes on to add, 'I think it's fun to have a woman dominant and let the man be the funniest.' Then Hawks describes how Cary Grant, appearing in drag in *I Was a Male War Bride*, wanted to produce a convincing simulation of a woman. Hawks had to stop him. He told Grant, 'Just act like a man in woman's clothes.' To demonstrate what he wanted, Hawks himself put on a red wig and a WAC's outfit to attend a party given by the military when the crew arrived in Germany to begin shooting. 'I want to tell you, I looked funnier than Grant did. I came in, pulled out a cigar and said, "Got a light, General?" He didn't know who or what I was. He thought I was a WAC. Cary was having convulsions, and he said, "You sold me, I know just what to do."' Hawks's films are full of similar scenes of burlesque transvestism.

For Hawks, it is not the accurate simulation of femininity which was important, but the element of travesty, of ridiculous disparity between signifier and signified. In her book on the male impersonator Vesta Tilley, Sara Maitland observed that Tilley's simulation of a man challenged the 'myth that the division between the genders was natural, immutable and absolute'. Hawks's aim was quite different. On the contrary, the effect which he wanted – the fun – was dependent on the preservation of the myth of sexual difference as something natural and absolute. His calculated use of burlesque transvestism depended precisely on the consciousness of its incongruity and what Hawks would call its 'craziness'. He was much closer to the world of the pantomime dame, as described by Peter Ackroyd in his account of theatrical cross-dressing – 'The dame is never effeminate; she is never merely a drag artist, since she always retains her male identity. The performer is clearly a man dressed as an absurd and ugly woman, and much of the comedy is derived from the fact that he is burlesquing himself as a male actor.'

As Ackroyd points out, this kind of burlesque, while it breaks sexual taboos up to a point, serves primarily to allay anxieties about feminine aggression, overt feminine sexuality and male homosexuality, by a kind of contained explosion, evoking laughter rather than panic. It is plausible to argue, I think, that Hawks's anxieties go back to the 1920s, the decade which saw the final collapse of a traditional Victorian concept of femininity and the advent of a physically active, sexually aggressive and professionally ambitious image of women. As Laura Mulvey points out, in her essay on *Gentlemen Prefer Blondes*, Hawks's obsession with gender and the perils of sexual difference goes back to the years of the flapper and gold-digger cycle of films (with Colleen Moore, Clara Bow, Joan Crawford and Louise Brooks) which were prominent during the 1920s, as Hawks first arrived in Hollywood and began his long career in the film industry.

In his eccentric little article on 'The Modernity of Howard Hawks' – a tribute to the director who first converted him to love of the cinema – the great French cinephile Henri Langlois argued that Hawks was the breakthrough director of American modernism in the cinema. Remembering back to the beginning of sound, Langlois considered that Hawks was the first film director to reject the expressionist and the ornamental in favour of a streamlined economy of means and a rationalized functionalism. His early works, from *The Dawn Patrol* to *Ceiling Zero*, are 'stripped bare almost to the point of abstraction'. The camerawork remains 'the simplest in the world', generally at eye-level, following the logic of sound film, dialogue combined with action. In Langlois's words, Hawks created a new dramaturgy 'derived from an agglomeration of facts, words, noises, movements, situations, as a motor is assembled'. Or, put another way, 'Hawks, like Gropius, conceived his films as one might conceive a typewriter, a motor or a bridge'.

Hawks was indeed trained as an engineer. This modernity of Hawks, which Langlois pinpointed – his view of a film as a well designed, well made and well functioning piece of engineering – is substantiated by Hawks himself. In *Hawks on Hawks*, he recounts his first step towards a Hollywood career:

I was sort of an assistant property man [as a summer job]. Douglas Fairbanks was making a picture, and he wanted a modern set, a modern apartment. Nobody knew what the hell a modern thing was, but I had studied about five or six years of architecture, and I knew, so I said, 'Oh, I can do that.'

7

However embroidered this memory may be (and Slim Hawks later accused Howard of being a compulsive mythomane) it certainly indicates Hawks's image of himself as a modernist. It is linked to his fascination with speed – both on the motor-racing track and in the delivery of dialogue – and his fascination with flight and aviation. In fact, the history of cinema runs absolutely in parallel with that of aviation. Hawks lived through the pioneering days of them both, through the two great twentieth-century conquests of space and time.

Aviation runs like a red thread through Hawks's early career – *The Air Circus* (1928), *The Dawn Patrol* (1932), *Ceiling Zero* (1936), *Only Angels Have Wings* (1939), *Air Force* (1943). This is the heroic period, of course, which saw the rise of Pan-American carrying the mail in South America and the triumph of Lindbergh flying the Atlantic. It is aviation, too, which linked Hawks to Faulkner. Hawks read Faulkner's first novel, *Soldier's Pay*, when it was published in the early 1920s and introduced it to his literary friends in New York, including Ben Hecht and Charlie MacArthur – not yet scriptwriters themselves, but eventually to be staple writers for Hawks in Hollywood, just like Faulkner. Significantly, while both Hawks and Faulkner told endless tales of their aviation adventures, Faulkner never in fact flew a plane (training as an engineer) and Hawks, according to Slim, got air-sick. Faulkner had enrolled as an air cadet at the very end of World War I, but in the RAF (across the border in Canada). *Soldier's Pay* is a book about pilots, about their cult of masculinity, the tragic impact of the war and its psychologically disturbing aftermath. It is surely significant that this post-war malaise coincided with the appearance of the new woman of the 1920s, a bewitching creature who provoked both fascination and fear.

Seen this way, Hawks is one of a group of artists decisively influenced by the war and by the heroic myth of aviation – Faulkner, Junger, Brecht, Malraux, Saint-Exupéry, even Auden and Isherwood. He belongs to a specific strand in modernism, one which sought to find a new, modern form of heroism in a world of machines and technology, which accepted functionalism, while seeking to transcend it in the heroic persona of the aviator. Hawks's modernity involved both his own fascination with the film as machine form and his identification with the myth of the aviator as hero of the machine age. In this context, the film-maker most like Hawks is Renoir. It is strange, though not surprising, that André Bazin never saw the connection between Hawks and Renoir, between *Only Angels Have Wings* and *La Règle du jeu*, both released in 1939.

La Règle du jeu has an aviator hero worshipped by the crowd – an explicitly modern hero, albeit one with suicidal tendencies. The main action is set in a house party cut off from the world, an elite group which is bound together by ritual and strictly preserves its exclusivity. The story revolves round three male friends who are all in love with the same woman. It has a long series of hunting scenes and the activities of hunting, gamekeeping and poaching are crucial metaphors structuring the film. It switches between crazy comedy and tragic drama, as chaos spreads uncontrollably throughout the house and aggressive female sexuality threatens to destroy the

8

solidarity of the group. The comedy ends in tragedy with the quasi-suicide of the aviator hero, a Hawksian climax of a kind in which, as Andrew Sarris put it, 'the moral arithmetic balances out because in each instance the martyr is a replacement in an obligatory situation'. Order and the solidarity of the group are finally restored through the expulsion of the poacher and the *raté* – a character played by Jean Renoir himself, the would-be professional who is an abject failure, who is simply not 'good enough'.

Jacques Rivette's seminal article on Hawks veered between acknowledging that Hawks was drawn towards 'dark forces and strange fascinations', that his view of life was bitter and pessimistic, and at the same time admiring the typical Hawksian hero for his 'pragmatic intelligence' and for his 'maturity', the mastery he exercises in an adult world threatened by the dark forces which generate the squalor and infantilism of the comedies. Rivette saw the modernity of *homo hawksianus* as precarious and under constant threat from the infantile, the primitive and the animal. It is as if reason and modernity are constantly overwhelmed by the death instinct, by the repetition of 'the same actions, endlessly recurring, which Hawks builds up with the persistence of a man obsessed' so that anger, hatred and passion finally break through the defence of professionalism and everything seems to 'whirl madly about, as if at the mercy of a capricious maelstrom'. Rivette can come to terms with this clash of dramatic extremes only by seeing it as an affirmation of life.

I see it rather differently – as a tragic recognition that the excitement of adventure, the aviator's philobatic thrill, can never be separated from the fascination of death, that the obsessive affirmation of the value of heroism and professionalism is constantly subverted by the irrational ('crazy') and self-destructive drives which undercut all human action and constantly subject us to a humiliation at which, if we are to avoid the failure of suicide, we can only laugh. This is not a heartening view of the world, any more than Faulkner's is, but it is one which Hawks gives us time and time again with his customary efficiency and inventiveness. For Hawks the remedy against the horror of life was to be found in the pleasure of making things, the kind of experience he enjoyed while working with Faulkner on *Land of the Pharaohs*, when, as Bruce Kawin recounts, he remembered the fun which they had working out the mechanics of 'a system of sand hydraulics to seal the pyramid'.

The mechanics of cinema were like the mechanics of the pyramids. Making a film was like working out a hydraulic system so that the movie would work without waste and be effective. It would also be a monument of sorts. Of course, for Hawks, this meant being good enough, and yet, at the same time, it also meant being ready to reveal unconscious obsessions and fascinations and flaws, repeated over and over again in every single story. Hawks's career was not marked simply by a modernist rationality (Langlois) or a 'pragmatic intelligence' (Rivette). He was driven. He was a fantasist. Like Hitchcock, Hawks found that, within the Hollywood system, he could make enough space for himself to tell the stories he wanted to tell more or less in the way he wanted to tell them. But, unlike Hitchcock, he was often uncertain where he was going. He worked intuitively and spontaneously, improvising on the set, repeating himself obsessively, but always looking for something 'different', something 'crazy'. He showed us both the pathos and the absurdity of modern life, both thrill and abjection, heroism and hysteria.

A note on sources

As well as the essays reprinted in this collection, I drew on Robin Wood's *Howard Hawks* (London: Secker & Warburg, 1968) and Joseph McBride's invaluable book-length series of interviews, *Hawks on Hawks* (Berkeley, Calif.: University of California Press, 1962, reissued in London by Faber & Faber, 1996), as well as his collection of critical essays, *Focus On Howard Hawks* (Englewood Cliffs, NJ: Prentice-Hall, 1972). I also looked at the crucial interview conducted by Jacques Rivette, François Truffaut and Jacques Becker (who happened to be chatting to Hawks when the other two arrived and stayed on at their request) which was first published in *Cahiers du Cinéma* no. 56, February 1956, and later reprinted in *La Politique des Auteurs* (Paris: Editions Champ Libre, 1972) and translated in Sarris, *Interviews with Film Directors* (see bibliography).

William Faulkner's extended relationship with Hawks is covered in Joseph Blotner's two-volume *Faulkner: A Biography* (London: Chatto & Windus, 1974) and studied in depth in Bruce Kawin's *Faulkner and Film* (New York: Frederick Ungar, 1967). Blotner's edition of the *Selected Letters of William Faulkner* (New York: Random House, 1977) contains frequent mentions of Hawks. I quoted from a Chandler letter cited in Frank MacShane's *The Life of Raymond Chandler* (London: Jonathan Cape, 1976). Further (not always complimentary) material on Hawks's life came from Lauren Bacall's autobiography, *By Myself* (London: Jonathan Cape, 1979) and Slim Keith's *Slim* (New York: Simon & Schuster, 1990), whose own early career as a model is described in Diana Vreeland's *D.V.* (New York: Random House, 1974).

On transvestism, I consulted and cited Sara Maitland's *Vesta Tilley* (London: Virago, 1986) and Peter Ackroyd's *Dressing Up. Transvestism and Drag: The History of an Obsession* (London: Thames & Hudson, 1979). For my theoretical approach I am particularly indebted to Michael Balint's *Thrills and Regressions* (London: Karnac, 1987). With Laura Mulvey, I had earlier investigated the relevance of Balint's ideas to the subject of aviation in our 1980 film, *AMY!*. My thoughts on Hawks, Renoir and aviation were first presented in a public lecture (1995) at the Wexner Center, Columbus, Ohio.

I dutifully reread, of course, the pages on Hawks in my own *Signs and Meaning in the Cinema* (London: Secker & Warburg; Bloomington: Indiana University Press, 1969) and I also revisited Andrew Sarris's fine introduction to Hawks in his classic reference book *The American Cinema* (New York: E. P. Dutton, 1968) and the euphoric notes in my now tattered copy of Yves Boisset and J.-P. Coursodon's *Vingt ans du cinéma américain* (Paris: Editions C.I.B., 1961), in which I once obsessively ticked off every

Hawks film that I saw. I also benefited from the chance to talk about Hawks with Todd MacCarthy, whose long-awaited biography is due to be published next year.

Where not given in the text, publication details of works cited are to be found in the Bibliography.

Howard Hawks, in 1965

A Girl in Every Port

JEAN-GEORGE AURIOL

From *La Revue du Cinéma*, December 1928.
Translated by John Moore.

There is nothing suspect about the unanimity of this film's success. Of the current American output, *A Girl in Every Port* was the film most likely to satisfy the jaded expectations of moviegoers; the most likely to divert. Whoever had the idea of showing it at the Ursulines is to be congratulated on their flair.

It is quite some time since I first drew attention to Howard Hawks, his simplifying style, the way he composes films through violent cuts, the astonishing seductiveness of his images. Hawks does everything we know he should be given to do with the same simplicity, the same comforting sureness. He is one of the directors who – without ageing, assisted by a well chosen group of courageous colleagues who know and love their profession, veritable magicians in their specialities – are keeping up the great American tradition.[1] Nearly all films of this sort give me the same degree of satisfaction and pleasure.

I hope that by now everyone will have seen *A Girl in Every Port*. But I will take my turn at mentioning the beauty of the little Dutch girl and the little Argentinian (Maria Alba); and the athletic perfection of Louise Brooks, alluring and slappable as usual. The hilarious consequences of McLaglen's fury each time he sees the mark of an unknown predecessor – always the same one – on the women he finds. The perfect inevitability of the brutal encounters between the two buddies and the naval shore patrol. And the scene of friendly teasing where Armstrong puts something on his shoulder to play the officer, and when he lets himself be assailed four times in succession and in four different ways, each time forcing McLaglen to

---

1. The cinema is still living on the habits (techniques, mannerisms) of the American school which have dominated it so far; even though Sternberg goes beyond these practices with his tremendous work Underworld, even though Murnau only accepts them from time to time, good-naturedly or as a ruse.

   Until a new order is established, the few works created in Europe, by poets, to have given us a glimpse of something different, can only be repeated through a miracle: for the cinema industry in our countries is in a ridiculous state, and very strangely run. So the next revolution will come from America again: indeed, it has already been proclaimed as that of the talking film with sound. It is not yet possible to have any idea of its consequences.

stop flirting with a beautiful girl to come to his rescue. And at the end where the two friends fall into each other's arms after bashing each other's faces in.

And all the rest of it. Yes! You eavesdrop on what happens in this film, like a lucky passer-by peering over a fence, doubled up with laughter.

It is very striking that our first entry should both acknowledge Hawks and speak of 'the great American tradition', and this in 1928, but then *La Revue du Cinéma* at this time also featured articles on directors such as King Vidor, Frank Borzage, Josef von Sternberg, Allan Dwan (though their interest in American cinema was balanced by an equal interest in Pabst and Lang, Eisenstein and Pudovkin, Man Ray, Walter Ruttman and Luis Buñuel, and Carl Theodor Dreyer). Jean-George Auriol was editor of the *Revue* in both its 1928–31 and 1946–9 phases. This journal was the forerunner of *Les Cahiers du Cinéma*, founded in 1951, in both its look and its aesthetic preferences. The first issue of *Cahiers* was dedicated to Auriol and in the hundredth issue of *Cahiers*, in 1959, Jacques Doniol-Valcroze commented that 'In the minds of the founders of *Cahiers* it was never anything other than continuing the work undertaken by Jean-George Auriol'. André Bazin contributed to the *Revue* in the 1940s, while developing many of his important ideas, and the way in which Auriol compares the state of the cinema in France, and Europe in general, with American cinema prefigures very precisely the way that *Cahiers* critics such as François Truffaut, Jacques Rivette, Jean-Luc Godard and others of the 1950s saw the relationship.

Henri Langlois, in his 1963 essay 'The Modernity of Howard Hawks', reprinted in this volume, returns to the moment at which Auriol was writing and in other ways picks up on his ideas. Langlois evokes 'the Paris of 1928, which was rejecting expressionism' and embracing the simplicity – the 'American-ness' – of American cinema.

Ceiling Zero

OTIS FERGUSON

From *The New Republic*, 5 February 1936.

Reprinted in *The Film Criticism of Otis Ferguson*, ed. Robert Wilson (Philadelphia: Temple University Press, 1971).

Unless the movie industry surprises everybody, including itself, *Ceiling Zero* will be one of the best pictures of 1936. In a sense this film is the kind of thing the movies do best; in another sense it is the sort of thing they seldom do at all. It has dash, vigor, the fascination of strange, deep, and meaningful devices; but it carries a sting, it has several things to say about the lives of men, without benefit of a happy ending. The story is about a group of fliers, sticking together since the war, now in the airmail business. One is already broken, feeble in the head from having flown through a tree. One is Stuart Erwin as Texas, a veteran flier, plodding, good-hearted, the comedy interest. One is the chief of the airport, Pat O'Brien. ('Get them feet moving – what are we flying, a lot of box-kites?') The fourth is James Cagney as Dizzy Davis, a brash lovable fool and crack pilot, romantic as anything, and the women can't leave him alone until, sooner or later in each case, he takes care of that matter for them.

The mere situation always has a strong and instant appeal: devil-may-care and shoulder-to-shoulder, and the life of danger we all would plunge into gladly, if we could get off our tails long enough and if it weren't so pesky dangerous. But although the early scenes – scrapes, reunions, the frictions and jollities of life at the airport – proceed lightly, with sly and witty competence and nice sentiment, there is soon indication that life is not all horseplay and kisses. Dizzy seems to have got tangled up with too many people's women, and with too many easy commitments. His friend Texas, duped into taking Dizzy's run, crashes; the Washington inspector lifts Dizzy's license for good, and he gets told off bitterly from several quarters. His friends and his flying have been his life, which now falls about his ears completely; and so he sneaks his last plane off the ground in suicide weather.

Outside of a few too-mellow lines on the life of action, none of this is wrong either as a whole or in details. The story moves along at a good clean pace, there is much snap to the lines and plenty of authentic color. Some of the scenes build up a high dramatic pressure, thanks partly to the story, partly to its background of curious instruments and procedures; but mostly to its acting and direction. There is an intricate art by which the line of feeling is kept uppermost and rising in the midst of a staccato din of commands, interjections, screams, speakers, plane-motors, tickers, sometimes as many as five or six voices going all the time, so that the crash of Erwin, coming in too low in the fog and blowing up on the wires, careening across the field on fire and smashing into the glass windows of the hangar, is a terrific bit of action. And there is a good simplicity and rightness to the last sequence – Dizzy, with the ice too thick on his wings and going into a spin, speaking a word for his chief and beloved friend, still ordering him profanely back to the field: 'Don't be mad at me, baby,' he says just before he hits; and O'Brien goes dully back to his routine, ordering out the crash truck, etc., listening to the monotone of the loudspeaker: 'Temperature, 30 degrees, wind, etc., etc.; visibility, zero; ceiling, zero.'

The dramatic high points of this story are mostly in the air and would be melodrama if it were not for the effect on those below, an effect made solid particularly by the work of Cagney and O'Brien. Cagney especially plays his best part here with fine feeling and wisdom, at last given a chance to fill out his own screen character – which is as tough and bright and endearing as life – with the other half of the story, which is the effect these irresistible happy-go-luckies invariably have on those who get left with the bag, and how, if they are true, decent chaps, it catches up with them in the end; and he does it beautifully.

But this is not all Hollywood's doing: outside of a few vivid seconds of fire, speed, and explosion, a few conventional shots of planes in the fog, fliers at the stick, people at the phone, the film is still a stage play with one main and two subsidiary sets. The fliers, the chief, the big shot, the salesman, the mechanics, together with their wives, girls, and other troubles, have to bring their lines and their crises into the control room, either personally, by radio, or by phone. It speaks very highly for the original stage play that the lack of diversity is not felt, that the whole thing was built right, constructed and tested under pressure at the start, so that it makes one of the very rare pieces to be transferred bodily to the screen as a good movie.

Otis Ferguson was one of several intelligent critics of American cinema of the 1930s – along with the likes of John Grierson, Pare Lorentz, Graham Greene (though all these achieved most fame in other areas of film, or in other arts). Ferguson contributed to *The New Republic* between 1934 and 1942, and his writings were collected in *The Film Criticism of Otis Ferguson* (edited by Robert Wilson, Philadelphia: Temple University Press, 1971). Ferguson's review of *Ceiling Zero* is typical of his critical approach in its recognition of the kind of cinema represented by Hollywood and of the director's role in its collaborative process. As Andrew Sarris recognizes in his Foreword to Ferguson's collected criticism, Ferguson (who died in the World War II) significantly influenced later critics such as James Agee and, more particularly, Manny Farber. *Ceiling Zero*, as Sarris remarks in his 1962 essay 'The World of Howard Hawks', was 'the Hawks film most highly regarded by the conventional critics of the time'. Sarris clearly felt an affinity with Ferguson's work and Sarris's own judgment concurs essentially with Ferguson's: 'one of Hawks's most fully realized films, *Ceiling Zero* is directed at a breakneck pace which emphasizes its lean fibre and its concentration on the essentials of its theme'. It is worth noting that the screenwriter of *Ceiling Zero*, Frank 'Spig' Wead, was the protagonist (played by John Wayne) of John Ford's 1957 film *The Wings of Eagles*.

Barbary Coast and Only Angels Have Wings

GRAHAM GREENE

From the *Spectator* 1 November 1935 and 20 October 1939.

Reprinted in Graham Greene, *The Pleasure Dome: The Collected Film Criticism 1935–40*, ed. John Russell Taylor (London: Secker & Warburg, 1972).

Barbary Coast is melodrama of the neatest, most expert kind, well directed, well acted and well written. The wit, vigour and *panache* of Mr Ben Hecht and Mr MacArthur have raised nearly to international halma form (in Mr Aldous Huxley's phrase) a conventional film story of a girl who comes to San Francisco one fogbound night in the 1840s to marry a gold-prospector and finds that he has been murdered. She stays to become the mistress of his killer, the Big Shot, and falls in love with a young prospector who reads Shelley and wants to write poetry. The Big Shot, himself pursued by Vigilantes, followed his mistress with the intention of killing her lover, but, taking pity on them both, goes to meet his lynchers. The story, it will be seen, belongs to the 'far, far better' school, but the character of the Big Shot has a sourness, of the girl an unscrupulousness, which is fresh and interesting. The conventionality of the plot has provided a challenge to the director and the authors to make something real out of the hocus-pocus.

They have succeeded triumphantly. There are moments as dramatically exciting as anything I have seen on the fictional screen. *Sous les toits de Paris* contained a sequence in which Préjean was surrounded by a gang with drawn razors in the darkness of a railway viaduct; the smoke blew continually across, and the dialogue was drowned in the din of shunting trucks. The steamy obscurity, the whispers, the uproar overhead combined to make the scene vividly sinister. There is a moment in *Barbary Coast* that takes its place with Clair's, when the Big Shot's gunman, on his way to commit another murder in the San Francisco of which he has long been one of the undisputed rulers, feels the pistols of the Vigilantes against his ribs. They walk him out to the edge of the acetylene-lighted town along streets ankle-deep in mud, holding a mock trial with counsel and witnesses as they go; the low voices, the slosh of mud round their boots, the rhythmic stride are terrifying because they have been exactly imagined, with the ear as well as the eye.

*　　*　　*

Only Angels Have Wings has everything a good film needs except a good story. It is admirably acted by Mr Cary Grant, Miss Jean Arthur, Mr Thomas Mitchell and Mr Richard Barthelmess (who makes another sombre and impressive return to the screen: he did it before in *Four Hours to Kill*; what happens to him in between returns?), and it is quite magnificently directed by Mr Howard Hawks – who made *Scarface*. Unfortunately, Mr Hawks has written his own story, a sentimental tough tale of a third-rate air line trying to make both ends meet somewhere near the Andes, the girl who steps off a cruise and stays behind (Miss Arthur) and a pilot who once parachuted from his plane and left his mechanic to die (Mr Barthelmess). At the airport, where he arrives with his wife seeking a new job under a new name, he meets the mechanic's brother (Mr Mitchell), and of course the wife was once engaged to the boss (Mr Grant), who is now forcefully loved by Miss Arthur. It's a regulation muddle which needs the regulation devices to untangle it – storm, sacrifice, heroism, redemption. What does remain in the memory is the setting – drab, dusty, authentic, and a few brilliantly directed scenes, as when a young pilot is trying to land in a ground fog; those below can't see the plane, but they can hear his engine and talk to him by telephone, warn him as he overshoots and hear from the vulcanite the regular record of his doomed descent – 1,000 feet, 500, 200, a long-drawn-out waiting for the inevitable crash.

Graham Greene is best known as a novelist but was also a playwright, screenwriter and, from the mid-1930s to early 1940, a regular film reviewer for the magazines *Night and Day* and the *Spectator*. Since much of Greene's creative output has been adapted into movies, by himself or others, his critical writing on film is of significant interest, even though he himself described it as entered into 'from a sense of fun' and as 'escape for an hour and a half from the melancholy which falls inexorably round the novelist when he has lived for too many months on end in isolation'. Most of Greene's reviews were collected in *Graham Greene: The Pleasure Dome*, edited by John Russell Taylor (London: Secker & Warburg, 1972, reprinted as a paperback by Oxford University Press, 1980). The more or less complete reviews, with other fascinating essays, articles and other material, are collected in *The Graham Greene Film Reader: Mornings in the Dark*, edited by David Parkinson (Manchester: Carcanet Press, 1993).

Greene's reviews of *Barbary Coast* and *Only Angels Have Wings* imply a real understanding of what the role of 'direction' might be, with his sense of the way in which setting and mood are evoked, beyond the level of plot. Noticeably, Greene's enjoyment of *Only Angels* echoes Ferguson's of *Ceiling Zero*. Greene's rather dim view of the story of *Only Angels* inaugurates a kind of debate about whether the story should be taken seriously, morally and dramatically, as claimed by, say, Jacques Rivette in his 1953 essay 'The Genius of Howard Hawks' (reprinted in this volume) and Robin Wood in his 1968 book *Howard Hawks* or whether it is, on the contrary, simply silly, as claimed by, among others, Manny Farber and Peter John Dyer in his 1962 'Swing the Lamps Low', whose views are echoed by Robert B. Ray in 'Classic Hollywood's Holding Pattern: The

Combat Films of World War II' (in this volume). In his 1957
'Underground Films' (reprinted in this volume), Farber calls it 'material
that is hopelessly worn out and childish', elaborating on this, in his 1969
essay 'Howard Hawks', with 'a ridiculous film of improbability and
coincidence' and 'a White Cargo melodrama that is often intricately silly'.
The implications of such divergent views for general assumptions about
Hollywood cinema are well discussed by Richard Maltby at the end of his
book *Hollywood Cinema*.

Hawks with Jean Arthur on the set of *Only Angels Have Wings*

To Have and Have Not

JAMES AGEE

From *Time*, 23 October 1944.

Reprinted in James Agee, *Agee on Film 2* (London: Peter Owen, 1963).

To Have and Have Not (Warner), having jettisoned a solid 90% of the Ernest Hemingway novel, for which Warner Bros. paid plenty, may make devotees of Hemingway the sourest boycotters since Carrie Nation.[1] But the sea change which Producer-Director Howard Hawks supervised – for the benefit of Humphrey Bogart, Hoagy (*Star Dust*) Carmichael, and a sensational newcomer named Lauren Bacall (rhymes with McCall) – results in the kind of tiny romantic melodrama which millions of cinemaddicts have been waiting for ever since *Casablanca*.

The screen story of *To Have and Have Not* is still about a couple of low characters named Harry Morgan and Marie, and Harry is still a rugged individualist who takes rich men out fishing and earns side money in whatever nefarious ways turn up. But Harry's beat is no longer the axis between bourgeois Key West and revolutionary Havana; he now works out of wartime Martinique, and the villains are Vichyites. Marie is no longer an idealized image of happy marriage; she is a tall, hoarse, egregious, 22-year-old tramp, so worldly-wise that when a policeman all but slaps her jaw out of joint she hardly bats an eye.

Harry Morgan's adventures are also considerably altered. He smuggles Gaullists, slams pistols against Vichyites. Harry Morgan becomes, in fact, one of Humphrey Bogart's most edged portrayals of Nietzsche in dungarees, without whose hard resourcefulness one is forced to infer that the rest of the effete world would quickly fall apart.

But *To Have and Have Not* is neither an action picture nor a Bogart picture. Its story is, in fact, just a loosely painted background for a kind of romance which the movies have all but forgotten about – the kind in which the derelict sweethearts are superficially aloof but essentially hot as blazes, and seem to do even their kissing out of the corners of their mouths. This particular romance is decorated by some sinister yet friendly bits of low-life café atmosphere. Hoagy Carmichael's performance as a cokey-looking ivory-prowler is especially useful for some spidery Caribbean jazz, and for two wryly elegant Carmichael songs. But the most valuable fixture in the show is 20-year-old Lauren Bacall.

Lauren Bacall has cinema personality to burn, and she burns both ends against an unusually little middle. Her personality is compounded partly of percolated Davis, Garbo, West, Dietrich, Harlow and Glenda Farrell, but more than enough of it is completely new to the screen. She has a javelin-like vitality, a born dancer's eloquence in movement, a fierce female shrewdness and a special sweet-sourness. With these faculties, plus a stone-crushing self-confidence and a trombone voice, she manages to get across the toughest girl a piously regenerate Hollywood has dreamed of in a long, long while.

Her lines have been neatly tailored to her talents. They include such easy lines of cryptic folk poetry as 'Was ya ever bit by a dead bee?' An even easier line, sure to bring down any decently vulgar house, is her comment on Bogart's second, emboldened kiss: 'It's even better when you help.' Besides good lines, there are good situations and songs for newcomer Bacall. She does a wickedly good job of sizing up male prospects in a low bar, growls a *louche* song more suggestively than anyone in cinema has dared since Mae West in *She Done Him Wrong* (1933).

Lauren (real name, Betty) Bacall was born on 103rd Street in New York City in September 1924. According to her employers, 'she is the daughter of parents who trace their American ancestry back several generations'. According to herself, she is part Rumanian, part French, part Russian (she thinks). Her father sold medical instruments. She is an only child. By the time she got out of Julia Richman High, Bette Davis was her idol, and she had seen enough Davis pictures to realize that it takes training to be an actress.

She got a certain amount of training at the American Academy of Dramatic Arts, more as a walk-on, more as an ingénue (directed by George Kaufman). She also worked as an usherette, and got a job modelling for *Harper's Bazaar*.

In April 1943 Mrs Howard Hawks, leafing through the *Bazaar*, caught on her face the way a skirt catches on barbed wire. She showed it to her husband; Producer Howard Hawks was caught too. He wired the magazine, asking whether she was available. The answer came fast, on the Hawkses's doorstep, in person. In May 1943 Miss Bacall signed a contract with Hawks; this was shared by Jack Warner as soon as he saw her screen test, a bit of *Claudia*. The test alone is proof of her abilities; for Lauren Bacall (as seen in *To Have and Have Not*) to make even a mediocre stab at such a role is like Tom Dewey's successfully impersonating Lincoln.

For the better part of a year Hawks worked her out mainly in a vacant lot, bellowing anything from Shakespeare to odd copies of shopping news. In the fullness of time Hawks had achieved his purpose: he had developed her voice from 'a high nasal pipe to a low guttural wheeze'. He instructed her now to speak softly and naturally, paying no attention to the traditional voice-culture style which he surrealistically compares with 'digging post-holes'.

Hawks carried his shrewdly contrived campaign of artificialized natural-ness still further. Time and again he left it up to Lauren to decide for her-self about how to play a scene, basing her decision on how she would handle the situation in real life. One of the most successful scenes in the picture is her own invention. After a highly charged few minutes with Bogart, late at night in a cheap hotel room, Marie reluctantly retires to her own quarters. At this point in the shooting, Miss Bacall complained: 'God, I'm dumb.' 'Why?' asked Hawks. 'Well, if I had any sense, I'd go back in after that guy.' She did.

Lauren Bacall may or may not become a star. Yet only last fortnight, Hawks turned down a rival producer's $75,000 bid for her services. He understands her pretty well, and he has plans.

1. The jettisoning was largely due to censor trouble, caused by the Hays office and by Government worries over Latin American relations.

James Agee reviewed movies from 1941 to 1948 for *Time* magazine and *The Nation*. His reviews were much admired and respected by the Establishment, partly simply because of his critical intelligence, but not least because Agee was already an established writer. Agee's *Let Us Now Praise Famous Men*, with Walker Evans's photographs, about poor Southern white sharecroppers in the Depression, had been received with some acclaim in 1939. Agee's reputation has been consolidated by his subsequent work: he contributed narration and dialogue to Sidney Meyers's film *The Quiet One* (1949), co-wrote John Huston's *The African Queen* (1951), adapted Stephen Crane's 'The Bride Comes to Yellow Sky' for *Face to Face* (directed by John Brahm and Bretaigne Windust, 1952) and was screenwriter of Charles Laughton's 1955 film *Night of the Hunter*; his posthumous novel *A Death in the Family* was awarded a Pulitzer Prize in 1958 (Agee died in 1955). Agee's reviews and essays on film were collected in *Agee on Film 2* (New York: McDowell, 1958; London: Peter Owen, 1963).

Journalist that he was, Agee's *Time* review of *To Have and Have Not* picks up on the buzz about the discovery of Lauren Bacall. Slim Keith recalls these events in the extract from *Slim*, 'Howard the Dreamer', as does Hawks himself in the Bogdanovich interview, and Bruce Kawin discusses Hawks's work with William Faulkner in the extract from *Faulkner and Film*, all reprinted in this volume. Kawin gives a very full account of the production background to the film in his introduction to the screenplay of *To Have and Have Not*, while Lauren Bacall gives her own account in *By Myself*.

Air Force

ANDRÉ BAZIN

From *Le Parisien Libéré*, 16 February 1945.
Translated by John Moore.

This is the Odyssey of a Flying Fortress crew that receives the news of Japan's attack on Pearl Harbor while on a mission. The base from which B-17 'Mary-Ann' has taken off is in flames. It flees from island to island across the Pacific, constantly threatened by enemy aviation and ground forces. Everywhere, American positions surprised by the treacherous Japanese attack are falling before the enemy's material superiority; but everywhere, there is growing determination to avenge these 'temporary' defeats and clamber back up the slope of disaster.

Nothing could be more different from Soviet war films than American war films. The Russian cinema is not much bothered with special effects. It owes it power to the authenticity of live documentary footage (of which, alas, there is a generous supply) and the violence of patriotic sentiment. American films are still primarily 'cinematic'. *Air Force*, although it deals with reality, is part of a whole traditional lineage in which skilful trickery and the acrobatic prowess of the camera work play an essential role. There is something in *Air Force* that recalls *Tarzan* and *Stagecoach*. (Isn't the vehicle in *Stagecoach* fleeing from a war, from one temporary haven to another?) *Air Force* is not just a prodigious documentary on the lives of American airmen; it will survive as a high point of the adventure film, an astonishing piece of pure cinema.

André Bazin is generally considered the most important of French film critics and theorists in the period after World War II. Though often associated most strongly with the magazine *Cahiers du Cinéma* in the 1950s, Bazin wrote a great deal, and developed many of his central ideas, in the 1940s. (Much of Bazin's most important critical work is collected in André Bazin, *What is Cinema?*, essays selected and translated by Hugh Gray (Berkeley and Los Angeles: University of California Press, 1967 and 1972, two volumes).) In his short review of *Air Force* Bazin offers no acknowledgment of Hawks as director. Given Auriol's earlier acknowledgment of Hawks, this may seem odd, but Auriol was writing in a specialist magazine and Bazin in a newspaper. This short piece is interesting from several points of view. First, French critics' predisposition to and consciousness of American cinema are thought to have been much affected by the sudden flood, after the Liberation, of American films which had been excluded during the German occupation. *Air Force* would have been part of this flood, and no doubt its reception would have been influenced by the events of the recent past in France. Second, Bazin in his reviews consistently formulated ideas which took him beyond individual films and into more general questions of, for example, style and generic evolution. *Air Force* clearly prompts several such lines of thought in Bazin. See also Bazin's 'How Could You Possibly Be a Hitchcocko-Hawksian?' in this volume.

The Genius of Howard Hawks

JACQUES RIVETTE

From *Cahiers du Cinéma*, no. 23, May 1953.

Translated in Joseph McBride (ed.), *Focus on Howard Hawks* (Englewood Cliffs, NJ: Prentice-Hall, 1972).

The evidence on the screen is the proof of Hawks's genius: you only have to watch *Monkey Business* to know that it is a brilliant film. Some people refuse to admit this, however; they refuse to be satisfied by proof. There can't be any other reason why they don't recognize it.

Hawks's *œuvre* is equally divided between comedies and dramas – a remarkable ambivalence. More remarkable still is his frequent fusing of the two elements so that each, rather than damaging the other, seems to underscore their reciprocal relation: the one sharpens the other. Comedy is never long absent from his most dramatic plots, and far from compromising the feeling of tragedy, it removes the comfort of fatalistic indulgence and keeps the events in a perilous kind of equilibrium, a stimulating uncertainty which only adds to the strength of the drama. Scarface's secretary speaks comically garbled English, but that doesn't prevent his getting shot; our laughter all the way through *The Big Sleep* is inextricable from our foreboding of danger; the climax of *Red River*, in which we are no longer sure of our own feelings, wondering whose side to take and whether we should be amused or afraid, sets our every nerve quivering with panic and gives us a dizzy, giddy feeling like that of a tightrope walker whose foot falters without quite slipping, a feeling as unbearable as the ending of a nightmare.

While it is the comedy which gives Hawks's tragedy its effectiveness, the comedy cannot quite dispel (not the tragedy, let's not spoil our best arguments by going too far) the harsh feeling of an existence in which no action can undo itself from the web of responsibility. Could we be offered a more bitter view of life than this? I have to confess that I am quite unable to join in the laughter of a packed theater when I am riveted by the calculated twists of a fable (*Monkey Business*) which sets out – gaily, logically, and with an unholy abandon – to chronicle the fatal stages in the degradation of a superior mind.

It is no accident that similar groups of intellectuals turn up in both *Ball of Fire* and *The Thing*. But Hawks is not concerned so much with the subjection of the world to the jaded, glacial vision of the scientific mind as he is with retracing the comic misfortunes of the intelligence. Hawks is not concerned with satire or psychology; societies mean no more to him than sentiments do; unlike Capra or McCarey, he is solely preoccupied with the adventure of the intellect. Whether he opposes the old to the new; the sum of the world's knowledge of the past to one of the degraded forms of modern life (*Ball of Fire, A Song Is Born*); or man to beast (*Bringing Up Baby*), he sticks to the same story – the intrusion of the inhuman, or the crudest avatar of humanity, into a highly civilized society. In *The Thing*, the mask is finally off: in the confined space of the universe, some men of science are at grips with a creature worse than inhuman, a creature *from another world*; and their efforts are directed toward fitting it into the logical framework of human knowledge.

But in *Monkey Business* the enemy has crept into man himself: the subtle poison of the Fountain of Youth, the temptation of infantilism. This we have long known to be one of the less subtle wiles of the Evil One – now in the form of a hound, now in the form of a monkey – when he comes up against a man of rare intelligence. And it is the most unfortunate of illusions which Hawks rather cruelly attacks: the notion that adolescence and childhood are barbarous states from which we are rescued by education. The child is scarcely distinguishable from the savage he imitates in his games: and a most distinguished old man, after he has drunk the precious fluid, takes delight in imitating a chimp. One can find in this a classical conception of man, as a creature whose only path to greatness lies through experience and maturity; at the end of his journey, it is his old age which will be his judge.

Still worse than infantilism, degradation, or decadence, however, is the fascination these tendencies exert on the same mind which perceives them as evil; the film is not only a story about this fascination, it offers itself to the spectator as a demonstration of the power of the fascination. Likewise, anyone who criticizes this tendency must first submit himself to it. The monkeys, the Indians, the goldfish are no more than the guise worn by Hawks's obsession with primitivism, which also finds expression in the savage rhythms of the tom-tom music, the sweet stupidity of Marilyn Monroe (that monster of femininity whom the costume designer nearly deformed), or the aging bacchante Ginger Rogers becomes when she reverts to adolescence and her wrinkles seem to shrink away. The instinctive euphoria of the characters' actions gives a lyric quality to the ugliness and foulness, a denseness of expression which heightens everything into abstraction: the fascination of all this gives *beauty* to the metamorphoses in retrospect. One could apply the word 'expressionistic' to the artfulness with which Cary Grant twists his gestures into symbols; watching the scene in which he makes himself up as an Indian, it is impossible not to be reminded of the famous shot in *The Blue Angel* in which Jannings stares at *his* distorted face. It is by no means facile to compare these two similar tales of ruin: we recall how the themes of damnation and malediction in the German cinema had imposed the same rigorous progression from the likable to the hideous.

From the close-up of the chimpanzee to the moment when the diaper slips off the baby Cary Grant, the viewer's head swims with the constant whirl of immodesty and impropriety; and what is this feeling if not a mixture of fear, censure – and fascination. The allure of the instinctual, the abandonment to primitive earthly forces, evil, ugliness, stupidity – all of the Devil's attributes are, in these comedies in which the soul itself is tempted to bestiality, deviously combined with logic *in extremis*; the sharpest point of the intelligence is turned back on itself. *I Was a Male War Bride* takes as its subject simply the impossibility of finding a place to sleep, and then prolongs it to the extremes of debasement and demoralization.

Hawks knows better than anyone else that art has to go to extremes, even the extremes of squalor, because that is the source of comedy. He is never afraid to use bizarre narrative twists, once he has established that they are possible. He doesn't try to confound the spectator's vulgar tendencies; he sates them by taking them a step further. This is also Molière's genius: his mad fits of logic are apt to make the laughter stick in your throat. It is also Murnau's genius – the famous scene with Dame Martha in his excellent *Tartuffe* and several sequences of *Der Letzte Mann* are still models of Molièresque cinema.

Hawks is a director of intelligence and precision, but he is also a bundle of dark forces and strange fascinations; his is a Teutonic spirit, attracted by bouts of ordered madness which give birth to an infinite chain of consequences. The very fact of their continuity is a manifestation of Fate. His heroes demonstrate this not so much in their feelings as in their actions, which he observes meticulously and with passion. It is *actions* that he films, meditating on the power of appearances alone. We are not concerned with John Wayne's thoughts as he walks toward Montgomery Clift at the end of *Red River*, or of Bogart's thoughts as he beats somebody up: our attention is directed solely to the precision of each step – the exact rhythm of the walk – of each blow – and to the gradual collapse of the battered body.

But at the same time, Hawks epitomizes the highest qualities of the American cinema: he is the only American director who knows how to draw a *moral*. His marvellous blend of action and morality is probably the secret of his genius. It is not an idea that is fascinating in a Hawks film, but its effectiveness. A deed holds our attention not so much for its intrinsic beauty as for its effect on the inner workings of his universe.

Such art demands a basic honesty, and Hawks's use of time and space bears witness to this – no flashback, no ellipsis; the rule is continuity. No character disappears without us following him, and nothing surprises the hero which doesn't surprise us at the same time. There seems to be a law behind Hawks's action and editing, but it is a *biological* law like that governing any living being: each shot has a functional beauty, like a neck or an ankle. The smooth, orderly succession of shots has a rhythm like the pulsing of blood, and the whole film is like a beautiful body, kept alive by deep, resilient breathing.

This obsession with continuity imposes a feeling of monotony on Hawks's films, the kind often associated with the idea of a journey to be made or a course to be run (*Air Force*, *Red River*), because everything is felt to be connected to everything else, time to space and space to time. So in films which are mostly comic (*To Have and Have Not*, *The Big Sleep*), the characters are confined to a few settings, and they move around rather help-lessly in them. We begin to feel the gravity of each movement they make, and we are unable to escape from their presence. But Hawksian drama is al-ways expressed in spatial terms, and variations in setting are parallel with temporal variations: whether it is the drama of Scarface, whose kingdom shrinks from the city he once ruled to the room in which he is finally trapped, or of the scientists who cannot dare leave their hut for fear of The Thing; of the fliers in *Only Angels Have Wings*, trapped in their station by the fog and managing to escape to the mountains from time to time, just as Bogart (in *To Have and Have Not*) escapes to the sea from the hotel which he prowls impotently, between the cellar and his room; and even when these themes are burlesqued in *Ball of Fire*, with the grammarian moving out of his hermetic library to face the perils of the city, or in *Monkey Business*, in which the characters' jaunts are an indication of their reversion to infancy (*I Was a Male War Bride* plays on the motif of the journey in another way). Always the heroes' movements are along the path of their destiny.

The monotony is only a façade. Beneath it, feelings are slowly ripening, developing step-by-step toward a violent climax. Hawks uses lassitude as a dramatic device – to convey the exasperation of men who have to restrain themselves for two hours, patiently containing their anger, hatred, or love before our eyes and then suddenly releasing it, like slowly-saturated batter-ies which eventually give off a spark. Their anger is heightened by their ha-bitual *sang froid*; their calm façade is pregnant with emotion, with the secret trembling of their nerves and of their soul – until the cup overflows. A Hawks film often has the same feeling as the agonizing wait for the fall of a drop of water.

The comedies show another side of this principle of monotony. Forward action is replaced by repetition, like the rhetoric of Raymond Roussel re-placing Péguy's; the same actions, endlessly recurring, which Hawks builds up with the persistence of a maniac and the patience of a man obsessed, suddenly whirl madly about, as if at the mercy of a capricious maëlstrom.

What other man of genius, even if he were more obsessed with continu-ity, could be more passionately concerned with the consequences of men's actions, or with these actions' relationships to each other? The way they in-fluence, repel, or attract one another makes up a unified and coherent world, a Newtonian universe whose ruling principles are the universal law of gravity and a deep conviction of the gravity of existence. Human actions are weighed and measured by a master director preoccupied with man's re-sponsibilities.

The measure of Hawks's films is intelligence, but a *pragmatic* intelli-gence, applied directly to the physical world, an intelligence which takes its efficacity from the precise viewpoint of a profession or from some form of human activity at grips with the universe and anxious for conquest. Marlowe in *The Big Sleep* practices a profession just as a scientist or a flier does; and when Bogart hires out his boat in *To Have and Have Not*, he hardly looks at the sea: he is more interested in the beauty of his passengers than in the beauty of the waves. Every river is made to be crossed, every herd is made to be fattened and sold at the highest price. And women, however seductive, however much the hero cares for them, must join them in the struggle.

It is impossible to adequately evoke *To Have and Have Not* with immediately recalling the struggle with the fish at the beginning of the film. The universe cannot be conquered without a fight, and fighting is natural to Hawks's heroes: hand-to-hand fighting. What closer grasp of another being could be hoped for than a vigorous struggle like this? So love exists even where there is perpetual opposition; it is a bitter duel whose constant dangers are ignored by men intoxicated with passion (*The Big Sleep, Red River*). Out of the contest comes esteem – that admirable word encompassing knowledge, appreciation, and sympathy: the opponent becomes a partner. The hero feels a great sense of disgust if he has to face an enemy who refuses to fight; Marlowe, seized with a sudden bitterness, precipitates events in order to hasten the climax of his case.

Maturity is the hallmark of these reflective men, heroes of an adult, often exclusively masculine world, where tragedy is found in personal relationships; comedy comes from the intrusion and admixture of alien elements, or in mechanical objects which take away their free will – that freedom of decision by which a man can express himself and affirm his existence as a creator does in the act of creation.

I don't want to seem as if I'm praising Hawks for being 'a genius estranged from his time', but it is the obviousness of his modernity which lets me avoid belabouring it. I'd prefer, instead, to point out how, even if he is occasionally drawn to the ridiculous or the absurd, Hawks first of all concentrates on the smell and feel of reality, giving reality an unusual and indeed long-hidden grandeur and nobility; how Hawks gives the modern sensibility a classical conscience. The father of *Red River* and *Only Angels Have Wings* is none other than Corneille; ambiguity and complexity are compatible only with the noblest feelings, which some still consider 'dull', even though it is not these feelings which are soonest exhausted but rather the barbaric, mutable natures of crude souls – that is why modern novels are so boring.

Finally, how could I omit mentioning those wonderful Hawksian opening scenes in which the hero settles smoothly and solidly in for the duration? No preliminaries, no expository devices: a door opens, and there he is in the first shot. The conversation gets going and quietly familiarizes us with his personal rhythm; after bumping into him like this, we can no longer leave his side. We are his companions all through the journey as it unwinds surely and regularly as the film going through the projector. The hero moves with the litheness and constancy of the mountaineer who starts out with a steady gait and maintains it along the roughest trails, even to the end of the longest day's march.

From these first stirrings, we are not only sure that the heroes will never leave us, we also know that they will stick by their promises *to a fault*, and will never hesitate or quit: no one can put a stop to their marvellous stubbornness and tenacity. Once they have set out, they will go on to the end of their tether and carry the promises they have made to their logical conclusions, come what may. What is started must be finished. It doesn't matter that the heroes are often involved against their wills: by proving themselves, by achieving their ends, they win the right to be free and the honor of calling themselves men. To them, logic is not some cold intellectual activity, but proof that the body is a coherent whole, harmoniously following the consequences of an action out of loyalty to itself. The strength of the heroes' will power is an assurance of the unity of the man and the spirit, tied together on behalf of that which both justifies their existence and gives it the highest meaning.

If it is true that we are fascinated by extremes, by everything which is bold and excessive, and that we find grandeur in a lack of moderation – then it follows that we should be intrigued by the clash of extremes, because they bring together the intellectual precision of abstractions with the elemental magic of the great earthly impulses, linking thunderstorms with equations in an affirmation of life. The beauty of a Hawks film comes from this kind of affirmation, staunch and serene, remorseless and resilient. It is a beauty which demonstrates existence by breathing and movement by walking. That which is, is.

Jacques Rivette's essay on Hawks is certainly the earliest attempt at a comprehensive account of the director's work, establishing some of the fundamental contours, such as its classicism and its moral basis, and particularly the division – and interrelationship – between the comedies and the dramas, taken up by later critics such as Wood and Wollen. Many later critics have recognized Rivette's analysis as an essential starting-point for further work. At the same time, we should not underestimate the *polemical* intent of the essay, with its claims for 'genius' and for Hawks as epitomizing 'the highest qualities of the American cinema'. Several months later in the pages of *Cahiers*, Eric Rohmer, in a review of *The Big Sky*, is claiming Hawks as 'the greatest film-maker born in America, except for Griffith' and ending with the flourish: 'I think that one cannot really love any film if one does not really love the ones by Howard Hawks.' As Bazin points out in 'How Could You Possibly Be a Hitchcocko-Hawksian?' (which follows), the *Cahiers* critics were apt 'to shock with abruptly expressed admirations and assertions', and the outrage such assertions engendered is what André Bazin sought to address.

Further examples of Rivette's writing from the 1950s and 1960s can be found in Jim Hillier (ed.), *Cahiers du Cinéma*, Vol. 1, *The 1950s: Neo Realism, Hollywood, New Wave* (London: Routledge; Cambridge, Mass.: Harvard University Press, 1985); Jim Hillier (ed.), *Cahiers du Cinéma*, Vol. 2, *The 1960s: New Wave, New Cinema, Re-Evaluating Hollywood* (London: Routledge; Cambridge, Mass.: Harvard University Press, 1986); and Jonathan Rosenbaum (ed.), *Rivette: Texts and Interviews* (London: British Film Institute, 1977).

31

How Could You Possibly Be a Hitchcocko-Hawksian?

ANDRÉ BAZIN

From *Cahiers du Cinéma*, no. 44, February 1955.
Translated by John Moore.

The issue of *Cahiers du Cinéma* devoted to Alfred Hitchcock caused a certain amount of fuss. As well as bringing a virulent correspondence, it earned us violent criticism from certain colleagues, including Georges Sadoul, Denis Marion and, most recently, Lindsay Anderson in *Sight and Sound*. This is because – let's admit it – it gave free rein to the small group of our contributors who never miss a chance to extol the virtues of American directors like Howard Hawks, Preminger, Nicholas Ray or Fritz Lang in his Hollywood phase. Their preferences, of course, run counter to the general body of received opinion; and as they are less concerned to justify them with reasoned arguments than to shock with abruptly expressed admirations and assertions, the irritation of their critics is just as deeply felt, beneath the irony or indignation, as the judgments they condemn.

Our returning yet again to the subject of Hitchcock with the taped interview (in this issue) is not, however, an attempt at provocation; and for those readers who may have been surprised or worried by it, I would like to seize this opportunity to justify the position of the *Cahiers du Cinéma* editorial board on this matter.

Anyone who does us the honour of taking in what we write will certainly have noticed that none of the editors of this review shares the enthusiasm of people like Schérer [Eric Rohmer], Truffaut, Rivette, Chabrol or Lachenay for the directors under discussion; nor indeed do we share the implicit critical system that gives these personal admirations their coherence and solidarity. That is why we can agree with them on, for example, Renoir, Bresson or Rossellini without feeling that this obliges us to admire *Gentlemen Prefer Blondes*.

It may be unnecessary, but I am spelling all this out to make sure that nobody assumes we have been converted to these views, or are unaware of them. On the contrary, we understood the implications perfectly when we published these paradoxical and 'scandalous' opinions in *Cahiers du Cinéma*. That decision was not the product of an indifferent liberalism, one that would give equal space to any and every critical position; it was made because, in spite of the great irritation caused by the divergences between

32

these young Turks and some of the rest of us, we believe their opinions to be respectable and fertile.

Respectable, because anyone who knows them can confirm, I won't say their sincerity, but their competence. I am not too keen on the emphasis Lachenay lays on the number of times they have seen the films under discussion; this is an authoritarian argument (and one that could be turned against them in the case of films *they* don't like). But it is certainly true that people say different things about a film when they have seen it five or ten times. The fact that their erudition is not based on the same values as that of more experienced (or British) critics does not detract from its effectiveness. They write about what they know, and it is always useful to listen to specialists.

And this is why their position is fertile. Where criticism is concerned I do not really believe in objective truths or, to put it more precisely, I would rather be forced to consolidate my own judgments in order to deal with opposing ones than have my principles supported by weak arguments. If I remain sceptical about Hitchcock's work, at least I do so for the best reasons; but I will never be able to see a Howard Hawks film through the same eyes again.

So if anyone asks now what can justify the publication of these opinions in *Cahiers*, I will start by saying that cinema magazines are far less numerous than literary ones, and the fact that an opinion is worth expressing is sufficient reason for us to print it. But I will then go on to risk suggesting that we all have something in common in spite of our disputes; not 'love of the cinema' – that goes without saying – but a vigilant refusal under all circumstances to *reduce* the cinema to the sum of what it expresses.

It is true that these worshippers of a certain strand of American cinema seem to be sliding towards the opposite heresy. This is a pity from their point of view, for they are perpetuating a misunderstanding whose removal would strengthen their position. Forgive me if I become their advocate for a moment: if they won't do it, I must. The reason why they place such a high value on the director's contribution is that they broadly perceive it as containing the very material of the film, an organization of beings and things (characters and objects) which is its own meaning, moral as well as aesthetic. What Sartre wrote about the novel is true of all the arts, cinema as well as painting. Every technique refers back to a metaphysics. Today we discern the unity and the moral message of German expressionism much more in the way the films are directed than in their subject matter; or, more exactly, it is those parts of expressionism's moral 'project' which are wholly interwoven with the visual universe that remain most significant in our minds. Personally, along with many others, I deplore the ideological sterilization of Hollywood, its growing timidity in treating 'big subjects' with a degree of freedom. This is another reason why *Gentlemen Prefer Blondes* makes me think longingly of *Scarface* or *Only Angels Have Wings*. But I have also learned, thanks to the admirers of *The Big Sky* and *Monkey Business*, to see with eyes opened by passion the extent to which the formal intelligence of Hawks's direction masks intelligence, full stop; and this in spite of the explicit idiocy of the scriptwriters. Hawks admirers may be wrong to miss this fatuity or try to ignore it; but we at *Cahiers* still find their prejudice more acceptable than its opposite.

As Bazin makes clear here, there were some important differences of perspective and assumption between himself and the 'young Turks', as well as much common ground. Bazin agrees, for example, with their conception of the 'director's contribution', in other words the role of *mise en scène* (his reference to Sartre relating to the idea that 'one is not a writer because one has chosen to say certain things, but because one has chosen to say them in a certain way', an idea central to later *Cahiers* debates on the role of *mise en scène* (as for example in Fereydoun Hoveyda's 'Sunspots', *Cahiers du Cinéma*, August 1960, reprinted in Jim Hillier, *Cahiers du Cinéma*, Vol. 2, *The 1960s: New Wave, New Cinema, Re-Evaluating Hollywood* (London: Routledge; Cambridge, Mass.: Harvard University Press, 1986)). On the other hand, here as elsewhere, Bazin takes a view of Hollywood which has implications for both the nature of its products and the possibilities for genuine 'authorship'. Bazin's fullest exploration of these issues came in his April 1957 *Cahiers* essay 'On the *politique des auteurs*' (also reprinted in Hillier, *Cahiers du Cinéma*, Vol. 2).

Underground Films

MANNY FARBER

From *Commentary*, November 1957.

Reprinted in Farber, *Negative Space* (New York: Praeger; London: Studio Vista, 1971).

The saddest thing in current films is watching the long-neglected action directors fade away as the less talented De Sicas and Zinnemanns continue to
fascinate the critics. Because they played an anti-art role in Hollywood, the
true masters of the male action film – such soldier-cowboy-gangster directors as Raoul Walsh, Howard Hawks, William Wellman, William Keighley,
the early, pre-*Stagecoach* John Ford, Anthony Mann – have turned out a
huge amount of unprized, second-gear celluloid. Their neglect becomes
more painful to behold now that the action directors are in decline, many
of them having abandoned the dry, economic, life-worn movie style that
made their observations of the American he-man so rewarding. Americans
seem to have a special aptitude for allowing History to bury the toughest,
most authentic native talents. The same tide that has swept away Otis
Ferguson, Walker Evans, Val Lewton, Clarence Williams, and J. R.
Williams into near oblivion is now in the process of burying a group that
kept an endless flow of interesting roughneck film passing through the
theaters from the depression onward. The tragedy of these film-makers lies
in their having been consigned to a Sargasso Sea of unmentioned talent by
film reviewers whose sole concern is not continuous flow of quality but the
momentary novelties of the particular film they are reviewing.

Howard Hawks is the key figure in the male action film because he shows
a maximum speed, inner life, and view, with the least amount of flat foot.
His best films, which have the swallowed-up intricacy of a good soft-shoe
dance, are *Scarface*, *Only Angels Have Wings*, *His Girl Friday*, and *The Big
Sleep*. Raoul Walsh's films are melancholy masterpieces of flexibility and
detailing inside a lower-middle-class locale. Walsh's victories, which make
use of tense, broken-field journeys and nostalgic background detail, include
They Drive by Night, *White Heat*, and *Roaring Twenties*. In any Bill
Wellman operation, there are at least four directors – a sentimentalist, deep
thinker, hooey vaudevillian, and an expedient short-cut artist whose special
love is for mulish toughs expressing themselves in drop-kicking heads and
somber standing around. Wellman is at his best in stiff, vulgar, low-pulp
material. In that setup, he has a low-budget ingenuity, which creates flashes
of ferocious brassiness, an authentic practical-joke violence (as in the

frenzied inadequacy of Ben Blue in *Roxie Hart*), and a brainless hell-raising. Anthony Mann's inhumanity to man, in which cold mortal intentness is the trademark effect, can be studied best in *The Tall Target*, *Winchester 73*, *Border Incident*, and *Railroaded*. The films of this tin-can de Sade have a Germanic rigor, caterpillar intimacy, and an original dictionary of ways in which to punish the human body. Mann has done interesting work with scissors, a cigarette lighter, and steam, but his most bizarre effect takes place in a taxidermist's shop. By intricate manipulation of athletes' bodies, Mann tries to ram the eyes of his combatants on the horns of a stuffed deer stuck on the wall.

The film directors mentioned above did their best work in the late 1940s, when it was possible to be a factory of unpretentious picture-making without frightening the front office. During the same period and later, less prolific directors also appear in the uncompromising action film. Of these, the most important is John Farrow, an urbane vaudevillian whose forte, in films like *The Big Clock* and *His Kind of Woman*, is putting a fine motoring system beneath the veering slapstick of his eccentric characterizations. Though he has tangled with such heavyweights as Book of the Month and Hemingway, Zoltan Korda is an authentic hard-grain cheapster telling his stories through unscrubbed action, masculine characterization, and violent explorations inside a fascinating locale. Korda's best films – *Sahara*, *Counterattack*, *Cry the Beloved Country* – are strangely active films in which terrain, jobs, and people get curiously interwoven in a ravening tactility. William Keighley, in *G-Men* and *Each Dawn I Die*, is the least sentimental director of gangster careers. After the bloated philosophical safe-crackers in Huston's *Asphalt Jungle*, the smallish cops and robbers in Keighley's work seem life-size. Keighley's handling is so right in emphasis, timing, and shrewdness that there is no feeling of the director breathing, gasping, snoring over the film.

The tight-lipped creators whose films are mentioned above comprise the most interesting group to appear in American culture since the various groupings that made the 1920s an explosive era in jazz, literature, silent films. Hawks and his group are perfect examples of the anonymous artist, who is seemingly afraid of the polishing, hypocrisy, bragging, fake educating that goes on in serious art. To go at his most expedient gait, the Hawks type must take a withdrawn, almost hidden stance in the industry. Thus, his films seem to come from the most neutral, humdrum, monotonous corner of the movie lot. The fascinating thing about these veiled operators is that they are able to spring the leanest, shrewdest, sprightliest notes from material that looks like junk, and from a creative position that, on the surface, seems totally uncommitted and disinterested. With striking photography, a good ear for natural dialogue, an eye for realistic detail, a skilled inside-action approach to composition, and the most politic hand in the movie field, the action directors have done a forbidding stenography on the hardboiled American handyman as he progresses through the years.

It is not too remarkable that the underground films, with their twelve-year-old's adventure-story plot and endless palpitating movement, have lost out in the film system. Their dismissal has been caused by the construction of solid confidence built by daily and weekly reviewers. Operating with this wall, the critic can pick and discard without the slightest worry about looking silly. His choice of best salami is a picture backed by studio build-up, agreement amongst his colleagues, a layout in *Life* mag (which makes it officially reasonable for an American award), and a list of ingredients that anyone's unsophisticated aunt in Oakland can spot as comprising a distinguished film. This prize picture, which has philosophical undertones, pan-fried domestic sights, risqué crevices, sporty actors and actresses, circuslike gymnastics, a bit of tragedy like the main fall at Niagara, has every reason to be successful. It has been made for that purpose. Thus, the year's winner is a perfect film made up solely of holes and evasions, covered up by all types of padding and plush. The cavity-filling varies from one prize work to another, from *High Noon* (cross-eyed artistic views of a clock, silhouettes against a vaulting sky, legend-toned walking, a big song), through *From Here to Eternity* (Sinatra's private scene-chewing, pretty trumpeting, tense shots in the dark and at twilight, necking near the water, a threatening hand with a broken bottle) to next year's winner, which will probably be a huge ball of cotton candy containing either Audrey Hepburn's cavernous grin and stiff behind or more of Zinnemann's glacéed picture-making. In terms of imaginative photography, honest acting, and insight into American life, there is no comparison between average underground triumph (*Phenix City Story*) and the trivia that causes a critical salaam across the land. The trouble is that no one asks the critics' alliance to look straight backward at its 'choices', for example, a horse-drawn truckload of liberal schmaltz called *The Best Years of Our Lives*. These ridiculously maltreated films sustain their place in the halls of fame simply because they bear the label of ART in every inch of their reelage. Praising these solemn goiters has produced a climate in which the underground picture-maker, with his modest entry and soft-shoe approach, can barely survive.

However, any day now, Americans may realize that scrambling after the obvious in art is a losing game. The sharpest work of the last thirty years is to be found by studying the most unlikely, self-destroying, uncompromising, roundabout artists. When the day comes for praising infamous men of art, some great talent will be shown in true light: people like Weldon Kees, the rangy Margie Israel, James Agee, Isaac Rosenfeld, Otis Ferguson, Val Lewton, a dozen comic-strip geniuses like the creator of 'Harold Teen', and finally a half-dozen directors such as the master of the ambulance, speed-boat, flying-saucer movie: Howard Hawks.

The films of the Hawks-Wellman group are *underground* for more reasons than the fact that the director hides out in subsurface reaches of his work. The hard-bitten action film finds its natural home in caves: the murky, congested theaters, looking like glorified tattoo parlors on the outside and located near bus terminals in big cities. These theaters roll action films in what, at first, seems like a nightmarish atmosphere of shabby transience, prints that seem overgrown with jungle moss, soundtracks infected with hiccups. The spectator watches two or three action films go by and leaves feeling as though he were a pirate discharged from a giant sponge.

The cutthroat atmosphere in the itch house is reproduced in the movies shown there. Hawks's *The Big Sleep* not only has a slightly gaseous, sub-surface, Baghdadish background, but its gangster action is engineered with a suave, cutting efficacy. Walsh's *Roaring Twenties* is a jangling barrel-house film, which starts with a top gun bouncing downhill, and, at the end, he is seen slowly pushing his way through a lot of Campbell's scotch broth. Wellman's favorite scene is a group of hard-visaged ball bearings standing around – for no damned reason and with no indication of how long or for what reason they have been standing. His worst pictures are made up simply of this moody, wooden standing around. All that saves the films are the little flurries of bulletlike acting that give the men an inner look of cred-ible orneriness and somewhat stupid mulishness. Mann likes to stretch his victims in crucifix poses against the wall or ground and then to peer intently at their demise with an icy surgeon's eye. Just as the harrowing machine is about to run over the wetback on a moonlit night, the camera catches him sprawled out in a harrowing image. At heart, the best action films are slicing journeys into the lower depths of American life: dregs, outcasts, lonely hard wanderers caught in a buzzsaw of niggardly, intricate, devious movement.

The projects of the underground directors are neither experimental, lib-eral, slick, spectacular, low-budget, epical, improving, or flagrantly com-mercial like Sam Katzman two-bitters. They are faceless movies, taken from a type of half-polished trash writing, that seem like a mixture of Burt L. Standish, Max Brand, and Raymond Chandler. Tight, cliché-ridden melo-dramas about stock musclemen. A stool pigeon gurgling with scissors in his back; a fat, nasal-voiced gang leader; escaped convicts; power-mad ranch owners with vengeful siblings; a mean gun with an Oedipus complex and migraine headaches; a crooked gambler trading guns to the redskins; exhausted GIs; an incompetent kid hoodlum hiding out in an East Side building; a sickly-elegant Italian barber in a plot to kill Lincoln; an under-paid shamus signing up to stop the blackmailing of a tough millionaire's depraved thumb-sucking daughter.

The action directors accept the role of hack so that they can involve themselves with expedience and tough-guy insight in all types of action: barnstorming, driving, bulldogging. The important thing is not so much the banal-seeming journeys to nowhere that make up the stories, but the tun-neling that goes on inside the classic Western-gangster incidents and stock hoodlum-dogface-cowboy types. For instance, Wellman's lean, elliptical talents for creating brassy cheapsters and making gloved references to death, patriotism, masturbation, suggest that he uses private runways to the truth, while more famous directors take a slow, embalming surface route.

The virtues of action films expand as the pictures take on the outer ap-pearance of junk jewelry. The underground's greatest mishaps have oc-curred in art-infected projects where there is unlimited cash, studio freedom, an expansive story, message, heart, and a lot of prestige to be gained. Their flattest, most sentimental works are incidentally the only ones that have attained the almond-paste-flavored eminence of the Museum of Modern Art's film library, i.e., *GI Joe*, *Public Enemy*. Both Hawks and Wellman, who made these overweighted mistakes, are like basketball's corner man: their best shooting is done from the deepest, worst angle. With material that is hopelessly worn out and childish (*Only Angels Have Wings*), the underground director becomes beautifully graphic and modestly human in his flexible detailing. When the material is like drab concrete, these directors become great on-the-spot inventors, using their curiously niggling, reaming style for adding background detail (Walsh); suave grace (Hawks); crawling, mechanized tension (Mann); veiled gravity (Wellman); svelte semicaricature (John Farrow); modern Gothic vehemence (Phil Karlson); and dark, modish vaudeville (Robert Aldrich).

In the films of these hard-edged directors can be found the unheralded ripple of physical experience, the tiny morbidly life-worn detail which the visitor to a strange city finds springing out at every step. The Hawks film is as good as the mellifluous grace of the impudent American hard rock as can be found in any art work; the Mann films use American objects and terrain – guns, cliffs, boulders, an 1865 locomotive, telephone wires – with more cruel intimacy than any other film-maker; the Wellman film is the only clear shot at the mean, brassy, clawlike soul of the lone American wolf that has been taken in films. In other words, these actioneers – Mann and Hawks and Keighley and, in recent times, Aldrich and Karlson – go completely underground before proving themselves more honest and subtle than the water buffaloes of film art: George Stevens, Billy Wilder, Vittorio De Sica, Georges Clouzot. (Clouzot's most successful work, *Wages of Fear*, is a wholesale steal of the mean physicality and acrid highway inventions in such Walsh-Wellman films as *They Drive by Night*. Also, the latter film is a more flexible, adroitly ad-libbed, worked-in creation than Clouzot's eclectic money-maker.)

Unfortunately, the action directors suffer from presentation problems. Their work is now seen repeatedly on the blurred, chopped, worn, darkened, commercial-ridden movie programs on TV. Even in the impossible conditions of the 'Late Show', where the lighting is four shades too dark and the porthole-shaped screen defeats the movie's action, the deep skill of Hawks and his tribe shows itself. Time has dated and thinned out the story excitement, but the ability to capture the exact homely-manly character of forgotten locales and misanthropic figures is still in the pictures along with pictorial compositions (Ford's *Last of the Mohicans* [*sic*; *Drums Along the Mohawk*?]) that occasionally seem as lovely as anything that came out of the camera box of Billy Bitzer and Matthew Brady. The conditions in the outcast theaters – the Lyric on Times Square, the Liberty on Market Street, the Victory on Chestnut – are not as bad as TV, but bad enough. The screen image is often out of plumb, the house lights are half left on during the picture, the broken seats are only a minor annoyance in the unpredictable terrain. Yet, these action-film homes are the places to study Hawks, Wellman, Mann, as well as their near and distant cousins.

The underground directors have been saving the American male on the screen for three decades without receiving the slightest credit from critics and prize committees. The hard, exact defining of male action, completely lacking in acting fat, is a common item *only* in underground films. The cream on the top of a *Framed* or *Appointment with Danger* (directed by two first cousins of the Hawks-Walsh strain) is the eye-flicking action that shows the American body – arms, elbows, legs, mouths, the tension profile line – being used expediently, with grace and the suggestion of jolting hardness. Otherwise, the Hollywood talkie seems to have been invented to give an embarrassingly phony impression of the virile action man. The performance is always fattened either by coyness (early Robert Taylor), unction (Anthony Quinn), historic conceit (Gene Kelly), liberal knowingness (Brando), angelic stylishness (Mel Ferrer), oily hamming (José Ferrer), Mother's Boy passivity (Rock Hudson), or languor (Montgomery Clift). Unless the actor lands in the hands of an underground director, he causes a candy-coated effect that is misery for any spectator who likes a bit of male truth in films.

After a steady diet of undergrounders, the spectator realizes that these are the only films that show the tension of an individual intelligence posing itself against the possibilities of monotony, bathos, or sheer cliché. Though the action film is filled with heroism or its absence, the real hero is the small detail which has arisen from a stormy competition between lively color and credibility. The hardness of these films arises from the esthetic give-and-go with banality. Thus, the philosophical idea in underground films seems to be that nothing is easy in life or the making of films. Jobs are difficult, even the act of watching a humdrum bookstore scene from across the street has to be done with care and modesty to evade the type of butter-slicing glibness that rots the Zinnemann films. In the Walsh film, a gangster walks through a saloon with so much tight-roped ad-libbing and muscularity that he seems to be walking backward through the situation. Hawks's achievement of moderate toughness in *Red River*, using Clift's delicate languor and Wayne's claylike acting, is remarkable. As usual, he steers Clift through a series of cornball fetishes (like the Barney Google Ozark hat and the trick handling of same) and graceful, semicollegiate business: stances and kneelings and snake-quick gunmanship. The beauty of the job is the way the cliché business is kneaded, strained against without breaking the naturalistic surface. One feels that this is the first and last hard, clamped-down, imaginative job Clift does in Hollywood – his one nonmush performance. Afterward, he goes to work for Zinnemann, Stevens, Hitchcock.

The small buried attempt to pierce the banal pulp of underground stories with fanciful grace notes is one of the important feats of the underground director. Usually, the piercing consists in renovating a cheap rusty trick that has been slumbering in the 'thriller' director's handbook – pushing a 'color' effect against the most resistant type of unshowy, hard-bitten direction. A mean butterball flicks a gunman's ear with a cigarette lighter. A night-frozen cowboy shudders over a swig of whisky. A gorilla gang leader makes a cannonaded exit from a barber chair. All these bits of congestion are like the lines of a hand to a good gun movie; they are the tracings of difficulty that make the films seem uniquely hard and formful. In each case, the director is taking a great chance with clichés and forcing them into a hard natural shape.

People don't notice the absence of this hard combat with low, commonplace ideas in the Zinnemann and Huston epics, wherein the action is a game in which the stars take part with confidence and glee as though nothing can stop them. They roll in parts of drug addicts, tortured sheriffs; success depending on how much sentimental bloop and artistic japery can be packed in without encountering the demands of a natural act or character. Looking back on a Sinatra film, one has the feeling of a private whirligig performance in the center of a frame rather than a picture. On the other hand, a Cagney performance under the hands of a Keighley is ingrained in a tight, malignant story. One remembers it as a sinewy, life-marred exactness that is as quietly laid down as the smaller jobs played by the Barton MacLanes and Frankie Darros.

A constant attendance at the Lyric-Pix-Victory theaters soon impresses the spectator with the coverage of locales in action films. The average gun film travels like a shamus who knows his city and likes his private knowledges. Instead of the picture-postcard sights, the underground film finds the most idiosyncratic spot of a city and then locates the niceties within the large nicety. The California Street hill in San Francisco (*Woman in Hiding*) with its old-style mansions played in perfect night photography against a deadened domestic bitching. A YMCA scene that emphasizes the wonderful fat-waisted, middle-aged physicality of people putting on tennis shoes and playing handball (*Appointment with Danger*). The terrorizing of a dowdy middle-aged, frog-faced woman (*Born to Kill*) that starts in a decrepit hotel and ends in a bumbling, screeching, crawling murder at midnight on the shore. For his big shock effect, director Robert Wise (a sometime member of the underground) uses the angle going down to the water to create a middle-class mediocrity that out-horrors anything Graham Greene attempted in his early books on small-time gunsels.

Another fine thing about the coverage is its topographic grimness, the fact that the terrain looks worked over. From Walsh's *What Price Glory?* to Mann's *Men in War*, the terrain is special in that it is used, kicked, grappled, worried, sweated up, burrowed into, stomped on. The land is marched across in dark, threading lines at twilight, or the effect is reversed with foot soldiers in white parkas (*Fixed Bayonets*) curving along a snowed-in battleground as they watch troops moving back – in either case, the cliché effect is worked credibly inward until it creates a haunting note like the army diagonals in *Birth of a Nation*. Rooms are boxed, crossed, opened up as they are in few other films. The spectator gets to know these rooms as well as his own hand. Years after seeing the film, he remembers the way a dulled waitress sat on the edge of a hotel bed, the weird elongated adobe in which ranch hands congregate before a Chisholm Trail drive. The rooms in big-shot directors' films look curiously bulbous, as though inflated with hot air and turned toward the audience, like the high school operetta of the 1920s.

Of all these poet-builders, Wellman is the most interesting, particularly with Hopper-type scenery. It is a matter of drawing store fronts, heavy bedroom boudoirs, the heisting of a lonely service station, with light, furious strokes. Also, in mixing jolting vulgarity (Mae Clarke's face being smashed with a grapefruit) with a space composition dance in which the scene seems to be constructed before your eyes. It may be a minor achievement, but, when Wellman finishes with a service station or the wooden stairs in front of an ancient saloon, there is no reason for any movie realist to handle the subject again. The scene is kept light, textural, and as though it is being built from the outside in. There is no sentiment of the type that spreads lugubrious shadows (Kazan), builds tensions of perspective (Huston), or inflates with golden sunlight and finicky hot air (Stevens).

Easily the best part of underground films are the excavations of exciting-familiar scenery. The opening up of a scene is more concerted in these films than in other Hollywood efforts, but the most important thing is that the opening is done by road-mapped strategies that play movement against space in a cunning way, building the environment and event before your eyes. In every underground film, these vigorous ramifications within a sharply seen terrain are the big attraction, the main tent. No one does this anatomization of action and scene better than Hawks, who probably invented it – at least, the smooth version – in such 1930s gunblasts as *The Crowd Roars*. The control of Hawks's strategies is so ingenious that, when a person kneels or walks down the hallway, the movement seems to click into a predetermined slot. It is an uncanny accomplishment that carries the spectator across the very ground of a giant ranch, into rooms and out again, over to the wall to look at some faded fight pictures on a hotel wall – as though he were in the grip of a spectacular, mobile 'eye'. When Hawks landscapes action – the cutting between light tower and storm-caught plane in *Ceiling Zero*, the vegetalizing in *The Thing*, the shamus sweating in a greenhouse in *The Big Sleep* – the feeling is of a clever human tunneling just under the surface of terrain. It is as though the film has a life of its own that goes on beneath the story action.

However, there have been many great examples of such veining by human interactions over a wide plane. One of the special shockers, in *Each Dawn I Die*, has to do with the scissoring of a stooly during the movie shown at the penitentiary. This Keighley-Cagney effort is a wonder of excitement as it moves in great leaps from screen to the rear of a crowded auditorium: crossing contrasts of movement in three points of the hall, all of it done in a sinking gloom. One of the more ironic crisscrossings has to do with the coughings of the stuck victim played against the screen image of zooming airplanes over the Pacific.

In the great virtuoso films, there is something vaguely resembling this underground maneuvering, only it goes on above the story. Egocentric padding that builds a great bonfire of pyrotechnics over a gapingly empty film. The perfect example is a pumped-up fist fight that almost closes the three-hour *Giant* film. This ballroom shuffle between a reforming rancher and a Mexican-hating luncheonette owner is an entertaining creation in spectacular tumbling, swinging, back arching, bending. However, the endless masturbatory 'building' of excitement – beautiful haymakers, room-covering falls, thunderous sounds – is more than slightly silly. Even if the room were valid, which it isn't (a studio-built chromium horror plopped too close to the edge of a lonely highway), the room goes unexplored because of the jumbled timing. The excess that is so noticeable in Stevens's brawl is absent in the least serious undergrounder, which attains most of its crisp, angular character from the modesty of a director working skilfully far within the earthworks of the story.

Underground films have almost ceased to be a part of the movie scene. The founders of the action film have gone into awkward, big-scaled productions involving pyramid-building, a passenger plane in trouble over the Pacific, and postcard Westerns with Jimmy Stewart and his harassed Adam's apple approach to gutty acting. The last drainings of the underground film show a tendency toward moving from the plain guttural approach of *Steel Helmet* to a Germanically splashed type of film. Of these newcomers, Robert Aldrich is certainly the most exciting – a lurid, psychiatric stormer who gets an overflow of vitality and sheer love for movie-making into the film. This enthusiasm is the rarest item in a dried, decayed-lemon type of movie period. Aldrich makes viciously anti-Something movies – *Attack* stomps on Southern racialism and the officer sect in war, *The Big Knife* impales the Zanuck-Goldwyn big shot in Hollywood. The Aldrich films are filled with exciting characterizations – by Lee Marvin, Rod Steiger, Jack Palance – of highly psyched-up, marred, and bothered men. Phil Karlson has done some surprising Gothic treatments of the Brinks hold-up (*Kansas City Confidential*) and the vice-ridden Southern town (*The Phenix City Story*). His movies are remarkable for their endless outlay of scary cheapness in detailing the modern underworld. Also, Karlson's work has a chilling documentary exactness and an exciting shot-scattering belligerence.

There is no longer a literate audience for the masculine picture-making that Hawks and Wellman exploited, as there was in the 1930s. In those exciting movie years, a smart audience waited around each week for the next Hawks, Preston Sturges, or Ford film – shoe-stringers that were far to the side of the expensive Hollywood film. That underground audience, with its expert voice in Otis Ferguson and its ability to choose between perceptive trash and the Thalberg pepsin-flavored sloshing with Tracy and Gable, has now oozed away. It seems ridiculous, but the Fergusonite went into fast decline during the mid-1940s when the movie market was flooded with fake underground films – plushy thrillers with neo-Chandler scripts and a romantic style that seemed to pour the gore, histrionics, decor out of a giant catsup bottle. The nadir of these films: an item called *Singapore* with Fred MacMurray and Ava Gardner.

The straw that finally breaks the back of the underground film tradition is the dilettante behavior of intellectuals on the subject of oaters. Esthetes and upper bohemians now favor horse operas almost as wildly as they like the cute, little-guy worshipings of De Sica and the pedantic, interpretive reading of Alec Guinness. This fad for Western films shows itself in the inevitable little-magazine review, which finds an affinity between the subject matter of cowboy films and the inner esthetics of Cinemah. The Hawks-Wellman tradition, which is basically a subterranean delight that looks like a cheap penny candy on the outside, hasn't a chance of reviving when intellectuals enthuse in equal amounts over Westerns by Ford, Nunnally Johnson, J. Sturges, Stevens, Delmer Daves. In Ferguson's day, the intellectual could differentiate between a solid genre painter (Ford), a long-winded cuteness expert with a rotogravure movie scene (Johnson), a scene-painter with a notions-counter eye and a primly naïve manner with sun-hardened bruisers (John Sturges), and a *Boy's Life* nature lover who intelligently half-prettifies adolescents and backwoods primitives (Daves). Today, the audience for Westerns and gangster careers is a sickeningly frivolous one that does little more than play the garbage collector or make a night court of films. With this high-brow audience that loves banality and pomp more than the tourists at Radio City Music Hall, there is little reason to expect any stray director to try for a hidden meager-looking work that is directly against the serious art grain.

While the *Cahiers* critics were developing their ideas about Hawks and American cinema more generally, in the USA Manny Farber was working towards some similar tastes and ideas but via a rather different route. Writing for *The Nation* in the late 1940s and early 1950s, then for *Commentary* and other journals in the 1950s, Farber developed an aesthetic which was less interested in moral themes – Hawks's or anyone else's – than in a muscular, no-nonsense visual and narrative style. Farber inherited something from Otis Ferguson but distanced himself significantly from James Agee's 'deep-dish criticism' (as Farber puts it in his 1958 essay 'Nearer My Agee to Thee', reprinted in Farber, *Negative Space*). Farber's particular perspective stemmed in part from the fact that he was a painter as well as a film critic, which accounts for the fact that he is one of the very few writers on film with as much enthusiasm for the avant-garde work of a Michael Snow as for the popular cinema of someone like Hawks. Farber's implied recognition of 'authorship' and his enthusiasm for not only Hawks but also Raoul Walsh, Robert Aldrich and Sam Fuller – all already, or soon to be, as much admired by the French critics – make him very much a precursor of the 'discovery' of Hollywood associated with Andrew Sarris. After the critical discovery of Hawks in the 1960s, Farber wrote another essay on Hawks further elaborating his independent line, and one which has remained important in critical thinking about Hawks ('Howard Hawks', *Artforum*, April 1969, reprinted in *Negative Space* and in Joseph McBride, *Focus on Howard Hawks*). In a kind of recognition of his importance in film critical history *Cahiers du Cinéma* published a fascinating interview with Farber (April 1982) in which, for example, *Rio Bravo* now puts Farber in mind of Chantal Akerman's *Jeanne Dielmann*.

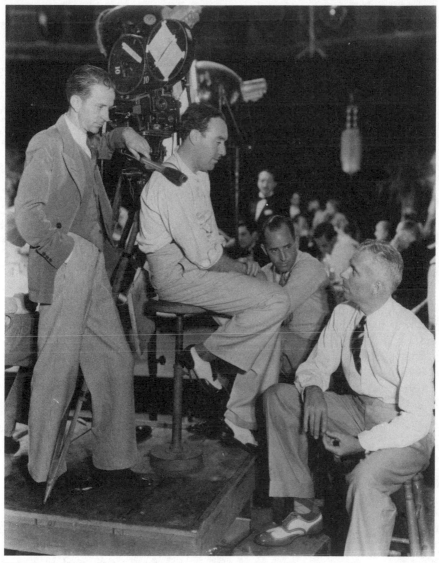

Hawks (rt.) on the set of *Scarface*

Cowboy Cop

G. CAIN (GUILLERMO CABRERA INFANTE)

From G. Cabrera Infante, *A Twentieth Century Job* (London: Faber, 1991).

sometimes,
the sureness of
cain
scares me:
did
von bismarck
really say
that?

Rio Bravo (Warner) poses a posse of problems. A critic should instantly recognize a masterwork but everywhere the film has gotten a thumbs-down at sundown.

In the Unites States it has been considered boring, slow and pretentious. Come on, fellas. *Rio Bravo* is a masterwork and something more: one of the most original films of the year.

Formally the movie is a Western, but it could just as well have been called *Lost Weekend on the Range*, because the central problem here is the means that the town drunk chooses for his rehabilitation – with a little help from John Wayne. At the same time it is a cop movie. For the first time the sheriff is a real policeman and the plot has all the astute legerdemain that Dashiell Hammett made his trademark in a novel that is at the antipodes, *The Maltese Falcon*. From another viewpoint – the formal – it is a study in what could be called the Frozen da Vincian Geometry of the movies. Howard Hawks, the director, has achieved a total mastery of that apparently easy game of chess, as if they were elements in a triangle in which the besieged hypotenuse always finds itself in danger of being crushed by the villainous Anglos.

Dude is the town drunk. The action takes place in Rio Bravo where Spanish is still the dominant language: everyone calls him 'Borrachón'. 'Borrachón' will do anything for a drink, even retrieve a coin that they throw in the saloon spittoon for him. This is what Joe Burdette does in the first scene of the movie, and when Dude masters his disgust and his shame for the sake of his thirst and tries to recover the coin, John T. Chance, the sheriff, kicks it away. Joe Burdette laughs. Dude comprehends, from within the haze of alcohol, his ruin, his total degradation, his vile self. Furious, he hits Chance with a club and leaves him unconscious. He goes after Burdette, who smiles like the villain he is. Dude tries to hit him. Two of Burdette's men pin him down and reduce him to a punching bag and the beast beats him mercilessly. A stranger, repelled, tries to stop the beating, Joe turns around, looks at the man who is holding his arm and, still smiling, draws and kills him. The stranger, unarmed, dies with a look of astonishment. Burdette is now a killer.

This is the first sequence of *Rio Bravo* and the one which engenders not only the movie, but also a new style in Howard Hawks. The whole scene is set up as if it were a pantomime, without words but with the maximum of movement, and only when the sheriff Chance meets up with Burdette in a cantina and tells him, 'Joe, you're under arrest', is the first word said and the movie really begins. The sequence is intended as an ironic response by Hawks to the movies that open with a prologue before the credits or with the credits that are printed over the prologue. This time the prologue is within the context of the film and not only explains the future behaviour of the characters but sets the melodramatic, cop-like and slow-moving tone of this frozen film.

The plot is mainly concerned with the rehabilitation of Dude – played in his now idiosyncratic vein, somewhere between humorous and lightly sarcastic, by Dean Martin, whom the separation from Jerry Lewis has benefited more than one thought. Who, from being a drunken good-for-nothing on account of a woman, goes up step by step in our estimation, thanks to the friendship of a man: Dude helps the sheriff Chance to guard the prisoner while the county marshal is coming for him from abroad. It is this wait – long, enriched by the least expected incidents – that is the subject of *Rio Bravo*. For some it is a stay in the dentist's waiting room. For the *cronista* it is a memorable experience, worthy of remembering: this is what makes masterworks.

Dude's anxiety for alcohol, his courage, his legendary marksmanship, the dry humour of Sheriff Chance – John Wayne is now the great actor of these epics in the dust, whom John Ford discovered in *Stagecoach*. He is the cowboy *par excellence* and aside from Gary Cooper there is no one who can outdo him with his slow drawl, his mincing walk and his aloofness towards life. In *Rio Bravo* Wayne has acted with an ease that the *cronista* has not seen in him for years. The explanation: Wayne was irritated because Dean Martin had all the breaks in his role and because they had put him in between two singers, one almost retired, the other a teenage idol, and he considered himself demeaned and his reputation diminished. Thus he engaged himself to do with a pencil point what it cost the other two God and a proud posse to do. They say that on one occasion Martin and Nelson had to repeat their takes fifteen times while Wayne did his fine on the first.

Then there is the griping bravura of Stumpy – which Walter Brennan has brought off with a competence very much his own: stereotyped but stealing all the scenes like candy from a papoose – the wait in the jail and the growing tension; the rounds of the town, charged with humour and fear; the arrival of Lou Burdette, dashing on his white horse, the unpolluted villain; the song played by the mariachis, Spanish and terrific, that one of the characters explains is 'El degüello', the tune that Santa Anna ordered played day and night before crushing the American resistance at the Alamo: its wailing sound in the night, its repeated macabre insolence; the fatal glass of beer in which the blood of the fugitive killer falls, when Dude is just about to let himself give in to the alcohol and the exacting death of the outlaw in the old style, updated here by that geometry of suspense that one thought Hitchcock had cornered for himself and that is now seen transplanted with easy success to the country of the six-shooter and the stagecoach; the inventive stratagems of the bad guys and the ingenuous, ingenious nature of the good guys, who dispatch their enemies one after another like square dancing without missing a step; the final killing, sportive and so dynamic; and the humorous note with which the movie ends, so like Hollywood and so like Hawks: so like the movies.

Howard Hawks declared once that he did not want to make any more Westerns, as if he thought that *Red River* was a masterwork and there was nothing more to say. Now, with *Rio Bravo* – and the choice of the title leaves nothing to chance: not even the chance in John T. – he has made another masterwork, and in passing he offers a retrospective review of his career: the parody of the genre and of his own work jumps into view. Note that:

Scarface opens with five minutes in which nothing is said and everything happens as in a pantomime: the first killing by Tony Camonte will set the tone for the whole film – and for a whole genre. *Rio Bravo* has the technique of a detective novel and precisely of those written by Dashiell Hammett and Raymond Chandler, who were Hawks's favourites in the past. As in *The Big Sleep, Farewell, My Lovely* or *The Maltese Falcon*, the spectator does not know what will happen next: at times, it is a silly thing, full of whimsy, at others a killing catastrophe, when a murderous bullet pierces the night.

One of Hawks's jerky jokes, noted this time by an English critic, is to have chosen Ward Bond for the character of a wagonmaster and to have killed him off in the first twenty minutes of the film: Bond, surprise, is an indestructible wagonmaster in a long-running television programme. Walter Brennan is in the film as a friendly recall of *To Have and Have Not*, since there he was also an old man, grumpy and lame, and the ending was entrusted to his jerky walk, while Lauren Bacall and Humphrey Bogart were kissing. Also Angie Dickinson – a discovery of Hawks, like Bacall – recalls something of Betty Bacall's role: one of the famous lines of the latter ('It's better when you help,' she said after Bogart showed himself cold to her kisses) is parodied blow by blow by the former: she says, after she has kissed Wayne and he returns the kiss: 'It's better when two people do it.'

The presence of the woman as the disgrace and the grace of a man and the femininely cynical lines of la Dickinson appear in the work of Hawks very frequently, especially in *Gentlemen Prefer Blondes*. The relationship between John Wayne and Rick Nelson – who is not as bad as the reviewers say nor as good as the teenagers wish – is very similar to the relationship between the same Wayne and Montgomery Clift in *Red River*. Throughout the film there are clues that relate to moments in the movie history of Hawks and to very precise moments in his work, which one must know well to be able to detect them.

In sum, *Rio Bravo* is a masterpiece of the genre and one of the most important and richest movies that Howard Hawks, a master, has made. A movie that the *cronista* has enjoyed enormously and that he recommends highly. Although beyond the humour and the sporting chance and the purely filmic he has been able to detect that bad seed of Hollywood, an element which is regrettably always present in Westerns: fascism. *Rio Bravo* shows it clearly in one single sentence. The powerful rancher Lou Burdette says when he sees some of the feats performed by Dude, considered until then an irredeemable derelict: 'Every man should have a little taste of power before he's through.' It happens that that sentence was pronounced some 100 years ago by Otto von Bismarck.

[11 October 1959]

Guillermo Cabrera Infante, the internationally known, idiosyncratic Cuban novelist, also for many years wrote film reviews, under the adopted name of G. Cain (presumably with James M. Cain, and maybe the biblical Cain, in mind), hence the cryptic comment which prefaces the review. Given his relative isolation from critical currents in France and the USA, Cabrera Infante's account of *Rio Bravo* is remarkably perceptive, at both stylistic and thematic levels, and particularly perhaps in its recognition of Hawks's borrowing from and reworking of his own earlier work. Cabrera Infante's writing on film is collected in *A Twentieth Century Job* (London: Faber, 1991).

Interview with Howard Hawks

PETER BOGDANOVICH

From Peter Bogdanovich, *The Cinema of Howard Hawks* (New York: Museum of Modern Art, 1962); also published in *Movie*, no. 5, December 1962.

1926   The Road to Glory
I was not in a very good frame of mind and wrote a complete tragedy. I was told it is not what people like to see, so I switched with my next picture.

1926   Fig Leaves
This opened in the Garden of Eden and moved into a modern story of an Adam and an Eve.
I just tried to say people haven't changed much and that they're the same today.

1927   Paid to Love
A comi-tragic love story, set in a mythical country, about a Parisian night-club performer and a Prince who falls in love with her.
It has no relation to my work. That happened to be a story that I didn't work on and had no sympathy with. I didn't care to do it but was forced to under contract.

'Paid to Love' had a lot of trick work.
It was made right after Murnau's *Sunrise*, which introduced German camera trick-work to Hollywood. I was beginning to direct and was feeling around. They liked it; I didn't. I don't like tricks. I only tried that one time. I've always been rather mechanically minded so I tried a whole lot of mechanical things, and then gave them up completely – most of the time my camera stays on eye level now. Once in a while, I'll move the camera as if a man were walking and seeing something. And it pulls back or it moves in for emphasis when you don't want to make a cut. But, outside of that, I just use the simplest camera in the world.

1928   A Girl in Every Port
This was the beginning of a relationship I have used in a number of pictures. It's really a love story between two men.

50

1928 Fazil
I'm not very fond of the picture. It was a story about a sheik and a modern French girl. It was a contractual thing, someone else's story, and I just shot it.

1928 The Air Circus
Very little story to it. It was just about how a boy learns to fly. I directed it alone and then they wanted to incorporate some talking sequences and they brought a man out who they said was an authority on dialogue and he turned out to be a burlesque comedian. I read the stuff he wrote and said, 'But nobody talks that way.' I said, if you want to do it go ahead, but I won't have anything to do with it. So Lew Seiler came in and did the mawkish dialogue stuff. And they generally botched up the picture.

1930 The Dawn Patrol
It was all for real, even the forced landings. There were a number of scenes where I piloted the air plane with the camera up front. That airplane footage has been used in a number of other pictures: *The Last Flight*, for instance, and the remake of *The Dawn Patrol* with Errol Flynn.

In 'Dawn Patrol', 'Road to Glory' and 'Twentieth Century', you end the picture as it began.
Yes, it's a form of story telling that I think is very fine. You create a character who has a problem and another man comes along and takes over his problem and in the finish he's spent himself and then another man has the problem and it keeps on going. It's like a great mechanic who builds racing cars and one man is killed and then another man is killed and you keep on going – you're not going to stop because of that.

1931 The Criminal Code
Could you say something about the making of 'The Criminal Code'?
The Criminal Code was a play that had merit but had failed on Broadway because of the ending. I got together with ten convicts and said, 'How should this end?' and they told me in no uncertain terms. They had a great deal to do with the formation of many scenes because it was built more or less on the convicts' code of not squealing. I used ex-convicts as extra men all through the picture to give it authenticity. Of course, Huston was one of the greatest actors we've ever had. His character was based on a district attorney we had here in California who was finally tried and sentenced to prison, and they put him in the prison hospital to protect him because the place was full of men he had sent there. Finally, he said, 'I can't take this any longer. I want to go out into the yard.' He went out into the yard, and the scene we did in the picture was just what he did. Things like his being shaved by a man he had sent up for cutting somebody's throat were all true. It was the first time that I discovered almost any tragedy can also be very amusing. In *The Big Sky* we made a comedy scene of Kirk Douglas getting his finger cut off and cauterized and it was very funny.

51

How did the scene in which Phillips Holmes learns of his mother's death evolve. Was it in the script originally?

I don't think so. It's just that when I reach a scene that is too sentimental, I try to turn it and keep it from being sentimental. In *Only Angels Have Wings*, I had a man talking to his friend who's been in an airplane wreck just say to him, 'Your neck is broken, kid.' Just a flat statement; just try to keep things from becoming mawkish. Play against it completely.

1932 The Crowd Roars

The racers in 'The Crowd Roars' seem to have a total disregard for the dangers of their profession.

They fall into the same category as the men in *Hatari!* catching wild animals in Africa. Every day is dangerous, terribly exciting, and they exist on that. They enjoy it and also they greatly understate their feats. After we left Africa, one of the men had a fight with a lion; he was terribly clawed and his reporting of it to me was the greatest piece of understatement I have ever known. He simply told me about the black boy who came up and took his gun and held it against the lion and killed the lion. And he said he was glad that he had trained him well.

1932 Scarface (Shame of the Nation)

How did 'Scarface' come to be made?

Scarface was really the story of Al Capone. When I asked Ben Hecht to write it, he said, 'Oh, we don't want to do a gangster picture.' And I said, 'Well, this is a little different. I would like to do the Capone family as if they were the Borgias set down in Chicago.' And he said, 'We'll start tomorrow.' We took eleven days to write the story and dialogue. We were influenced a good deal by the incestuous elements in the story of the Borgias. We made the brother–sister relationship clearly incestuous. But the censors misunderstood our intention and objected to it because they thought the relationship between them was too beautiful to be attributed to a gangster. We had a scene in which Muni told his sister that he loved her, and we couldn't play it in full light. We wound up playing it in silhouette against a curtain with the light coming from outside. It was a little bit too intimate to show faces – you wouldn't dare take a chance.

How did Raft's coin flipping originate?

There were two or three killings in Chicago where in the fist of the victim they found a nickel. That was a mark of contempt. When we cast Raft in this picture, a coin seemed to be a good thing to use as a mark for the man. It was his first picture and it also helped him fill in things. It became his trade mark.

1932 Tiger Shark

In 'Tiger Shark' you use the idea of a man not being admitted to heaven unless he is whole, and you use it again in 'The Big Sky'. How did this develop?

I knew a man who believed that. He had lost a couple of fingers and he had saved the fingers because he believed that when he died he would have to go to heaven whole. It amused me and I used it several times.

How did the Robinson character develop?
The character was written as a very sedate, solid citizen. It was duller than hell so I stopped on the first day and said to Robinson, 'We're really going to make a horrible thing here.' And I told him about a man I knew that talked a great deal and very fast, and covered up his shyness by doing it. I said, 'If you have enough nerve to try it I'll give you as much help as I can.' So we changed a morose, silent, single-minded man into a very volatile character, who could also be pretty tough.

1933   Today We Live
The picture was written just as it had appeared in the *Post*. It was the story of some men in England during the First World War. It was again our little love theme about two boys who get together. Well, Metro didn't have a picture for Joan Crawford, so a week before we started they announced to me that she was in the picture. We had to change it considerably from what we had started with; to make it worse, she tried to talk like the men. It didn't come out the same.

1934   Twentieth Century
The extremely fast pace of your comedies, like 'Twentieth Century', is not achieved through cutting, is it?
No, it isn't done with cutting. It's done by deliberately writing dialogue like real conversation – you're liable to interrupt me and I'm liable to interrupt you – so you write in such a way that you can overlap the dialogue but not lose anything. It's just a trick. It's a trick getting people to do it too – it takes about two or three days to get them accustomed to it and then they're off. You must allow for it in your dialogue with just the addition of a few little words in front. 'Well, I think—' that's all you need, and then say what you have to say. All you want to do is to hear the essential things; if you don't hear those in a scene, you're lost. You have to tell the sound man what lines he must hear and he must let you know if he does. This also allows you to do throwaways – it keeps an actor from hitting a line too hard. Actually we started to use speed in *Scarface* and that had probably a twenty percent faster tempo than anything that had been made to date. And, of course, if I have a scene today that I don't think is very interesting the quicker I can play it the better off I am.

How did you arrive at your techniques of pacing?
As far as speed is concerned, I was trained in the old two-reel comedy school where all we were after was speed. People seemed to like it, so I thought why not play all comedy fast. The only other picture that was supposed to be fast was *The Front Page*; I said it had a false sense of speed. In *Dawn Patrol* we underplayed, dispensing with the emoting and ham-acting

which was habitual up until then. Consequently I had one communication after another from the front office telling me I was not taking advantages of my scenes, but I was simply playing them a different way, you see.

The scene in the train compartment, when she tried to kick him, looks particularly impromptu. Was it?
That was the first scene we shot in the picture. Lombard had never done that kind of comedy before, but I cast her because I'd seen her at a party with a couple of drinks in her and she was hilarious and uninhibited and just what the part needed. But when she came on the set she was emoting all over the place. She was trying very hard, but it was just dreadful. Barrymore was very patient and we tried it a few times but she was so stilted and stiff. Then I said to her, 'Come on, let's take a walk,' and we went outside, and I asked her how much money she was getting for the picture. She told me and I said, 'What would you say if I told you that you'd earned your whole salary this morning and didn't have to act any more?' And she was stunned. So I said, 'Now forget about the scene; what would you do if someone said such and such to you?' And she said, 'I'd kick him in the stomach.' And I said, 'Well, he said something like that to you, why don't you kick him?' And she said, 'Are you kidding?' And I said, 'No.' So we went back on the set and I gave her some time to think it over and then we tried that scene and we did one take and that was it. And afterwards, Barrymore said, 'That was fabulous!' And she burst into tears and ran off the set. She never began a picture that she didn't send me a telegram saying, 'I'm gonna start kicking him.'

1935   Barbary Coast
I don't remember the story too well except it was about a girl who arrived in the San Francisco Bay, in a ship that came round the Horn, only to discover that the man she was going to marry had been shot in a gambling game. I didn't like the picture much. I thought it was a contrived thing, more or less done to order, and a lot of trouble. As Ben Hecht said, 'Miriam Hopkins came to the Barbary Coast and wandered around like a confused Goldwyn Girl.'

1936   The Road to Glory
The men in your war and adventure films never question the impossible conditions under which they work.
They know there's nothing to be gained by it. It's part of the game. They take planes up and test them; they take cars out and test them. And having been schooled to the Army, they accept commands, no matter what the command. And that's what makes an army function. It's just a calm acceptance of a fact. In *Only Angels Have Wings*, after Joe dies, Cary Grant says, 'He just wasn't good enough.' Well, that's the only thing that keeps people going. They just have to say, 'Joe wasn't good enough, and I'm better than Joe, so I go ahead and do it.' And they find out they're not any better than Joe, but then it's too late, you see.

1938   Bringing Up Baby

In 'Bringing Up Baby' and several of your other comedies, aren't you expressing your annoyance with scientists and academicians?
No, if you're going to do a picture, the fun of it is to do a characterization, something very close to caricature. And the moment you caricature it, you're accused of disliking it. But really you're just picking things that make a caricature – the attitude of newspapermen, the attitude of scientists – and it's bound to make people think you're poking fun at them. That's why a scientist or inventor or a man who's in a location that's interesting is fun to do. But it's a form of caricature work that you're doing and we do it with Westerns, we do it with every picture. If you don't do a caricature, you don't have a character.

By the end of 'Bringing Up Baby', hasn't Grant abandoned his scientific life?
Well, let's say he's mixed it. He had an awfully good time and if you had to choose between the two girls, you'd certainly choose Hepburn. You see, you start off, as I say, with a complete caricature of the man and then reduce it to give him a feeling of normality because he certainly wouldn't have had fun going through life the other way, would he? He becomes more normal as the picture goes along, just by his association with the girl. Grant said, 'I'm kind of dropping my characterization.' I said, 'No, she's having some influence on you. You're getting a little normal.'

Is Hepburn then the normal one in the picture?
I think the picture had a great fault and I learned an awful lot from it. There were no normal people in it. Everyone you met was a screwball. Since that time I have learned my lesson and I don't intend ever again to make everybody crazy. If the gardener had been normal, if the sheriff had been just a perplexed man from the country – but as it was they were all way off centre. And it was a mistake that I realized after I made it and I haven't made it since. Harold Lloyd told me though that it was the best constructed comedy he had ever seen and that to him it was a classic.

It is much darker in terms of lighting than most comedies.
They're inclined to start a comedy with a very funny main title and animated stuff that seems to say, 'Now we're gonna be funny.' In *Hatari!* we started almost with tragedy and not until they discovered the man was going to live did it become funny. It crept up on people; they weren't told to laugh. And the more dangerous and the more exciting, the easier it is to get a laugh.

There seems to be a very dark, though nonetheless hilarious, quality to the night scenes when Grant and Hepburn are looking for the bone.
Well, it was a complete tragedy to Cary, wasn't it? You see, you get a certain dignity with a scientist. Now if he gets down on all fours and scrambles for something, he becomes funny. And that's the thing Chaplin was always so good at. And it goes way back to the scene in *A Girl in Every*

55

Port where they push policemen into the water. They didn't like cops. They weren't vicious or mean about it, but policemen interfered with their fun and so they disposed of them. The more dignified somebody is – Katie Hepburn in *Bringing Up Baby* – losing the back of her dress became funny because she was dressed up and superior to the whole situation and she became ridiculous.

1939   Only Angels Have Wings
In 'Only Angels Have Wings' you established for the first time the theme for your love scene, variations of which you use in 'To Have and Have Not', 'Red River', 'The Big Sleep', 'Rio Bravo', and 'Hatari!' You rather like a relationship where the woman is the aggressive one.
Yes, it was first used in *Only Angels Have Wings*, and it was in *To Have and Have Not* and *The Big Sleep*, and very definitely in *Rio Bravo* and *Hatari!* I do that on purpose every once in a while because it amuses people, especially the people I like. How many times are you going to use that? Just as often as they'll laugh at it. It's just a method of thinking and it becomes attractive because they don't act like a heroine or a hero. They're just kind of normal people. I call it honesty and it allows you to make a scene that's a little different. Hitchcock tried it in *North by Northwest*.

Were a lot of the incidents in 'Only Angels Have Wings' things that you had heard about or experienced?
Yes, every character was taken from life. Barthelmess was a man I saw jump out of an airplane, leaving another behind. The linking of those incidents was done fictionally but actually the character of Jean Arthur and her relation to Cary Grant was a true story, based on fact. The bird coming through the windshield was a fact, and the place was real – a little Grace Line port in South America.

The characters in your films make a point of ignoring tragedy, as in 'Only Angels' where Grant says 'Who's Joe—' after Joe is killed.
Well, that's a simple thing. You take two viewpoints. One is Josef von Sternberg's. Somebody had a bright idea that if the two of us made a picture together we could make a super-picture, but I said it's utterly ridiculous. You can start the two of us off on the same story and you'd never recognize it as we'd change the characters. He blows up a little bit of a thing (and at that time he was one of the greatest directors we had) into a great big situation, and I take a great big situation and play it way down. So we'd have exactly opposite viewpoints. And I think you get a sigh of relief from an audience when they see a familiar old situation come up and you don't bore them with it – just hit it and go on. But, anyway, the men that I show and choose to show, they don't dramatize those things, they underplay them, which is normal with that type of man. The average movie talks too much; you have to make your scenes and plant them and then let the audience do a little work so they become part of it. Any script that *reads* well is no good. If you have to read it three times to understand it, you've got a

chance of getting a movie out of it. But if it starts out saying, 'He looks at her and the yearning of ten years shows in his eyes . . .' I've never found an actor who can do that.

Also in 'Only Angels', as in many of your films, there is the theme of professionalism. You have strong feelings about this, don't you?
And the men in it have too. It's their job, they're supposed to do it. You get a stunt team in acrobatics in the air – if one of them is no good, then they're all in trouble. If someone loses his nerve catching animals, then the whole bunch can be in trouble. I have a complete tape of all the sound of the British bombing the three dams that really changed the course of the war. And they got out there early in the morning and the leader said, 'You fellows stick around and I'll take a run through and see if they've got any cables stretched.' And then one of them said, 'I'll buy you a beer when you get back.' And the man says, 'There's no cable, you can go right on through.' He says, 'I'll go a little off to one side and a little ahead of you and maybe I can draw their fire.' And they got every other one through – first, third, fifth – but second, fourth and sixth were shot down. I was going to film that. They had a complete record of the entire conversation; Mr Churchill sent it to me. And these were kids – twenty-one was the oldest – but they were fifty or sixty in their training. And that's the attitude they have. It isn't anything I've invented. It's just something I've seen and it interests me and so I use it.

1940   His Girl Friday
I was going to prove to somebody one night that *The Front Page* had the finest modern dialogue that had been written, and I asked a girl to read Hildy's part and I read the editor and I stopped and I said, 'Hell, it's better between a girl and a man than between two men,' and I called Ben Hecht and I said, 'What would you think of changing it so that Hildy is a girl?' And he said, 'I think it's a great idea,' and he came out and we did it.

1940   The Outlaw
The original story I heard in New Mexico was that Pat Garrett had blown the face off somebody and buried him as Billy the Kid and let Billy the Kid go – so we started from that and we wrote a story. I found Jane Russell and Jack Buetel and I thought it was just a little Western and I had my fun with it. But I had a chance to do *Sergeant York*, and I wanted to do that, and Hughes wanted to direct, so I said, 'You go ahead and direct and finish it.' I made the introduction of Billy the Kid and Doc Holliday on location, and then Hughes messed up the rest. I directed a couple of weeks of it. Probably a thousand or fifteen hundred feet of what I did remained in it.

1941   Sergeant York
Huston and I wrote the script. We just kept ahead of shooting. We threw away the written script and did what Jesse Lasky told us about the real

57

Sergeant York. Huston and I were very much in accord and it became very easy to tell the story simply.

You particularly enjoyed making this film?
Especially because Lasky gave me my first good job and he was broke at the time and after I talked to him, I called up Gary Cooper and I said, 'Coop, didn't Lasky give you your first job?' and he said, 'Yes,' and I said, 'Well, he's broke and he needs a shave and he's got a story and I think we could do it and I don't think he would hurt us.' So Coop came over and we talked about everything but the story – he talked about a new gun and finally I said, 'Let's talk about the story,' and he said, 'What's the use of talking about it, we're going to do the damn thing, you know that.' And I said, 'Well, let's go over to Warners and make a deal, and if I say "Isn't that right, Mr Cooper?" you say yes.' So I said, 'We'll do it if you let us alone – isn't that right, Mr Cooper?' 'Yes.' 'If you come in, if you butt in on us, we'll be really hard to handle. Isn't that right, Mr Cooper?' He'd say, 'Yes.' So we made the deal and we made the film. And Lasky made two million out of it and we were terribly pleased to have helped somebody. And the funny thing about it was that it turned out to be a hell of a picture and Cooper got an Academy Award and we had no idea it was going to be anything like that. (*Hawks was nominated for an Oscar for his direction; it was the first and last time to date.*)

The ending of 'Sergeant York' is actually quite tragic, in that a very religious man is rewarded for going against his beliefs. Did you want it to appear that way?
Well, it was based on the theory you are talking about. It was based on a man who actually was very religious; and so they told him to go out and do everything his religion said not to do, and he became a great hero doing it. So there was bound to be a good deal of confusion in his mind and actually it *was* a form of tragedy. I asked him hundreds of questions, as you are asking me questions, and he answered them. I asked him how he got religion. 'I got it in the middle of the road,' he said. So my visualization of that was a mule, getting hit by lightning in the middle of the road. They wrote a remarkable scene of how he got religion and I didn't believe it. I said if anyone talked to me like that, I wouldn't get religion. So we got some real people from Tennessee to sing, they got excited, and we brought him to a little meeting house, and while they were singing he got religion. But if you will notice, again, it's underplaying. If they want to believe it, fine, but you don't cram it down their throats. I went back down there after the picture was made to see how good a job I had done and I heard some people talking and one of them said, 'I saw me a picture last night – it was about hill people and the fellow certainly knew what he was doing when he made that picture. He's got them to look just like hill people – they talk just like hill people.' Well, I had some of those people to help me, and they would say a line and then the actors would say the line, and things changed, you see. One of the best things in the picture was the mother who

58

didn't do much talking. The writers had given her a lot of great lines and I kept taking them away from her and finally I said, 'I know what we're after – I want somebody who doesn't talk.' 'That I can understand,' she said. But they're very childlike, those people, they're extremely backward – the little scenes in the store indicated that – so you are not treating a sophisticated man – he was bewildered. And we tried to show a bewildered man. I don't attempt to preach or prove anything – I just figure out what I think was in the man and tell it. His comment was interesting. He said, 'I supplied the tree and Hawks put the leaves on it.' I thought it was kind of a nice comment.

1944   To Have and Have Not

How did the Bacall character in 'To Have and Have Not' develop?
We discovered that she was a little girl who, when she became insolent, became rather attractive. That was the only way you noticed her, because she could do it with a grin. So I said to Bogey, 'We are going to try an interesting thing. You are about the most insolent man on the screen and I'm going to make a girl a little more insolent than you are.' 'Well,' he said, 'you're going to have a fat time doing that.' And I said, 'No, I've got a great advantage because I'm the director. I'll tell you just one thing: she's going to walk out on you in every scene.' 'You've won already.' So as every scene ended, she walked out on him. It was a sex antagonism, that's what it was, and it made the scenes easy. But it wouldn't be any good with John Wayne, because he is not the insolent type. There's a place in *Hatari!* where the girl says, 'I was chased by a bull once,' and he says, 'Are you sure it wasn't the other way around?' That's more like Bogey.

'To Have and Have Not' and 'The Big Sleep' seem to me the two most perfect elaborations of the Bogart character, and the most complete. How do you feel about that?
Well, that's just taking advantage of what I think about Bogart. To me, they are rather like the same picture. He was extremely easy to work with, really underrated as an actor. My kind of actor, you know. And the little queer things he did because he had a nerve cut in his upper lip – so his upper lip wouldn't smile – only his lower lip would smile. We seemed to understand one another and work very well together. Without his help I couldn't have done what I did with Bacall. The average leading man would have gotten sick and tired of the rehearsal and the fussing around. Not very many actors would sit around and wait while a girl steals a scene. But he fell in love with the girl and the girl with him, and that made it easy.

'To Have and Have Not' is basically a love story. You don't think much of the political intrigues in the picture, do you?
Oh, well, you notice how long it took us to fill in the other plot. As a matter of fact, the writer got terribly worried. He said, 'I'm going to quit.' I said, 'Why?' He said, 'Here we are four reels into the picture and you're afraid to tell the plot – will you go on and do these scenes!' I said, 'I guess

I've just been steering away from them because they're so dull.' But we had to have a plot, you know, a secondary plot, but it was just an excuse for some scenes. Out of the wounded man we got a marvellous scene about one girl fainting, and the other girl fanning ether fumes on her. And lines of hers as when Bogart is carrying the fainted girl, she says, 'You trying to guess her weight?' That goes way back to Dietrich – in *Morocco*, Sternberg made Dietrich come in and find Cooper with two native girls on his lap, and she kind of congratulated him – she didn't get angry at it. So Bacall is a warmer version of Dietrich. Dietrich knew it the moment she saw the picture. She said, 'That's me, isn't it?' and I said, 'Yeah.'

1946   The Big Sleep
What does the title, 'The Big Sleep', refer to?
I don't know, probably death. It just sounds good. I never could figure the story out. I read it and was delighted by it. The scenario took eight days to write, and all we were trying to do was to make every scene entertain. We didn't know about the story. They asked me who killed such and such a man – I didn't know. They sent a wire to the author – he didn't know. They sent a wire to the scenario writer and he didn't know. But it didn't stop the picture from being very fast and very entertaining. Then, when the picture was getting ready to go to New York, the publicity man said, 'Howard, what will I tell them about this picture?' And I said, 'Well, tell them it's kind of interesting because it's told from the point of view of the detective and there are no red herrings. And if anybody can follow the plot they have to follow what he is thinking.' And I can't, and he can't, so an audience might be amused. The picture turned out to be very good from an audience stand-point. And it disarmed the critics because they were trying to be as smart as the fellow in the picture and they ended up being no smarter.

It is really kind of a parody of private eye pictures, isn't it, with all the girls falling for Bogart?
Oh, yeah, you're just having fun. The main idea was to try and make every scene fun to look at. A place where Bogey was to walk into a book store I said, 'This is an awfully ordinary scene. Can't you think of something to do?' And he just pushed up his hat brim, put on glasses and got a little ef-feminate. The moment he did that, I said, 'O.K. come on, we're off, I'll write some new dialogue when we're inside.' But just going in that way made it fun. It was just two people a little bit bored. About eight months after we had finished it, they asked me to make some more scenes between Bogart and Bacall – they said they didn't have enough scenes of them together. It was during the racing season at Santa Anita and I had some horses out there and so I made them talk about riding a horse, and it ended with 'It depends on who's in the saddle.' And it was just that I was think-ing about racing and I thought, well, I'll do a scene about a little love ar-gument about racing.

So, again, the plot mattered very little to you.

It didn't matter at all. As I say, neither the author, the writer, nor myself knew who had killed whom. It was all what made a good scene. I can't follow it. I saw some of it on television last night, and it had me thoroughly confused, because I hadn't seen it in twenty years.

1948   Red River
In 'Red River', as well as in 'The Big Sky', 'Hatari!', and even in 'A Girl In Every Port', you have two strangers meet, have a fight, and then become the best of friends. How did you come upon this idea?
Oh, I don't know. Probably the best friend I ever had I ran off a race track through a fence before I met him, and then we met and became friends. And you are always more interested in an antagonist than somebody who's terribly nice to you. In *Red River*, Wayne admired Clift's spirit. It was done to try and show why there is a relationship between people.

There is a certain ambiguity in Wayne's character, isn't there? What was your opinion of his character?
Well, Wayne is a man who made a big mistake and lost the girl he was really in love with because of ambition and the great desire to have land of his own. Having made a mistake, it would make him all the more anxious to go through with his plans. Because a man who has made a great mistake to get somewhere is not going to stop at small things. He built up an empire, and it was falling to pieces. He warned them about what they were getting into and said there would be no quitting. And they quit on him. We were walking a tightrope in telling a story like that. Are you still going to like Wayne or not? Fortunately, we ended up with a good characterization and you did like Wayne. Let's say his motive was entirely self-centered. In contrast, Cary Grant in *Only Angels Have Wings* had no selfish motivation at all. He was doing a job for a man he liked – a man who was unable to do it himself – so it was pure friendship. He could look at the Dutchman and say, 'I can't let this fellow get away with this;' so he said, 'You're fired, you're through, because you want to quit.'

You were criticized for not ending 'Red River' with someone getting killed – either Wayne or Clift – but that would not have fitted in with your point of view, would it?
No, the premise of the scene, I think, is logical. If we overdid it a little bit or went too far, well, I didn't know any other way to end it. I certainly would have hated to kill one of them. It frustrates me to start killing people off for no reason at all. I did it in *Dawn Patrol*, but when I finished, I realized how close I'd come to messing the thing up, and I didn't want to monkey with that again. I'm interested in having people go and see the picture, and enjoy it.

1949   I Was a Male War Bride (You Can't Sleep Here)
What would you say 'I Was A Male War Bride' was really about?
Oh, I don't know. Two people get married and red tape keeps them from

sleeping together. There's a Polish version of the same story done dramatically, *The Eighth Day of the Week*, with one funny sequence in it, but basically it's a complete tragedy. Like that picture about the suicide, *Fourteen Hours*. I said the only way I would have done that was if the man had been Cary Grant and he'd been making love to this woman and her husband came in so he jumped onto the window ledge and pretended to be attempting suicide. After *War Bride*, Zanuck said, 'I've got a great idea – you and Grant do *Charley's Aunt*' and I said, 'We just did it.' One of the good scenes in *War Bride* is where the brides marrying GIs had to say if they had any woman trouble or had they ever been pregnant, and it was a beautifully written scene, and Grant, being a man, was supposed to be embarrassed. And I said, 'Try it the opposite way. Let the sergeant be embarrassed at having to ask you these things. Say, "Oh, many times, Sergeant. Oh, I have a great deal of trouble."' Then it became funny, and the other way, it wasn't. And that's the good thing about Grant. You say, 'Cary, let's try it the opposite way. It will change your dialogue, but don't let it worry you. Say anything you think, and if you can't think of the right thing, I'll write it down for you.' But he thinks of the right thing and we go ahead and do it. We have a scene in *Bringing Up Baby* where he's angry. I said, 'Pretty dull. You get angry like Joe Doaks next door. Can't you think of somebody who gets angry and it's funny?' And then I remembered a man who practically whinnies like a horse when he's angry – so he did it.

1951   The Thing (From Another World)
Were you purposely criticizing scientists in 'The Thing'?
Oh, no, it just worked out that way. You see we had to make it plausible – why they let the thing live. In order to make it plausible we turned them into heavies – it had to be an honest sort of dedication on their part. That was fun to do, taking a stab at science fiction. I bought the story; it was just four pages long, and we took about a week to write it. We had trouble the first two days finding a way of telling the story. Finally we got the idea of the reporter and we told it through his eyes.

1952   The Big Sky
Wasn't the end of 'The Big Sky' intended to be tragic, in that Martin stays behind with the girl, not because he loves her, but because if he doesn't stay with her he will lose the friendship of Douglas, who actually does love her?
Yes, that's very much what we were trying to do there, but I don't think I did a good job of it. Oddly enough, I don't think there was any warmth in the relationship of those two people. I had planned it but it just didn't come off. And I think it is very much of a failure on my part in telling the story of friendship between two men. I look on Kirk as being one of our great heavies – every time he's played that kind of thing he's been awfully good. And when he attempts to be too pleasant or show friendship, it doesn't come off. I think he was the wrong person to put into that picture to make it really come off as I had planned.

1952   O. Henry's Full House
This episode was cut on some parts of its release.
I imagine it was cut because it wasn't really O. Henry. I started out just to make a comedy and got a long way from O. Henry. They probably didn't think it fit with the other episodes that had been made for the picture.

1952   Monkey Business
What are your feelings about 'Monkey Business'?
I don't believe the premise of *Monkey Business* was really believable and for that reason the film was not as funny as it should have been. The episodes that directly concerned the monkey were unbelievable. The other episodes seemed to work out very well where you could accept the premise. But I think we got the audience started on the wrong foot. I don't think they believed a monkey could put those things together, so it became a little too much of a farce. Also the great trouble with the scenes where Ginger Rogers becomes adolescent was that they were completely repetitive. Cary Grant had already done it and he had the best of it because he had done it first – and his part was written better.

1953   Gentlemen Prefer Blondes
Don't you find it ironic that some people found Monroe and Russell sexy in 'Gentlemen Prefer Blondes', when you actually intended the opposite?
It's ironic. Actually to me they were very amusing and it was a complete caricature, a travesty on sex. It didn't have normal sex. Jane Russell was supposed to represent sanity and Marilyn played a girl who was solely concerned with marrying for money. She had her own little odd code and she lived by it. The child was the most mature one on board the ship, and I think he was a lot of fun. We purposely made the picture as loud and bright as we could, and completely vulgar in costumes and everything. No attempt at reality. We were doing a musical comedy, pure and simple.

1955   Land of the Pharaohs
Why do you like this least of your own films?
I don't know how a Pharaoh talks. And Faulkner didn't know. None of us knew. We thought it'd be an interesting story, the building of a pyramid, but then we had to have a plot, and we didn't really feel close to any of it.

Is the last line, 'We have a long way to go', your comment on humanity?
Yes, on that phase of humanity. You see, the Pharaoh was a little too narrow, too one-sided a character. He had one belief and he stuck to it and you heard it too many times. I got a feeling we were doing repetitive scenes and it was awfully hard to deepen them because we didn't know how those Egyptians thought or what they said. All we knew about them was this strange desire to amass a fortune to be used in their second life, as they called it. So you don't know what to try for at all. You don't know whether to make the girl a little more evil or the Pharaoh a little more dominating. You kind of lose all sense of values. You don't know who somebody's for

and if you don't have a rooting interest and you're not for somebody then you haven't got a picture.

'Land of The Pharaohs' is the only film you've made in CinemaScope. What do you think of the process?
I don't think that CinemaScope is a good medium. It's good only for showing great masses of movement. For other things, it's distracting, it's hard to focus attention, and it's very difficult to cut. Some people just go ahead and cut it and let people's eyes jump around and find what they want to find. It's very hard for an audience to focus – they have too much to look at – they can't see the whole thing. If you are going to cut to a close-up, you should have a man speaking in the same relative position on the screen. It's hard to form those compositions. I like the 1.85 to 1 ratio better than any other – the one we used for *Rio Bravo* and *Hatari!* – it gives you just a little more space on the sides. If the CinemaScope size had been any good, painters would have used it many years ago – and they've been at it a lot longer than we have.

1959   Rio Bravo
After 'Pharaohs', you waited three years before making 'Rio Bravo'. Why?
Well, I just got to thinking of how we used to make pictures and how we were making them now, and I reviewed the making of a lot of pictures that I had liked. Today they want you to stick to a script and the easiest, simplest way for the physical facilities of a studio is the best way to do it. So I determined to go back and try to get a little of the spirit we used to make pictures with. We used to use comedy whenever we could and then we got too serious about it. So, in *Rio Bravo* I imagine there are almost as many laughs as if we had started out to make a comedy. I also decided that audiences were getting tired of plots and, as you know, *Rio Bravo* and *Hatari!* have little plot and more characterization. And so far it has worked out very well. People seem to like it better. I don't mean that if a story comes along you shouldn't do it, but I think the average plot is pretty time-worn. Television has come in and they have used so many thousands of plots that people are getting tired of them. They're a little too inclined – if you lay a plot down – to say, 'Oh, I've seen this before.' But if you can keep them from knowing what the plot is you have a chance of holding their interest. And it leads to characters – so that you may write what the character might think and the character motivates your story and the situations – and it's when a character believes in something that a situation happens, not because you write it to happen.

But haven't most of your pictures dealt with characters rather than situations?
Well, sometimes it takes you a little while to realize what you did unconsciously, and then you can begin to do it purposely, and then it makes working very much simpler. But harder, too, because it is easy to follow a plot but without one it's pretty hard sometimes to tell what to do.

Was 'Rio Bravo' made up as you went along?

No, it was just an elaboration of the characters. We'd say, now here we have a scene; let's put a little character in it. What do you think this man would do? And, no, he wouldn't do that, he'd do this. And you can't do it in an office. With a play the writer sits and watches dozens of rehearsals and things change. We can't change. Once we've got a scene in the can, as it were, it's going to be there on the screen, so we have to feel our way as we go along and we can add to a character or get a piece of business between two people and start some relationship going and then further it. In *Rio Bravo*, Dean Martin had a bit in which he was required to roll a cigarette. His fingers weren't equal to it and Wayne kept passing him cigarettes. All of a sudden you realize that they are awfully good friends or he wouldn't be doing it. That grew out of Martin's asking me one day 'Well, if my fingers are shaky, how can I roll this thing?' So Wayne said, 'Here, I'll hand you one,' and suddenly we had something going. Or like the baby elephants in *Hatari!* and what they did. You can't just start out to do a thing like that I don't think the average studio would be pleased to spend six or seven million dollars on a picture of that sort without any story. But it isn't as odd as it sounds. You may have a perfectly good scene, but as the character develops in the story, as he becomes clearer to you, you realize that the scene you are doing has little or no characterization; so you begin to add character to the man. You're actually doing the same scene but you're giving him a few different words and you're getting new attitudes into it. The crux of *Rio Bravo* is not Wayne – it is Dean Martin's story. As a matter of fact, Wayne said, 'What do I do while he's playing all these good scenes?' 'Well,' I said, 'you look at him as a friend.' And he said, 'OK. I know what to do.' Actually it becomes a great part for Wayne because he's going through all these things because of friendship. He's wondering how good this man is, whether he's been ruined or whether he's going to come out all right. You watch a man develop and end up well and the friend is glad for it.

How did you come to make 'Rio Bravo'?

It started with some scenes in a picture called *High Noon*, in which Gary Cooper ran around trying to get help and no one would give him any. And that's rather a silly thing for a man to do, especially since at the end of the picture he is able to do the job by himself. So I said, we'll do just the opposite, and take a real professional viewpoint: as Wayne says when he's offered help, 'If they're really good, I'll take them. If not, I'll just have to take care of them.' We did everything that way, the exact opposite. It annoyed me in *High Noon* so I tried the opposite and it worked, and people liked it. And then, of course, we had a lot of fun in the picture. I mean crazy reactions – I don't think they're crazy, I think they're normal – but according to bad habits we've fallen into, they seemed crazy. Everyone was urged and egged on to find new things. Things like the explosion of dynamite at the end – that was the art director's creation. He overdid it one time and in our big explosion he put in red and yellow and green paper and when it went up the whole house looked like a big Chinese firecracker. We all started to laugh and I said, 'What did you do?' And he said, 'Well, I figured that that building would have invoices of different colours, but,' he said, 'it's the most horrible looking thing I've ever seen.' He rebuilt it and we did it normally, but it looked like some huge marvellous bomb going off at Monte Carlo – it was very funny.

1962   Hatari!

'Hatari!' was largely improvised while on location, wasn't it?
Well, you can't sit in an office and write what a rhino or any other animal is going to do. From the time we saw one of them to the time we either caught it or failed to, it wouldn't be more than four minutes. So we had to make up scenes in an awful hurry; we couldn't write them. We threw out many good scenes – maybe we can use them in another picture sometime. But the whole story was outlined when we started. We were lucky enough to catch every kind of animal in Africa – everything we'd hoped for – usually if you get one-third you're lucky.

Then you really caught those animals yourselves?
Oh, yes, there was no doubling at all – the actors caught the animals. We chased sixteen rhinos and caught four with ropes. You know, there is a lot of excitement when you get hold of one of those things. They caught a number of animals not shown in the film – you can't keep going forever. I've got enough footage for another hour.

The picture is really a series of vignettes, isn't it?
I'd rather say that the form of the picture is a hunting season, from beginning to end. It's what happens when a bunch of fellows get together and hunt during a season. Elsa Martinelli is the famous girl photographer, Ylla, who was so damned attractive that men would put her in the places where she could get the best pictures in the world. She fell off a truck and got killed in South Africa. I heard about some of her romances and that's where that character started. The character of the younger French girl was based on a true story of a girl with a famous father who was killed by a rhino and these men used his farm, and the girl grew up with these men around her. Instead of getting a little, frail girl, I got a big, lusty kid who's just growing up, you know, who kind of lumbered around, and had fun with it.

How did the scene of Buttons repeatedly asking them to tell him about the rocket develop?
Have you ever seen *Of Mice and Men*?

You mean where Lennie asks George to tell him about the rabbits. Was that scene your take-off on it?
Yes. I brought down a copy of the book and let Red read it, and wrote some dialogue and said, 'Go ahead and make it.' First take and we made it.

Which of your pictures do you like best?
Oh, I imagine I like *Scarface*, and I like *Male War Bride*, and I like the last one, *Hatari!*

Interview recorded in Hawks's office in Paramount Studios, Hollywood, April 9th and 10th, 1962.

Peter Bogdanovich and Andrew Sarris were among the first American critics (following Manny Farber) to establish Hawks's reputation in the USA. Bogdanovich wrote *The Cinema of Howard Hawks* for the New York Museum of Modern Art, as the programme for their July 1962 Hawks season, and the programme included this interview, which was reprinted in *Movie* no. 5, December 1962, and reprinted again as the programme for the National Film Theatre Hawks season (November 1962 to January 1963). Though there had been an earlier interview with Hawks in *Cahiers* (February 1956, translated and reprinted in Andrew Sarris (ed.), *Interviews with Film Directors* (New York: Bobbs-Merrill, 1967) and many later interviews (see the Bibliography in this volume), the Bogdanovich interview was without doubt the one which had most influence on ways of thinking about Hawks among British and US critics in the 1960s. Hawks's ideas and attitudes to his work as evidenced in the interview enabled *Movie* to preface its Hawks issue with the assertion that 'When one talks about the heroes of *Red River*, or *Rio Bravo*, or *Hatari!*, one is talking about Hawks himself'.

Hawks's Comedies

V. F. PERKINS

From *Movie*, no. 5, December 1962.

In his interview with Peter Bogdanovich, Howard Hawks criticizes *Bringing Up Baby* for just the quality which makes it one of the screen's greatest comedies. 'If only the gardener had been normal': that would have been a cardinal error. Standards which would be relevant to, say, Cukor's naturalistic comedies are quite inapplicable here. Cukor's comedies are funniest when they are most 'real', but Hawks's depend on the reversal of all our preconceptions about character and behaviour. Thus in Cukor's *Born Yesterday* the 'dumb blonde' reactions come from a dumb Brooklyn blonde (Judy Holliday). In *Bringing Up Baby* they come from an intelligent Connecticut society girl (Katharine Hepburn). Hawks's achievement is to create a world in which the abnormal is the norm and where, in consequence, the rational seems outrageous. In this world a postman's reaction to your announcement that you are about to be married is not 'Congratulations!' but a sombre 'Don't let it throw you, buster.'

The Ransom of Red Chief, Hawks's contribution to the Fox omnibus picture *Full House*, is a concentrated exercise in the reversal of normal patterns of behaviour. Its heroes, two 'confidence men without confidence' (Fred Allen and Oscar Levant), kidnap a little boy, 'J.B.' Dawson. They are observed in this by the child's mother. She offers a languid commentary. 'Now they're puttin' a sack over his head . . . Now they're takin' him away.' Her husband sways placidly in his rocking-chair. 'Must be strangers,' he says. Mom wanders away with an apathetic 'More'n likely.' J.B. terrorises and humiliates his captors. Mr Dawson demands a cash payment before he will take his son back. The kidnappers pay the ransom, their entire savings. As Slick Sam hands over the money he tells the Dawsons, 'You gotta gold mine in that boy.'

Red Chief turns inside out all the devices of a 'mechanics of crime' picture. *Monkey Business* and *I Was a Male War Bride* (*You Can't Sleep Here*) similarly proceed with a remorseless logic from very simple premises. What if the elixir of youth endowed its discoverers with the mental, as well as the physical, attributes of youngsters? What if the protocol devised for the transport of war brides to the States were applied to the *husband* of an American service*woman*?

Bringing Up Baby has no such premise. Its plot is either non-existent or frantically complicated, as you wish. Turn it inside out and it would still be crazy. In every other respect, though, the Hawks law of reversal applies. David Huxley (Cary Grant) learns that Katharine Hepburn has gone off to catch, not her aunt's tame leopard 'Baby', but a ferocious circus beast who has recently mauled its trainer. 'Poor darling Susan,' he says, 'she's in danger and she's helpless without me.' Cut to an exasperated Susan determinedly dragging the said beast up the steps of the local constabulary. The most consistently 'reversed' of the characters in *Bringing Up Baby* is Major Horace Applegate, a big-game hunter. He is presented as an effeminate pedant who cannot distinguish between the cries of leopard and loon. He is also a coward and a rotten shot.

Normal relationships as well as consistent characterization are over-turned. *Monkey Business*, like *Red Chief*, reverses the adult–child relation-ship. George Winslow, the eight-year-old baritone, overcomes by a neat piece of blackmail Hugh Marlowe's reluctance to act as maypole for a gang of infant savages: 'Don't you like children?' 'Of course.' 'Why are you mean to them, then?'

Most of all Hawks likes to upset the relationship between the sexes. Cary Grant, the Male War Bride, resents the fact that a soldier's wolf-whistle is meant for his wife, not for him. In *Monkey Business*, under the influence of the youth drug 'B-4', he goes off on a spree with Marilyn Monroe. When he returns his wife (Ginger Rogers) observes that his face is 'breaking out in red blotches'. 'That's not red blotches,' he insists, 'that's lipstick.' Ginger Rogers, in her turn, consumes B-4 and becomes a shy virgin. She drives her husband from the bedroom of the hotel to which they have returned for a second honeymoon. The cord of his pyjama trousers is caught in the slammed door. When he draws attention to his predicament, she takes the cord and puts a knot in it. The symbolism is unstressed, but clear and beautiful.

The hero of *Bringing Up Baby* is completely dominated by women. Firstly by Alice, who regards a chaste peck on the cheek as a violation of public decency: 'What will professor Latouche think!' The professor is a tolerant man. 'After all,' he concedes with an understanding smile, 'you *are* getting married tomorrow.' Alice rules out David's tentative suggestion that they might perhaps have a honeymoon. Nothing, *nothing*, must be allowed to distract him from his work for the Stuyvesant Museum of Natural History. He is no less ruthlessly exploited by Susan. A psychiatrist has told her that 'the love impulse in man frequently reveals itself in terms of con-flict'. David shows some mild irritation at, among other things, having his car stolen and wrecked, and at being tripped up in the bar of the Ritz Plaza Hotel. Therefore, according to Susan's free-association method of reason-ing, he is in love with her. Therefore he must be tricked into escorting her to Connecticut a couple of hours before his wedding is due to begin. And once there, of course, he must not be allowed to escape. So deprive him of his clothes.

Susan's mind here works along true Hawksian lines. A course of action, once decided upon, must be carried through (as Rivette says) *jusqu'au bout*. Hawks's motto for comedy seems to be 'Everything in excess'. Thus once Cary Grant has been labelled as a war bride, male, it can only be a matter of time before we see him in skirts. But Hawks is, happily, not willing to leave the matter there: the uniform which his wife borrows must be a nurse's. And why put him in nurse's uniform if he is not to do any nursing? So let him be called on to assist at a childbirth. Similarly, in *Monkey Business*, what could be more natural than that the 'ten-year-old' Cary, having had his face covered in whitewash, should use it as the basis for an Indian war-paint? Then he can join in a children's game and suggest scalping his wife's one-time sweetheart, Hugh Marlowe. Now George Winslow must step forward to ensure that the rules are obeyed: 'You can't scalp anybody unless you do a war-dance first . . . That's no good. You gotta sing when you do it!'

Bringing Up Baby is one of the most 'excessive' of Hawks's films. (The other is *Gentlemen Prefer Blondes*.) 'I'll be with you in a minute, Mr Peabody,' David shouts to his influential golf-partner as he leaves the course. The words are repeated many times, with uncertainty giving way to desperation, as he becomes ever more frantically involved with Susan. They are last heard as he walks closely and speedily behind her through the doors of the Ritz Plaza Hotel. Susan's loss of the rear panel of her evening dress is thus concealed but David's top hat (trampled) and frock-coat (torn) are clearly displayed.

In this chaotic world language aids confusion, not comprehension. Susan attempts to account for the 'theft' of another woman's purse, but 'it never will be clear' says David, 'as long as she's explaining it'. She either ignores or over-exploits verbal logic. When David protests that she has just taken his golf ball and is about to drive away his car, she asks 'You mean *this* is *your* car? *Your* golf ball? *Your* car? Is there anything in the world that doesn't belong to you?' She uses words mainly for camouflage: when David emerges from the shower and asks what has happened to his clothes, she says that the gardener is taking them into town to be cleaned. 'Well stop him. I've got to leave here immediately.' 'But David! You can't leave here without your clothes!' She tells her aunt what she really means by this apparent nonsense: 'If he gets some clothes, he'll go away. And he's the only man I've ever loved.' Susan's is a logic of the emotions, not of the syllogism. All that she does, however crazy it seems, is justified rationally by her love for David. As Hugh Marlowe says in *Monkey Business*, 'The language may be confusing, but the actions are unmistakeable.'

Humiliation plays a very important part in all Howard Hawks's comedies, a humiliation the greater because its victims are established as persons of a certain dignity. I see no need, however, for the assumption that this director's view of the world is pessimistic. All comedy is more or less 'black'. Hawks has simply learnt the lesson of Stan Laurel: if you wear a bowler hat, it's all the funnier when you slip on a banana skin. His comedies do not lament human degradation so much as celebrate human resilience. *I Was a Male War Bride* is the blackest of the comedies. Its hero is relegated to the final position on the transit order, after dogs, cats, canaries and other domestic animals. But even he retains enough of his human dignity to protest when his wife starts to make a wig for him from a horse's tail: 'Can't you at least take if off the mane?' he asks.

In *Monkey Business*, humiliation is the direct result of a refusal to accept life's terms. Charles Coburn drags his secretary, Marilyn Monroe ('Anyone can type!'), to the laboratory with him to see the success of an experiment in rejuvenating an aged chimpanzee. 'Look at that old chimp, Miss Laurel,' he splutters. 'Eighty-four years old. Fourteen years older than I am! And just look at him!' A husband and wife suffer 'maladjustment, near-idiocy, and a series of low-comedy disasters' when they return to youth. But they learn from their experience and come to regard B-4 as 'the most dubious discovery since itching powder, and just about as useful'. For a genuinely pessimistic treatment of the subject of *Monkey Business* see Nicholas Ray's *Bigger than Life*, which, with the substitution of cortisone for B-4, is virtually a remake of Hawks's picture.

David Huxley certainly shed a good deal of surplus dignity in the course of *Bringing Up Baby*. He wanders around in the middle of the night, wearing an ill-fitting suit with the trousers rolled up, no socks, and carrying in one hand a butterfly net, in the other a croquet mallet. He becomes so accustomed to associate Susan with disaster that when she appears in the museum with the lost Brontosaurus bone his immediate reaction is panic and flight. But even David finally realizes that 'one catastrophe after another' actually constituted 'the best day I ever had'.

V. F. Perkins, one of the central core of critics associated with *Movie* since its beginnings at the start of the 1960s (and with *Oxford Opinion* before that), offers a very perceptive account of Hawks's comedies which has some relationship to Rivette's 'The Genius of Howard Hawks', above, and some relationship to Robin Wood's later account of the comedies in his 1968 book, but manages to be individual in its emphasis on the functions of excess and, countering Rivette's idea about the bitterness of Hawks's world view, on the celebration of 'human resilience'. Perkins's critical output has been frustratingly small, but Hawks's classical style is a frequent reference point in Perkins's *Film as Film* (Harmondsworth: Penguin Books, 1972).

The Modernity of Howard Hawks

HENRI LANGLOIS

From *Cahiers du Cinéma*, no. 139, January 1963.

Translated in Joseph McBride (ed.), *Focus on Howard Hawks*.

It seems that *A Girl in Every Port* was the revelation of the Hawks season at the Museum of Modern Art in New York.

For New York audiences of 1962, Louise Brooks suddenly acquired that 'Face of the Century' aura she had had, many years ago, for spectators at the Cinéma des Ursulines.

Because for Paris *A Girl in Every Port* is not a recent event, but one which occurred in the 1928 season.

It was the Paris of the Montparnassians and Picasso, of the surrealists and the Seventh Art, of Diaghilev, of the 'Soirées de Paris', of the 'Six', of Gertrude Stein, of Brancusi's masterpieces.

That is why Blaise Cendrars confided a few years ago that he thought *A Girl in Every Port* definitely marked the first appearance of contemporary cinema.

To the Paris of 1928, which was rejecting expressionism, *A Girl in Every Port* was a film conceived in the present, achieving an identity of its own by repudiating the past.

To look at the film is to see yourself, to see the future which leads through *Scarface* to the cinema of our time.

The modern man – that's Hawks, completely.

When you look back over his *œuvre* today what is striking is the degree to which the cinema of Hawks was ahead of its time.

To be more precise – since there is generally a time lag between the main currents of contemporary art and the cinematic art – what is striking is the degree to which Hawks's art is up-to-date, and even in the vanguard of artistic movements.

The art he created is that of an America which has now been exposed and which did exist, but whose evolution was then still in progress.

Thus, five years before the appearance of the first modern construction in the streets of New York, on 53rd Street[1] – fifteen years before the appearance of the first modern skyscrapers which have transformed Manhattan – Hawks, like Gropius, conceived his films as one might conceive a typewriter, a motor, or a bridge.

That is why, today, when America has discovered Hawks, his old films like *The Crowd Roars* have such an impact when shown on television.

In these forgotten Warners films, the people of New York and America, much to their surprise, recognize themselves: the depiction of the American scene now seems very accurate.

It is this which has caused people to write that Hawks is the most American of film-makers.

He is certainly American, not more so than Griffith or Vidor, but his work is rooted in contemporary America in its spirit as well as in its surface appearance. It is now clear that Hawks's is the only *œuvre* the American public can totally identify itself with, in terms of both simple admiration and criticism:

> It has no relation to my work. . . . I didn't care to do it but was forced under contract. . . . It was made right after Murnau's *Sunrise*, which introduced German camera trick-work to Hollywood. . . . They liked it; I didn't. . . . I've always been rather mechanically minded so I tried a whole lot of mechanical things, and then gave them up completely – most of the time my camera stays on eye level now. . . . I just use the simplest camera in the world.[2]

So many excuses for three or four shots made as a concession to Fox in *Paid to Love*, which anticipates Lubitsch.

It must have meant a lot to him.

Thus, at the time when Paris was rejecting expressionism, at the very moment when Babelsberg was conquering the United States and Hollywood, Hawks too rejected it and for the same reasons, because it was in conflict with the demands of the new age.

Curiously, *A Girl in Every Port*, so novel for people at the time, seems much less so today than *Fig Leaves*, in which Hawks's art operates in complete freedom.

But *Fig Leaves* was at that time too new a film for contemporary audiences not to be blinded by it.

With the coming of the sound film, the problem arose of cinematic construction in terms of speech, of the editing of dialogue in terms of movement.

A new dramaturgy was about to be born: it had to be discovered, explored, established.

Hawks applied himself directly to the task, without trying to evade the difficulties.

He immediately arrived at the heart of the problem: dramatic film construction in terms of the roles played by dialogue and sound.

From *The Dawn Patrol* to *Ceiling Zero*, Hawks was totally preoccupied with this construction. As a result, he became the Le Corbusier of the sound film, in the way he handles lines and volume.

His works, then, are stripped bare almost to the point of abstraction – but it is as if they are made of concrete.

The essential. The truth of the dialogue, the truth of the situations, the truth of the subjects, of the milieux, of the characters: a dramaturgy derived from an agglomeration of facts, words, noises, movements, situations, as a motor is assembled. There is nothing superfluous: no stopping, no meandering, no fleshing out. What is most impressive is Hawks's progressive mastery, culminating in *Ceiling Zero*, a totally accomplished film, and one which is diametrically opposed to filmed theater, except for those who no longer see its originality and its extraordinary achievement because they have learned too much from it and thus find it too familiar.

The dialogue: what one says, what one is, what one does. Hawks puts great emphasis on dialogue and intonation: on the meaning of the dialogue, the construction of the dialogue, the delivery of the dialogue.

No, it isn't done with cutting. It's done by deliberately writing dialogue like real conversation . . .

All you want to do is to hear the essential things . . .

And, of course, if I have a scene today that I don't think is very interesting the quicker I can play it the better off I am.[3]

As in every man's work, there is one exception to his general rule:
Twentieth Century, lit up by the radiance of Carole Lombard's femininity, and that is enough. Thanks to it everything is balanced, everything comes alive, through cutting which makes the dialogue into cinema.

The period characterized by *Scarface* is coming to an end.

In 1937 there is a short pause.

The explosion of *Bringing Up Baby*.

And, suddenly, in 1939, that night at the Marivaux when they showed *Only Angels Have Wings*, a charm was reborn, that trance-like spell which had seemed lost since the advent of sound.

Out of cinema, mastered anew, magic was reborn. And with it, Hawks rediscovered that total freedom which let him dispense with all heaviness of touch. Already there was a hint of things to come: the play of colors and light in the brilliant facets of *Red River* and *The Big Sky*.

From *The Dawn Patrol* to *Only Angels Have Wings*: the circle is closed.

Another stylistic exercise, as if for the pleasure of a private gamble: *His Girl Friday*.

And now the great masterpieces.

Hawks is himself again, as before, as he was at his debut in the silent period.

The same arabesque, and this art of giving birth, from a void, to miraculous life.

The 'concrete' period has been transcended. The logical force of *To Have and Have Not* and *The Big Sleep* is hidden beneath the sheen of an art as dense and translucent as the extraordinary vegetable-like growth of the new New York.

The constructivist, almost abstract art of Hawks becomes colorful.

Pared down further – and because it is in color – *Rio Bravo* is a construction of psychological impulses.

All of Hawks's intelligence is confirmed and exercised in *Land of the Pharaohs*, the only epic film which has style, rigor, and plastic beauty, qualities whose meaning we had long since forgotten.

1. Langlois is punning with the word 'construction'; it refers both to buildings and to modern 'constructivist' sculpture – the Museum of Modern Art is located on 53rd Street. – *Translator's Note.*
2. From Bogdanovich's interview with Hawks in his *The Cinema of Howard Hawks.* – *Ed.*
3. Also from *The Cinema of Howard Hawks.* Hawks's remarks came when Bogdanovich asked, 'The extremely fast pace of your comedies, like *Twentieth Century*, is not achieved through cutting, is it?' – *Ed.*

Henri Langlois was co-founder of the Cinémathèque Française in 1936 and indelibly associated with that archive, and it with him, for the rest of his life. The Cinémathèque was a crucial element in French film culture from the 1940s to the 1960s, screening material of all kinds and allowing for critical discoveries which fed into journals like *Cahiers du Cinéma* and led to critics and later film-makers like François Truffaut and Jean-Luc Godard being dubbed 'the children of the Cinémathèque'. Langlois was an occasional contributor to *Cahiers*, as with this piece, which appeared alongside others (including Jean Douchet's piece, below, on *Hatari!*) devoted to a Hawks retrospective. Langlois's essay, returning as it does to the moment at which Jean-George Auriol was writing about *A Girl in Every Port* in 1928, is especially interesting for its comments on Hawks's silent films.

Hawks (rt.) with John Wayne during the making of *Hatari*!

Hatari!

JEAN DOUCHET

From *Cahiers du Cinéma*, no. 139, January 1963.
Translated by John Moore.

Perhaps *Hatari!* is not Hawks's best film. It nevertheless appears to be his most revealing work. A (very relative) lack of rigour in the canvas, a certain indolence in the progress of the narrative, combined with day-to-day improvisation, not only give it a singular sort of charm but seem to become virtues when we see that they authorize the auteur to attempt his first meditative work. Freed from the 'how' of the action and the dramatic conflicts caused by it, his reverie is able to wander at will through the 'wherefore' of this action, the *raison d'être* of man, woman and the world. It leads him into a return to his original sources, in the post-Eden world of *Fig Leaves* from which his *œuvre* emerged. So it is in no way surprising that, after that long and roundabout journey, *Hatari!* reassembles Hawks's *œuvre* into a whole, recalling each of its parts through a scene, a situation, a word, a character: all references whose 'retrospective' nature makes it much easier to decode them.

So what does *Hatari!* tell us about Howard Hawks that we did not know already (especially since Jacques Rivette's capital study [reprinted above])? Not much, I admit, except perhaps another way of looking at his creative imagination. This draws its strength from a sensibility engaged directly with the world; from a need to confront it, not to dominate it but to learn more about it and the self; and from a literally *physical* sense of the real relations of force. This word 'physical', as always when a term characterizes and summarizes a form of imagination, should be understood in its fullest sense. It implies an immediate, instinctive rapport with matter, an absolute respect for its properties, an *a priori* refusal to interpret them, a desire to penetrate their secrets using the knowledge and method of the physical sciences. The 'imagining' form, to use one of Bachelard's words, submits totally to reality and abjures all concepts lacking a factual basis. It is the fruit of an acceptance of the world as it is, not of a flight from it.

So, for Hawks, the core of the problem will always be to record physical necessity in man. Man has only one duty, which is his privilege: to prove through work his superiority over matter, in all its forms. The only real problems that confront him are problems of conservation or accumulation, and of loss of energy, his own and the world's.

Whether tragedy or comedy, the energy deployed to capture or tame the energy of matter always – even in the ridiculous – projects human greatness. So, in Hawks, what we see is an unending alternation of static energy, which is the product or conflicting tensions in balance, and real energy which is the product of mass times velocity. His films contain a succession of scenes in which the characters are crowded into a restricted space – less a refuge than a place where they are subjected to the influence of time and the tensions, both internal and external, that it generates – and others in which they emerge into a reconquered larger space and release this condensed energy, sometimes amplifying it with a vehicle (aircraft and cars) or a rapid and effective action (perilous adventures), sometimes on the contrary wasting it in vain enterprises (comedies). *Hatari!* mixes all these three elements; and its refuge, the white hunters' house, becomes a place without conflict, almost a haven of peace. Hence the internal dynamic of Hawks's films, subject with the rest of his imagination to the imperative, not of his private reverie, but of the actual laws of dynamics. A spring is slowly compressed, then suddenly released: compression-explosion, compression-explosion . . . the same cycle as an internal combustion engine fuelled by the energy of matter, life creating its own perpetual motion.

Here perhaps lies the secret of the Hawksian style. The economy and efficiency of his methods result from a strict application of the law of conservation of energy. Conflict is created by simply showing the forces present in the world, making any dramatization – which is a representation and therefore an *a priori* conception – redundant. *Hatari!* is exemplary in this respect. Hawks achieves the miracle of making us interested in characters whose situation suggests a rousing theatrical crisis, but between whom practically nothing happens. The actual dramatic events are calmed down before they have even occurred. We have only to see the combination of characters and temperaments to become aware of the possibility of conflict. And the mere detection of this possibility is enough to satisfy our expectations.

The real conflict in *Hatari!* is not between men, but between man and the world. Man must impose himself physically on the world, put his stamp on it through his labour. The resulting discharge of energy is not just proof of his creative genius; it is the reason for his presence in the world. Hence the importance of profession in Hawks's films. Men are defined in terms of their working skills, to which they feel duty bound to devote all their energy. Tragedy and comedy both begin where this energy is first diverted from its proper objective. Catastrophe arrives when man yields to his emotiveness, his sensibility, his excitability, his affects; when he stops regarding matter as a sum of energy to be overcome, and instead allows himself to be seduced by the world's appearance, by *nature*.

Nature here is the enemy, the seductress, the source of degradation. It is the deadly trap that matter springs on man to sap his creative energy. In Hawks, drama springs in effect from the fact that man is also part of the physical universe. He is just a superior kind of animal. The moment he abdicates his higher qualities – intelligence, will, reflection, maturity, and so on – he falls back to the level of the next animals in the hierarchy of species, the apes. Witness 'Pockets'. This not-too-bright, although droll and appealing (qualities shared with apes) character merits a short digression. Incapable of dealing with the world's energy, in this film embodied in wild animals (represented typically by the rhinoceros, whose huge bulk and formidable turn of speed figure at the beginning and end of the film's hunting scenes), this character aspires to prove himself a man like the others: a pathetic ambition doomed to ridicule. Unable to associate them in himself he dissociates creation from energy and, after wasting a phenomenal amount of the latter, manages, with the aid of a rocket, to capture his anthropoid brothers. This is certainly a victory, but a grotesque one, further underlining the scene in which the hunters, got up like Martians and medieval knights, set out to conquer quadrupeds: a satirical reference to all crusades, past and future, that play no part in man's true adventure.

This adventure, which is purely internal, resides in the conflict between his energy and his nature (this last pulled remorselessly towards nature itself). The drama is hinged on his capacity for feeling, a source of misery but also the reason for his greatness. If you do away with the feeling and keep the energy you are left with a monstrous being, a thing from another world, inviting immediate destruction. One way to avoid this danger (*hatari*) is to keep oneself in splendid isolation. Which is what John Wayne and his companions are doing at the beginning of the film.

What they do not allow for is nature's subtlest ally: woman. The profound misogyny of Hawks's – quintessentially American – *œuvre* may have something to do with the pioneer spirit that imbued Hollywood trailblazers like Griffith, Ince, Mack Sennett, Walsh, Dwan, Ford and Hawks himself. Unlike the others, however, Hawks started early to highlight the contradictory double relations between men of action and women. The hero dreads woman, considering her a hindrance to his action (and in a double way: if he feels strong, he is handicapped by the woman's weakness and the obligation to protect her; and as soon as he conceives a weakness for her, his partner's maternal nature, the part of her that makes her a 'refuge', becomes invasive and hampers his work). But at the same time he desires her as a reason for his actions (again in a double, contradictory fashion: he imagines that she should justify his effort, in other words give him an excess of energy; but he also, converting motive to objective, sees her as a worthy recipient of all this energy). This diversity of woman in relation to the adventurous man, which other American film-makers convey by depicting several types of woman (mother, wife, fiancée, adventuress, and so on), in Hawks's films is found complete in each of the heroines. Indeed, his films are no more than a sequence of variations on the multiple and complex combinations made possible by the double, contradictory relationship with a rejected and desired woman, seen as inimical but necessary to man. So that in these films woman is more beautiful than ever before, but also more denigrated and accused.

The tragedy or comedy of the war between the sexes is not based solely, for Hawks, on this distinction between man inhabited by strong sentiments

79

– in other words, a sensibility controlled by reason and will – and woman possessed by her emotions, relying on intuition or instincts. The difference is more physical than that. Woman is linked physiologically to nature, open to its influences, subject to its cycles. She has its capriciousness, its instability, its shifting variations. She is in perpetual change, because time rules and conditions her life. She is dependent. Man, by contrast, has no physiological obligations to time, which acts on him only externally. This action is nevertheless sufficient to degrade him: childhood, youth, old age are all states that detract from his fullness. But in *maturity* he is liberated from time. All that counts for him then is the confrontation with the space containing the world, matter, nature. He is independent, in charge.

Solitude, like an exclusively male universe, is thus perfectly suited to the man shaped by comradeship and sporting rivalry (which is no more than an effort to capture space). Man exists only when in pursuit of space. Woman exists only when she is hunting man. Whence their impossible dialogue: woman needs to attach herself to a master, and in the process attaches man to nature and time. The Hawksian hero, who always exists in a present focused on a near or distant future, has no past except in relation to women. So it is with John Wayne, whose whole comportment is a *fuite en avant* to banish memories of an unhappy affair. To achieve her ends, the woman seeks to gain entry to this masculine universe by embracing the profession. The work gives her the feeling of escape from her condition, of having her turn at mastering space and the world, of being man's equal. In the event it causes nothing but catastrophes. Since the woman cannot escape from her own nature, she inevitably introduces nature, its excesses, its uncontrolled forces, its waste of energy, into this domain reserved for men. She undermines their work of controlling and governing nature; especially as the man is taken in by her apparent boldness, which he finds admirable and endearing. He allows himself to be invaded by emotion and sensibility, and is lost.

This theme was already present in *Fig Leaves*, from the moment that Eve, purely to satisfy a desire for luxury, secretly agrees to work as a model. It is a hundred times more evident in *Hatari!* Brandy (Michèle Girardon), one of the two women, has been raised in this society of men and is seen by them as a boy. 'Has been seen', rather, since her first appearance (and the first by a woman) in the film shows Kurt (Hardy Kruger) buttoning her dress for her and noticing that his tomboy pal has unmistakably become a pretty girl. However, nothing in her behaviour distinguishes her from the other hunters until, falling in love, she suddenly displays her femininity. She shows that she is more of a woman than other women. Disdaining the two young stallions, she falls for the weakest, the most ill-favoured and least manly character, the one on whom she can best exercise her maternal and protective nature, and who only wants to be petted: Pockets (Red Buttons), the brother of apes.

The other woman, Dallas, has come to Africa for her 'career'. She sets out to conquer space, and pays for her temerity with a comprehensive series of tumbles and pratfalls. But her modesty and 'touching' confession earn her the forgiveness of the clan of men. This frees her to begin the work of destruction. She saves a baby elephant from a cruel death. This leads to the acquisition of a flock of goats to supply milk for the animal; the goats run amok and devastate the camp of the fierce hunters, who laugh at themselves in their new role as protectors of nature. And nature continues its invasion: soon there are three baby elephants; then savages giving free rein to their own equally excessive affectivity. In the end nature itself revolts against this orgy of heart (the mother elephant's threatening behaviour at the water hole). Obviously Dallas will eventually be hoist with her own petard. Her love of nature will be reciprocated a hundredfold, at the moment when she tries to flee. And a triumphant nature then invades the men's domain. All energy is annihilated; mass and inertial forces begin their work of devastation, the film ending on a shot of the young elephants trampling a bed underfoot.

It would, however, be unfair to blame woman alone. Woman, in Hawks's films, is what man is in the depths of his being. She embodies his true aspiration. The reason why the feeling of nature is so strong from the very first shots of *Hatari!* – sunsets, great plains, magnificent mountains and all the animals roaming free – is that it is already anchored in all the hunters' hearts. There is already an implicit decay in their spiritual or moral life. All these men who have confronted space and the world – the ex-matador, the former racing driver, the adventurer down on his luck, the descendant of Indians – are on a false scent, nourishing illusions. They are devoting their energy, their hunger for space, to a cause – a task – which they feel in their hearts to be dishonourable: depriving living beings, albeit only animals, of their space, therefore their energy. The resulting prickings of conscience explain why they are so prompt to yield to nature, to offer it a love that flies in the face of their man's nature. Only Pockets is capable of marvelling at the capture of animals: so much so that he weeps like a sissy, thinking the achievement has made a man of him (something that really makes him all the more hopelessly despicable). None of the others ever – not even once – shows the slightest elation over a capture. The Indian – a great womaniser – can only just bring himself to look at the downed rhinoceros (to fend off the evil eye).

Perhaps it is because he senses this malaise more deeply than the others that Sean shuts himself in splendid isolation and seeks by all means to counter the invasion of nature. The struggle he must wage is a struggle against himself, all the more relentless because he is the one most attached to this part of Africa (his first wife having left him over her loathing of nature). He is the group's centre of energy, the atomic nucleus around whom the others gravitate. But he is a nucleus ready to split. He falls for Dallas because she incarnates his penchant for nature and, on an even deeper level, his aspiration to peace, in other words the dream – an impossible dream that will destroy him – of a reconciliation, through love, of man with space and the world. In doing so, he surrenders himself to time, a time cleared of all static energy, flowing forward without shocks, conflict or tension in a sort of natural prelapsarian harmony. This sin against what he is physically – a nucleus – can only lead to his rapid disintegration. All those around him, the electrons or protons (whichever you prefer), the people who used to energize him and draw energy from him, will disperse. Some – like the two virile young heroes – will resume their energetic careers as space-conquering men; others will continue to decline. Sean, a nucleus deprived of his energy for ever, a unit of human matter henceforth dissolved into the mass, has committed suicide. 'Hatari', danger: the physical (and thus, for Hawks, spiritual and moral) end of man.

But also the end of an enterprise that bears an extraordinary resemblance to the shooting of a film (with the communal life of its crew, its plan for the next day's work improvised every evening, its idle periods and bursts of effort), perhaps even to a cineaste's life. There is a confident tone here that is not usual with Hawks. *Hatari!* is a documentary on what his life had been, on his profession as film director. In it, he reveals the secret of his aesthetic and his morality, the determination to get as close as possible to reality, to capture it with the lasso of his camera like a daring sportsman attempting a difficult exploit. What we get is the portrait of a man of feeling concealed behind the façade of a haughty manner, whose amused, cool, sometimes ferocious humour hides a secret tenderness for the strange human fauna that surround him. In the autumn of a well filled life Hawks surrenders at last to memories, to the charm of his professional existence, to the love of women that he has always tried to resist, to the enthusiasm and beauty of youth. A repudiation of all his previous work? Surely something simpler than that: a lesson in wisdom from a great master of cinema who has always looked the world in the eye and who knows, from his constant struggles with himself, that man's fate – both his grandeur and his weakness – is his attachment to an order of things that he knows he must try to govern without love. Nostalgia shows through the open and good-humoured gaiety; a certain bitterness can be discerned behind the lucid simplicity of a master's technique; disenchantment accompanies an enjoyment of life just as intense as ever. The pessimism balances the optimism, and vice versa.

Jean Douchet was one of the most regular critics writing in *Cahiers du Cinéma* in the early 1960s (and one who also later directed films, though these did not achieve the recognition accorded those of Truffaut, Chabrol, Godard and Rivette). A true 'Hitchcocko-Hawksian', Douchet also wrote on Hitchcock: see 'Hitch and His Audience' in *Cahiers du Cinéma*, November 1960 (translated in Jim Hillier (ed.), *Cahiers du Cinéma*, Vol. 2, *The 1960s: New Wave, New Cinema, Re-Evaluating Hollywood* (London: Routledge; Cambridge, Mass.: Harvard University Press, 1986)). Though Douchet's piece shares some perceptions with V. F. Perkins's interesting short article on *Hatari!* in *Movie*, no. 5, December 1962, its philosophical tone, stressing the film's meditative aspect and its looseness of narrative, and ending with ideas about hunting as a metaphor for film-making, differentiates it sharply from the more moral concerns and textual detail of Robin Wood's 1960s writing on Hawks and much other later writing in English.

Howard Hawks

LEE RUSSELL

From *New Left Review*, no. 24, March–April 1964.

'I do not think one can love any film deeply if one does not deeply love the films of Howard Hawks.' This dogma – to be found in a review of *The Big Sky* in *Cahiers du Cinéma*, no. 29, 1953 – has rightly infuriated many film viewers. Their fury, in turn, has provoked the *Cahiers* critics into reiterating their adulation of Hawks time and time again. Despite the reasoned and corrective interventions of André Bazin (*Cahiers*, nos 44 and 70), an attitude to Hawks – and to Hitchcock – has become a touchstone of critical commitment. In England, the new magazine *Movie* polemically flew Hawks and Hitchcock at its masthead; in America, Hitchcocko-Hawksianism has been endorsed by the authority of Andrew Sarris in *Film Culture*. These beachheads of 'Parisian' criticism have undoubtedly invigorated local discussion of cinema. Always, Hawks has been at the centre of controversy.

Why Hawks? Rather than, say, Borzage or Vidor? One obvious reason is that Hawks is such a convincing demonstration of the 'politique des auteurs': the theory, which underlies all *Cahiers* criticism, that the director of a film is its author, that he gives it any distinctive quality it has and that his personal themes and style can be traced throughout his career, so that the corpus of his work can be discussed as a whole. This is, of course, a quite normal critical procedure when applied to the other arts. Its acceptance for cinema – or rather for American cinema – has been delayed so long mainly because of the conviction of most critics that the industrial conditions of work in Hollywood have necessarily imposed an undifferentiated anonymity on every American director. This has not been the case. Most people are now aware how Hitchcock has consistently made films which, while recognizably 'Hollywood', are equally recognizably 'Hitchcock'. Hawks, during his long career (his first film, *The Road to Glory*, was made in 1926), has directed Westerns, gangsters, war films, farce, musical comedies, science fiction, even a film about ancient Egypt. Yet all of them are recognizably made by Hawks; they exhibit the same preoccupations, the same recurring situations, the same visual style and tempo. It is possible to extract from Hawks's films a whole Hawksian ideology.

Hawks is, first and foremost, a director of adventure films. He subordinates the Western, for instance, to the adventure film at large. In this he is unlike, say, John Ford, for whom the Western as such is paramount, because it expresses his fervent interest in pioneer American history. Hawks has little historical sense. His ideology is primitive and anachronistic. For Hawks the highest human emotion is the camaraderie of the exclusive, self-sufficient, all-male group. Hawks's heroes are cattlemen, marlin-fishermen, racing-drivers, pilots, big-game hunters, etc., habituated to danger and living apart from society, actually cut off from it physically by dense forest, sea, snow or desert. Their aerodromes are fog-bound; the radio has cracked up; the next mail-coach or packet-boat doesn't leave for a week. The elite group strictly preserves its exclusivity. It is necessary to pass a test of ability and courage to win admittance. The group's only internal tensions come when one member lets the others down (the drunk deputy in *Rio Bravo*, the panicky pilot in *Only Angels Have Wings*) and must redeem himself by some act of exceptional bravery, or occasionally when too much 'individualism' threatens to disrupt the close-knit circle. The group's security is the first commandment: 'You get a stunt team in acrobatics in the air – if one of them is no good, then they're all in trouble. If someone loses his nerve catching animals, then the whole bunch can be in trouble.' The group members are bound together by rituals (in *Hatari!* blood is exchanged by transfusion) and express themselves univocally in communal sing-songs. In *Dawn Patrol* the camaraderie of the pilots stretches even across the enemy lines: a captured German ace is immediately drafted into the group and joins in the sing-song.

Hawks's heroes pride themselves on their professionalism. They ask: 'How good is he? He'd better be good.' They expect no praise for doing their job well. Indeed, none is given except: 'The boys did all right.' When they die, they leave behind them only the most meagre personal belongings: often a handful of medals. Hawks himself has summed up their utterly barren view of life: 'It's just a calm acceptance of a fact. In *Only Angels Have Wings*, after Joe dies, Cary Grant says: "He just wasn't good enough." Well, that's the only thing that keeps people going. They just have to say: "Joe wasn't good enough, and I'm better than Joe, so I go ahead and do it." And they find out they're not any better than Joe, but then it's too late, you see.' The only relieving features of life are 'danger' (*Hatari!*) and 'fun'. Danger gives existence pungency: 'Every time you get real action, then you have danger. And the question, "Are you living or not living?" is probably the biggest drama we have.' This nihilism, in which 'living' means no more than being in danger of losing your life – a danger entered into quite gratuitously – is augmented by the Hawksian concept of having 'fun'. The word 'fun' crops up constantly in Hawks's interviews and scripts. It masks his despair.

When one of Hawks's elite is asked, usually by a woman, why he risks his life, he replies: 'No reason I can think of makes any sense. I guess we're just crazy.' Or Feathers, sardonically, to Colorado in *Rio Bravo*: 'You haven't even the excuse I have. We're all fools.' But when Hawks has his dramatic heroes describe themselves as crazy, he is being ironic. In fact, as his 'crazy' comedies make clear, it is the normal – for most people, rational

– world which he thinks of, he portrays, as lunatic. He himself is quite aware of this play on 'crazy': 'I mean crazy reactions – I don't think they're crazy, I think they're normal – but according to bad habits we've fallen into, they seemed crazy.' Hawks believes that his heroes are the only sane people and the rest of the world is mad. But in reality his heroes, his 'kind of men', are a dwindling band of eccentrics. He cannot expect them to be taken seriously: hence his bitter sense of 'fun'. Often Hawks resorts to gallows humour. He becomes obsessively macabre. The butt of the farce in *His Girl Friday*, for instance, is a condemned murderer who has escaped from the death-cell on the day fixed for his execution. Hawks's fun is grim. In *Sergeant York* it is 'fun' to shoot Germans 'like turkeys'; in *Air Force* it is 'fun' to blow up the Japanese fleet. In *Rio Bravo* the geligniting of the bad-men 'was very funny'. Hawks's heroes can articulate no rational ground for their lives: their fun is only too often reprisals on rationality and human progress. At worst, it is crudely destructive.

Outsiders, other people in general, are an undifferentiated crowd. Their role is to gape at the deeds of their heroes, whom, at the same time, they hate. The crowd assembles to watch the showdown in *Rio Bravo*, to see the cars spin off the track in *The Crowd Roars*. Most dehumanized of all is the crowd in *Land of the Pharaohs*, employed in building the pyramids. Originally this film was to have been about Chinese labourers building a 'magnificent airfield' for the American army, but the victory of the Chinese revolution forced Hawks to change his plans ('Then I thought of the building of the pyramids; I thought it was the same kind of story') and substitute the Pharaohs for the US army. But the presence of the masses poses no threat to the security of the Hawksian elite or the order of the Hawksian universe. They are, after all, 'not living'.

There is only one force that threatens: woman. Man is woman's 'prey'. Women are admitted to the male group only after much disquiet and a long ritual 'courtship', phased around the offering, lighting and exchange of cigarettes, during which they prove themselves worthy of entry. Even then, though, they are never really full members. A typical dialogue sums up their position:

Woman: You love him, don't you?
Man (embarrassed): Yes . . . I guess so . . .
Woman: How can I love him like you?
Man: Just stick around.

Hawks sees the all-male community as an ultimate; obviously it is very retrograde. His Spartan heroes are, in fact, cruelly stunted. Hawks is not unaffected by this: his comedies are the agonized exposure of the underlying tensions of his heroic dramas. Their two principal themes are infantilism (Hawks has said of *Gentlemen Prefer Blondes*: 'The child was the most mature one on board the ship, and I think he was a lot of fun.') and sex-reversal (*I Was a Male War Bride*). Hawks himself described *A Girl in Every Port* as 'really a love story between two men', but we never find in his films

85

the kind of considered working-out of the logic of all-male situations which marks Penn's 'resolutely homosexual' Western, *The Left-Handed Gun*, or Peckinpah's *Ride the High Country*, in which a young bride in a gold-camp is forced to sleep on her wedding-night not only with her husband but with all his younger brothers as well. The Hawksian ethic is a faked-up ethic, born from freakish and stunting social conditions. For Hawks it has become an absolute; the unnatural conditions have become natural and their victims heroes. And the real world, human society, has become a monstrous farce and a constant humiliation.

Hawks brings to his job, directing films, the professionalism he portrays in his heroes. Just as they distrust intellectuals, he distrusts artistic devices – though he confesses he was once influenced by Murnau's camera movements. His camera stays firmly at eye-level; close-ups are rare; angled shots even rarer. Hawks disliked his experience with CinemaScope, because of the difficulty of cutting – 'people's eyes jump around' – and the consequent distraction and weakening of dramatic effect. His direction is a model of dealing with his kind of material: this is his highest merit. Occasionally, as in *Scarface*, which deserves close attention, he has been magisterial. But cinema critics must be ruthless: cinema must advance far beyond Hawks, to express a far more advanced vision, in the far more advanced style which that will demand. The editors of *Movie*, in their eulogy of Hawks, stated, quite rightly: 'Maturity is a rare enough quality in the cinema.' But the works of Howard Hawks are not where maturity is to be found.

Lee Russell began writing on the cinema from an auteur standpoint in the early 1960s. His articles in the 'Motifs' section of *New Left Review* made a clean break with the previous policy of the journal, which had been a strong supporter of the new British cinema of Lindsay Anderson, Karel Reisz and Tony Richardson. In a radical change of direction, Lee Russell analysed the work of auteurs as various as Samuel Fuller, Jean-Luc Godard, Budd Boetticher, Roberto Rossellini and Jean Renoir. His detailed and innovative study of Hawks was written partly in response to the Leavisite approach of Robin Wood to the work of Hawks and Hitchcock and others. Russell's work later formed the basis for Peter Wollen's influential discussion of Hawks in *Signs and Meaning in the Cinema*. Wollen, however, abandoned the concept of 'world view', which Russell had taken from Lucien Goldmann, and replaced it with Claude Lévi-Strauss's concept of 'structure'. Many commentators have felt that Wollen, in true Hawksian style, stole many of his best ideas from Lee Russell, while giving them a new theoretical twist. By the end of the 1960s, Lee Russell had abandoned writing. Claire Johnston and Paul Willemen's 1975 book *Jacques Tourneur* (Edinburgh Film Festival), which pioneered a new path for auteurist studies, influenced by both psychoanalysis and feminism, was generously, if ironically, dedicated 'To the memory of Lee Russell . . .'

Rio Bravo

ROBIN WOOD

From Robin Wood, *Howard Hawks* (London: Secker & Warburg/BFI, 1968).

The genesis of *Rio Bravo* was Hawks's reaction against *High Noon*: the hero of *High Noon* spends the whole film asking for help and in the end he doesn't need it. Hawks decided to reverse the process: the hero of *Rio Bravo* never asks for help and often rejects it; and he needs it at every crisis. The relationship between the two films is not quite as simple as that; the two exceptions to this general reversal-pattern are interesting, as they may both have suggested to Hawks, whether he was aware of it or not, aspects of *Rio Bravo*: (1) The Marshal (Gary Cooper) in *High Noon* does once reject the help of a one-eyed drunken cripple who sees in his offer of assistance the possibility of regaining his self-respect: 'I used to be good,' he tells Cooper, a line doubtless as common in Westerns as certain musical phrases were common in late eighteenth-century music, yet one which Hawks (like Mozart with *his* contemporary clichés) can fill with intensity. Are we to see in this the genesis of Dude and Stumpy? In one way obviously not, because both these characters, and their relation to the film's main hero-figure, have their ancestry in Hawks's own work, notably Eddie in *To Have and Have Not*. Yet, given the admitted relationship of *Rio Bravo* to *High Noon*, and the complexity of influence and reminiscence that can underlie any great work of art, it may not be far-fetched to feel some significance in this passing resemblance. (2) Grace Kelly's final intervention (shooting a man in the back to save her husband, against her Quaker principles) is one point where Cooper *does* need help, and may point forward to *Rio Bravo*'s celebrated flower-pot scene and Angie Dickinson's subsequent distress at having been responsible for the deaths of four men.

The reputation of *High Noon* – it is still widely regarded as one of the best Westerns, a film that confers dignity on a low genre by infusing into it a seriousness of moral purpose – is very revealing, as regards current attitudes to the Western and to film in general. This reputation is my only reason for undertaking a brief comparison of the two films: *High Noon* in itself doesn't offer anything that the critic who regards the cinema as, in its potentialities and to some extent its achievements, the equal of the other arts is likely to find worth serious consideration. It strikes me as the archetypal 'Oscar' film, product of the combined talents of the archetypal 'Oscar'

87

director (Zinnemann), the archetypal 'Oscar' writer (Carl Foreman), and the archetypal 'Oscar' producer (Stanley Kramer): three gentlemen whose work has been characterised by those Good Intentions with which we understand the road to hell to be paved. *Mental* intentions, not emotional or intuitive intentions: intentions of the conscious, willing mind, not of the whole man. The film reeks of contrivance. Every sequence is constructed to lead up to, and make, a simple moral point, character, action, and dialogue being painstakingly manipulated to this end. Nowhere is there that sense of inner logic, of *organic* development, of the working-out of natural processes through the interaction of the characters, that one finds in the best films of Hawks. This characteristic is not only in the script. Zinnemann's direction, external and shallow, matches it perfectly. His handling of the actors is almost uniformly abominable, cliché-gesture following cliché-gesture (see, for instance, poor Thomas Mitchell, whose Kid in *Only Angels Have Wings* is among the American cinema's great supporting performances, in the church scene), just as cliché-set-up follows cliché-set-up in the camera positioning.

Quite fundamental issues are involved here, including the question of what constitutes cliché. But in *High Noon* not a single character or situation is spontaneously-intuitively *felt* – everything is in the head, a painstaking application of carefully learnt lessons. One could attack Carl Foreman's script for its contrivance, but, ultimately, to understand why *High Noon* is a bad film is to understand that the cinema is a director's art. There are situations, such as the scene between Katy Jurado and Lloyd Bridges where her contempt for him finally erupts after long suppression, which are perfectly valid emotionally, but which Zinnemann relentlessly turns into cliché-melodrama with his academically conceived jumps into close-up at the most obvious moments, his insistence on acting that is conventional in the worst sense (it isn't the actors' fault), the obviousness of gesture and expression exactly corresponding to the obviousness of the editing.

Judgments of this kind are notoriously difficult to enforce when dealing with the cinema (how great an advantage the literary critic has in being able to quote!): one has to appeal not only to the reader's common experience, but to his memory of that experience. One can, however, in the case of *High Noon*, point to several obvious major inadequacies which are symptomatic of the quality of the film as a whole – its quality as a work of art, as a record of lived and felt experience (however indirectly expressed). There is the entire church sequence, where the cliché-treatment both of the congregation *en masse* and of individuals reaches risible extremes. There is the handling of the Cooper–Kelly relationship. It is presumably of importance that the audience feel this as meaningful, that a sense of frustrated mutual needs and resulting tensions is communicated. Yet if we look at what Zinnemann actually offers us we find, apart from one or two tentative attempts at inwardness from Grace Kelly in the early stages of the film, nothing at all convincing. The wife remains a mere puppet, manipulated according to the requirements of the plot: no understanding of her reactions is communicated, beyond the explicit statement of her Quakerism, which is then merely taken for granted. Everything important, in fact, is taken for granted: Cooper's need for her, the importance of the marriage to him, is reduced to a bit of data, never *felt* as real. Someone, indeed, seems to have felt that there was something missing there, that the marriage-theme needed a bit of artificial bolstering; hence the tiresome repetition on the soundtrack of the lines from the theme-song, 'I'm not afraid of death but Oh! what will I do if you leave me?' – the importance of the marriage is only there in the song, an explicit statement of intentions that remain quite unrealised.

But most interesting of all, in relation to Hawks and *Rio Bravo*, is the motivation of the hero's actions. It is clear, I think, that for the Marshal, as for Hawks's heroes, the essential motivation is the preservation of self-respect – he goes back to face Frank Miller because a failure to do so would be, for him, a failure to live up to his own conception of manhood. One may reflect that this is a theme that lends itself readily to (could even be said to be implicit in) the Western genre. It is not its theme that makes *Rio Bravo* great, but the intensity and emotional maturity with which it is felt. The level on which the theme is handled in *High Noon* can be, I think, fairly represented by the scene where Grace Kelly confronts Katy Jurado and asks her *why* Cooper is determined to stay. Cut to close-up of Jurado, who says, with heavy emphasis, 'If you don't know, I can't explain it to you.' The reader who doesn't see what I mean by cliché (in terms of acting, editing, camera-position) couldn't do better than study that moment. The reputation of *High Noon* rests, in fact, on two things, both quite superficial in relation to what the film actually *is*: its strict observation of the unities (which it never lets us forget), and its 'Message'. Its message is really its whole *raison d'être*.

Rio Bravo is the most traditional of films. The whole of Hawks is immediately behind it, and the whole tradition of the Western, and behind that is Hollywood itself. If I were asked to choose a film that would justify the existence of Hollywood, I think it would be *Rio Bravo*. Hawks is at his most completely personal and individual when his work is most firmly traditional: the more established the foundations, the freer he feels to be himself. Everything in *Rio Bravo* can be traced back to the Western tradition, yet everything in it is essential Hawks – every character, every situation, every sequence expresses him as surely as every detail in an Antonioni film expresses Antonioni.

List the stock types of Western convention, and your list will almost certainly include the following:

1. Hero: strong, silent, infallible.
2. Hero's friend: flawed, fallible, may let him down or betray him (through cowardice, avarice, etc.).
3. Woman of doubtful virtue, works or sings in saloon, gambles; will probably die saving hero's life.
4. Nice girl, schoolteacher or farmer's daughter, open-air type, public-spirited; will marry hero when he settles down.

5. Hero's comic assistant, talks too much, drinks.
6. Singing cowboy, plays guitar.
7. Comic Mexican, cowardly, talks too much, gesticulates.

In six of these seven stock types we can recognise the basis of the six lead-ing characters of *Rio Bravo*; only the clean-living farmer's daughter is miss-ing. These stock figures are used without the slightest self-consciousness or condescension. Hawks builds on these traditional foundations; he also builds on his actors, exploring and using their particular resources and limi-tations creatively. Just as *To Have and Have Not* gave us the fullest ex-pression of Bogart, so here John Wayne, Dean Martin, Walter Brennan, and others are able to realise themselves, to fulfil the potentialities of their fam-iliar screen *personae*. The extraordinary thing is that, while they can all be referred back to traditional Western types and to the personalities of the ac-tors, the characters of *Rio Bravo* are at the same time entirely and quintes-sentially Hawksian, unmistakable in their behaviour, their attitudes, their dialogue. The film offers, I think, the most complete expression we have had of Hawks himself, the completest statement of his position. There are no clichés in *Rio Bravo*.

The complex flavour of the film can be partly defined in terms of appar-ent contradictions: it is strongly traditional yet absolutely personal; it is the most natural of Westerns, all the action and interrelationships developing organically from thematic germs that are themselves expressed as actions, yet it is also stylised; if one looks at it dispassionately, one becomes aware of an extreme austerity – a few characters, the barest of settings, no con-cessions to spectacle (with the exception of the dynamite at the end) or prettiness, yet if one submits to the atmosphere and 'feel' of the film one is chiefly aware of great richness and warmth. These characteristics are all very closely interconnected. It is the traditional qualities of the Western that allow Hawks to make a film so stylised in which we are so little aware, until we stand back and think about it, of stylisation; the stylisation and the aus-terity are but two ways of naming the same thing; the richness and warmth emanate from Hawks's personality, which pervades the whole; and it is the traditional and stylised form that sets him free to express himself with the minimum of constraint or interference.

The term 'traditional', applied to the Western, can mean two things, and two very different kinds of Western. The genre gives great scope to the di-rector with a feeling for America's past, for the borderline of history and myth, the early stages of civilisation, primitive, precarious, and touching. But the genre also offers a collection of convenient conventions which allow the director to escape from the trammels of contemporary surface reality and the demand for verisimilitude, and express certain fundamental human urges or explore themes personal to him. If the classic Westerns of John Ford, with their loving and nostalgic evocation of the past, are the supreme examples of the first kind, *Rio Bravo* is the supreme example of the second. The distinction, obvious enough yet very important, can be exemplified by comparing the town in Ford's *My Darling Clementine* with the town in *Rio*

Bravo. Ford's Tombstone is created in loving detail to convey precisely that sense of primitive civilisation against the vastness and impersonality of nature, the profound respect for human endeavour and human achievement exemplified in even the simplest of men that is so characteristic of this director: on the one hand the Bon Ton Tonsorial Parlour and the honey-suckle-scented hair-spray, the tables in rows neatly laid with cloths in the dim hotel dining-room; on the other, the vast expanses of wilderness from which strange-shaped rocky projections grandly rise. Ford places his community against the wilderness, the wooden hotel, the skeletal wooden church tower, the dancers on the uncovered church floor unselfconsciously enjoying themselves under the sky, surrounded on all sides by the vast emptiness of desert.

There is nothing like this in *Rio Bravo*. Here the whole Ford theme of the defence of civilised order and civilised values against destructive elements is compressed into the single strong reaction evoked so powerfully by the murder, brutal, gratuitous, stupid, that precipitates the entire action. Hawks's town consists of jail, hotel, saloons, and rows of unadorned and inconspicuous housefronts; inhabitants appear only when the narrative demands their presence, and there is never the least attempt to evoke that sense of community that is one of the finest and most characteristic features of the work of Ford. If a barn contains agricultural implements, they are there to provide cover in a gun-fight, not to suggest a background of agricultural activity; if the barn is littered with dust and straw, this is not to create atmosphere or a sense of place, but simply to use to blind a character momentarily. Every item of décor is strictly functional to the action. The social background is kept to the barest minimum below which we would be *aware* of stylisation. Even the jail and hotel which are the two main centres of the action are not felt as having any real social function (no one seems to stay in the hotel unless the plot requires them: mainly only Angie Dickinson); but there is a certain unobtrusive symbolic opposition between them (women tend to dominate in the hotel, and are excluded from the jail, where a miniature all-male society develops in isolation). The bar in which the action begins is so neutral in atmosphere that it scarcely registers on the spectator as a 'presence': Hawks uses it neither to suggest any potential fineness of civilisation (however primitive) nor to create a background of incipient violence and disorder: it is just a bar. Neither is there any attempt at 'period' evocation: the costumes, while not obtrusively stylised, are quite neutral in effect.

The result of all this is twofold. It frees Hawks from an obligation to fulfil the demands of surface naturalism, the accumulated convention of the Western tradition allowing him the simplest of frameworks which can be taken on trust; and this enables him to concentrate attention on the characters and their relationships, and the characteristic attitudes and themes developed through those relationships, to an extent impossible in an outdoor Western: we feel far more intimate with the characters of *Rio Bravo* than with those of *Red River*, let alone *The Big Sky*. The neutral background of the opening scene throws the initial confrontation between

91

Wayne and Martin into forceful relief. But it would be a mistake to see the stark simplicity of setting in this film as *merely* a convenience. It has also, and more importantly, an expressive function, providing a perfect environment for the stoicism that characterises Hawks's attitude to life. The action of *Rio Bravo* is played out against a background hard and bare, with nothing to distract the individual from working out his essential relationship to life. The virtual removal of a social framework – the relegating of society to the function of a *pretext* – throws all the emphasis on the characters' sense of *self*: on their need to find a sense of purpose and meaning not through allegiance to any developing order, but within themselves, in their own instinctual needs.

The value of existing conventions is that they not only give you a firm basis to build on but arouse expectations in the spectator which can be creatively cheated. We can study this principle in any art form in any period where a highly developed tradition is available to the artist. One can see it very clearly in Mozart: much of the freshness of his music, its ability continually to surprise and stimulate the listener into new awareness, derives from his use of the 'conventional' language of the age in order to arouse and then cheat expectations – from a constant tension between the conventional background and the actual notes written. The effect depends very much on our awareness of the background, which needn't necessarily be a *conscious* awareness. This tension between foreground and background, between the conventions of the Western and what Hawks actually does with them, is everywhere apparent in *Rio Bravo*. It will be immediately evident, for anyone who has seen the film, in the relationship of the actual characters on whom the film is built to the stereotypes I listed above. Consider, for example, how Hawks uses John Wayne – both his qualities and his limitations. He is the archetypal Western hero, strong, silent, infallible. His taciturnity becomes the occasion for humour (especially in the scenes with Angie Dickinson) which is dependent partly on our awareness of John T. Chance as a genre-character; at the same time, the concept of stoical heroism Wayne embodies provides the film with one of its major touchstones for behaviour. For all the sophistication and unobtrusive but extreme virtuosity, Hawks's art here has affinities, in its unselfconsciousness, its tendency to deal directly with basic human needs, its spontaneous-intuitive freshness, with folk-song: consider, for instance, the refusal to identify most of the characters with anything beyond descriptive-evocative nicknames: Dude, Feathers, Stumpy, Colorado . . . even Chance *sounds* like a nickname. Colorado has a surname somewhere, but who remembers it? One feels the characters as coming from a folk-ballad rather than from any actual social context: they have that kind of relationship to reality.

Feathers is the product of the union of her basic 'type' – the saloon girl – and the Hawks woman, sturdy and independent yet sensitive and vulnerable, the equal of any man yet not in the least masculine. The tension between background (convention) and foreground (actual character) is nowhere more evident. We are very far here from the brash 'entertainer' with a heart of gold who dies (more often than not) stopping a bullet intended for the hero. Angie Dickinson's marvellous performance gives us the perfect embodiment of the Hawksian woman, intelligent, resilient, and responsive. There is a continual sense of a woman who really grasps what is important to her. One is struck by the beauty of the character, the beauty of a living individual responding spontaneously to every situation from a secure centre of self. It is not so much a matter of characterisation as the communication of a life-quality (a much rarer thing). What one most loves about Hawks, finally, is the aliveness of so many of his people.

Stumpy (Walter Brennan) and Carlos (Pedro Gonzalez-Gonzalez) are brilliant variants on the Western's traditional 'comic relief' stock types. Both are so completely integrated, not only in the action, but in the overall moral pattern, that the term 'comic relief' is ludicrously inadequate to describe their function. With Stumpy, as with Chance/Wayne, the traditional figure merges indistinguishably into the personality of the actor. Brennan's *persona* of garrulous and toothless old cripple has been built up in numerous other films (some of them Hawks's – *To Have and Have Not*, *Red River*). Hawks's method with Brennan/Stumpy is the same as with Wayne/Chance: the character is pushed to an extreme that verges on parody. With Chance this has the effect of testing the validity of the values the *persona* embodies by exposing them to the possibility of ridicule. With Stumpy the effect is dual: on the one hand we have Brennan's funniest and richest, most completely realised impersonation; on the other, the character's position in the film ceases to be marginal (as 'comic relief' suggests). His garrulity gradually reveals itself as a cover for fear and a sense of inadequacy; it plays an essential part in the development of the action, contributing to Dude's breakdown. With Stumpy, humour and pathos are inseparable. The response the characterisation evokes is remarkably complex: he is funny, pathetic, maddening, often all at the same time; yet, fully aware of his limitations, we never cease to respect him.

Carlos raises a more general problem: what some critics have described as Hawks's racialist tendencies. I feel myself that Hawks is entirely free of racial feeling; with Carlos, with the Dutchman in *Only Angels Have Wings*, with the French-Canadians in *The Big Sky*, he is simply taking over genre-figures (and often the character-actors associated with them) and building on them. One can say that the very existence of such stock figures is itself insulting, and this is fair enough; one can, I suppose, go on from that to complain that Hawks is unthinkingly helping to perpetuate the insult; but that is rather different from finding actual racial malice in his attitude. He is simply – and very characteristically – making use of the conventions (and the actors) that are to hand, and not questioning their initial validity. He takes the stock figure of the comic, cowardly, gesticulating, garrulous Mexican and, by eliminating the cowardliness while playing up the excitability, builds up a character whose dauntlessness and determination win our sympathy and respect even as we laugh at him. Hawks's handling not only revivifies and humanises the stock type, but greatly increases his dignity and (moral!) stature.

But it is the figure of the Hero's Fallible Friend that is most fully worked on and transformed in *Rio Bravo*. Significantly, perhaps, this is the least stereotyped, the most uncertain and unpredictable, of the traditional Western ingredients. What I have in mind, however, is a character the variations on which the reader will have little difficulty in recognising, whose function is usually to act as a foil to the hero, to set off his integrity and incorruptibility. Usually, he falls from grace either through weakness, personal inadequacy, or (more often perhaps) his betrayal of the hero, and gets killed. The characters played by Arthur Kennedy in two of Anthony Mann's excellent Westerns, *Where the River Bends* and *The Man from Laramie*, are interesting variants on the basic type; Lloyd Bridges in *High Noon* is another example. A part of this function – a foil to set off the hero's moral infallibility – is still clearly operative in *Rio Bravo*; but Dude takes on such importance in the film that it becomes a question at times who is a foil for whom. Hawks says *Rio Bravo* is really Dean Martin's picture; and if one disagrees, it's not because it's John Wayne's, but because what gives *Rio Bravo* its beauty is above all the interaction of all the parts, the sense that its significance arises from the ensemble, not from any individual character in isolation. Otherwise Hawks (who said of the ending of *Red River* that he couldn't see the sense of killing people off unnecessarily) exactly reverses the Fallible Friend's usual progress: instead of decline and betrayal, we have a movement (despite setbacks) towards salvation. And it is very important that the first step in that salvation is the mainspring of the film's whole action: it is typical of Hawks that everything should hang, ultimately, on a matter of *personal* responsibility, not social duty.

Rio Bravo, then, is firmly rooted in a certain Hollywood tradition, and awareness of the tradition and its conventions can help to enrich our response to it. Nevertheless, it is equally true to say that the film can be understood without reference to 'the Western' at all. It is as firmly rooted in Hawks's own past. Hawks has never rejected his past, and never really left it behind. In a sense, *Rio Bravo* subsumes almost everything he had done previously (without, of course making the other films redundant). The expository first few minutes, where the situation from which all the action develops, and the film's central relationship, are established without a word being spoken, constitute, whether intentionally or not, a homage to the silent cinema that takes us right back to Hawks's roots. The whole pattern of relationships in the film will be familiar to those who have seen *Only Angels Have Wings* and *To Have and Have Not*. Consider the following parallels between the three films: the three heroes (Grant, Bogart, Wayne) are all variations on a basic concept; the women (Arthur, Bacall, Dickinson) all share a strong family resemblance, and there are clear similarities in their relationships with the films' respective heroes. Stumpy, obviously, can be traced back to Eddie in *To Have and Have Not*: the fact that both are played by Walter Brennan makes the similarity very conspicuous. But Dude can be traced back to Eddie too, and also to Bat in *Only Angels Have Wings* (one would not readily have connected Bat and Eddie without this sense that they are both partly subsumed in Dude). Stumpy is also related

94

to Kid in *Only Angels Have Wings* – there is the same fear of growing old and no longer being of any use. Carlos has something in common with the Dutchman in *Only Angels Have Wings* and with Frenchy in *To Have and Have Not*; further, the 'responsibility' he is given of putting Feathers on the stagecoach recalls the task of putting Slim on the plane entrusted to Crickett (Hoagy Carmichael). Both fail.

What is important to note are the differences that such juxtapositions force on the attention. The quite different 'feel' of the three films is largely determined by the differences between their heroes. Grant in *Only Angels Have Wings* is much younger than the other two men, and strikes one as essentially more vulnerable (he is, I think, the only Hawks hero who ever cries), less finally formed by experience, his maturity and balance less secure. Hence the more extreme and drastic – almost exhibitionistic – nature of his rejection of sentimentality: it almost becomes the rejection of feeling itself, a trait criticised and qualified during the film. With the other two, especially Wayne, we are made aware of limitations rather than imperfections. Also, while Wayne and Bogart are both confronted with the *possibility* of their associates' death or collapse, Grant is the only one confronted with death itself. The possibility of desperation, which seems always, almost invisibly, to underlie the good-humoured surface of the adventure films, is much more apparent in *Only Angels Have Wings* than in the later works, and it is largely the nature of the protagonist that makes this possible. Bogart, on the other hand, of the three is the one most completely in command of the situations he finds himself in. Wayne appears to be in command; but a leading point of *Rio Bravo* – it amounts almost to a 'running gag' – is that he isn't: his safety and success depend at every crisis on the timely intervention of others. *To Have and Have Not* and *Rio Bravo* are probably the two Hawks films which are closest to each other (if one excepts *Ball of Fire* and its inferior remake *A Song Is Born*): the likeness of *El Dorado* to *Rio Bravo* may be more immediately obvious, but it proves on closer acquaintance also more superficial. *Rio Bravo* and *To Have and Have Not* give us closely parallel patterns of character-relationships, and even stretches (in the Bogart/Bacall and Wayne/Dickinson exchanges) of almost identical dialogue. The real difference between them rests not on obvious differences of location and plot-twists, but on the different relationship of the hero to the total work. In fact, the more one thinks about the three films, the more different they seem.

The wordless first minutes of the film are a good example of Hawks's use of actions to speak for themselves. Why does Dude strike Chance down? Why does Chance, despite his injury, so rashly – on the face of it hopelessly – follow and try to arrest Joe Burdett? Why does Dude help him? We feel we know the answers to all these questions, though they are never spelt out. All are essential to the film, and to what Hawks stands for.

The flooring of Chance establishes the basis on which Dude's whole development is built – his reluctance to be dragged up from his gutter when it is so much easier to sink further; and the resentment of the fallen man for the apparently infallible. Chance's single-handed attempt at arresting Joe

Burdett in a saloon full of Joe's friends gives us a perfect image of the Hawks hero. There is no element of showing-off nor of self-willed martyrdom: Chance's attitude is rooted in a personal need for self-respect, which demands that an action that must be done be done unquestioningly, without fuss, and alone, even in the teeth of hopeless odds. Dude's intervention sets the pattern for the whole film, where at every crisis Chance is saved by assistance he hasn't asked for or has rejected; but its motivation is equally fundamental to the spirit of the film. When Chance prevented Dude from taking the coin from the spittoon, Dude was made conscious of his degradation; his beating-up by Joe intensifies this consciousness. Above all, he is confronted by two opposite examples: the moral disintegration of Joe, the moral integrity of Chance. On his choice between them depends his salvation as a human being: his decision to help Chance (physically) commits him to an attempt to save himself (morally and spiritually). To express all this purely through simple physical actions is profoundly characteristic of Hawks; so is the immediately established positive trend of the character-development. There is nothing glib or sentimental about Hawks's treatment of his characters, but if he can possibly steer them towards salvation, he does. This spirit of generosity, the most creative human characteristic, vivifies all his best films. Even Tony Camonte, in *Scarface*, obviously an exception to any general rule one could make about Hawks's protagonists, becomes most interesting when self-awareness begins, belatedly, to break on him. It is consistently a moral rather than a psychological interest: the cure is always therapeutic, never psycho-analytical (though what happens to Dunson in *Red River* has certain affinities with the process of psycho-analysis).

If in *Rio Bravo* the traditional Western theme of the defence of civilised values is reduced to little more than a pretext, where, then, does Hawks put the emphasis? On values below the social level, but on which social values, if valid, must necessarily be built: man's innate need for self-respect or self-definition. As a motif, it will be easily seen that this pervades the film, as a unifying principle of composition. It is stated through virtually every character, usually on his first appearance, like the subject of a fugue, and developed throughout contrapuntally with fugal rigour. The film's first actions constitute a negative statement (Dude grovelling for the coin in the spittoon) and a positive one (Chance's intervention, and the ensuing arrest of Joe Burdett). The first words of Colorado (Ricky Nelson) insist on his rights as an individual: when Chance questions Pat Wheeler (Ward Bond) about him in his presence, he interrupts with, 'I speak English, Sheriff, you wanna ask me.' Pat, too old and unsteady to be of direct use, risking (and giving) his life to get others to help Chance; Stumpy asserting his independence by disobeying Chance's orders and standing in the jail doorway; Feathers refusing to stop gambling and wearing feathers as a way of escaping a suspect past ('That's what I'd do if I were the kind of girl that you think I am'); Carlos insisting with sudden touching dignity on his right to arrange matters as he pleases in his own hotel: all these constitute variants on the theme.

Variants, not repetitions: the statements range from broad humour (Stumpy) to near tragedy (Dude): each is distinct from the others in tone and in moral weight. Examples could be multiplied throughout the film. There is a continual sense of the contrapuntal interaction of the various levels of seriousness and humour, so that great complexity of tone often results. Consider for example the way in which Stumpy's comic need to emphasise his alertness and mastery to offset his sense of disability ('Old cripples ain't wanted') precipitates Dude's breakdown when Stumpy shoots, as ordered, the moment someone fails to give the word on entering the jail (Dude, bathed and shaved, was unrecognisable). Everything in the film can be referred back to this unifying motif, yet, as always, it is nowhere given explicit statement. The density of the thematic development is increased by the element of parody introduced through the villains. Nathan Burdett (John Russell) goes to such lengths to get his brother out of jail not from motives of affection but from pride in his position: his actions are dictated, that is to say, by the desire not to lose face, a caricature of the motives for which the heroes act, rendered further invalid by the fact that he is defending a morally indefensible action. When Nathan tells Dude that everyone should have a taste of power before he dies, we are made strongly aware of the distinction between the kind of power Dude is experiencing in overcoming his tendency to disintegration, and the sort of power Burdett experiences.

By shifting the emphasis from man's responsibility to society (still there as a starting-point but no more than that) to his responsibility to himself, Hawks strips everything down to a basic stoic principle. From this follows his conception of friendship as a relationship based on mutual respect and mutual independence. Throughout the film we see Chance training Dude for the independence and self-respect that constitutes true manhood – for a relationship based on a balance of equality between free men. There are those who can see no more to this theme of close friendship between men in Hawks's films than the endorsement of a hearty, superficial matiness: nothing could be further from the truth. These relationships in Hawks almost invariably embody something strong, positive, and fruitful: at the least (*The Thing*) a warmth of mutual response; at the most (*Rio Bravo*) the veritable salvation of a human being.

Here, too, the essential things are conveyed through – or more accurately perhaps *grow out of* – physical actions. It is worth quoting Hawks here – a passage from the earlier of the two interviews he gave Peter Bogdanovich which throws much light on his methods:

> . . . we have to feel our way as we go along and we can add to a character or get a piece of business between two people and start some relationship going and then further it. In *Rio Bravo*, Dean Martin had a bit in which he was required to roll a cigarette. His fingers weren't equal to it and Wayne kept passing him cigarettes. All of a sudden you realize that they are awfully good friends or he wouldn't be doing it. That grew out of Martin's asking me one say 'Well, if my fingers are shaky, how can I

roll this thing?' So Wayne said, 'Here, I'll hand you one', and suddenly we had something going.

There is a beautiful example in *Only Angels Have Wings* of the establishment of a relationship purely through actions: the scene where Cary Grant and Thomas Mitchell try to guide Joe down through the fog. Hawks builds the scene on a sense of instinctive awareness between the two men, Mitchell using his ears and Grant his voice as if they were two aspects of the same human being; at the end, when Joe has crashed, Mitchell holds out a cigarette he has rolled and Grant takes it, as if he knew it would be exactly there at exactly that moment, without looking. One moment in *Rio Bravo*, in itself very small, beautifully defines the relationship between Chance and Dude. Chance takes Dude out to patrol the streets, mainly to help him overcome the strain he is under from his need for alcohol, pauses by the paid gunman who has been appointed by Burdett to watch the jail, says 'Good evening' to him and stands there till the man shuffles uneasily and moves away. We see Dude watching from the other side of the street, and from his face the impact on him of this expression of moral force, the authority that comes from integrity.

But for Hawks there comes a point where these friendships, valuable and creative as they are, reach the limit of their power to influence and affect, beyond which point the individual is alone with his own resources or sheer chance to fall back on. We saw this in the treatment of Kid's death in *Only Angels Have Wings*; in *Rio Bravo* Dude's salvation rests ultimately, not on Chance, but on chance. At the climax of his relapse, when he has failed in his responsibilities and decided to hand in his badge, he clumsily pours out a glass of whisky, nerves gone, hands trembling helplessly: it is his moment of defeat, from which it seems likely that he will never recover. Chance's example, combined with his stoic refusal to indulge him, no longer reaches him. Then, as he raises the glass, the 'Alamo' music starts up again from the saloon across the street, and we see its immediate implications ('No quarter!' – it is being played on Burdett's orders) and its heroic associations strike him. He pauses, then pours the whisky back into the thin-necked bottle unfalteringly – 'Didn't spill a drop.' It is his moment of victory, and one of the great moments of the cinema. Its power to move derives partly from its context (it is, after all, one of the central moments in a film singlemindedly concerned with self-respect), partly from the irony (the tune played to undermine courage in fact has the opposite effect), and partly in our sense of the precariousness of everything.

One of the concerns common to *Red River* and *Rio Bravo* – though it takes very different forms in the two films – is a preoccupation with heroism, the conditions necessary to it, and the human limitations that accompany those conditions. This will be obvious enough in the earlier film, with its examination of the limits of the acceptability of Dunson's ruthlessness. The concept of the hero in *Rio Bravo* – of Hawks's attitude to him – may at first sight appear less complex, in that Chance is presented throughout as morally infallible. Yet Hawks's conception here is subtler. Without qualifying our sense of moral infallibility, Hawks defines in the course of the action the limitations that not only accompany it but are to some extent the conditions for its existence. Consider, for example, the song sequence, one of the film's focal points (it is often regarded as an irrelevance, forced into the action to give Ricky Nelson something to sing). It occurs just after Dude's triumph over his weakness, which in its turn was preceded by Colorado's intervention, his ceasing to 'mind his own business', in the flower-pot scene. Earlier, his refusal to commit himself helped to make possible the murder of his boss, Pat Wheeler: Colorado, like Dude, was guilty of a failure of responsibility. In the song sequence he, Dude, and Stumpy sit in a circle in the jail, Stumpy accompanying on the harmonica while the other two sing. It is perhaps the best expression in Hawks's work of the spontaneous-intuitive sympathy which he makes so important as the basis of human relations. The compositions and the editing (by making us aware of the exchange of glances) as well as the acting contribute gradually to link the three men in a bond of fellow-feeling through the shared experience of the music. Throughout it, Chance stands outside the circle looking on, a paternally approving smile on his face, but none the less excluded from the common experience. The three physically or morally fallible men – cripple, reformed drunk, boy who failed once in his responsibility – are able to achieve a communion which the infallible man is denied, excluded by his very infallibility.

More obviously, Chance's limitations are revealed in his relationship with Feathers. For, if *Rio Bravo* as a whole is a summing-up of Hawks's adventure films, its love relationship, with the repeated discomfiture of the hero, succinctly recapitulates Hawksian comedy, and the film is enormously enriched by the interaction of the two. It is the first time in Hawks's work that this kind of relationship, so basic to the comedies, appears in an adventure film. Certainly the Grant/Arthur and Bogart/Bacall relationships in *Only Angels Have Wings* and *To Have and Have Not* have points in common with it; but Grant and Bogart, while they may have *resisted* their women for a time, were always able to handle them. *Rio Bravo* marks the beginning of a tendency (here kept beautifully under control and in balance) to satirise the hero – a tendency carried further with Wayne in *Hatari!*, and taking different forms in the parodistic 'Wildcat Jones' song of *Red Line 7000* and in *El Dorado*, where the challenge comes not from women but from age.

Feathers's first appearance constitutes a humorous inversion of the fugue theme – Chance, the seemingly invulnerable, almost mythic figure of the 'strong, silent man', finding his dignity abruptly undermined when the scarlet bloomers ordered for Carlos's wife are held up against him for Carlos's approval, and the woman greets him with, 'Those things have great possibilities, Sheriff, but not on you.' She has to take the initiative throughout their relationship; but – and this is what makes it so different from the man–woman relationship in, say, *I Was a Male War Bride* – its development is repeatedly given impetus by her attempts to drive him to establish authority over her, thereby completing his mastery of his world. Feathers, in fact, trains Chance rather as Chance trains Dude – trains him for a relationship of spiritual equals, for it is always clear that the establishment of male authority will be a matter of voluntary surrender on her part. It is true that Hawks never shows his man–woman relationships developing beyond a certain point; nevertheless, the relationship reached at the end of *Rio Bravo* carries a beautiful and satisfying sense of maturity, with both partners strong enough to preserve a certain independence and to come together on terms of equality. Again, it is a relationship of free people, each existing from an established centre of self-respect. The final scene between them, where Chance 'tells her he loves her' by ordering her not to go down to the saloon to sing in the very revealing 'entertainer's' costume which she wore before she knew him, far from seeming an anti-climax after the gun-and-dynamite showdown with Burdett and his men, is the true climax of the film. The lightly humorous treatment shouldn't blind us to its underlying seriousness and beauty.

There is a sense in which Chance's independence and self-sufficiency is illusory. He goes through the film systematically rejecting the help of others; yet every crisis without exception, from the arrest of Joe Burdett on, would end in disaster were it not for the unsolicited intervention of others. Without the cripple, the drunk, the comic Mexican, the teenage boy, a girl on hand to fling a well-timed flower-pot, the superman would be defeated before he had the chance to perform a single decisive action. Yet if the others are physically indispensable to him, it is never in doubt that Chance is spiritually indispensable to them. Remove him from the film, and you would be left largely with human wreckage; for it is abundantly clear that it is Chance, partly by direct influence, partly by example, by the very fact of his existence, who gives meaning, coherence, and integrity to the lives of those around him. As a concrete embodiment of the Hawksian values, he is the nucleus round which the others can organise themselves, without which there would be no possibility of order.

I am aware that this account of *Rio Bravo* is open to one serious objection: anyone reading it, with its talk of fugues, of stylistic and structural rigour, of moral seriousness, will be totally unprepared for the consistently relaxed, delightful, utterly unpretentious film that *Rio Bravo* is. In fact, when it first came out, almost nobody noticed that it was in any sense a serious work of art. Furthermore, it would be a great mistake to assume that there is any split here between the relaxed tone and the serious content – that Hawks has 'something to say', a 'message', and has deliberately (and compromisingly) made it 'entertaining', sugaring the moral pill, so to speak, for the masses. One can feel confident that *Rio Bravo* is precisely the film he wanted to make. The immense good humour is, in fact, essential to the moral tone, and, together with the leisurely tempo, manifests an achieved serenity of mind; the relaxed mood of the film as a whole is never incompatible with the consistent tension in the relationships that shows the intensity of Hawks's involvement in his work.

The source of *Rio Bravo*'s richness is threefold: there is the sense of it as the product of a whole vital tradition, acting as a fruitful soil in which the film is rooted, nourishing it invisibly from beneath; and there is the sense of the film's working on many levels and for different sorts of spectator, the strength derived from its being the product and the representative of a popular art form, appealing to 'groundlings' and intellectuals alike, and with no sense of discrepancy or conflict between these levels of appeal. But above all the richness derives from Hawks himself, from the warmth and generosity of his personality, pervading every scene of the film; from the essentially positive and creative nature of all the film's leading relationships; from the good humour and sanity that colour every sequence. Everything in *Rio Bravo* ends happily; not a hero dies, the final battle becomes a kind of joyous celebration-party for Dude's regeneration. Yet always one is aware of the extreme precariousness of everything. In the background, never very far away, is the eternal darkness surrounding human existence, against which the Hawksian stoicism shines; over everything, colouring each scene, is the marvellous good-natured humour and balance of Hawks when he is at his best.

Robin Wood has been probably the most influential English-language critic during the last thirty years. He brought a Leavisite concern with the moral implications and value of works and emphasis on close textual analysis to bear on a number of film-makers within the commercial cinema. Wood's first acknowledgement at the end of his book on Hawks is of his debt to F. R. Leavis, and in *Hitchcock's Films Revisited* (New York: Columbia University Press, 1989; London: Faber, 1992) Wood returns to the subject of Leavis and criticism. Wood's first two book-length studies were on Hitchcock (*Hitchcock's Films*, first published London: Tantivy Press, 1965) and Hawks (*Howard Hawks*). As well as excitement and enthusiasm, they also generated – and in many ways courted – controversy. In part, of course, Wood was picking up on the 'Hitchcocko-Hawksian' tendencies of *Cahiers du Cinéma* in the 1950s (*Cahiers* did in fact publish Wood on *Psycho*), but Wood's approach to both film-makers was essentially very different, particularly in its close attention to textual detail, which was not a major characteristic of most *Cahiers* work. Though Wood had already written extensively – his lifetime output has been prodigious – for journals like the Cambridge-based *Granta*, *Oxford Opinion* and early issues of *Movie* (which grew out of *Oxford Opinion*), his first work on *Rio Bravo* appeared in *Movie*, and Lee Russell's *New Left Review* essay on Hawks is in part a response to this material, just as Wollen's discussion of Hawks in *Signs and Meaning in the Cinema* responds to Wood's 1968 book. (Wollen was, in fact, Wood's editor in the British Film Institute Education Department for the Hawks book.)

Wood's magistral reading of *Rio Bravo* bases itself upon an introduction which stresses the 'conservative' and classical nature of Hollywood (likened by Wood in some ways to Elizabethan London or Mozart's Vienna), with Hawks seen as 'a survivor from the past whose work has never been afflicted with the disease of self-consciousness'. Though Wood's approach is unashamedly authorial – Hawks as the determining factor in the works – Wood always retains some sense of Hollywood tradition as a vitally informing element. Wood's moral emphasis can be inferred from the title of the chapter which includes his discussion of *Rio Bravo*: 'Self-Respect and Responsibility' (the chapter also discusses *Only Angels Have Wings* and *To Have and Have Not*). In the wake of Wollen's *Signs and Meaning in the Cinema*, Wood's humanist assumptions were much attacked in the politicized and theorizing 1970s, particularly in the pages of *Screen*. Wood's responses (along with essays on Sternberg, Ophuls, Tourneur, Welles and Mizoguchi – which give some idea of the range of his interests) were collected in *Personal Views*. Particularly relevant are 'Reflections on the Auteur Theory' and 'Hawks De-Wollenized'. Despite the obvious implications of Wood's first two books being on Hitchcock and Hawks, Wood has also written at length on Bergman, Godard, Dusan Makavejev, Antonioni, Arthur Penn and Claude Chabrol.

Howard Hawks

ANDREW SARRIS

From Andrew Sarris, *The American Cinema: Directors and Directions 1929–1968* (New York: Dutton, 1968).

Howard Hawks was until recently the least known and least appreciated Hollywood director of any stature. His name is not mentioned in the indices of Kracauer's *Theory of Film, Grierson on Documentary* (which discusses many Hollywood directors), Lewis Jacobs's *The Rise of the American Film*, and Roger Manvell's *Penguin Film* series. Paul Rotha's *The Film Till Now* makes one brief reference to Hawks: 'A very good all-rounder [who] stays in the mind with *The Crowd Roars, Scarface, Ball of Fire*, and *The Big Sleep*.' By contrast, Hawks had been greatly admired in France since *Scarface* in 1932. But then it was easier to see *Scarface* in Paris than in New York through the thirties and forties. Many revival houses featured a double bill of *The Public Enemy* and *Little Caesar*, but *Scarface* was always withheld from circulation by the Howard Hughes interests. (It would be interesting to know where and when the late Robert Warshow saw *Scarface*, to which he refers briefly in his famous essay on *The Gangster as Tragic Hero*.) Once Hawks was discovered, however, he revealed a consistent personal style and view of the world. If anything, *Man's Favorite Sport, Red Line 7000*, and *El Dorado* are quintessentially and self-consciously Hawksian. The same lines and basic situations pop up in film after film with surprisingly little variation. Call it classicism or cliché, the fact remains that for a director whose credentials are so obscure to English-speaking critics, Hawks has retained a surprising degree of control over his assignments, choosing the ones he wanted to do, and working on the scripts of all his films. The Hawksian hero acts with remarkable consistency in a predominantly male universe.

If Ford's heroes are sustained by tradition, the Hawksian hero is upheld by an instinctive professionalism. Even during the Depression, Hawksian characters were always gainfully employed. The idea that a man is measured by his work rather than by his ability to communicate with women is the key to Hawksian masculinity, as the converse is the key to Antonioni's femininity. Whereas Ford's attitude to his women can be defined in terms of chivalry, the Hawksian woman is a manifestation of the director's gallantry.

Like his heroes, Howard Hawks has lived a tightrope existence, keeping his footing in a treacherous industry for more than forty years without surrendering his personal identity. It is impossible to single out any one of his films as a definitive summation of his career, and it is unlikely that he will ever discard the mask of the commercial film-maker, although he comes very close in *El Dorado* when one of his characters recites Poe's 'Eldorado' almost as a tribute to perceptive French criticism of both Poe and Hawks.

Throughout his career Hawks has adjusted to technological changes without blazing a trail for others to follow. He came late to the talking film after Vidor, Lubitsch, Sternberg, and Mamoulian had explored its potentialities, extremely late to the color film, and, despite an honorable effort in *Land of the Pharaohs*, he does not seem to have been enchanted by the world of the wide screen. His technique is a function of his personality and the material with which he has chosen to work. His scenarios, which invariably emphasize action within a short time span, do not lend themselves to decorative mannerisms. When he has been confronted with epic subjects in *Red River* and *Land of the Pharaohs*, he has split his story into two short segments of time a decade or so apart. He has never used a flashback, and even in the thirties he seldom resorted to the degenerative montage of time lapses. His tracking, cutting, and framing have never attracted much attention in themselves, and this is not so much a virtue as it may seem. Critics who argue that technique should not call attention to itself are usually critics who do not wish to call attention to technique. If Hawks does not choose to use technique as reflective commentary on action, it is because his personality expresses a pragmatic intelligence rather than a philosophical wisdom.

Hawks has an uncanny technical flair for establishing the mood of the film at the outset and sustaining this mood to the end. The atmosphere established in the opening fog-enshrouded shots of *Barbary Coast*, *Road to Glory* and *Only Angels Have Wings* casts a spell that is uniquely Hawksian. The opening, wordless sequences in *Rio Bravo* present all the moral issues of the film. The low-angle shot of Wayne looking down at Martin with sorrowful disdain tells the audience all it has to know about the two men, and Hawks even tilts his camera to isolate the relationship from its background and to intensify the reciprocal feelings of shame and disappointment. However, Hawks never tilts his camera again in the film, and the intensity of the opening tapers off into comic understatement. This is typical of the director's tendency to veer away from dramatization and verbalization of feelings that are implicit in the action.

Hawks consciously shoots most of his scenes at the eye level of a standing onlooker. Consequently, even his spectacles are endowed with a human intimacy which the director will not disturb with pretentious crane shots. Hawks will work within a frame as much as possible, cutting only when a long take or an elaborate track might distract his audience from the issues in the foreground of the action. This is good, clean, direct, functional cinema, perhaps the most distinctively American cinema of all. It is certainly not the last word on the art of film-making, but its qualities are more unusual than most critics have imagined. However, even at the time of their release, the Hawks films were generally liked for their solid professionalism. The director has worked with the most distinguished cameramen in Hollywood: Gregg Toland, Lee Garmes, James Wong Howe, Tony Gaudio, Ernest Haller, Russell Harlan, and Sid Hickox. Hawks himself has never been less than a professional, but he has been more as well. His technique has served ultimately to express his personal credo that man is the measurer of all things.

Aside from a few gibes at red-baiting in *His Girl Friday*, Hawks has never indicated any specific political orientation. The religious lunatic in *Twentieth Century*, the revivalism in *Sergeant York*, and the mordant piety after the brutal fact in *Red River* constitute what little there is of religion in the world of Howard Hawks. Except for *Sergeant York*, Hawks has never dealt with the very poor as a class, and except for *Bringing Up Baby*, he has never dealt with the very rich as a class. To the best of my memory there has never been a divorce or a gratuitous suicide in any of the director's films. Hawks rejected *Fourteen Hours* as a directorial assignment because he explicitly disapproved of the theme of suicide as a form of neurotic escape. (Henry Hathaway later accepted this assignment.) Curiously, however, *Dawn Patrol*, *Today We Live*, *Ceiling Zero*, and *Road to Glory* have quasi-suicidal climaxes in which characters accept fatal missions, but the moral arithmetic balances out because in each instance the martyr is a replacement in an obligatory situation. However, it may be significant that all these sacrificial episodes occurred in films of the thirties, an era in which the Hawksian virtues were most appropriate. A director of parts as well as a unified whole, Hawks has stamped his distinctively bitter view of life on adventure, gangster and private-eye melodramas, Westerns, musicals, and screwball comedies, the kind of thing Americans do best and appreciate least. Now that his work has been thoroughly revived and reevaluated throughout the English-speaking world, there is little point in belaboring the point for the few remaining stragglers who maintain that his art is not really Art with a serving of espresso in the lobby. That one can discern the same directorial signature over a wide variety of genres is proof of artistry. That one can still enjoy the genres for their own sake is proof of the artist's professional urge to entertain.

During the 1960s Andrew Sarris was certainly the principal advocate of 'auteurism' in the USA, credited with bringing the 'politique des auteurs' developed in France in the 1950s into film criticism in North America as 'the auteur theory'. One should note the slippage in translation from 'politique' – policy or principle – to 'theory', since there was usually precious little theory in its use. The 'theory' claim was generally not deployed by the *Movie* critics who were simultaneously developing an authorship approach in Britain, though with much greater emphasis on close textual analysis. Hawks was as central to Sarris's thinking about American cinema as he was to French and British thinking, and Sarris's two-part overview of Hawks's work, 'The World of Howard Hawks' (*Films and Filming*, July and August 1962, reprinted in Joseph McBride (ed.), *Focus on Howard Hawks*) was certainly the first substantial critical analysis of the span of Hawks's work. But probably more significant than this was Sarris's development of a polemical perspective on American film history and the role of authorship, first in the pages of *Film Culture* in the early 1960s and then in the hugely influential *The American Cinema: Directors and Directions 1929–1968*. This was less about American cinema as a whole than about selected directors, classified into value categories – 'Pantheon Directors', 'The Far Side of Paradise', 'Expressive Esoterica', 'Less Than Meets The Eye', 'Lightly Likable', 'Strained Seriousness', and so on. Needless to say, Hawks appears among the 'Pantheon Directors', in the company of Chaplin, Griffith, Ford, Hitchcock, Lang, Ophuls, Welles, and others. Sarris's incisive capsule overviews and value judgments informed the thinking of a whole generation of critics and cinephiles, though Sarris's impact on thinking about US cinema has not been so significant since the 1970s.

Man's Favorite Sport? (Revisited)

MOLLY HASKELL

From *The Village Voice*, 21 January 1971, and in revised form in Joseph McBride (ed.), *Focus on Howard Hawks* (Englewood Cliffs, NJ: Prentice-Hall, 1972).

American films, especially the action and thriller genres, flourish to an unusually large degree on an unconscious level. Most of the signals and symbols sent up from this region are sexual, a result both of the restrictions of a masculine genre and the repressions of a Puritan society. The earrings of Madame de resonate quite explicitly with accumulated meanings – sexuality, passion, longing, and finally despair, whereas the spectacle of blood in a Hitchcock film makes a covert appeal to the darker side of our natures. The fact that American directors are less intellectual and more instinctive than Europeans has been used to evade serious analysis of their work, considered conventional and commercial. Actually, genre films operate on more levels than subjective cinema (though they are sometimes imperfectly resolved), and demand more rather than less exploration to uncover these meanings which relate directly to our collective unconscious – especially in this dark hour of our cultural confusion.

Critics will spend hours with divining rods over the obviously hermetic mindscape of Bergman, Antonioni, etc., giving them the benefit of every passing doubt. But they will scorn similar excursions into the genuinely cryptic, richer, and more organic terrain of home-grown talents.

I recently watched for the second time Howard Hawks's *Man's Favorite Sport?*, a film which was universally ridiculed when it appeared in 1964, and which I myself hadn't much liked. I wanted to watch it again just to make sure – it is almost impossible for a great director to make a worthless film, and a few years in a film's life can change our perspective a great deal. This time I was both delighted and deeply moved by the film – delighted by the grace and real humor with which the story is told, and moved by the reverberations of a whole substratum of meaning, of sexual antagonism, desire, and despair.

The two layers, narrative and allegorical, interweave in such a way that the cruelty is constantly tempered by compassion and the ridiculous is redeemed by risk and anguish. As a result, the intrigue is not only richer, but the humor is funnier. In describing the substratum, I don't mean to suggest that Hawks is an unconscious artist. He is far more deliberate and articulate in his vision of the American male than, say, John Cassavetes, who in *Husbands* arrives at truths almost (but not quite) accidentally. The control and precision, the economy and follow-through of a Hawks film is assurance that he has mastered his material, that he *knows* it in a way that is more than intuitive but short of theoretical.

In a Hawks film, men and women are on their own, starting out in, and trying to fill, a vacuum. In *Man's Favorite Sport?* he gives us Rock Hudson and Paula Prentiss as primordial man and woman, Adam and Eve in the lush, hazardous Eden of a hunting and fishing resort. But an Adam and Eve saddled with a bitter, comical heritage of sexual distrust, bravado, and fear, archetypes that are infinitely closer to the American experience than such articulate *angst*-mongers as Jeanne and Monica and Marcello and Max and Harriet and Jean-Paul (Sartre or Belmondo).

Rock Hudson works as a salesman in the sporting goods department of Abercrombie and Fitch. He has written an authoritative book on fishing, although he has never gone fishing in his life and finds the idea repugnant. His professional standing, therefore, is a hoax. Or, in the vocabulary of the sexual allegory to which the film implicitly alludes, Hudson is a virgin, who has written a 'How to' book on sex while harboring a deep, fastidious horror of it. His masculinity is a lie. (Interestingly, he is engaged, but has never told his fiancée he can't 'fish'.)

Paula Prentiss, an aggressive, outdoorsy girl with a *soupçon* of butch (the female equivalent of a man's man), arrives on the scene to browbeat Hudson into entering a fishing competition at the lodge where she works. (They first collide in a parking lot, in a scene which has been cut from the print now shown on television.)

But certain modifying characteristics emerge. Although Paula Prentiss seems strident and overbearing in her action, there is something in the way Hawks directs her behavior – her soft, nervous gestures and the odd rhythm of delivery – which suggests vulnerability. And although Rock Hudson seems inoffensive and gentle – just a man trying to mind his own business and have peace – there is something flaccid and unresponsive about him, a self-satisfaction which is untested and therefore undeserved. Paula Prentiss, in a remarkable performance, is the girl we knew at college, smart and good at everything but terrified of (and therefore hostile to) men. She spends all her time in the smoker while other girls come and go; she has a shell of genial sarcasm to protect her from the humiliation of desire and rejection.

But she is competent – even sexually, in the film's metaphor – and it is she who must take the initiative in Hudson's sexual initiation, for which the fishing exploit is metaphor. Fish are phallic symbols, of course, and there is even a scene in which a loose fish thrashes around inside Hudson's pants, causing him to jump and jerk uncontrollably.

Hawksian comedy, as Peter Wollen and other critics have pointed out, is the underside of, and compensation for, the action drama. Heroism and danger are replaced by adolescence and sexual failure, the way falling in a dream compensates for our overweening aspirations. The progression, in drama, from life to death, giving birth to an ideal, becomes, in the comedy,

108

a progression from death (Hudson's inertia) to life, with the burial of a false ideal. Alongside Hudson's false-hero there is even a phoney Indian – a cynic, European-style, who poses as an Indian for the tourists and continually tries to blackmail Hudson. (He is finally disarmed by the very naïveté of Hudson; the sleeping bag episode suggests that whereas Europeans cheat romantically without ever being caught, Americans don't do anything and are immediately suspect.)

Without giving a play-by-play analysis, I will mention several of the loveliest and most complex images:

In a small clearing – his own Garden of Eden – Hudson tries unsuccessfully to pitch his (pink) tent, while Paula Prentiss and her girlfriend, serpents in frog suits, hide behind the bushes laughing, and finally intrude upon his privacy. The tent collapses, wrapping the inept Hudson in swaddling clothes. (This sequence is reversed in the end of the film, in which Hudson, now the aggressor, comes to Prentiss's tent, in a well-constructed, firelit campsite.)

When Hudson finally learns to 'fish' it is not by reading his book of instructions, not by the rules, but by accidents of nature . . . or, instinct. (Before he learns, there is a 'men in groups' scene at the lodge bar, where Hudson gives the men 'tips' – an approximation of the locker room ritual of sexual tall tales.) But when Hudson wins the tournament, he has the confidence (or virility) to tell the truth.

An incident that disturbs many people occurs when Rock Hudson has given her the long-awaited kiss, and Paula Prentiss cries 'That was terrible', and runs off. But how eloquently this expresses her desperate resistance at being overwhelmed; her defensiveness over the kiss she has longed for and for which, when it comes, she is totally unprepared.

The head-on collision of trains in the film-within-a-film – the explosion, the electricity – is one side of the Hudson–Prentiss relationship; their drifting in peace and communion along the river of mutual fulfillment is the other. For both Hudson and Prentiss there is embarrassment and humiliation, and they are finally closer to each other than to those graceful members of society who establish rapports more easily.

Hawks's conception of woman, as a creature both equal and threatening to man, can be seen as adolescent and anthropomorphic, but never idealizing or domesticating. He may not penetrate the secrets of a woman's heart and her unique dilemma the way the so-called 'woman's directors' do. But at the same time he never excludes them from the action, never even implicitly suggests that a woman occupies a fixed place – the home, society – or that she is man's subordinate. Instinctively, he strikes a very modern note in the image of a couple united not by the attraction of opposites but the unanimity of similarities. The male–female polarity is reconciled by the struggle to assert oneself in life, in the crazy American scene, in which man and woman can be – as much as man and man – natural allies.

It is entirely appropriate that Molly Haskell should be the first woman critic to be represented in this volume and should initiate the major shift in writing about Hawks, from the 1970s onwards, brought about by 'feminist' film writers. Haskell brought a keen, feminist intelligence to bear on the representation of women in cinema in her book *From Reverence to Rape: The Treatment of Women in the Movies*. Hawks's films are central to Haskell's arguments about progressive elements in the representation of women in films of the 1930s and 1940s. It has been suggested that the wide publicity given to Haskell's ideas (along with those of Marjorie Rosen in *Popcorn Venus: Women, Movies and the American Dream* (New York: Coward, McCann & Geoghegan, 1973)) were responsible in part for the opening up of more and different roles for women in Hollywood films of the mid and late 1970s. It should be emphasized that Haskell is not only interested in the representation of women in Hawks's work. Her essay on Hawks in Richard Roud (ed.), *Cinema: A Critical Dictionary* is one of the best overviews of Hawks's career. While feminist concerns inform that overview, they are not its focus. Haskell's fine 1974 *Film Comment* essay, 'Howard Hawks: Masculine Feminine', centres much more obviously on the sexual politics of Hawks's work, and this perspective is evident in her short analysis reprinted here on *Man's Favorite Sport?* While Haskell's approach to Hawks is always highly accessible, its Freudian underpinning perhaps opened the way to more theoretical work by later feminist critics.

Hawks with Paula Prentiss on the set of *Man's Favorite Sport?*

The Hawksian Woman

NAOMI WISE

From *Take One*, vol. 3 no. 3, January–February 1971.

We all know how idiotically women have been portrayed in Hollywood movies – most of which have been written, directed, and photographed by men. This has been especially true of the adventure genre. Since the adventure film (including such subgenres as Westerns, war films, aviation dramas, detective movies, etc.) is considered a male-oriented genre, women in these films have generally represented the most stereotyped male concepts of women.

While males initiate and carry on the action, women usually play a passive, and largely incidental role in these films: they are an excuse for the hero to get upset, or something for him to leave behind. Within the genre, 'reality' is usually defined as a situation involving physical peril, and this situation is one that, for the most part, excludes women. Women function as 'love interest', remaining largely outside the main thread of the plot, or else they are precious objects whose peril impels the hero to action. (King Kong is merely an interesting, if scary, specimen until he takes a fancy to Fay Wray.)

Within this framework, heroines can be further divided into two categories: the sexless, and the sex object. For many years, fair-haired virgins were the most common heroines. When placed in danger, their reaction is non-utile: they scream and/or faint. In a genre where reality is defined as danger, they are unable to deal with danger, hence with reality; this chicken-heartedness is the guarantee of their innocence.

On the other hand, we have the sex object. She is sexy. She chews gum. Frequently she speaks with a Brooklyn accent. And, since she is not innocent, she is allowed to participate, to some extent, in the action. Frequently she is tainted with evil – the fact that she can keep her head when danger threatens is a mark against her, for it proves that she's had some soiling contact with the real world. Sometimes, however, she appears as the good-bad-girl, and in this role she may sacrifice herself to save the hero (what else are 'used women' good for?). It is her willingness to make this sacrifice that defines her as a *good* bad-girl; without it, she'd simply be a slut.

The work of Howard Hawks is remarkable as the single most consistent exception to these rules. In most of Hawks's adventure films, women play consequential roles; in fact, the heroines are, if anything, superior to the heroes. The good girl and bad girl are fused into a single, heroic heroine, who is both sexual and valuable.

Hawks began directing in 1926 (*The Road To Glory*), when the Flapper Age was at its height, and he came into his own in the 30s. Betty Friedan notes in *The Feminine Mystique* that magazine stories of the 30s and 40s commonly presented career women as heroines: women who remained independent, and to whom romance was a secondary (though welcome) consideration. Hawks's most prolific period occurred during these relatively egalitarian years, when the Depression and the war made it desirable for women to work. It was during this period that the 'Hawksian heroine' was defined.

Her prototype appears in 1932, in *The Crowd Roars*, although she is still dualistic: there is a good girl, Lee (Ann Dvorak), and a good-bad-girl, Ann (Joan Blondell). Conflict centers on Lee's ambivalence toward her sweetheart's dangerous career of car racing, and on Ann's involvement with the hero's younger brother. The hero (James Cagney) is seen from the heroines' points of view – as a fanatic regarding racing (P.O.V. Lee) and as a bigot regarding women (P.O.V. Ann) – a rare viewpoint in the action genre.

The characters of Lee and Ann are fused in *Scarface* (1932) in the character of Cesca (Ann Dvorak), younger sister of mobster Tony Camonte (Paul Muni). Cesca is not yet the complete Hawksian woman, as she has no past of her own. Sheltered and protected by Camonte, and by the Italian family system, she's had no opportunity for experience. However, in typical Hawksian fashion, she takes the initiative in courting Camonte's buddy (George Raft). Ann Dvorak, a delightful actress who combines delicacy with a gentle earthiness, plays the role with such natural ease that Cesca's forthright, 'un-feminine' course of action in no way mars her character. Like later Hawks heroines, Cesca has a sense of her own value, which enables her to go after what she wants without fearing other people's judgments. That she chooses to go after a mobster reflects on her environment, not her taste. She is the good girl and the good-bad-girl fused into a single, balanced personality.

Her role in the film is central. Throughout the film, Camonte exhibits an incestuous sexual jealousy toward Cesca. Indeed, his death derives from his confusion between women and property, since sexual jealousy stems from the concept that women are owned by their men. Camonte's emotional development is arrested and, like a baby, he refuses to recognize the existence of the wills of other humans. This allows him to become a murderer, and it kills him in turn. He refuses to acknowledge that his little sister has not only a right to her own life, but the will and intelligence to make her own choices.

Again, in *Tiger Shark* (1932), we have the good-bad-girl; Quita (Zita Johann) is a somewhat-used young woman who marries fisherman Mike Mascarena (Edward G. Robinson) for the protection and security otherwise denied unmarried non-virgins in the Portuguese community. Unlike Dietrich in Raoul Walsh's near-remake, *Manpower* (1941), she's not a glamorous figure, but simply a human one. She's honest about her motives, but since she doesn't have the resources to live independently, her choice is a forced one.

In *Only Angels Have Wings* (1939), the completely independent Hawksian heroine finally appears – Jean Arthur as Bonnie Lee. Like Lee in *The Crowd Roars*, she's attracted to a man (Jeff, played by Cary Grant) who makes his living by taking physical risks (flying mail planes through the Andes), although she's turned off by the danger itself. Typically, Hawks heroines learn to accept danger as a natural part of life; in his later films, in fact (*Red Line 7000*, *El Dorado*, *Rio Lobo*), the heroine is frequently attracted to the risks as well as the men who undergo them, and actively participates in the danger.

This raises the central question of whether the love of physical danger is a *machismo* neurosis in a technological culture (where courting such danger may be atavistic), or whether, in fact, it's a healthy, natural drive women lack because of rigorous and distorted cultural conditioning.

The typical point of view of male action directors supports the *machismo* theory, since it includes an assumption that the audience will be largely male, and that women viewers will be repelled or bored. In Hawks, however, this viewpoint is frequently reversed: in *Only Angels Have Wings* (as Robin Wood points out) the audience identifies with the heroine, sharing her shocked reaction to Jeff's stoicism in the face of his friend's death. For a change, the audience of an adventure film is given a female sensibility! But Hawks undercuts the 'feminine' role as well as the 'masculine'; one of his central (and running) points is that *someone* must deliver the mail, and Bonnie Lee learns stoicism within this concrete situation. Although her emotions are running strong, she stops fussing over them since fussing would be a liability within the situation. On the other hand, she awakens Jeff to his own emotions – he is finally enabled to accept his feelings.

Like most Hawksian women, Bonnie Lee functions beautifully in the human sphere – while tough and experienced (as a nightclub singer travelling solo through South America, she's obviously no fragile flower), she retains an untouched center, a fine sense of balance between human warmth and personal endurance. Unlike Jeff, she has no compulsion to prove her integrity by constant and exaggerated displays of toughness; her integrity has been fully assimilated as her *self*.

Jeff, on the other hand, is stiff-necked; the sensible prohibition against giving in to emotion in times of crisis has become generalized to *all* situations, and it's deleterious to Jeff's functioning. He nearly loses Bonnie Lee because he's almost incapable of showing his love for her – he isn't merely anti-sentimental, he seems to fear that any emotional response whatever will un-man him. Bonnie Lee finally breaks down his exaggerated stoicism, forcing him to admit that he is, in fact, human and emotional, and that it's *all right*.

Hawks's films frequently show a merging of sexual roles for the benefit of both sexes – the women learn certain 'masculine' values while the men become 'feminized'. Frequently, the men have more to learn (and to gain) than the women, who are already mature at each film's beginning. (In Hawks's comedies, this situation plays a pivotal role, cf. *I Was A Male War Bride*). The men tend to suffer from emotional blocks that keep them from full self-realization, while the women need merely to adjust to a particular situation.

This is attributable to the 'experienced' nature of nearly all of Hawks's heroines. They're mostly saloon singers of one kind or another – good-bad-girls, but without the Brooklyn accents and chewing gum used to depict 'cheapness' in Hollywood films. What kind of experiences define Hawks's women? Evidently, all the heroines have experienced suffering in the past (this is explicit in the films' dialogue, and implicit in the heroines' maturity); evidently, their sufferings have had largely to do with their roles as sex objects, since saloon singers are prototypical sex objects. Yet they refuse to regard themselves as objects of any kind; in this lies their special maturity and integrity. Since they are independent, self-supporting, and competent, their choices are made by personal will rather than by social or economic pressures. They can choose a man or refuse a man, because they are valuable people – and aware of their own value. While the men in Hawks's adventure films are professionally skilled (as fliers, gunmen, racing drivers, etc.), Hawksian women are professional human beings.

As a 'very entertaining, nervy, adolescent new blonde' (James Agee's appraisal), Lauren Bacall (Slim) in *To Have and Have Not* (1944) is in many ways Hawks's arch-heroine. Aggressive, gutsy, sexually experienced (but not an *object*), with her John Wayne delivery and baritone voice, Bacall may be the most masculine of Hawks's female leads. In *To Have and Have Not* her characterization of Slim is remarkably free of sex-linked behavior. Even her name is unisexual, and in keeping with it Slim courts physical danger, rather than flinching from it.

Her past is similar to Bonnie Lee's: she's been knocking around the Caribbean, singing and surviving, learning to take slaps without grimacing. She, too, projects an integrity that's an essential part of her personality, independent of action and circumstance (e.g., if necessary, she can shamelessly steal the wallet of the chiselling Johnson). And, despite the toughest façade of any Hawksian heroine, she's not emotionally constipated like some of his heroes.

In *The Big Sleep* (1946), Bacall appears again, playing Bacall-via-Chandler. This is the first Hawks film to be scripted by Leigh Brackett (a woman; writing here in collaboration with William Faulkner and Jules Furthman), and in it the role of Vivian Regan (Bacall) is changed from villainess (as in Chandler's novel) to heroine. Although one of the film's chief *raisons d'être* appears to be to match Bogey and Bacall again, the romantic involvement between the private eye and the rich girl is left unresolved; a mutual attraction exists, but the characters are unlikely to live happily ever after. This casual resolution of the romantic aspects of the plot will recur frequently in Hawks's films from this point onward, particularly in the films written by Leigh Brackett: *Rio Bravo* (again with Jules Furthman), *Hatari!*, *El Dorado* and *Rio Lobo*. Also worth noting, these are films in which the female leads become increasingly courageous and the romances even more casual.

In the 13 years following *The Big Sleep*, Hawks made a number of adventure films in which women play conventionally peripheral roles. In *Red River*, *The Big Sky* and *Land of the Pharaohs*, the chief function of the female characters is to cause reactions in the male characters (although *The Thing* – officially credited to Hawks's editor, Christian Nyby – does include a woman scientist as a major character, functioning both as 'one of the boys' and as romantic interest). This was the post-war repression period in America; magazines were full of the familiar, soppy 'women's stories', in which heroines 'found' themselves only through love and marriage. The Baby Boom and Joe McCarthy reigned. But by the end of the 50s a change was occurring. The Civil Rights and Ban-the-Bomb movements appeared, bringing many women out of their homes and into political action. At this point, in 1959, *Rio Bravo* appeared – and the Hawksian woman returned at her very best.

Rio Bravo – in many ways a remake of *To Have and Have Not* – has a script by Leigh Brackett (her first for Hawks since *The Big Sleep*). It also has Angie Dickinson (as Feathers) in the Bacall part, eschewing Bacall's mannerisms but speaking some nearly word-for-word repeats of Slim's dialogue. This time the heroine is a gambler (presumably a better one than her late husband, who had to cheat) who also sings in saloons now and then.

Feathers embodies the clearest depiction of female superiority in Hawks's action films: she has all the Hawksian 'masculine' virtues (decisiveness, courage, professionalism and style) plus the 'feminine' ones (warmth, humor, openness). The hero, John T. Chance (John Wayne) is, in contrast, somewhat immature even in middle age. For Feathers, both men and women exist as individuals, whereas Chance seems to despise (and fear) women. Perhaps this is because he has lived his life in a purely male world; many of the film's comic moments derive from Chance's social immaturity, his adolescent proneness to sexual embarrassment. Chance's rationalization for misogyny is that his best friend, Duke (Dean Martin), was driven to drink by a woman's duplicity; Feathers, however, has an even better excuse for hating men (if she wanted one) – she's been hurt far more directly by her late husband.

Chance is probably the most stiff-necked of Hawks's heroes. While Jeff (in *Only Angels*) was certainly a rigid character, he had the excuse of youth. Chance is older. Unwilling to accept help from anyone, his behaviour towards his friends is paternalistic to the point of condescension; he clearly considers himself their moral superior. It's Feathers's role to wear him down (and build him up) to humanness. First, she embarrasses him repeatedly – at their first meeting, for example, she teases him about holding up a pair of women's bloomers to himself in a moment of accidental sex-role reversal. Then, more significantly, she makes him admit that he's misjudged her: because she's an uppity woman, and treats Chance as no more than her equal, he had assumed, quite incorrectly, that she was 'bad'. Finally, she supplies crucial help during a gunfight by flinging a flowerpot through a window at precisely the right moment. She's willing to risk her life to help him, not in a useless sacrifice but in a calculated attempt to change the odds in his favor. Feathers proves her courage and wins Chance's respect. Chance is transformed: he discovers his own emotions and his need for help, and in that discovery he comes to maturity as a human being in a world where two sexes exist as equals.

Unfortunately, it's at precisely this moment where Hawks's sexual egalitarianism fails. Feathers taunts Chance into forbidding her to wear a revealing costume; this is the expression of love that she wants, but it's also an expression of the proprietorship of male over female. Feathers's body, evidently, now belongs to Chance, and can no longer be exhibited to other men. Although Feathers has indisputably proven herself to be Chance's moral equal, their relationship now becomes one of dominance and subordination. At her own insistence, Feathers takes the traditional subordinate position.

Feathers has accepted the necessity for Chance to face physical peril in his specific situation, and is willing to risk her own life to help him. In *Red Line 7000* (1965), there are three female leads, and they are actually attracted to the danger *per se*.

In a society where, outside of warfare, opportunities for physical risk are rare, dangerous sports draw a very special type of person. The women of *Red Line* haven't entered the world of car racing by accident. In earlier films, female leads were attracted to men who happened to be involved in perilous situations. Bonnie Lee, Slim and Feathers were only coincidentally thrust into dangerous environments; they weren't seeking them specifically. In *Red Line*, however, all the women characters have specific personal involvements in car racing; evidently, they have made a considered choice.

Gaby (Marianna Hill), the Hawksian 'professional human' at her best, would like to race herself. Since the rules of the track exclude women drivers (although in real life this is changing), Gaby chooses the most dangerous of the men within her environment: Mike Marsh (James Caan). Mike's psychotic insistence that his women be virgins makes him *physically*, as well as emotionally, a dangerous man – he attempts to murder Dan McCall, Gaby's former lover. Excluded from actual participation in car racing, Gaby's derring-do reveals itself in her choice of lovers.

Another of the *Red Line* leads, Julie (Laura Devon), is first seen on a motorcycle – riding superbly. Like some of Hawks's earlier male leads, she's had more experience with physical risks than with human relations, and she foolishly chooses Ned Arp (John Robert Crawford), a success-freak, for her sweetheart. Perhaps the relationship between Julie and Ned illustrates the kind of past that the mature Hawksian woman has endured *prior* to her appearance as Bonnie Lee, Feathers, etc. Julie has no idea of her own value, as a person or as a woman. Sister of the team manager, she has defined herself, so far, by her skill in relatively 'masculine' pursuits. A tomboy, she's been friendly with many men (taking a 'kid brother' role, as Robin Wood points out); now, when she's ready to deal with men sexually, she chooses a man who's incapable of valuing her. As the film ends, the couple is still trapped in a false cultural ethos, wherein success is everything, and a woman is valueless except as a plaything for her man.

The third female lead, Holly (Gail Hire), reveals the possibility of a sick involvement with danger – and is the only Hawks heroine to exhibit neurosis of any kind. Three of Holly's lovers have died, and she shies away from further involvement with racing drivers, feeling herself a jinx. But what, then, is she doing hanging around the track?

The ingenue of *El Dorado* (1966, written by Leigh Brackett) is a reworking of the Julie character. Dressed in men's clothing and with a male name, Joey Macdonald (Michele Carey) is another female 'kid brother'. Like 'the kid' in conventional Westerns, she's eager to become involved in physical violence, and goes so far as to shoot the hero, Cole (John Wayne), in a moment of hot-headedness. Later, she meets Mississippi (James Caan) by ambushing him, and it's only at the very end of their wrestling match that he realizes she's a girl. Finally, it is Joey who kills the professional gunfighter hired by the bad guy, demonstrating both her commitment and her competence. Since her family has been the target of the bad guy's oppression, she takes an active, deliberate role in opposing him. Clearly, Hawks has made his decision regarding women and danger – in his latest films, the heroines are as eager for peril (and as competent in dealing with it) as are the heroes. For him, attraction to violence is not a *machismo* neurosis, but a natural part of life for both sexes, and this is particularly evident in those scripts written by Ms Brackett.

The Feathers character reappears in *El Dorado* as Maudie (Charlene Holt). She's an old friend of both Cole Thornton and his buddy, J. P. Harrah (Robert Mitchum), and her previous incarnation as Feathers is made explicit in some dialogue wherein she discusses her past. Maudie's role in *El Dorado* is small (though pivotal), but even here the Hawksian woman shows through – Maudie is calm, collected and aggressive, aware of her own worth. 'I'm woman enough for the both of you,' she tells Cole and Harrah, once again taking the active role in courtship.

It's unclear, at the end, whether Maudie and Cole will resume their old romance, and whether or not Mississippi and Joey will be permanently united. There's no final romantic scene to wrap it up; Hawks's and Brackett's interest is elsewhere.

In his most recent film, *Rio Lobo* (1970, again scripted by Brackett), Hawks continues to show women eager for, and competent in violence. The female lead (Jennifer O'Neill) shoots the first shot in a bar-room confrontation with the bad guys. Later, she is only barely prevented from joining the final shoot-out by Frenchie (Jorge Romero), who's taken a proprietary romantic interest in her.

Another woman, however, takes a major part in the film's last battle. A Mexican girl, much oppressed by the villains, has sworn to kill the chief bad guy. After blasting him with a shotgun she breaks down, unable to take it lightly as the men do. While in *Only Angels* Bonnie Lee shoots Jeff accidentally, in *Rio Lobo* (as in *El Dorado*), the young woman's action is premeditated and deliberate. Like Joe, she is not content to let men free her from her oppression; she, herself, must take positive action. She bears the full realization of what she's done, and her tears represent one of the few instances in film when an honest reaction to a killing is shown. The sorrow which mars her relief reveals that she has killed for the right reason – not from hunger for violence, but from thoughtful, righteous anger.

While Leigh Brackett has written yet another archtypically Hawksian script for *Rio Lobo*, the film is something of a failure – partly because of pacing, partly because of unfortunate choices for the leads. While John Wayne and Chris Mitchum do all right, the other actors and actresses seem stiff. Jennifer O'Neill, playing a young woman who has endured many tragedies (I've forgotten the character's name), is supposed to be self-sufficient and collected. When she tells her story to Frenchy, he finds her attractive because, 'You don't cry.' Alas, O'Neill sounds as though she *is* crying. She plays the character with more than a touch of shrillness and neurosis, and neurosis is anathema to the Hawks heroine. Hawks's women are always relaxed with themselves, even when excited over a tense situation. At their best, they have an easy, Western style: O'Neill has a New York whine. In *Rio Lobo*, the Hawksian woman is surely in the script, but she doesn't appear on the screen.

As in *El Dorado*, the romances in *Rio Lobo* are loosely resolved at the end. Everyone goes off arm in arm with someone of the opposite sex – but how long the O'Neill character will put up with Frenchy's overprotectiveness is left unstated, as is the exact nature of John Wayne's relationship with the much younger woman whom he befriends. Romance has, I think, lost its interest for Hawks: other questions occupy him now.

If most action films are made for men, there's little wonder that women find them unappealing. Hawks's films, however, are exceptional. They include some of the most honest portrayals of women in any movies (most especially including 'women's movies'). In addition, Hawks is truly unusual in constantly placing his audience in the woman's position regarding the heroes. In those films where the interaction between hero and heroine is a central concern – from *The Crowd Roars* to *Rio Bravo* and, to some extent, *Red Line 7000* – the audience sees the hero and his situation with both the sympathy and the annoyance of the heroine. Then, too, the Hawksian woman is never effeminate. A central theme throughout Hawks is the shedding of sexual roles in both men and women for the creation of a single, *human* role.

Women have very few role models to look to within popular culture. While I'd hesitate to suggest the Hawksian heroine as a general model for all of us, she can be very helpful as a guide for competent behavior in certain specific situations. While she is still far from the ideal 'liberated' woman, she represents an important step toward that ideal.

Naomi Wise's central argument here is not that Hawks's films offer women positive role models but rather that, given the generally very limited roles which have been offered traditionally to women within Hollywood films, Hawks's films were in important respects an exception – 'the single most consistent exception', as Wise puts it. This is very much the position of Molly Haskell in her 1974 book *From Reverence to Rape: The Treatment of Women in the Movies*, and such views began to reshape much thinking about Hawks. But these were not the only way in which women critics looked at Hawks. As the title of her short article implied, Barbara Bernstein in 'That's Not Brave, That's Just Stupid' (*Focus!*, no. 8, Autumn 1972, reprinted in Karyn Kay and Gerald Peary (eds), *Women and the Cinema* (New York: Dutton, 1977)) argued, taking a line owing something to the Manny Farber tradition of Hawks criticism, that what Hawks had to say – his themes and particularly his sexual politics – was essentially adolescent and not to be taken seriously, and that what was to be admired in Hawks lay elsewhere, in his 'artistry'.

A Comment on 'The Hawksian Woman'

LEIGH BRACKETT

From *Take One*, vol. 3, no. 8, July–August 1971.

I read 'The Hawksian Woman' with enormous interest. I've been working with Howard Hawks, off and on, since 1944, but I never really stopped to think what exactly he was doing with his women. I only knew that I liked them and was comfortable with them. Naomi Wise has done a brilliant job of analyzing them and their relationships with their men.

I learned some things very quickly when I first began to work for Hawks. Conventional heroines bore him; he can't 'have fun' with them, and if a character or situation develops that Hawks can't have fun with, it gets lost, pronto. His heroines must never become shrill, or bitchy, or coy, or cute. They must be honest, and they must have a sense of humor. He likes them with long handsome legs, not too much bosom, and hair that looks well no matter how hard the wind blows. They dress with style, but simply, and wear very little make-up . . . the natural, straightforward look, without fussy frills and hairdos. As Naomi Wise points out, they often take over and push the whole plot. More than once I've argued with Hawks that the girl was getting too pushy, and couldn't we let the poor boob of a hero make just one decision all by himself? I was always overruled, and I guess Hawks knew what he was doing, because it came out right in the end.

There were some other Hawksian conventions about men/women. The word 'love' is not heard, and there is no scene where hero and heroine declare their tender feelings for each other. It's done obliquely. Usually the hero's friend comes to the girl and says, 'I think he likes you.' Marriage is not mentioned; it's 'Are you going to ask her to stay?' Hawks's people are not domestic types; nobody ever talks about getting that little spread and settling down to raise a family.

Generally, far in the background, there is the girl who wasn't any good ('I tried to tell him she wasn't any good but he wouldn't listen.') (As though anyone ever did!) Or the woman who hated whatever it was the hero was doing and tried to make him stop it; i.e., attempted to destroy his individuality and make him over into something he didn't want to be. The hero is woman-shy, living in a male world where he is comfortable with his relationships. When the new girl arrives he tries at first to get rid of her. She insists on staying, and now she has to win her place in this closed group *as a man* (or asexual human being, if you prefer) proving that she is as honest and courageous and loyal as any of them. Somewhere along the line she is likely to say to the hero, 'Any time you want me to go, just tell me, and I'll go.' In other words, no strings. When the hero can accept her as he would another man, with the masculine virtues he values, then he can start thinking about her as a woman; i.e., lose his fear of falling in love again, because he knows she is not going to be like those others. In the meantime, as Naomi Wise says, the woman herself emerges as a whole and complete human being in her own right, and minus the hero's hang-ups.

This brings up a couple of questions. Why should Howard Hawks, almost alone among producers, have this attitude toward the women in his pictures? He is an intensely masculine person, with an intensely masculine outlook on life. He has done most of the things he makes pictures about . . . driven racing cars, piloted planes, ridden motorcycles. He doesn't like losers, or anti-heroes. He values bravery, strength, expertise, loyalty, all the 'masculine' virtues (though Lord knows I've known women who had a damned sight more of them than some of the men I've known; it isn't the sex, it's the individual). So why should he give his women a position of equality . . . often, indeed, dominance . . . in a genre that usually relegates them either to being decorative in the hero's relaxed moments, or to looking doleful as the hero goes off about his business?

I suspect that it's because Hawks doesn't like women in their *negative* aspect, and until he can accept a female character, as the hero must, as another man, or an asexual *human being* with the attributes he respects, he can't like her. And if he didn't like her, he wouldn't know what to do with her. Hawks has to like all his people (the villains are kept down to a minimum) and this is why such a deal of affectionate good humor comes through in films like *Rio Bravo* and *Hatari!*

All right for Howard Hawks, he's a man, he's supposed to value the masculine virtues. What about me?

Well, there's a curious parallel there. A friend who reads my science fiction once asked me, 'Why do your heroines always come down out of the hills swinging their swords like Genghis Khan?' And I said, 'I suppose it's because conventional heroines bore me.' Actually, only a small number of my sci-fi heroines swing swords. But they are all, by God, *people*, with independent lives and thoughts of their own, capable of being comrades and mates but always of their own free choice and always as equals. (*Earned* equality. Men have to earn it. So do they.) So the Hawksian woman fitted my typewriter very well.

How come?

Partly, I suppose, I was just born hatefully independent. Partly it was because my father died when I was a baby and I was womaned to death by my mother, grandmother, and a great aunt. They were very high on femininity and the segregation of the sexes, and they had an attitude that I find most interesting now, in the light of Women's Lib. Far from feeling in the slightest degree inferior to men, they believed that Woman was a sacred and special creation, infinitely superior to the lower orders, such as males, who

121

were put here simply to serve them, support them, protect them, and take their orders. Any attempt to make women equal with men was not to elevate them, but to degrade them. They were proud of their physical frailty, which was prodigious. They were constantly lecturing me on what little girls/young ladies could/couldn't (mostly couldn't) do, and the core of it all was that one *never* did anything for oneself.

I couldn't relate to any of this even as a small child. I took my values from the boys' books I read, that taught the sterling values of self-reliance and good sportsmanship. And I realized, from observation, that no other human being, in this uncertain world of death and taxes, can ever be a permanent possession. Your own self is the only person you can always be certain of having around.

I think Howard Hawks knows this, too, and that is why there is so little of the living-happily-ever-after in his films. His heroes and heroines are what he calls 'grown up'. They don't expect the moon with a string around it, they do not expect or desire to own each other. They are content with what they have, for as long as they have it, and this is possible because the Hawksian woman is not husband-hunting or looking for 'security'. She is secure in herself, and she is giving her love as a free person, with open hands.

It has often been said that Hawks's films, in recent years, are concerned chiefly with friendship and its obligations. And in this context, the Hawksian woman has first to become a friend, before she can become a lover.

Which isn't at all a bad idea.

Leigh Brackett was a science-fiction and a crime novelist and occasional screenwriter, whose best and most characteristic work for movies was for Howard Hawks. She worked on the scripts for *The Big Sleep* (1945), *Rio Bravo* (1959), *Hatari!* (1962), *El Dorado* (1967) and *Rio Lobo* (1970). Other notable credits included Robert Altman's *The Long Goodbye* (1973) and *The Empire Strikes Back* (1979, appearing after Brackett's death in 1978). Given her close collaboration with Hawks, her postscript comments on Naomi Wise's essay are of particular interest.

I Was a Male War Bride

JOHN BELTON

From *The Velvet Light Trap*, no. 3, Winter 1971–2.

I Was a Male War Bride, though one of Howard Hawks's funniest films, is also one of his bleakest, blackest, and most serious works. This deeply un-settling paradox underlies almost every scene – even, for instance, the film's tenderest, gentlest, and perhaps most intimate sequence in which Henri Rochard (Cary Grant) rubs liniment on the sore back of Lt Catherine Gates (Ann Sheridan). Rochard's consideration and concern for her throughout this scene reflects itself in the warmth and deliberation of his gestures, e.g. as he screws the bottle cap back on, and in the sympathetic kindness of his actions (opening the window, putting out the light, turning the lampshade). The sound of the rain outside throughout the scene reinforces our sense of the intimacy that exists between the two central characters. But the whole effect of the scene's intimacy depends upon the rather cold premise that Gates only allows Rochard to touch her when ministering to her. Our fur-ther realization is that this intimacy is possible only because she is asleep, and the conclusion of the scene, when the innkeeper's wife pushes Rochard out of Gates's window, completely obliterates the sense of harmony, privacy, and mutual understanding with which the scene began. (Aspects of this scene are very similar to those in a later scene when Rochard, alone on a driverless motorcycle, tells Gates that he likes her. Hawks works the scene for comedy, but we also realize that her presence would probably destroy the intimacy of what Rochard says.) It is this overall seriousness in *Male War Bride* that brings it closer in mood and theme to a film like *Red River* than one like *Gentlemen Prefer Blondes* or *Man's Favorite Sport?* and which justifies my more or less sober approach to the film and its ideas.

Film as Journey

Like the cattle drive in *Red River* (1948), the journey from Heidelberg to the Statue of Liberty in *Male War Bride* (1949) becomes a sort of trial or test of the film's central characters. The greater part of *Male War Bride* con-sists of travelogue, journeys from one place to another: Rochard's taxi ride in the credit sequence, the motorcycle trip to Baden-Auheim, the voyage to the United States. Hawks fills his frames with characters in transit, like the people in the foreground and background of the credit sequence walking or riding bicycles, like the war brides and their children on their way to the USA in the background of the second half of the film, and with various modes of transportation – cars, motorcycles, trains, rowboats, planes, buses, horses and ships. Yet, at the same time, the film contains a confused sense of destination: its characters, quite unlike those in *Red River*, never seem to know, either literally or figuratively, where they are going, their ultimate destination.

In the credit sequence, for example, Rochard asks directions for Heidelberg; later, Lt Gates gets them lost, in spite of her maps, on their way to Baden-Auheim. Both scenes introduce a theme which culminates in Rochard's wandering search for a bed and a night's rest in Bremerhaven. As Rochard goes from one place to another, each character he meets (the unfriendly, pipe-smoking sergeant with a bed and a wife in it, the private from Brooklyn, the MP from Yonkers, the knitting desk clerk – all men without women and women without men, like the film's characters except for the innkeeper and his wife who never appear together) presents a different attitude towards him and his predicament. All these brilliant minor figures, because of the great variety of their characterizations, turn Rochard's sleepless night into an odyssey of moods and attitudes – each character becoming a further test of his endurance and flexibility.

Hawks, clearly, treats the Sheridan–Grant relationship as a journey, but what's most interesting about this treatment of it is its to-and-fro motion, its seeming lack of destination. Their first scene together in the corridors of Army HQ captures this perfectly: the tracking camera follows them, first down one corridor, then another. They seem to be moving in a maze, and their occasional exchange of positions in the frame heightens this sense of geographic confusion. (This scene recalls Rochard's similar movements earlier when he goes from door to door, reading abbreviations, in search of Gates's office.) Later, the marriage application montage sequence becomes a visual equivalent to this earlier scene – their application form now representing their relationship. It goes from office to office, back and forth across hallways, gets roughly stamped (as they do) on its journey through bureaucracy, and finally gets lost somewhere in someone's desk. On the surface, Hawks's red-tape montage appears quite conventional, something recognizable from dozens of dull, uninspired films. What makes the Hawks sequence different – and better – is that he varies the convention: he interrupts this sequence for a pair of scenes that uncover the application's whereabouts. By breaking up the continuity of the montage sequence, Hawks neatly foreshadows the difficulty the couple has with army red tape which *separates* them in the last half of the film. While satirizing the convention, Hawks subtly uses it to satisfy his thematic needs.

The action of this sequence is, of course, comic and the mood optimistic. The final stamp of approval sanctions their wedding and looks ahead to the direction, i.e. the happy ending, the film ultimately takes. The trip from Heidelberg to the Statue of Liberty, then, reflects the progression in their relationship both geographically and emotionally but Hawks, strangely enough, shows this progression towards realization in terms of the restrictions placed upon the couple.

Entrapment

The movement of Rochard's car at the beginning of the film, shown by means of pans, tracks, and fluid dissolves, gives him a sense of freedom; his ability to get directions to Heidelberg, a sense of power. As the film continues, however, he loses more and more of his ability to move, his freedom, his power. Hawks conveys this progressive confinement which parallels Rochard's commitment to Gates in several ways.

(1) *Framing* In the credit sequence, when his car stops for directions, Rochard is shown in the center-background of the frame, sandwiched between his driver and a traffic cop in the foreground. The framing gives a sense of powerlessness and corresponds to the narrative content of the scene. But when Rochard gets the directions from an American soldier, Hawks cuts to a different, less constrictive two-shot set-up and frees Rochard from his boxed-in position in the frame. At critical moments throughout the film, Hawks suggests Rochard's entrapment and powerlessness by framing him in three-shot between two other characters, one of whom is quite often Lt Gates – in Prendergast's office when he gets his assignment with Gates, in Rumsey's office, at the motor pool, at the hotel when Billings interrupts him on his wedding night. In almost all of the scenes, Gates stands on one side, the Army on the other.

(2) *Sets* The dark, narrow hallways within Army HQ, the claustrophobic sidecar of the motorcycle, the jail in Baden-Auheim, the small cabin of the ship at the end all reflect a gradual imprisonment of Rochard during the course of the film.

(3) *Gags* Even the baldest comedy routines – when the train's signal gate lifts Rochard high into the air, the business with the door handle, his discomfort in the chair and the bathtub, his arrest at the black market – become funny, in part because of Rochard's isolation, in part because of his awkward confinement. Behind the comic gags, with all the restrictions they place upon Rochard's movement, lies a more serious thread: the trap-like nature of Rochard's relationship with Gates.

In this light, the motorcycle-and-sidecar becomes a perfect visual metaphor for their initial relationship: it binds them together physically, but places Rochard in a position of inferiority. At the same time, the first motorcycle gag, in which the sidecar gets left behind by the motorcycle, is more than a gag: it visualizes their initial physical antagonism and their apparent inability to work together as a cohesive unit.

Although Robin Wood's article on *Male War Bride* in his Hawks book suggests that many of the film's episodes are 'loosely strung together', I find that they are, on the contrary, tightly interwoven thematically. The door gag episode, for example, in which Rochard locks himself into Gates's hotel room, comments rather directly on the confining nature of their relationship. Even within this scene, their chair gag – a beautiful bit in itself – further strengthens the sense of confinement, but does so with unusual subtlety. Although the chair itself does not imprison Rochard, as the bathtub does later in the film, his use of it as a bed sets up an awkwardly comic disparity between the shape of the container and that of the thing contained – a device Hawks uses later with almost as much success when Rochard puts on the innkeeper's too-small clothes or when he dresses up as Florence in the nurse's uniform. What's interesting about the scene is that Rochard restricts himself spatially in his attempt to fit himself into the chair. Rochard's fantastic flexibility within a constricting environment is, in a sense, his greatest characteristic. It is this flexibility which prevents his loss of identity and masculinity in the second half of the film. The trouble he has with his hands in this sequence betrays his actual helplessness and, in a larger sense, reflects the temporary awkwardness in his relationship with Gates. Yet his ultimate flexibility (he finally falls asleep, albeit gracelessly, in the chair) underscores the optimism with which we must ultimately regard their relationship. There is freedom in confinement: what Rochard does within a limited space he is given defines the strange form of freedom his relationship with Gates allows him.

Structurally, *I Was a Male War Bride* falls into two parts. In the first half of the film, Hawks traps Rochard and Gates together, starting with the motorcycle and building to the inn sequence; in the second half, he reverses this process and traps them apart: a single-shot sequence shows us Gates sleeping with Kitty, Rochard in the bathtub. At the same time, it becomes clear that the restrictions on their relationship in the first half are self-imposed (the chair gag); they come from within, from her prudishness, his reluctance to commit himself. In the second half, as the bathtub sequence illustrates, the restrictions are imposed by society, i.e. the Army; they come from without.

Paradoxically, their entrapment together in the first part, at least until the mission is completed, seems to bring out their antagonism – an antagonism based upon their unwillingness to admit that they really want each other. Yet the film's second half, which separates them, also unites them together against society, red tape, and the Army. The final image of them locking the world out and, simultaneously, locking themselves in defines their paradoxical relationship beautifully. In order to achieve this freedom in confinement their love must first be tested before it is allowed to be consummated. Their 'confession' of love in the haystack demands a test, and the second half of the film provides one.

Sexual Reversals

The first half of the film concludes with the haystack scene. In a sense, this scene is parallel to the film's last scene in the ship's cabin. In both, Rochard and Gates are enclosed together and, ironically, their love seems free and without restrictions. Although one assumes from the jokes later in the film that they do not have intercourse in the haystack, the scene itself, like the last scene, is shot as if there could have been a consummation. What's important about the haystack sequence is that it is a culmination of the first stage of their relationship and, at the same time, the final test of Gates's womanhood. For if the last half of *Male War Bride* is a testing of Rochard's masculinity (his final disguise as Florence), then the first half of the film tests the femininity of Lt Gates. Her masculine traits, her domination of Rochard throughout the first half of the film, although more or less objectified because of the action and situation of the film, nevertheless rob her of her femininity. For example, the action of the film dictates that she must wear pants to drive the motorcycle and that her uniform be, by necessity, somewhat masculine, but when she puts on her helmet over her already-short hair, she loses the last visual trace of her femininity. In the very first scene, when Rochard returns her laundry, Gates seems outraged not only by his suggestions of sexual intimacy but also, apparently, by the articles which represent her own feminine nature. Her attempts at being a woman are weak and awkward. When she stops for a train and tries to put on some make-up, she drops her lipstick; Rochard ends up the victim of another harrowing, emasculating experience. Although she wants Rochard and, seemingly, puts on make-up to attract him (whatever it is, it is one of her few feminine gestures), she bungles it. Even when she gets out of her uniform, she puts on masculine pajamas – a stark contrast to the frilly, feminine nightgown she wears on her wedding night at a later point in her trial.

If Lt Gates is a failure at being a woman (in the first half of the film), she's also not quite a success at being a man. Even though she does complete the mission, she botches up parts of it, nearly sending their boat over a waterfall in the process. After the mission is completed, however, she does become a little more womanly. In a romantically-lit outdoor scene, Hawks shows her, without helmet, chewing on a stalk of grass and looking dreamily off into the countryside – at the same time allowing Rochard to sleep. The following scene in the haystack, then, with its dialogue about Frenchmen and kissing, tests both her femininity ('If I only had a French girl') and his masculinity ('That was no good. Is that all there is to it?'). Their final kiss re-establishes, for the moment, her femininity and Rochard's masculinity, just as the last scene on the boat, after another series of tests, reaffirms their basic sexuality and consummates their relationship.

The testing of Rochard's masculinity in the second half concludes with him in nurse's uniform – an ironic travesty of Gates's militantly masculine femininity. The final few shots are of Rochard locked in a ship's cabin. He rolls down his pants leg, throws away his phony wig, confronts and triumphs over the ship's captain and chaplain who want to 'forget the whole thing' and bunk him in with some of the ship's officers. These shots restore Rochard's masculinity and his power; although entrapped, he maintains control over his trap.

At the end of his fine essay on *Male War Bride*, Wood, discussing the confinement theme, writes that, 'the irony of the concluding shot of the Statue of Liberty (as seen from Henri's cabin-cell) is its final masterstroke and perhaps the nearest thing in Hawks to overt comment on modern society.' Although I disagree with Wood's conclusion that the final shot is a comment on modern society, it is, without doubt, the film's masterstroke. This final shot draws all the thematic threads of the film together into a single image. It is, above all else, an extremely sexual shot – a phallic object seen through a round porthole – and clearly represents sexual union. At the same time, the internal frame of the porthole is, as Wood suggests, confining, but the object confined is the Statue of Liberty. Perhaps it is – as Wood says – ironic, yet it seems to me to convey the thematic notion of freedom in confinement perfectly. Finally, this last shot comments directly on the relationship-as-journey motif. A geographical landmark, the statue stands at the terminus of their journey, and symbolizes the realization of their relationship. The last shot of the film conveys the consummation of this relationship and, at the same time, its paradoxical nature, i.e., that Henri and Catherine find freedom in confinement.

John Belton has written extensively on Hawks, as our Bibliography makes clear. A great admirer of Robin Wood's work on Hawks, Belton nevertheless comes up with finely detailed readings of Hawks films with differently nuanced interpretations. His essay on *I Was a Male War Bride* adds a useful additional perspective on Hawksian comedy to put alongside those of Rivette, Perkins, Haskell and Cavell in this volume. Belton's interest in Hawks is centred in an overall research interest in American cinema. Belton's other work includes *Widescreen Cinema* (Cambridge, Mass.: Harvard University Press, 1992) and *American Cinema/American Culture* (New York and London: McGraw-Hill, 1994).

Leopards in Connecticut: *Bringing Up Baby*

STANLEY CAVELL

From Stanley Cavell, *Pursuits of Happiness* (Cambridge, Mass.: Harvard University Press, 1981).

Speaking of the relationship of the principal man and woman of our comedies as one, as revealed in *It Happened One Night*, in which what they do together is less important than the fact that they do whatever it is together, I said that Howard Hawks's *Bringing Up Baby* (1938) is the member of the genre that presents the purest example of this quality of the relationship. I called this quality the achievement of purposiveness without purpose (or say directedness without direction). In thus invoking Kant's characterization of the aesthetic experience I am thinking of his idea as providing an access to the connection of the aesthetic experience with the play of childhood, a connection to whose existence many aestheticians have testified. This is not to recommend that we take an aesthetic attitude toward our moral lives; this would not overcome our distance from childhood and its intimacies, but merely cover one distance with a further one. The idea is rather to measure our capacity for perception by the condition of childhood, as for example Wordsworth does, or Freud. I am reminded here of the poignant concluding words of Freud's *Wit and Its Relation to the Unconscious*: 'the mood of childhood, when we were ignorant of the comic, when we were incapable of jokes and when we had no need of humor to make us feel happy in our life'.

The fact of remarriage between the central pair is even less directly present in *Bringing Up Baby* than in *It Happened One Night*. In the essay to follow I justify its inclusion in the genre of remarriage by emphasizing the pair's efforts to extricate their lives from one another, in which the attempt at flight is forever transforming itself into (hence revealing itself as) a process of pursuit. I should like to add that this transformation can be said to provide the structure of the tale *Gradiva: A Pompeiian Fancy*, by Wilhelm Jensen, the work of fiction to which Freud allotted his most extended consecutive interpretation. It is pertinent for us that Freud's interest in this romance would have been elicited by its being a tale of the therapy of love. It is the woman who provides this therapy by virtue of her knowledge, whatever the man may think, that she is the object of his (repressed) desire, and her ability to bring him back to this knowledge by virtue of her willingness for the time to live out his delusions (call this sharing his fantasies). The therapy of love provided by the woman making an initial marriage possible (as though women can bear up, where men buckle, under the injunction not to look back, as if either they trust the past or else they can look at it without distorting it – as if they do not succumb to skepticism about love) is a condition that will perhaps not fully manifest itself in these chapters until the final one, on *The Awful Truth*. But it is well to leave the idea as a current underlying the repeated emphases on the saving education provided by the man, which makes the remarriage possible.

To include the principal pair in *Bringing Up Baby* among the pairs in remarriage comedies is, put otherwise, to imply that their conversation is such, their capacities for recognition of one another are such, that what they are is revealed by imagining them as candidates for the trials of remarriage – as though we are here in the earliest phases, say the prehistoric phases, of the myth I began sketching in the Introduction, something I claimed represented an inheritance in which we must conceive the members of a genre to share. I conclude these transitional short subjects by remarking that it sweetens my sense of relevance that the title *Bringing Up Baby*, while suggesting something about the etiquette of conversation, is directly that of an education manual, one of those cute ones, written for the millions who find it reassuring to be told that babies are not scary and mysterious, and that a brand new baby and a brand new parent will naturally educate one another, with no difficult decisions ever having to be made. (Or maybe this mode of discourse is now confined to modern sex manuals.) But it is time for the movie.

It's the one that opens in a museum of natural history where an absent-minded professor (Cary Grant) is trying to finish his reconstruction of the skeleton of a brontosaurus. Standing as it were before the curtain, he finds out, or is reminded of, five or six things: that the expedition has just found the crucial bone, the intercostal clavicle, to complete the skeleton; that he is getting married tomorrow to his assistant, Miss Swallow; that after their wedding there will be no honeymoon; that the reconstructed skeleton will be their child; that he has an appointment to play golf with a Mr Peabody and discuss a donation of a million dollars to the museum; and that he is to remember who and what he is. Call this Prologue the first sequence. There is a natural breakdown into ten further sequences. (2) On a golf course, the professor is drawn from his game and conversation with Mr Peabody by a young woman (Katharine Hepburn) who first plays his golf ball and then dents and rends his car unparking it, amused at his claim that she has made a mistake and that the car, too, belongs to him, and then drives off with it while he is hanging onto its side as perhaps the bull did with Europa. The sequence ends with his yelling back for the third or fourth time: 'I'll be with you in a minute, Mr Peabody.' (3) At night, in the restaurant of some Ritz Hotel, Grant slips on an olive dropped by Hepburn and sits on his hat on the floor. Their argument is resumed concerning who is following whom. After further parapraxes, each rips open part of the other's clothing: she splits the tails of his swallow-tail coat up the back and he rips off the back

130

of her skirt of the evening dress. He walks out behind her, guiding her, to cover what he's done (not, however, what he's doing). As he does so, Mr Peabody appears again, with whom he again had an appointment, and again he says, I'll be with you in a minute, Mr Peabody.' (4) In her apartment Hepburn sews Grant's tails, after which they set out to find Mr Peabody, whom she knows and whom she throws stones at after giving Grant his second drive around. They are on a first name basis by now. David tells Susan that he's getting married tomorrow. (5) The prehistoric bone is delivered to Grant's apartment and he rushes to hers, the bone in a box under his arm, to save her from a leopard, who turns out to be Baby, a tame present from her brother. Susan and Baby arrange that the leopard is not to be Susan's problem alone. (6) Driving Baby to Susan's house in Connecticut, they hit a truck of fowls, buy thirty pounds of raw meat, and Susan steals, this time quite consciously, another car. (7) At the house, Susan does not rip David's clothes off but steals them while he is showering. So David puts on Susan's negligee, and later is discovered in bits of her brother's riding habit, which is appropriate since they soon have to hunt for something rare and precious, the bone which the dog George has taken from the box on the bed. David says to Susan's Aunt (May Robson) that he went gay all of a sudden. He learns that the aunt is the potential donor of the million and that Susan expects to inherit it. He asks Susan most earnestly not to tell her aunt who he is. Susan tells her that he's had a nervous breakdown and that his name is Bone, and that is what the Aunt tells her friend the Major (Charles Ruggles) who appears for dinner. (8) The four are at dinner during which David stalks George. The Major gives the mating cry of the leopard, which is answered. He asks, 'Are there leopards in Connecticut?' (9) Baby escapes, George disappears, and David and Susan spend most of the night exploring the woods. Susan enjoys it. They are captured, she by a recurring psychiatrist, he by a recurring sheriff. (10) They are behind bars; eventually most of the household is, from trying to identify them. Susan talks her way out of her cell, then out a window, to get the proof that there really is a leopard in Connecticut. She returns dragging a circus leopard behind her, whom we know to be a killer. David does what he once ran to her apartment to do – saves her from a wild beast. (11) In the Epilogue, back in daylight at the museum, Susan shows up, having recovered the bone and inherited the money. Running up high ladders, they talk across the back of the brontosaurus; he says he thinks he loves her. He rescues her again as she has jumped from her swaying ladder onto the brontosaurus, pulling her by one arm up the ledge as the skeleton collapses under her weight. They embrace.

At some point it becomes obvious that the surface of the dialogue and action of *Bringing Up Baby*, their mode of construction, is a species of more or less blatant and continuous double entendre. The formal signal of its presence in the dialogue is the habitual *repetition* of lines or words, sometimes upon the puzzlement of the character to whom the line is addressed, as though he or she cannot have heard it correctly, sometimes as a kind of verbal tic, as though a character has not heard, or meant, his own words properly. I qualify this presence of doubleness thus heavily (calling it a 'species' and claiming that it is 'more or less blatant') for two reasons.

(1) While an explicit discussion, anyway an open recognition, of the film's obsessive sexual references is indispensable to saying what I find the film to be about, I am persistently reluctant to make it very explicit. Apart from more or less interesting risks of embarrassment (for example, of seeming too perverse or being too obvious), there are causes for this reluctance having to do with what I understand the point of this sexual glaze to be. It is part of the force of this work that we shall not know how far to press its references.

At some juncture the concept and the fact of the contended bone will of course threaten to take over. (Its mythical name, the intercostal clavicle, suggests that it belongs to creatures whose heads are beneath their shoulders, or anyway whose shoulders are beneath at least some of their ribs.) This threat will occur well before the long recitative and duet on the subject (beginning with Grant's thunderous discovery of the empty box and the lines 'Where's my intercostal clavicle?' 'Your *what*?' 'My intercostal clavicle. My bone. It's rare; it's precious,' and continuing with Hepburn's appeal to the dog: 'George. George. David and Susan need that bone. It's David's bone'; hence well before the quartet on the words 'Mr Bone', a title that both claims Grant as the very personification of the subject at issue (as someone may be called Mr Boston or Mr Structuralism) and suggests, pertinently, that he is an end man in a minstrel show).

By the close of the sequence in the restaurant, the concept and the fact of the behind will be unignorable. Neither the bone nor the behind will give us pause, on a first viewing, in Grant's opening line, the second line of the film: gazing fixedly down at a bone in his hand he says: 'I think this one belongs in the tail.' His assistant, Miss Swallow, corrects or reminds him: 'You tried that yesterday.' That we are not given pause on a first viewing means both that this film is not made for just one viewing and also that this early line works well enough if it underscores the plain fact that this man is quite lost in thought, and prepares us for amazement when we discover what it is he is lost in thinking about, and for discovering that his preoccupation is the basis of the events to come. This is not asking too much. The broad attitude of this comedy is struck at once, at Miss Swallow's opening line, 'Sh-h-h. Professor Huxley is thinking', as the camera rises to discover Cary Grant in the pose of Rodin's *The Thinker*, a statue already the subject of burlesque and caricature. (The rightness in its being Cary Grant who takes this pose is a special discovery of Howard Hawks's about Grant's filmic presence, his photogenesis, what it is the camera makes of him. What Grant is thinking, and that what he is doing is thinking, is as much the subject of *His Girl Friday* as it is of the time he reverts to playing professor, in *Monkey Business*.)

Then are we to pause over the lines started by Grant to Hepburn when they discover that Baby has escaped?: 'Don't lose your head.' 'My *what*?' 'Your head.' 'I've got my head; I've lost my leopard.' And how much are

132

we to do with Hepburn's line, genuinely alarmed, to Grant as he is trying to cover her from behind in the restaurant? 'Hey. Fixation or no fixation . . . Will you stop doing that with your hat?' (What does she think he is doing and what does she think he should be doing it with?) And we are to gasp as Hepburn, in the last scene before the Epilogue, in jail, drops what she calls her 'society moniker' and puts on a society woman's version – or a thirties movie version – of a gun moll, drawling out, in close-up: 'Lemme outta here and I'll open my puss and shoot the works.' I say we do not know how far to press such references, and this is meant to characterize a certain anxiety in our comprehension throughout, an anxiety that our frequent if discontinuous titters may at any moment be found inappropriate. If it is undeniable that we are invited by these events to read them as sexual allegory, it is equally undeniable that what Hepburn says, as she opens the box and looks inside, is true: 'It's just an old bone.' Clearly George agrees with her. The play between the literal and the allegorical determines the course of this narrative, and provides us with contradicting directions in our experience of it.

(2) The threat of inappropriateness goes with a slightly different cause of my reluctance to be explicit, namely that the characters are themselves wholly unconscious of the doubleness in their meaning. This is a familiar source of comic effect. But so is its opposite. In particular, the effect here contrasts specifically with Shakespearean exchanges in double entendre, where the characters are fully conscious of the other side of their words. The similarity between our characters and comparable ones in Shakespeare is that the women in his plays are typically virgins and the men typically clowns. They are, that is to say, figures who are not yet (or by nature not) incorporated into the normal social world of law and appropriateness and marriage and of consonant limitations in what we call maturity and adulthood.

The critical problem in approaching these characters, or the problem in describing them, can then be put this way: If we do not note the other side of their words and actions, then we shall never understand them, we shall not know why the one is in a trance and the other in madcap. But if we do note the other side of their words and actions, we shall lose our experience of them as individuals, we shall not see their exercises of consciousness. We have neither to know them nor to fail to know them, neither to objectivize nor to subjectivize them. It is a way of defining the epistemological problem of other minds.

Let us note some further features of the world of this film that there should be no reluctance or difficulty in making explicit. Not surprisingly, given that the film is some kind of comedy, it ends with a marriage, anyway with a promise of marriage, a young pair having overcome certain obstacles to this conclusion. Apart from these central characters, we have a cast of humors – an exasperated aunt; a pedant (in the guise, not uncommon in Hollywood films, of a psychiatrist); a sexless zany who talks big game hunting; an omni-incompetent sheriff; a drunken retainer – none of whom can act beyond their humorous repetitions. The exposition of the drama takes

133

place, roughly, in the town, and is both complicated and settled in a shift to the countryside. It carefully alternates between day and night and climaxes around about midnight.

Are we beginning to assemble features whose combination, could we find their laws, would constitute a dramatic genre? And should such a genre be called 'a Hollywood comedy'? This seems unpromising. Not all the considerable comedies made in Hollywood will contain even the features so far mentioned; and the label hardly captures our intuition that the mood, to go no further, of this film is quite special. Yet Northrop Frye, in an early statement of his work on comedy, allows himself to say: 'The average movie of today [he is writing in 1948] is a rigidly conventionalized New Comedy proceeding toward an act which, like death in Greek tragedy, takes place offstage, and is symbolized by the final embrace.' This is a nice example of academic humor, and strikes a conventional note of complacency toward movies in general. But is it true?

I cannot speak of the 'average movie' of 1948 or of any other time, but of the Hollywood comedies I remember and at the moment care most about, it is true of almost none of them that they conclude with an embrace, if that means they conclude with a shot of the principal characters kissing. It is, in particular, not the way the other members of our genre conclude.

So let us not speak hastily and loosely of final embraces and happy endings. There are few festivals here. The concluding moments I have cited are as carefully prepared and dramatically conclusive (if, or because, fictionally inconclusive) as the closing of an aphorism, and it may be essential to a certain genre of film comedy that this should be so.

Bringing Up Baby, it happens, does conclude with an embrace, anyway with some kind of clinch. It is notably awkward; one cannot determine whether the pair's lips are touching. And it takes place on the platform of a work scaffold, where the film began, and in the aftermath of a collapsing reconstructed skeleton of a brontosaurus. What act does *all* of this symbolize? The collapsing of the skeleton poses the obvious discomfort in this conclusion, or shadow on its happiness. One is likely to ask whether it is necessary, or positively to assert that it is not. Is it meant to register the perimeter of human happiness, or the happenstance of it – like the breaking of glass at the end of a Jewish wedding? Both surely comment upon the demise of virginity, but in this film it is the woman who directly causes it. Perhaps, then, our question should be, not whether it is necessary, but how it is that this man, afterwards, can still want to embrace. Are we to imagine that his admission of love requires that he no longer cares about his work? Or can we see that he finally feels equal to its disruption and capable of picking up the pieces?

It should help us to recognize that the pose of the final clinch – something that to me accounts for its specific awkwardness – is a reenactment of a second popular statue of Rodin's, *The Kiss*; a concluding *tableau vivant* to match the opening one. So what? Are we accordingly to conclude that the opening man of stone after all retreats into stone? But surely the intervening events have produced some human progress, or some progress toward

134

the human? At least he now has company. The isolation of the scaffold has emphatically become the isolation of a pedestal. It looms so large and shadowy in the final shot as to mock the tiny figures mounted on it. Surely they will make it down to earth? How did they get up there? It started as Hepburn entered the museum holding the recovered bone, upon which Grant instinctively ran up the scaffold – perhaps *in order* to be followed up. In any case he does at least acknowledge, over the skeleton, that he ran because he is afraid of her, which prepares his declaration of love. So he, or his prehistoric instinct, was as much the cause of the collapse of science as she was; as much the cause of its collapse as of its construction.

The issue of who is following whom presides over their relationship from its inception. At the end of the first scene, on the golf course, he responds to her accusation by denying that he is following her, and in the conventional sense he is not; but it cannot be denied that literally he is. Whereupon she gallops off with him. (She does this again later, and again in a stolen chariot, after their stop in Connecticut to buy food for Baby.) At the close of the restaurant sequence, their walk-off – the man leading the woman yet following her pace, as in some dream tango, dog fashion – identifies the issue of who is following whom with the matter of who is behind whom, which remains thematic in subsequent scenes. Notably, as the two are hunting through the night woods for Baby, Grant with a rope and a croquet mallet, Hepburn with a butterfly net, he turns around to discover her on all fours (she is trying to avoid his wake of branches swinging in her face) and he says, 'This is no time to be playing squat tag'; she replies that she is not playing and, upon asking whether she shouldn't go first, is told, 'Oh no. You might get hurt.' The question of who belongs where reaches its climax inside the jailhouse in the last scene before the Epilogue. We will get to that.

I have suggested that the work of the romance of remarriage is designed to avoid the distinction between Old and New Comedy and that this means to me that it poses a structure in which we are permanently in doubt who the hero is, that is, whether it is the male or the female, who is the active partner, which of them is in quest, who is following whom. A working title for this structure might be 'the comedy of equality', evoking laughter equally at the idea that men and women are different *and* at the idea that they are not. The most explicit conclusion of this theme among the films I can recognize as of this genre is arrived at in *Adam's Rib*. Once more we are in the expensive Connecticut countryside; once more the pair is alone. And we are given what sounds like a twice-told, worn-out joke. Tracy says: Vive la différence. Hepburn asks: What does that mean? Tracy replies: It means, Hooray for that little difference. Then they climb behind the curtains of a fourposter bed and the film concludes. If what I have claimed about the conclusions of such films is correct, then a film so resourceful and convincing as *Adam's Rib* cannot vanish on the sounding of a stale joke. And it does not. It vanishes with a joke on this joke. It is not conceivable that this woman – to whom Tracy had cracked earlier, when she was turning on a superior note, 'Oh. Giving me the old Bryn Mawr business, eh?' – it is not conceivable that this woman does not know what the French words mean. She is asking solemnly, what difference is meant by that little difference. So it is upon the repetition of a question, not upon the provision of an answer, that they climb together out of sight into bed, with, surrealistically, their hats on. (How their hats get put on makes a nice story. Her putting hers on is a reacceptance of an important and intimate present from him. His putting his on acknowledges that hers is on. He puts his on without thinking, as another man would take his off in the presence of a lady. This pair is inventing gallantry between one another.)

The equality of laughter at the idea of difference is enough to ensure that, unlike the case of classical comedies, there can in general be no new social reconciliation at these conclusions, for society does not regard the difference between men and women as the topic of a metaphysical argument; it takes itself to know what the difference means. So the principal pair in this structure will normally draw the conclusion on their own, isolated within society, not backed by it. The comedy of equality is a comedy of privacy, evoking equal laughter at the fact that they are, and are not, alone. In particular, the older generation will not be present. Where this rule seems to be infringed, say in *The Philadelphia Story*, the moment is radically undercut; we are ripped from our supposed presence at this wedding festival by being shown that we are looking at a gossip shot – one way of looking at a movie – giving us the sort of inside knowledge that merely underlines our position as members of an outside public. Contrariwise, the pull of the private conclusion can mislead a director into supposing that his picture has earned it. I am thinking of Cukor's *Holiday*, which he concludes with a kiss. This conclusion feels wrong, feels like violation, every way you look at it – from Grant's point of view, from Hepburn's, but especially from the point of view of their older friends, a couple who in this case, themselves being shown out of sympathy with the conventional world, have provided an alternative social world for this young pair and who therefore deserve to be present, whose presence therefore feels required. I mention this in passing partly to enlist another item of evidence for investigating the idea of the final embrace, but also to suggest that the wrongness of this conclusion cannot be accounted for by appealing to a lack in the psychological development of the characters (their development is complete), nor excused by appealing to a general movie convention of the final embrace, first of all because there is no such general convention, and second, and more important, because the wrongness in question consists in breaking the structure of this narrative.

Is there present a definite structure of the kind I have named the comedy of equality? And if there is, what has it to do with the thematic or systematic allegory in *Bringing Up Baby*? How does it help us to understand who or what Baby is, and where a Baby belongs, and where a Baby comes from?

I might bypass my intuition of a definite structure in force here and directly seek an interpretation of the moods of sexuality in play, in particular, of the ambivalence or instability in it: the situation between this pair cannot remain as it is. Here I would wish to put together the following facts: first, the texture of certain speeches and actions that I have noted as

136

a play between their literal and their allegorical potentialities; second, the sense that the principals' actions consist of, or have the quality of, a series of games (from actual golfing, to rock-throwing at the windows of the rich, to various species of follow-the-leader and hide-and-seek, to playing dress-up and playing house, to finding the hidden object, all framed by pinning the tail on the brontosaurus); third, the fact that the female of the pair likes the games whereas the male plays unwillingly and is continuously humiliated by their progress; fourth, the mystery of their behavior to everyone around them (to Mr Peabody, from before whose eyes Grant is continually disappearing; to the man's fiancée and to the woman's aunt and to the aunt's major and her cook's husband; to the psychiatrist and the sheriff; and even to the butcher from whom Grant orders thirty pounds of meat for Baby to eat raw).

Such facts add up to a representation of a particular childhood world, to that stage of childhood preceding puberty, the period Freud calls latency, in which childish sexual curiosity has been repressed until the onset of new physiological demands, or instincts, reawakens it. In this film we are attempting to cross the limit of this stage, one whose successful and healthy negotiation demands a satisfaction of this reawakened curiosity, a stage at which the fate of one's intelligence, or ability and freedom to think, will be settled. This stage is confirmed by the air of innocence and secrecy between the two; by the obviousness of the sexuality implied, or rather by the puzzles of sexuality seeming to concern merely its most basic mechanics; and by the perception we are given of the humorous collection of figures surrounding them, a perception of these figures as, one might simply say, grown-ups – not exactly mysterious, yet foreign, asexual, grotesque in their unvarying routines, the source primarily of unearned money and of unmerited prohibitions.

This representation of this period implies two obstacles in the way of this pair's achieving some satisfactory conclusion in relation to one another and to the world, a conclusion both refer to as 'marriage'. Or, two questions stand in the way of man's awakening from his entrancement ('I can't seem to move') and of the woman's doffing her madcap ('I just did whatever came into my head'). One question is: If adulthood is the price of sexual happiness, is the price fair? If the grown-ups we see around us represent the future in store for us, why should we ever leave childhood? A second question is: If virginity at some point becomes humiliating and laughable, then why must departing from it be humiliating and laughable? Why are the vaunted pleasures of sexuality so ludicrous and threatening? In the middle of their chase through the woods, they come upon Baby and George growling and rolling in one another's arms on a clear, moonlit patch of ground. Thus seeing themselves, the female is relieved ('Oh look. They like one another' – but she had earlier said that she doesn't know whether, having been told that Baby likes dogs, that means that he is fond of them or eats them); the male is not happy ('In another minute my intercostal clavicle will be gone forever'). I think it would be reasonable, along such lines, to regard the cause of this comedy as the need, and the achievement, of laughter at

137

the physical requirements of wedded love, or, at the romance of marriage; laughter at the realization that after more than two millennia of masterpieces on the subject, we still are not clear why, or to what extent, marriage is thought to justify sexual satisfaction. (That such comedies are no longer made perhaps means that we have given up on this problem, or publicized it to death.) Accordingly, we should regard the midsummer's eve in the Connecticut forest not as the preparation for a wedding ceremony but as an allegory of the wedding night, or a dream of that night. Grant, sensing his entrancement, at one point almost declares himself asleep: 'What I've been doing today I could have done with my eyes shut.' (At the beginning of the end of the Ritz sequence, he said: 'Let's play a game. I'll close my eyes and count to ten and you go away.') And just before they discover Baby's escape and leave for the woods, he behaves as if he is walking in his sleep, rising stiffly from the dinner table and following George out of the house, his soup spoon still in his hand, stopped in midair on the way to his mouth.

But while I find such considerations pertinent, they seem to me to leave out too much, in particular they do not account for the beginning and the ending of this narrative, for why just this couple finds just these obstacles on their road to marriage. More particularly, they do not account for the overall drive of the plot, which appears to be a story not of a man seeking marriage but of a man seeking extrication, divorce. One might say that according to this plot he is seeking extrication from Hepburn in order to meet his engagement with Miss Swallow. But that hardly matches our experience of these events, which could just as well be described, attending to the introductory sequence, as his attempt to extricate himself from Miss Swallow, who promises him, or threatens him with, a marriage that, as she puts it, must 'entail [that word again] no domestic entanglements *of any kind*'. Upon which promise, or threat, he leaves to seek his fortune.

The film, in short, poses a question concerning the validation of marriage, the reality of its bonding, as that question is posed in the genre of remarriage comedy. Its answer participates in, or contributes its particular temperament to, the answer of that structure – that the validity of marriage takes a willingness for repetition, the willingness for remarriage. The task of the conclusion is to get the pair back into a particular moment of their past lives together. No new vow is required, merely the picking up of an action which has been, as it were, interrupted; not starting over, but starting again, finding and picking up the thread. Put a bit more metaphysically: only those can genuinely marry who are already married. It is as though you know you are married when you come to see that you cannot divorce, that is, when you find that your lives simply will not disentangle. If your love is lucky, this knowledge will be greeted with laughter.

Bringing Up Baby shares, or exaggerates, two of the features of this structure. First, it plots love-making in the form of aborted leave-taking. It adds to this, more particularly, the comic convention according to which the awakening of love causes the male to lapse into trances and to lose control of his body, in particular to be everywhere in danger of falling down or of breaking things. *The Lady Eve* contains, as we saw, another virtuoso

138

treatment of this convention. And even Spencer Tracy, whom it is hard to humiliate, is asked by the genre to suffer these indignities. Second, it harps upon repetition. Beyond the texture of verbal repetitions and the beginning and ending *tableaux vivants*, and beyond the two 'I'll be with you in a minute, Mr Peabody' exits, and the two kidnappings in stolen cars, and the two scenes of serenade under the second-story windows of respectable houses, and two golf balls and two convertible coupés and two purses and two bones and two bent hats, there is the capping discovery that there are two leopards in Connecticut. My idea, then, is that this structure is to be understood as an interpretation of the genre of remarriage in the following way: the principals accept the underlying perception that marriage requires its own proof, that nothing can show its validity from outside; and its comedy consists in their attempts to understand, perhaps to subvert, to extricate themselves from, the necessity of the initial leap, to move directly into the state of reaffirmation. It is as though their summer night were spent not in falling in love at first or second sight, but in becoming childhood sweethearts, inventing for themselves a shared, lost past, to which they can wish to remain faithful. (Among the other, nonexclusive, perceptions of their final setting, it can be read as a tree house or a crib.) It is a kind of prehistoric reconstruction. That this must fail is not exactly funny. Grant, in particular, never smiles.

The concluding tableau is a repetition, or interpretation, not alone of the opening shot of Grant, but of the image upon which the final scene (preceding the Epilogue) had closed. There Grant faces the second leopard, the wild one, the killer, using correctly this time an appropriate implement, a tamer's tool before him, and coaxes the beast into a cage, or rather a cell; it is, as it happens, the particular cell in which Hepburn had been locked. In this final game (playing tamer and rescuer), the woman is now standing behind the man, and, after their victory, he turns to face her, tries to say something, and then loses consciousness, collapsing full-length into her arms for their initial embrace. Somewhat to our surprise, she easily bears his whole weight. Nature, as in comedies it must, has taken its course.

This sub-conclusion is built upon a kind of cinematic, or grammatical, joke. The cutting in this passage back and forth between the leopards emphasizes that we are never shown the leopards within the same frame. It thus acknowledges that while in this narrative fiction there are two leopards, in cinematic fact there is only one; one Baby with two natures; call them tame and wild, or call them latent and aroused. It is this knowledge, and acknowledgement, that brings a man in a trance of innocence to show his acquisition of consciousness by summoning the courage to let it collapse.

Common to some who like and some who dislike *Bringing Up Baby* is an idea that the film is some kind of farce. (It would be hard to deny that some concept of the farcical will be called upon in dealing with the humor in marriage.) But if the home of this concept of farce lies, say, in certain achievements of nineteenth-century French theater, then, as in other cases, this concept is undefined for film. I do not deny that such achievements are a source of such films, but this merely asks us to think what a source is and why and how and by what it is tapped. Nor would I put it past Howard Hawks, or those whose work he directed, to be alluding in their title to, even providing a Feydeauian translation of, Feydeau's *On purge Bebé*. This would solve nothing, but it might suggest the following line of questioning: Why, and how, and by what, is such a source tapped in this film since neither the treatment of dialogue nor of character nor of space nor of the themes of sexuality and marriage in *Bringing Up Baby* are what they are in Feydeau?

One line of response might undertake to show that this question encodes its own answer, that *Bringing Up Baby* is what it is precisely in negating Feydeauian treatments. This would presumably imply a negation or re-demption of (this species of) farce itself, that is, an incorporation, or subla-tion, of the bondage in marriage into a new romanticizing of marriage. Would an implied criticism of society be smaller in the latter than in the for-mer case? Not if one lodges one's criticisms of society irreducibly, if not ex-clusively, from within a demand for open happiness. Feydeauian comedy cedes this demand on behalf of its characters; Hawksian comedy, through its characters' struggles for consciousness, remembers that a society is crazy which cedes it, that the open pursuit of happiness is a standing test, or threat, to every social order. (Feydeau and Hawks are as distant conceptu-ally as the Catholic and the Protestant interpretations of the institution of marriage, hence of the function of adultery.)

What is it about film that could allow the 'negation' of theatrical 'treat-ments'? Take the treatment of character, and film's natural tendency to give precedence to the actor over his or her character. This precedence is ac-knowledged in the capping repetition of the line – the curtain-line for each of the first two scenes – 'I'll be with you in a minute, Mr Peabody.' It scans and repeats like the refrain of a risqué London music-hall ballad, of course to be sung by a woman. This contributes to an environment for our re-sponse to the *expertness* of the pair's walk-off through the revolving door of the restaurant. (That they are as on a stage is confirmed by the inset cut, in mid-walk, to a tracking shot past the astonished Mr Peabody, who takes the place of an audience.) The authority of this exit, which calls for a bent hat held high in salute in the hand upstage, is manageable only by a human being with Cary Grant's experience and expertise in vaudeville.

As well as in its allusions to, and sources in, farce and vaudeville, this film insists upon the autonomy of its existence in its allusions to movies. When I took in Grant's line, in the jailhouse scene, 'She's making all this up out of old motion pictures', I asked myself, Which ones? (There is a similar jail-house scene in John Ford's earlier *The Whole Town's Talking*.)[1] But of course one is invited further to ask oneself why, in so self-conscious a film, Hawks places this allusion as he does. It is a line that immediately confesses the nature of movies, or of a certain kind of movie-making: the director of the movie is the one who is making all this up out of old motion pictures. (As Hitchcock will incorporate the conclusion of *Bringing Up Baby* into the conclusion of *North by Northwest*, where Grant's powerful hand and wrist save another woman from falling, and we see that the ledge he hauls her onto is his cave-bed.) Or: a director makes a certain *kind* of movie; or: a director works within, or works to discover, a maze of kinships. Anyway *this* director does, demanding his inheritance. So Hepburn is characterized by Grant as having or standing for some directional function. The implication is that the spectator is to work out his or her relation to (the director of) this film in terms of Grant's relation to Hepburn. So, after all, criticism comes down to a matter of personal attachment! This is why we must adopt some theoretical position toward film! But I rather imagined that Grant's relation to Hepburn itself might provide a study in personal attachment. At any rate, a theory of criticism will be part of a theory of personal attachment (including a theory of one's attachment to theory, a certain trance in thinking).

I have thus, encouraged by this film, declared my willingness, or commitment, to go back over my reading of it, construed as my expressions of attachment to it. Reconsideration of attachments, and of disaffections, ought to be something meant by education, anyway by adult education, by bringing oneself up. Since for this film I am to proceed in terms proposed by Grant/David's relation to Hepburn/Susan, then before or beyond testing any given form in which I have so far expressed myself about the film, for its accuracy at once to what is there and to what I feel in what is there, I am to ask what I know and do not know about this relation, and what Grant knows and does not know about it. The principal form this question takes for him is, in essence: What am I doing here, that is, how have I got into this relation and why do I stay in it? It is a question all but continually on his mind. So I, as his spectator, am to learn to ask this question about my relation to this film. It will not be enough to say, for example, that I like it, for however necessary this confession may be, that feeling is not apt to sustain the amount of trouble the relation may require, or justify its taking me away from other interests and commitments in order to attend to it. Nor will it be enough to say that I do not like it, should that be required of me, for perhaps I am not very familiar with my likes and dislikes, having overcome them both too often. If this is a good film, it ought to, if I let it, help teach me how to think about my relation to it.

Earlier, in registering the pace of this narrative as one in which a complete exposition is comically compressed into a stilted prologue, I described the hero as leaving to seek his fortune. His first name for this fortune is, conventionally enough, 'a million dollars'; but the first thing he finds on his quest, the first of the nonaccidental accidents which punctuate quests, is a mix-up with an oddly isolated, athletic woman, suddenly appearing from the woods, who looks like a million dollars. (The camera's attraction to Katharine Hepburn's body – its interpretation of her physical sureness as intelligence self-possessed – is satisfied as fully in Cukor's comedies with her as in this of Hawks.) This hero's entanglements with this Artemis from the beginning, and throughout, threaten the award of his imagined fortune, both because she compromises him in the eyes of those who are to award it and because she herself seeks the same million. Yet when at the conclusion she confers it upon him, together with all other treasures, he seems unsatisfied. He gets the money, the lost bone, and the girl, yet he is not happy. What can he, do we think, be thinking of? Why is he still rigid; why is his monstrous erection still false? Do we think: He cannot accept these powers from her, as if these things are her dowry, for in accepting her right to confer them he must accept her authority, her fatherhood of herself? Or do we think: He still cannot think about money any more than he can (or because he cannot) think about sexuality? Or is it: The fate of sexuality and the fate of money are bound together; we will not be free for the one until we are free from the other? Perhaps we shall think, for Luther's reasons, or for Marx's, or Freud's, that money is excrement. I find that I think again, and I claim that such comedies invite us to think again, what it is Nietzsche sees when he speaks of our coming to doubt our right to happiness, to the pursuits of happiness. In the *Genealogy of Morals*, he draws a consequence of this repressed right as the construction of the ascetic ideal, our form of the thinker. He calls for us to have the courage of our sensuality, emblematized for him by Luther's wedding. For this priest to marry, the idea of marriage, as much as that of ordination, is brought into question. I do not say that the genre of remarriage thinks as deeply about the idea of marriage as does, say, the *Pagan Servitude of the Church*. Doubtless our public discourse is not as deep on these matters as it once was. I do say that a structure depicting people looking to remarry inevitably depicts people thinking about the idea of marriage. This is declared by a passage in each of these films in which one or both of the principals try a hand at an abstract theoretical formulation of their predicament. (Among the central members of our genre, *The Awful Truth* contains the most elaborated instance of this, with its concluding philosophical dialogue on sameness and difference, answering to its opening pronouncement about the necessity for faith in marriage.) It is why their conclusions have that special form of inconclusiveness I characterized as aphoristic. Nothing about our lives is more comic than the distance at which we think about them. As to unfinished business, the right to happiness, pictured as the legitimacy of marriage, is a topic that our nation wished to turn to as Hollywood learned to speak – as though our publicly declared right to pursue happiness was not self-evident after all.

About halfway through *Bringing Up Baby*, Grant/David provides himself with an explicit, if provisional, answer to the question how he got and why he stays in his relation with the woman, declaring to her that he will accept no more of her 'suggestions' unless she holds a bright object in front of his eyes and twirls it. He is projecting upon her, blaming her for, his sense of entrancement. The conclusion of the film – Howard Hawks's twirling bright object – provides its hero with no better answer, but rather with a position from which to let the question go: in moving toward the closing embrace, he mumbles something like, 'Oh my; oh dear; oh well', in other words, I am here, the relation is mine, what I make of it is now part of what I make of my life, I embrace it. But the conclusion of Hawks's object provides me, its spectator and subject, with a little something more, and less:

with a declaration that if I am hypnotized by (his) film, rather than awakened, then I am the fool of an unfunny world, which is, and is not, a laughing and fascinating matter; and that the responsibility, either way, is mine. I embrace it.

1. Andrew Sarris provided this answer at the New York Conference at which a version of this reading was presented. I have not seen the Ford film.

Stanley Cavell, Harvard professor of the philosophy of aesthetics, has made significant contributions to film theory and criticism, though usually not in accord with the fashionable film theory of the day. His analysis of *Bringing Up Baby* brings together in an idiosyncratic blend a range of philosophical and Freudian psychoanalytic concepts with close textual analysis. His account of the film forms a central chapter in Cavell's book-length study of 1930s/1940s screwball comedy, *Pursuits of Happiness: The Hollywood Comedy of Remarriage*. Hawks is central to this study, which also contains a fine detailed analysis of Hawks's *His Girl Friday* (along with analyses of Preston Sturges's *The Lady Eve*, Frank Capra's *It Happened One Night*, George Cukor's *The Philadelphia Story* and *Adam's Rib* and Leo McCarey's *The Awful Truth*). In the sense that Cavell's studies of these films place central importance on their spirited, independent female protagonists, Cavell's perceptions probably owe something to the work being undertaken in the 1970s by feminist film critics such as Molly Haskell and Naomi Wise.

Cavell is also the author of an earlier book on film, *The World Viewed* (New York: Viking, 1971; enlarged edition Cambridge, Mass. and London: Harvard University Press, 1979), which extended some of André Bazin's theoretical interest in the ontological status of the film image.

Hawks and Faulkner

BRUCE KAWIN

From Bruce Kawin, *Faulkner and Film* (New York: Ungar, 1977).

One of the things that amused Hawks was the way his friends Hemingway and Faulkner were always asking him about each other, admiring each other's work but refusing to meet. On a fishing trip with Hemingway, Hawks tried to interest him in adapting one of his own novels for the screen. When Hemingway answered that he was happy as he was, and had no interest in 'bucking hours', Hawks called him 'a damned fool', then offered this challenge: 'I can make a picture out of your worst book.' 'What', asked Hemingway testily, 'is my worst book?' 'That goddamned piece of junk called *To Have and Have Not*.' 'You can't make a picture out of that,' said Hemingway, and Hawks replied: 'OK, I'll get Faulkner to do it. He can write better than you can anyway.'

To Have and Have Not, by the way, is no piece of junk; it is, however, about losers, and as Hawks says, 'I *hate* losers.' It is the story of Harry Morgan, a tough and bitter fisherman who runs liquor and revolutionaries between Cuba and Florida when his other means of support are exhausted. In the course of the novel he loses his arm, his boat, his shipmate, and finally his life, having learned that 'No matter how a man alone ain't got no bloody fucking chance.' Harry's wife, Marie, is autonomous, hard, and passionate, but even she is beaten down at the end. In one sense, they both go from having to not having; in another, however, Marie and Harry are the 'haves' in this story; the moral 'have nots' are the artists and businessmen who loll in their boats and bars, congratulating themselves on their talents.

'You've drawn the character of Harry Morgan,' said Hawks; 'I think I can give you the wife. All we have to do is make a picture about how they met.' For ten days the fishermen drew up that story, switching the location to Vichy-controlled Martinique. Faulkner, as it happened, had recently written *The De Gaulle Story*, an anti-Vichy screenplay, and was quite interested in that aspect of the new picture. With his brilliant collaborator, Jules Furthman, Faulkner expanded the story-outline Hawks had delivered him, turning Morgan into Hawks's idea of a 'winner' and Marie into 'Slim' (the nickname of Hawks's wife). By the time the picture was finished, however, these characters could hardly be described as anything but Bogart and Bacall.

According to Hawks, Furthman got along well with Faulkner. They had apparently met at MGM in 1933, in connection with *Honor*. Furthman was disliked by many of his collaborators because he was demanding and obnoxious, and also because he owned some of the most valuable real estate in Culver City. He had been forced to move from his former home (to what was then worthless property) because his retarded son's bellowing disturbed the neighbors. It is not far-fetched to speculate that Furthman warmed up to Faulkner as the creator of Benjy. Hawks enjoyed working with Furthman because he could taunt him into doing good work. When Furthman wrote a scene for *To Have and Have Not* in which Marie has her purse stolen, Hawks teased him until he stalked out and wrote the scene in which Marie steals a wallet. (Hawks was quite as direct with Faulkner, but less loud.)

To Have and Have Not is central to Hawks's work, but marginal to Faulkner's. It might even be considered marginal to Furthman's, since most of the script was thrown away on the set. A great many extraliterary elements influenced the picture: for one, Warner's was interested in making another *Casablanca*, and wanted emphasis thrown on Bogart's conversion from isolationism to Resistance activity; for another, Bogart did not want to have to deliver the kind of lengthy patriotic speech Faulkner had been writing for Warner's for the past two years. Furthman had become expert at creating tough female roles – he worked on several pictures for Josef von Sternberg and Marlene Dietrich – but the character of Marie, for all her resemblance to other Furthman heroines, is largely the result of Hawks's and Bacall's improvisations, with some help from a chorus girl Hawks calls 'Stuttering Sam', – who had been around quite a bit herself. The *Casablanca* influence extended beyond Jack Warner's directives; Hawks had once swapped assignments with the director of that film, Michael Curtiz (who had been stumped by his assignment, *Sergeant York*), and was now going to show, rather playfully, how *he* might have made *Casablanca*. Faulkner's work is most evident in the characterization of the Resistance fighters (particularly the woman), and in the treatment of the themes of patriotism and fear. The film's basic device was hit on by Hawks during that first fishing trip: each of the losses suffered by Hemingway's Morgan (notably those of his money and fishing tackle) pushes Hawks's Morgan deeper into an involvement not with politics but with politicos, some of whom he likes and therefore helps, some of whom he dislikes and therefore fights. Where considerations of expediency lead Hemingway's Morgan to consider killing his rummy shipmate, Eddie (played in the film by Walter Brennan), Hawks's Morgan continues to support his old friend because Eddie used to be a good man and has stuck by him. An unspoken law in Hemingway's novels is that a man with a healthy emotional life will at some point in the story be castrated or killed or otherwise sexually ruined; Hawks reverses this structure completely, leaving Morgan not dead and bankrupt but autonomous, witty, politically engaged, and sexually fulfilled. Faulkner

145

probably did not find these changes distasteful; the point is that he did not make them. . . .

The superstars of *To Have and Have Not* were reunited on *The Big Sleep*, Jules Furthman excepted. Contrary to legend, Furthman had nothing to do with the screenplay as published; he was called in only when shooting was nearly completed.[1] His assignment was to condense the final third of the screenplay into a few brisk scenes. For one thing, the film was getting too long; for another, the censors had refused to pass the ending devised by Faulkner's collaborator, Leigh Brackett. Hawks challenged the censors to give him a better ending, and to his surprise they outlined the extremely crisp and violent scene that now closes the picture. That scene was written by Furthman and Hawks, long after Faulkner and Brackett had gone on to other projects.

The Big Sleep went through three major stages of generation, and it will simplify this discussion to clarify them at the start. The first temporary screenplay was written by Faulkner and Brackett in eight days; Faulkner outlined the story and divided up the work. They expanded this into a final screenplay,[2] which was rejected by the censors. Furthman wrote most of the new final scene, then helped Hawks condense the rest during shooting. Warner's liked the picture so much that they decided to hold up its release for more than a year, so that it finally came out as part of Warner's 'twentieth anniversary of sound on screen'. During the interim, however, it was shown to American servicemen overseas; their reactions led Hawks to write and shoot several new scenes, most of them romantic banter between Philip Marlowe (Bogart) and Vivian Sternwood (Bacall). When the picture was released, then, it was much faster and funnier than Brackett and Faulkner had intended. Hawks began with a 'film noir', a hard-boiled detective story with sexy undertones; he ended with a wacky, elliptical, contradictory film that, because it plays by no known rules, decisively influenced such New Wave films as Godard's *Breathless*, Truffaut's *Shoot the Piano Player*, and Chabrol's *A Double Tour* (*Web of Passion*), not to mention Altman and Brackett's later version of Raymond Chandler's *The Long Goodbye*. As Hawks told a group of critics before its release, 'You're not going to know what to make out of this damned picture; it holds out its hand for a right-turn signal, then takes a left.'

Chandler's novel is romantic, fog-bound, and depressing. It is set in an expanding, poisonous Los Angeles, paving itself into an ethical oblivion. Its hero-detective, Marlowe, is more than tough: he is a throwback to the old virtues of professionalism, honor, and integrity. On the novel's first page Marlowe describes a stained-glass panel in the Sternwood mansion, 'showing a knight in dark armor rescuing a lady who was tied to a tree and didn't have any clothes on'. This panel is a miniature of the entire novel, in the course of which this knight in unshining armor learns that 'knights had no meaning' in the Sternwoods' chess game.

Marlowe is hired by General Sternwood to protect his nymphomaniac daughter, Carmen, from a blackmailer. What really upsets the General is the possibility that the villain is Rusty Regan, the husband of his other daughter, Vivian. Several murders and reversals later, it develops that Regan was killed by Carmen when he rejected her advances, and that Vivian is collaborating with a gambler named Eddie Mars, protecting Carmen and misleading Marlowe. The climax occurs when Carmen tries to shoot Marlowe (who in his turn has rejected her), near the sump in which Regan's body has been mouldering. Vivian sends Carmen to a sanitarium, the General is kept in the dark, and Marlowe feels that he has been made 'a part of a nastiness now'. Such an ending, of course, could not possibly satisfy Hawks, and a variation of the cleanup he had called for in *To Have and Have Not* soon came into play.

Faulkner and Brackett, working on alternate sections of the script, downplayed Chandler's imagery of existentially empty eyes, cyanide factories, oil wells, and a fog so thick that one of the characters is described as leaning against it, leaving the question of visual atmosphere to Hawks. They reduced the number of scenes in which Marlowe and various policemen explain who killed whom and why, but left in enough to make it *possible* to follow the story. Neither they nor Hawks, however, could figure out who killed the Sternwoods' chauffeur; Hawks wired Chandler, who didn't know either, so the matter was left unresolved.[3] The major change they introduced was to make Marlowe and Vivian Sternwood fall in love and plan to marry. This necessitated two related changes: Regan became the General's employee instead of Vivian's husband, and Vivian became not tough and evil but strong and good/bad. Carmen (Martha Vickers) remained the villain, but Brackett introduced (and Chandler approved) a marvelous climax, set not at the sump but in the house of the now-dead blackmailer, Arthur Geiger. Marlowe enters the house, outside which Mars (John Ridgely) and his gunmen are waiting to shoot him when he leaves. Carmen arrives; she had been locked in her room, but climbed down a drainpipe to rendezvous with Marlowe, whom she intends to seduce. (This part of the scene is Faulkner's contribution, an echo of Quentin II's escape in *The Sound and the Fury*, as described – and misremembered – in the 1945 Appendix to that novel.) When Marlowe rejects her, she shoots at him with a gun he has unloaded; then she taunts Marlowe who, because of his love for the General (Charles Waldren), could never reveal the truth about her and cause a scandal that would break the old man's heart, if not kill him.[4] Marlowe snaps off the light as she leaves the house, so that Mars – thinking he is shooting Marlowe – guns her down. Mars enters, and Marlowe kills him. Marlowe tells the General that Carmen has died in a car crash, and that Regan 'sends you his affection and respect, but he won't come back'. The General, Marlowe, and Vivian come to a happy end, and Carmen and Mars are punished – but the censors would not stand for Marlowe's causing Carmen's death.

As the picture now ends, Marlowe and Vivian are at Geiger's with Eddie Mars; Marlowe forces Mars to go out and be shot by his own men, then arranges with Vivian to have Carmen 'sent away' to be cured. It is in this final scene that the series of crimes is 'explained', much too fast for the audience to put it together. Even if one could follow this speech, however, one would find that it contradicts most of what has gone before, making Mars out to be the principal villain. This is more of a fast curve than the plot can support; it is at this moment, then, that *The Big Sleep* blasts the genre of detection and teaches the audience how to 'read' film in a new way. One follows the action because it is action; one responds to each scene on its own terms, without probing beneath them for some secret, coherent structure. The first half of the film, then, which is played much as Faulkner and Brackett wrote it (except for Hawks's interjection that Marlowe and Regan are old friends – which allows Marlowe to take a personal and masculine interest in the case – and a number of comic scenes), gives the audience the impression that all the clues will form *some* kind of pattern. Furthman, however, cut out almost all of the later explanatory scenes and introduced (as the censors had demanded) the nearly impossible suggestions that Mars had been deluding Vivian and that Carmen might not have killed Regan. Hawks compounded this shift by adding romantic scenes that completely derail the rhythm of Marlowe's quest and the audience's attempt at concentration, and by directing the picture for *speed*.

The genesis of one crucial scene shows the interplay of these creative forces and gives a sense of how Faulkner saw the story. In Chapter 24 of the novel, Marlowe enters his apartment and finds Carmen, naked, in his bed. Her 'small sharp teeth' glint; her giggle reminds him of 'rats behind a wainscoting in an old house'. There is a chessboard on his card table, with a problem he can't solve; he moves the knight, then tells Carmen to get out. Then he moves back the chess-piece: 'Knights had no meaning in this game. It wasn't a game for knights.' Carmen curses him; her eyes are blank, and her lips move 'as if they were artificial lips and had to be manipulated with springs'. He realizes that he cannot endure her violation of his home, the only private space he has. When he threatens to throw her out by force, she gets dressed and leaves. The imprint of her body on the pillow and sheets drives him into a fury, and he tears the bed to pieces 'savagely'.

In Faulkner's version of this scene (no. 123), Carmen and Marlowe have a long exchange of cute, witty dialogue; Carmen (in the chair, dressed) is still bent on seduction, but also meditates on her fall from what she thinks is innocence. As in the novel, she has a nervous habit of biting her thumb; she appears to be doing this throughout the scene, but when Marlowe tells her to take her thumb and get out, she shows him that she is biting the white queen from his chess set. The scene continues:

> Marlowe stares at her for a moment, then he slaps her terrifically across the face, rocking her back. The chessman falls from her hand and she stares at Marlowe, frightened now, as he walks toward her.
> CARMEN: Do that again.
> MARLOWE: (seething with repressed rage; almost whispering) Get out.
> CARMEN: Maybe if people had done that to me more often, I would have been good now.
>
> Marlowe reaches her, grasps her arm, hurries her across to the door,

jerks the door open, almost hurls her through it, flings the wrap after her, slams the door, turns the bolt as she rattles the knob, then begins to hammer on the door. He turns and crosses the room rapidly to the bath while she still beats on the door, and washes his hand savagely with soap and water, his face now actually beaded with sweat. . . . [He then pours Scotch on his hand, 'when what he needs is carbolic acid.'] . . . While the knocking still continues, he kneels at the hearth, lays the delicate chess-piece on it and with a heavy fire-dog hammers the chess-piece into dust, still beating even after the piece has vanished, his blows at last drowning out the sound of the knocking on the door.

FADE OUT.

Allowing for the censors, this is the finest adaptation of Chandler's scene one could hope for. Marlowe's thoughts are expressed in action, and both chapter and master-scene black out on an image of Marlowe's 'savage' attempt to destroy the effects of Carmen's intrusion on his privacy and all that it represents. It is the one place, in novel and screenplay, that he *cracks* – where one sees that the Sternwoods have left their mark on him. Faulkner introduces a significant change in emphasis, however, evident in the shift from knight to white (virginal) queen. The issue now is not male honor but female dishonor, not the threat to his professional code but the violation of his image of womanhood. Although this change of chess-piece can be explained as a means of compensating for the necessary writing-out of the bed and its nude defiler, it is a change that is typical of Faulkner's moral imagination. (It was less than one year after finishing *The Big Sleep* that he wrote the Appendix to Malcolm Cowley's *Portable Faulkner*, in which he portrayed Caddy Compson as the mistress of a Nazi official; in a lighter version of the same tone, he identified her husband of 1920–25 as 'a minor moving picture magnate'.) Faulkner's Carmen surpasses all her sources – in both Faulkner and Chandler – in her capacity for innately sexual evil.

When Hawks rewrote this scene, he kept Faulkner's humor but dropped any indications of strain on Marlowe's part. Both chess-piece and -game are dispensed with; instead, Carmen starts to bite her thumb (which irritates Marlowe), then thinks better of it, and then says, 'See, I remembered.' When Marlowe advises her that he has a tough friend, she asks, 'Is he as cute as you are?' and he answers, 'Nobody is.' While we can all be grateful for this wonderful line, the climax of the scene is disappointing. Marlowe simply throws Carmen out after she bites his hand. She tries to protest; he says 'Shut up' and slams the door; then there is a quick fade-out. There is no breakdown, no still point, no resonance. When I told Hawks that I thought he had wrecked the scene, he told me I didn't understand the picture. After thinking about it for some time, I realized he was right.

The point is that Hawks had no intention of putting Bogart through the kind of professional crisis and moral self-examination basic to a picture like *The Maltese Falcon* and to Chandler's novel. *The Big Sleep*, on its surface, is dark and violent *fun*. The undercurrents of perversity and amorality suc-

149

ceed in disturbing the audience because they are so rapidly and efficiently passed over. Hawks's Marlowe, like his Harry Morgan, is a winner who can take his licks. When the darkness does surface, it is in connection with other characters – notably Jones (Elisha Cook, Jr) and Canino (Bob Steele), whose deaths are the strongest moments in the picture. Yet even these brilliantly violent scenes are counter-balanced by the comic interludes Hawks improvised on the set, such as Bogart's impersonation of a prissy book-collector and his subsequent encounter with Dorothy Malone (by far the sexiest bookseller on film). The next time Faulkner handed Hawks an evil, lusty woman – Princess Nellifer in *Land of the Pharaohs* – Hawks had no idea how to balance her out, and the picture flopped. Although there is no place in Hawks's universe for Faulknerian depravity, it is unfortunate that the two men could not have worked out some compromise on the character of Vivian, who is simply too *good*-under-it-all to hold up her end of the story. It is possible, of course, that the problem with Vivian is Bacall, who is visibly being coached by Bogart in most of her scenes, and who (thanks to Jack Warner) has the burden of being Vivian and Slim at once; it is, in any case, her least effective performance.

1. According to Leigh Brackett; see Donald Chase, *Film-making: The Collaborative Art*, ed. James Powers (Boston: Little, Brown/American Film Institute, 1975), pp. 54–5.
2. It is this version of the screenplay that has been published in *Film Scripts One*, ed. Garrett, Hardison, and Gelfman (New York: Appleton-Century-Crofts, 1971; distributed by Irvington Publishers), pp. 137–329. The final, amended shooting script, with Furthman's and Hawks's contributions, is on file in the UCLA Theatre Arts Library and at Warner's.
3. In the film it is suggested but not proved that Joe Brody killed the chauffeur. Chandler's remark to Hawks that 'the butler did it' was a joke.
4. Faulkner's scenes between Marlowe and General Sternwood make much of the question of heartbreak. Hawks revised and cut these so that the one remaining scene is very close to Chandler's original (except for the detail of Marlowe's friendship with Regan).

As the more reductive conceptions about authorship in the context of Hollywood cinema have been jettisoned, so there has been greater interest in exploring the way directors interacted with their collaborators, particularly with writers. It is generally recognized that Hawks, though a good 'story man' himself and always collaborating closely with writers to get what he wanted, was also *dependent* on his writers – pre-eminently Ben Hecht, Jules Furthman, Charles Lederer and Leigh Brackett (the only woman, but before he met her, Hawks was expecting a man!). Richard Corliss, among others, has helped to open up the ways in which Hawks and his writers collaborated: see the entries for Hecht, Furthman, Borden Chase and Lederer, for example, in *Talking Pictures*. For more than twenty years, Hawks was also both a close friend and a collaborator of William Faulkner. Bruce Kawin's book *Faulkner and Film*, from which this entry is extracted, gives some fascinating insights into Hawks's working methods. In the same chapter, though excluded in our extract, Kawin discusses Faulkner's other film work, including his work with Hawks on *Today We Live* (1933), *The Road to Glory* (1936), *Air Force*

(1943) and *Land of the Pharaohs* (1955). Kawin gives a very detailed account of Hawks at work in his introduction to the screenplay of *To Have and Have Not.*

Hawks shooting *Land of the Pharaohs*

Empire to the West: *Red River*

ROBERT SKLAR

From John E. O'Connor and Martin A. Jackson (eds.), *American History/American Film* (New York: Ungar, 1979).

Red River is one of the curiosities in American film history. Nearly every-one pays homage to it, almost no one pays attention to it. Howard Hawks's first Western – incredibly, after two decades of directing and nearly thirty films, this was his first Western – was hailed on its release in September 1948 as an archetypal Western, the quintessential Western, the kind that tingles all the nerve endings but never touches the brain. A rattling good outdoor adventure movie, was *Time* magazine's assessment. Peter Bogdanovich in *The Last Picture Show* caught the core of its iconographic value by showing the commencement of the cattle drive on a small-town Texas theater screen. 'Take 'em to Missouri, Matt,' crusty Tom Dunson says, the music flares, and we see that classic sequence of cowboys in close-up yelling, 'Ya hoo. Hi yaa. Ya hoo. Whoopee. Yaa. Ya hoo. Yaa Yaa.' A magnificent horse opera, Pauline Kael called *Red River*, and there is no denying that a chorus of 'ya hoos' does not address the deeper issues of that time, our time, or any time.

'When things get tough in Hollywood they start the horses galloping,' wrote Kyle Crichton, in the midst of the backlash from the blacklist, in his 1948 *Collier's* review of *Red River*. 'Nobody can yell "propaganda" at a motion picture full of cows, horses, gunplay, brave women and daring men.' It became the central theme of *Red River* criticism, that here was a motion picture happily innocent of ideology, and the great French critic André Bazin a few years later gave this attitude toward *Red River* its definitive expression.

'Howard Hawks, indeed,' Bazin wrote, 'at the height of the vogue of the superwestern should be credited with having demonstrated that it had always been possible to turn out a genuine western based on the old dramatic and spectacle themes, without distracting our attention with some social thesis, or, what would amount to the same thing, by the form given the production. *Red River* (1948) and *The Big Sky* (1952) are western masterpieces but there is nothing baroque or decadent about them.'

Ultimately the critical consensus on *Red River* succeeded too well. It enshrined the film on a pedestal, a masterpiece of old-fashioned movie entertainment, a spectacle without, thankfully, social significance; it rendered the film irrelevant. Some of the most penetrating interpretations of Hawks's career ignore *Red River* completely. Those who aspire to complete coverage generally notice *Red River* for its *mise en scène*, its spectacular (what else?) set-pieces, the stampede, the river crossing, the final confrontation between Dunson and Matt.

No one noticed that there might have been a motive in the dual gesture of honoring and dismissing *Red River*, that there is a curious note of overkill in Bazin's and the reviewers' remarks – that they protest a little too much *Red River*'s mindlessness, as if trying too hard to keep us from seeing some things they prefer us not to see. No one noted that film criticism as much as any other intellectual or artistic pursuit has its ideological foundation, even when its ideological project is to deny the presence of ideology. No one observed the most obvious fact of all: that *Red River* is rich in social significance, is as teeming with messages as it is with meat on the hoof.

Red River announces itself, in fact, boldly. It is a film about the issues of empire. It is a film about the territorial expansion of one society by the usurpation of land from others, and the consequences arising therefrom – in the relations between men and women, in the relations between men and other men, in the social compact that binds people together for a common purpose. And these human themes, important as they are, are subordinate to even more fundamental issues of economic survival, of commodity production, above all of the need to find a market for one's goods. *Red River* is a film about cows, horses, gun play, brave women, daring men – and capitalism.

When Matthew Garth brings Tom Dunson's herd into Abilene, opening the Chisholm Trail route for Texas cattle to reach a Kansas railhead, Chicago stockyards, and distant consumers, the *Red River* dialogue continuity script has a voiceover line (later eliminated from the completed film) spoken by Groot the cook: 'It was just the first of thousands of such drives bringin' beef to the world.' That the issues *Red River* raises of empire and markets were also central issues of American economic power and expansion after World War II should come as no surprise to anyone, except those film critics who prefer their masterpieces to be meaningless.

Red River is not only about capitalism; its form and its destiny were also the products of capitalism, specifically of the changing economic structure of the Hollywood film industry in the postwar years. The film's director and producer, Howard Hawks, was a man not unlike its hero Thomas Dunson, a man with a vision, a man leaving the ordinary ways and trying to establish himself independently, struggling to find a market and gain a return on his investment of time and toil. He was to face as many challenges as Tom Dunson in reaching his goal.

Hawks was among the half dozen or so long-time studio directors – Frank Capra, William Wyler, Leo McCarey, Preston Sturges, and George Stevens were others – who aspired after World War II to work independently of the Hollywood factory system. They wanted to break away from

153

assembly-line studio production methods, to develop their own properties, and maintain control of the film-making process from beginning to end. What they wanted was soon to be commonplace in post-television Hollywood, but for some of them the desire was a few years premature. Hawks was actually one of the few to accomplish what he set out to do.

In December 1945 Hawks took part in establishing a corporation, Monterey Productions, Inc., with himself as president. *Red River* was Monterey Productions' only product. The last one hears about Monterey Productions is some six years later, when Pathe Labs tries to sell the negative and soundtrack of *Red River* to recover four thousand dollars it claims Monterey still owes them. The intervening years are replete, as Hawks himself delicately put it, with 'unforseen production difficulties'.

The genesis of *Red River* was an original story by Borden Chase, later published in *Saturday Evening Post* as a serial, 'The Chisholm Trail'. Chase wrote the first *Red River* screenplay and Charles Schnee was called in to tighten Chase's somewhat unwieldy and rambling narrative. The story of Tom Dunson and his cattle drive seems straightforward enough, but Hawks obviously came to feel the plot needed more explanation than the shot continuity provided. At some point in postproduction he added a voiceover narration, and as late as the dialogue continuity script those lines were to be spoken by Groot. The cutting continuity script, however, dated the same time as the dialogue script, lists the shots of the 'Early Tales of Texas' manuscript, the narrative backbone Hawks finally chose to use.

There may be no such source with the precise title 'Early Tales of Texas', but at least one of many first-hand accounts of cattle drives was almost surely used by Chase in developing his story. Joseph G. McCoy was an Illinois businessman who set up a shipping center for Texas cattle in Abilene in 1867 and wrote *Historic Sketches of the Cattle Trade of the West and the Southwest*, published in 1874. McCoy seems clearly to have been the model for Melville, who greets Matthew Garth in Abilene with the words, 'Matt, I'm the Greenwood Trading Company of Illinois.' Around the basic economic tale of a commodity finding its outlet to markets, the screenwriters and director wove their stories of men with and without women, of tyranny and rebellion and reconciliation, of a man and a boy grown up.

Hawks cast John Wayne as Dunson, Walter Brennan as Groot, and a young New York stage actor, Montgomery Clift, as Matthew Garth. Joanne Dru replaced Margaret Sheridan in the role of Tess Millay at the last minute when the latter actress became pregnant and left the cast. Location shooting began early in September 1946 at Rain Valley Ranch and other ranches south of Tucson, Arizona, and production ended in December 1946 after more than seventy shooting days. *Red River* was budgeted at approximately 2.4 million dollars, much of it provided as a production loan by Motion Picture Investors Corporation, a firm established to channel funds from individual investors into independent productions.

Rain Valley Ranch unfortunately lived up to its name, and bad weather was the first of the 'unforeseen production difficulties' to beset *Red River*.

Extra location days began to drive up the picture's cost, and years later an outfit called the Arizona Wranglers, the men who cared for the cattle, was still trying to collect 32,000 dollars in wages from Monterey Productions for the additional days. 'As you know,' Hawks wrote to Donald Nelson, president of the Society of Independent Motion Picture Producers, in May 1947, 'unforeseen production difficulties have caused this picture to cost far beyond what was originally intended,' and there were 'difficulties which still have to be met in finishing this picture.' Ultimately *Red River* was estimated to cost 4.1 million dollars, including prints and advertising.

Hawks's letter to Nelson may have had something to do with his efforts to get out of his distribution deal with United Artists and seek a distributor who would guarantee him a larger minimum return, to compensate for the additional production costs. *Red River* was completed by October 1947 but it sat on the shelf for nearly a year while Hawks wrangled and finagled. At one point there was talk of having the Motion Picture Investors Corporation foreclose on Monterey Productions and have its assets placed in the hands of a trustee; the trustee, in turn, would be free to find a new distributor.

United Artists succeeded in holding on to *Red River* through an arbitration hearing. It was the only picture that troubled company had at the time that was believed capable of realizing substantial profits. Hawks continued to balk, however. He resisted UA's plan to open the picture at its four Los Angeles Music Hall theaters, then acquiesced when Fox West Coast theaters rejected UA's offer to turn over the picture for a fifty-fifty split of the box office (*Red River* also opened at 265 theaters affiliated with the Interstate Circuit in Texas, Oklahoma, and Kansas – Chisholm Trail country).

Then *Red River* was hit with an unforeseen postproduction difficulty. In August 1948, a few weeks before the picture's scheduled opening, Howard Hughes, through the Hughes Tool Company, sued Monterey Productions for plagiarism. Hughes maintained that the climactic battle between Dunson and Matt had been copied from his controversial Western, *The Outlaw* (1943), where Billy the Kid refuses to reach for his gun though he is nicked in the ear by a shot fired by his one-time friend Doc Holliday. It so happened that Hawks had developed *The Outlaw* for Hughes and had directed at least part of the film, receiving, however, no screen credit. Within a week a settlement was reached: twenty-four seconds were cut from the *Red River* fight scene.

At last *Red River* made it to market. United Artists promoted it by a perhaps unfortunate comparison to two earlier historical epics of the West, *The Covered Wagon* (1923) and *Cimarron* (1931), dull, earnest films, much honored but quickly forgotten. Reviews were generally strong but box office was soft. *Variety*, reporting the final 4.1-million-dollar total cost for the picture, set a figure of 5 million dollars gross as its break-even point. The trade paper predicted a gross of between 4.5 and 5 million dollars from domestic box office and 2 million dollars from overseas bookings (the term 'gross' in the language of motion picture economics generally refers to rentals paid to the distributor, not total ticket sales). Though information about actual motion picture revenues is notoriously unreliable, it is estimated that *Red River* earned just under 4.5 million dollars domestically; foreign revenues are not recorded. Monterey Productions disappeared – leaving behind, as noted, several disgruntled creditors – but Hawks's 'unforeseen production difficulties' on *Red River* did not deter him from further capitalist ventures. He was to produce, through his own companies, nearly two-thirds of the dozen or so films he directed during the remainder of his career.

Themes of contract and compact are central to *Red River*. The social use of contracts goes back a long way, of course, but in modern society contracts denote economic relationships, exchanges, promises, or commitments enforceable by law; they are how business gets done in a capitalist economy. Compact, though sometimes a synonym for contract, generally has a wider meaning, as in Mayflower Compact: an agreement among many to pursue a common purpose, a tacit community of shared goals enforceable more by moral or social suasion than by law. In Hawks's visual style contract relationships are presented in closeups and two-shots, compact situations in medium and long shot, panoramas not of spectacular events but of men in groups, standing or sitting horse, talking or silently observing. On one fundamental level *Red River* is a film that asserts the superiority of compact over contract in the achievement of economic and social goals.

Tom Dunson is a man who believes in contract. The opening shots of the film define him. He is leaving the wagon train. The colonel rides up and says, 'You can't do that. You signed on. You agreed with the others.' Dunson replies, 'I signed nothing. *If I had, I'd stay.* (Emphasis added.) If you'll remember, I joined your train after you left Saint Louis.' In Borden Chase's original script Dunson *had* signed a contract and broke it to set off on his own, but Hawks and Charles Schnee wisely changed that because it destroys the grounds for his later actions.

The sanctity of contract animates Dunson's behavior throughout *Red River*. He makes his cowboys sign a contract and is willing to kill those who break it. He makes a contract with Matt to add the boy's initial to the cattle brand when he has earned it. And he contracts with Fen to come and get her. The climactic conflict in *Red River* is ultimately founded not only on the opposition between contract and compact but between two kinds of contracts Dunson and Matt have made – one between each other and one that each of them has with a woman.

The role of women in *Red River* disconcerted many of the film's contemporary reviewers. 'This is a movie about men, and for men,' *Time* magazine insisted, and both the *New Yorker* and the *New York Times* complained that the film was spoiled by Tess Millay's intervention in the fight between Dunson and Matt. For some spectators, the final scene of Millay stopping the fight does not seem to work; in fact, however, without that scene *Red River* would not hold together as it does. Instead of spoiling the film, Millay's act serves to unite its many themes.

For *Red River* also asserts the importance of women to the society and economy of the expanding American empire. After Dunson has announced his intention to leave the wagon train, he must tell Fen that he does not want to take her with him. 'Oh, you'll need me!' she argues, in her desire to go along. 'You'll need a woman. Need what a woman can give you. To do what you have to do!' Much of this scene of parting is shot so that we see only the back of Dunson's head, hiding his emotions from us. 'But you're wrong,' Fen cries, the first of many times Dunson is told that. He puts the snake bracelet on her wrist, a gift that binds him to her, emblem of his promise someday to rejoin her.

The next time Dunson sees that bracelet it is on the wrist of an Indian he has just fought and killed. 'Oh, I wish . . .' he whispers to himself, and we can complete the sentence for ourselves. The Indian raid that took Fen's life had broken Dunson's contract with her, but the snake bracelet continues to embody that obligation. The shot of the bracelet on Fen's wrist is duplicated three more times in the film – Dunson's shock of recognition exemplified in the gesture of his hand grasping another person's wrist: once it is the dead Indian's, once it is Matt's, the last time it is Millay's. This final view of the bracelet reveals a contract between Matt and Millay with which Dunson, with his views on the sanctity of contract, must come to terms.

Fen had insisted on the importance of a woman in Dunson's life. After seeing the bracelet on the Indian's wrist his face contorts momentarily, on the verge of tears. That is the first and almost the only expression of emotional vulnerability John Wayne portrays. Otherwise he plays Dunson as cold, hard, stone-faced. The second time he breaks this mask comes after Dan Latimer is trampled to death in the stampede. With his wages from the cattle drive Dan was planning to buy presents for his wife, including the red shoes she always wanted. After Dan's burial, Dunson makes arrangements for the widow. 'And . . . uh . . . get her . . . ah, anything you can think of,' he instructs Matt. 'Like a pair of red shoes, maybe?' Matt replies. Dunson blinks, as if again about to cry. He turns his back to the camera and says, 'That's the way he wanted it, wasn't it?'

Dunson's separation from the company of women also separates him from the company of men. Perhaps he would not have been so ruthless and successful a rancher and empire-builder if Fen had been along to divert and restrain him; but his human feelings would not have so atrophied that he becomes a tyrant, believing only in contractual relations, with himself as their enforcer. Yet *Red River* makes clear that even without a woman Dunson is dependent on the feminine for his achievements. In the Indian attack on Dunson and Groot the bull is spared but both his cows are slain. No cows, no herd, no ranch – a blasted dream. Before this fact has time to register on the spectator, however, the boy Matthew Garth appears with a cow; the cow had strayed and Matthew had gone searching for it, and thus escaped the slaughter of the wagon train. Matthew restores to Dunson the indispensable feminine.

Matthew serves as bearer of the feminine principle in a society of men without women. This is one of the most subtle aspects of *Red River*, brilliantly achieved by the choice of Montgomery Clift to play Matthew, and by Clift's performance. But Clift did not completely create the ambiguous elements of Matthew's character; some of those elements are even stronger in Borden Chase's original script than in the film itself. There, Cherry Valence several times tells Matthew he has the look of a man who needs a woman. He also tells him he's 'as tender as a mother and child'.

How are we to understand Matthew Garth? On one side he is a superb gunfighter, and he went off to fight in the Civil War. The boy Matthew shows his toughness when Dunson confronts Don Diego's men after crossing the Red River into Texas. Knowing a gunfight is at hand, Dunson waves the boy to step back. Matt shakes his head, no. Dunson says, 'Get away, Matt.' The boy remains by Dunson's side, and draws his gun when Dunson does.

But on the other side is the Matthew who is sensitive, virginal, soft. One of the film's most revealing moments is the first shot when Wayne and Clift appear together. Dunson has been sitting, Matt standing with one knee bent. Preparing to rise, Dunson puts his hand on Matt's knee, Matt reaches out to help Dunson straighten up. Then he rolls a cigarette, lights it, and hands it to Dunson. This is no longer the hard, slightly-crazed, boy Matthew; as Clift plays him, he is more like an androgynous Matthew.

It is the 'feminine' side of Matthew that supports Dunson, literally and figuratively, in Dunson's rise to become a powerful rancher. It is this 'soft' side that reluctantly drives Matthew to side with the cowboys against Dunson, to preserve the compact that is their hope for survival, as Dunson insists ever more cruelly on enforcing the terms of contract. But after Matthew becomes a leader of men, he must become fully a man. Hence the appearance of Millay and her seduction of him, hence the need to fight it out physically with Dunson.

'It's gonna be all right,' Groot cries when Matt at last fights back. 'For fourteen years I've been scared . . . but it's gonna be all right.' Was Groot scared that Matthew's androgyny was going to tip to the feminine side? Perhaps part of Dunson's pleasure at Matt's violent manhood, as well, is relief, a release of sexual tension aroused by the youth's feminine role in his life. Finally, with Matt fully a man, and Dunson and Matt able to express an asexual love for each other, Millay assumes the feminine influence and imposes part of what a woman, in the terms of *Red River*, can give – reconciliation between men and the promise of a normal social order.

The taming of Tom Dunson's tyranny, the proving of Matthew Garth's manhood, the assertion of Tess Millay's feminine will: these are the human elements that critics refer to, along with the spectacular scenes of the cattle drive, of course, when they speak of *Red River* as a magnificent horse opera, as a 'genuine' Western without 'some social thesis' to bother our minds. But these human struggles and events take up only the foreground of *Red River*'s larger canvas, only part of the foreground at that, and the film's critics have rarely stepped back for a wider look, for a complete view of *Red River*, seeing the human stories and the spectacle within their given frame. That frame, as *Red River* insists we recognize, is the history of American westward expansion. But many critics and spectators find it hard to recognize, because we have learned to accept the westward movement as, well, a darn good excuse for a movie, in the same class with a haunted house.

The westward movement was, of course, a series of historical events: the Indians actually were defeated and driven onto reservations, Texas actually was wrested from Mexico, Texas cattle actually did meet the railhead at Abilene. But we know all this already. That is one of the reasons we pay attention to the human and not the historical drama; the individual's destiny appears more contingent, more open, more uncertain, than the national destiny. Hawks in *Red River* is interested, however, in more than individual destiny. One of his major themes is the values and behavior of men in groups. His human concerns in *Red River* are as often social as they are individual, and the social theme inevitably links men to the process, to the contingency, to the actual events of history.

First and foremost in the historical process of the westward movement was the taking of the land. *Red River*, typical of its time and genre, could not care less about the Indians' claim to the land. The Indians appear as no more than cruel savages, obstacles to be overcome. But the Spanish-Mexican claim to the land is something else: a European title, a legal document. How can Dunson, the believer in contract, usurp the land from Don Diego, who holds land grants from a Spanish king? Groot supplies the justification: 'That's too much land for one man. Why, it ain't decent. Here's all this land aching to be used and never has been! I tell you, it ain't decent.'

The seizure of the land has a larger social purpose than personal wealth or aggrandizement: morality and utility are invoked. Dunson endorses these wider aims in his narration behind the montage sequence depicting the building of his personal empire: 'Wherever they go, they'll be on my land. My land! I'll have the brand on enough beef to . . . to feed the whole . . . country. Good beef for hungry people. Beef to make 'em strong . . . make 'em grow.' The hesitation in his voice suggest he is just discovering, indeed creating, the link between his personal empire and the nation's imperial future. It is one of the classic American visions – to do good by doing well.

And we in the audience learn that our own fates are linked with Dunson's: it was his beef, or beef from someone like him, that fed our forebears. When historical forces intervene, clouding Dunson's dream, we know that more than one man's success hangs in the balance. The Civil War impoverishes the South, leaving Texas rich in commodities – cattle – but poor in capital. Without a market, all of that meat on the hoof is not worth a cent. 'He learned that a ranch ain't only beef, but it's money,' says Groot of Dunson. 'But the war took all the money out of the South. He never knew about money, Matt, he never had none. He . . . he didn't know what to do.' Dunson begins to realize that his personal destiny is linked not only to hungry consumers, but also to Northern and Eastern capital.

Matthew makes a significant reply to Groot's explanation. 'You mean', Matthew says, 'he just doesn't know who to fight.' Dunson's skill is as a fighter – he fought the Indians, he fought Don Diego's emissaries, he fought the men who lie in seven graves on his ranch. He never knew about money, because he never had money. He is a feudal lord, and Texas is preparing to undergo the transition from feudalism to capitalism. His cowboys are not mere hired hands. They are, or were, landowners and cattle ranchers too, though their properties were destroyed, scattered, or stolen by war and postwar 'carpetbaggers'. For them the cattle drive is not simply a way to earn a living, it is their opportunity to accumulate capital, to qualify for full participation in the rewards of the new capitalist era. Their need for solidarity, for an effective working compact, is no abstract or sentimental thing, it is essential for their economic advancement.

Nowhere in *Red River* is this theme presented more vividly than in the shot that precedes the stampede. In the background of the frame, in deep focus, stand Buck Keneally, the sugar thief, pots falling all around him. In the foreground are six men in closeup, expectation and fear on their faces, looking not toward Buck but away from him and off screen, looking toward the herd. This economic theme also gives meaning to the many shots in *Red River* of men in groups, standing around, looking and listening as other men talk. Hawks in fact frames many shots with men in profile on both sides of the frame, witnessing conversations or confrontations. They are not casual observers, they are part of the compact, their futures are involved.

Far more is at stake here, for example, than a husband's wish to buy a present for his wife, 'a pair of red shoes'. Dunson's sentimentality over Dan Latimer's widow is a welcome sign of humanity but it also reveals his limitations. The loss of his woman seems in fact at times so to control his feelings that he cannot even recognize the larger issues at stake for his men. Perhaps he thinks all they want to do with their earnings is buy presents for their families, rather than what they actually do want – land, cattle, income-producing property. 'I'll do the thinking,' Dunson says, but it becomes clearer and clearer that his mode of thinking is inadequate. 'Don't tell me what to think,' Matthew at last tells him. 'I'll take your orders about work but not about what to think.'

The critical turning point comes after Teeler, Laredo, and Bill Kelsey run off. Estranged from Matt, completely drained of human feelings for his men, Dunson sends Cherry Valance to bring them back. He returns with Teeler and Laredo, having killed Kelsey. 'I'm the law,' Dunson says, preparing to hang them, marking the extreme point of his tyranny. Teeler then speaks for the compact among the men. 'You're crazy. . . . This herd don't belong to you. It belongs to every poor hopin', prayin' settleman in the whole wide State. I shouldn't have run away. I should have stayed and put a bullet in you. I signed a pledge, sure. But you ain't the man I signed it with.'

As Teeler speaks, Matt edges slowly away from Dunson's side – the opposite of the boy Matthew's behavior when Dunson tried to wave him off in the confrontation with Don Diego's men. Matthew rebels against Dunson, and Cherry Valance, the gunfighter whose last name means an ornamental piece of drapery, sides with Matthew. Ornamental Cherry may be, particularly for his taunting of Matt and his threat to get Matt's gun (symbol-readers may do what they will with the fact that a man named Cherry wants another man's 'gun'); but he understands the capitalist imperatives as well as any other of the men.

The cattle get to Abilene, Northern capitalism makes its appearance ('I'm the Greenwood Trading Company of Illinois'), and Thomas Dunson, by proxy, is introduced to capitalism by means of a bank check for his cattle. The heroes and heroines of the American West have suffered their struggles and tribulations, have made their legends, in service of a larger social purpose. Texas beef will make Americans strong in body; sold to the world, it will make America strong in balance of payments.

Red River was an imperialist film for an imperialist era in American life. That it ends with a woman firing a gun at two brawling Texas gunmen, who, it turns out, are expressing their love for each other, only serves to remind us, after all, how benign the behavior and purposes of Americans really are.

Notes

The Howard Hawks Collection in the Arts and Communications Archives, Harold B. Lee Library, Brigham Young University, contains considerable material on *Red River*, including the original Borden Chase script, final dialogue continuity and cutting continuity scripts, and files pertaining to production, advertising copy and strategy, correspondence, and newspaper reviews. I wish to express my thanks to James V. D'Arc, Curator, Arts and Communications Archives, for his aid in my use of this material. A useful file of materials on *Red River*, mainly clippings, is in the Margaret Herrick Library of the Academy of Motion Picture Arts and Sciences, Los Angeles.

Red River dialogue quotations are taken from the dialogue continuity script in the Harold B. Lee Library and checked against the actual film.

Information on *Red River* reviews comes from the Academy files. Dates of cited reviews are as follows: *Time*, 11 October 1948; *Collier's*, 9 October 1948; *New Yorker*, 9 October 1948; *New York Times*, 10 October 1948.

Information on *Red River* production and postproduction, as well as financial data, comes from the Production and Correspondence files in the Howard Hawks Collection, and from clippings in the Academy file, including the following: *Variety*, 30 July, 16 August, 23 August, and 7 December 1948; *Daily Variety*, 3 August 1948; *Hollywood Reporter*, 16 August 1948; *Los Angeles Times*, 20 August 1948; *New York Times*, 2 February 1948; *Hollywood Citizen-News*, 18 August 1952.

Hawks's letter to Donald Nelson, 9 May 1947, is in the Correspondence file of the Howard Hawks Collection.

André Bazin's remarks on *Red River* appear in his essay, 'The Evolution of the Western', in *What Is Cinema?*, Volume II, essays selected and translated by Hugh Gray (Berkeley, Calif.: 1971), p. 154. Pauline Kael's description of *Red River* is in *Kiss Kiss Bang Bang* (Boston: 1968), p. 338. An extensive treatment of *Red River* is in Donald C. Willis, *The Films of Howard Hawks* (Metuchen, NJ: 1975), pp. 43–55. Among other writings on the film see Robin Wood, *Howard Hawks* (Garden City, NY: 1968) and Leo Braudy, *The World in a Frame* (Garden City, NY: 1976). A significant critique of Hawks that does not mention *Red River* is in Peter Wollen, *Signs and Meaning in the Cinema* (Bloomington, Ind.: 1969). George N. Fenin and William K. Everson, *The Western* (New York: 1962), consider *Red River* 'pedestrian', p. 331. Information on Hawks's dealings with United Artists is in Tino Balio, *United Artists: The Company Built by the Stars* (Madison, Wis.: 1976).

Robert Sklar's essay on *Red River* offers an analysis of the underlying ideological assumptions and implications of the film. The project of ideological analysis derives from the Marxist-inspired theorizing about film developed in the late 1960s and 1970s within *Cahiers du Cinéma* and elsewhere in France and then, inspired particularly by French thinking, in *Screen* in Britain. For example, Jean-Louis Comolli and Jean Narboni's 'Cinema/Ideology/Criticism', first published in *Cahiers du Cinéma*, October 1969, was translated in *Screen*, vol. 12, no. 1, Spring 1971 (reprinted in, for example, Bill Nichols (ed.), *Movies and Methods*, Vol. 1 (Berkeley: University of California Press, 1976). Just as Sklar's analytical approach could be said to be of its time, so the imperialist ideology which he discovers at work in *Red River* is of its time (and place), as Sklar argues. The additional interest of Sklar's essay is his attempt to tie his ideological analysis to Hawks's attempt, as an independent producer, to change the nature of the way films were made in Hollywood, at a time when Hollywood was in the throes of the anti-trust legal moves which were to lead to the demise of the 'studio system' as it had been known. This additional perspective relates Sklar's essay to other contemporary and later explorations, like Richard B. Jewell's essay on the production of *Bringing Up Baby* which follows, of how film production actually worked and how a producer-director like Hawks could function within it.

Very different interpretations of *Red River* are offered by, for example, Robin Wood in *Howard Hawks* and David Thomson in his intriguing account in *Sight and Sound* of his changing responses to the film over the years, 'All Along the River'.

Retrospect

ROBIN WOOD

From Robin Wood, *Howard Hawks*, 2nd edition (London: British Film Institute, 1981).

I am on principle against revising one's past work: it can lead only to confusion and anomaly. Inevitably, one moves on; were I to write a book on Hawks today, it would differ not merely in occasional sentences and a few judgments, it would be written differently throughout. In the rapidly evolving discipline of film criticism, any interest that one can hope one's earlier work will continue to have must be seen in two interacting historical contexts: the state of criticism when the work was produced, and the stage of the critic's personal growth. Revision blurs the clarity of these contexts without significantly translating the work into their present equivalents. I have therefore left this book exactly as it was written, preferring to add a further essay that speaks from my current position.

The book's general approach and emphasis were clearly determined by the evolution of the auteur theory in the early 70s. This was responsible for two tendencies (both here and in film criticism of that period generally) that now appear as failings, or at least serious limitations: the tendency to restrict one's sense of a film's interest and value to what could be shown to be the contribution of its director; the tendency to abstract individual artists from their society – a tendency epitomised by the widespread impulse to construct 'pantheons', the significance of whose gods was somehow eternal and unchanging. The significance of a work of art can only be grasped, in fact, within the contexts of two cultures (or states of culture): the culture that produced it, and the culture within which it is experienced. Our relationship to (hence our reading of) Shakespeare's plays, for example, unless we fossilise them as museum exhibits (the ultimate distortion), cannot possibly be the same as that of an Elizabethan, or of spectators in the eighteenth or nineteenth centuries.

My own work, and the position underlying it, have evolved considerably since the mid-60s when the book was written – a development provoked partly by professional challenges (notably the work of *Screen* and the wider critical movement of which *Screen* is one representative), partly by changes in my personal life (notably my 'coming out' as gay). I now see Hawks's films from a different perspective (in which Gay Liberation and Feminism have major roles); accordingly, the films change, reveal new aspects, new

163

implications, new uses. This is not, I think, to distort the films, to twist them to particular ends. In a sense, *any* interpretation distorts, since no reading can escape particular personal/cultural emphasis. But semiology has confirmed what the more intelligent traditional criticism has always observed: that a given work of art, or a given artist, does not have a single, finite meaning that can be fixed for all time, but is the point of intersection of a multiplicity of interacting codes, hence capable of surrendering a range of meanings, the choice of which will be determined by the requirements of the situation within which work or artist is perceived.

Hawks and Hollywood Ideology

By the term 'Hollywood ideology' I wish to convey the set of assumptions which classical Hollywood cinema tends *overall* to reproduce and reinforce. I do not mean to suggest that it corresponds closely to the ways in which individual Americans live and think or to the ways in which individual films actually work (if the latter were true, one would not need to bother oneself with Hollywood beyond the sort of cursory blanket dismissal favoured by intellectuals prior to the 50s). But it is clear enough that Hollywood has part-created, and done much to perpetuate, a body of myth (in the sense in which Barthes uses the term in *Mythologies*) which one must feel has played a dominant role in our culture, shaping our values, assumptions and aspirations.

The simplest embodiment of this ideology is the Hays Office Code, a set of rules explicitly elaborated to protect the American Way of Life. The *need* for such a code itself testifies eloquently to the continual conflict in the Hollywood cinema between the dominant ideology and the powerful impulses driving to its subversion, which go far beyond the attempts to get away with being 'naughty' to which conventional film historians and *aficionados* of Mae West tend to reduce them. The basic principles can be put quite simply: capitalism, the right to ownership; the home, the family, the monogamous couple; patriarchy, with man as adventurer/pioneer/ builder/breadwinner, woman as wife/mother/educator/centre of civilisation (the 'feminine' sensibility); the 'decent' containment of sexuality/love within its structure, its permitted manifestations governed by the foregoing principles and deviation from them punished; the general sense that all problems can be resolved within the system – that, although it may be in need of a bit of reform and improvement here and there, the system is fundamentally good (natural, true) and radical change inappropriate. (Indeed, one of the main functions of this ideology is, by 'naturalising' cultural assumptions, to render alternatives literally unthinkable.)

This ideology is challenged implicitly across the whole spectrum of the Hollywood cinema, most obviously in certain genres (for example, film noir) or in the work of certain directors (for example, Sirk); though it must be said that this obviousness was not apparent to audiences when the films were made. Crucial here is the concept of 'entertainment', that extraordinary two-edged weapon of the capitalist establishment. Entertainment is the means whereby the exploited are kept happy and unaware; it is also (because, by definition, not taken seriously – 'it's only entertainment' is a phrase commonly used to render any further discussion superfluous and even foolish) the means whereby in disguised forms, like Freudian dreams evading the 'censor' in sleep, the most subversive impulses can find expression in an apparently harmless or insignificant form.

The interest of Hawks's work – from the general ideas and attitudes abstractable from it, down to the vivid detail of performance that gives his best films their inexhaustible freshness – derives from its ambiguous relationship to the dominant Hollywood ideology. Safely contained within the 'entertainment' format, and invariably discussed by their director in terms of character and action with very little thematic (let alone ideological) awareness, the films maintain this ambiguity on every level. Consider the relationship of the male groups of the adventure films to established capitalist society. Dependent upon, and supportive of, that society, the groups actually embody values which are either irrelevant or antagonistic to it. The mail-plane fliers of *Only Angels Have Wings*, the sheriff and deputies of *Rio Bravo*, the animal catchers of *Hatari!*, all nominally serve the interests of society, yet are never motivated by that aim, which is relegated to the status of pretext. The values the films celebrate – a sort of primitive existentialism rooted in notions of self-respect, personal integrity, intuitive recognition and loyalty between individuals (the account expounded in this book seems to me still to stand up) – render irrelevant the accumulation of wealth and the development of civilisation.

Most striking – and so much commented on that it is unnecessary to do more than glance at it here – is the films' treatment of the whole monogamy/family/home syndrome, conspicuous mainly for its absence. Almost no Hawks film is centred on a stable marriage relationship; the one obvious exception (*Monkey Business*) is concerned, characteristically, with the release of all the impulses which 'stability' represses. Children in the Hawks world are wizened little grotesques (George Winslow in *Monkey Business* and *Gentlemen Prefer Blondes* is the definitive embodiment) who seem to have sprung from nowhere: one scarcely imagines them having parents or family backgrounds. Hawks was always content to work within the established genres, and the narrative structures of the films are therefore determined overall by the ideological system the genres variously embody: they move inevitably towards the establishment of the monogamous heterosexual couple. The strength and conviction of such generic resolutions, however, are everywhere undermined by the pervasive sense of impermanence that characterises Hawks's world. This conflict sometimes produces flaws in the films' narrative coherence, a danger that even *Rio Bravo* (still in my opinion Hawks's masterpiece, the definitive elaboration of his 'world') does not escape. The final John Wayne/Angie Dickinson scene in that film is curiously redundant: the tension it appears to be resolving was resolved much earlier in the film. What the logic of the narrative demands is a further *development* of the relationship; Hawks, unable to imagine this, produces only repetition. Interestingly, the corresponding scene in *El Dorado*, resolving the Wayne/Charlene Holt relationship, is simply absent, a curious and troubling hiatus in the narrative (troubling, that is, in terms of the expectations Hollywood narrative traditionally satisfies). In the Hawks universe there is no past (except as an unfortunate experience to be got over and forgotten) and no future (everyone may be dead by tomorrow); life is lived, spontaneously and exhilaratingly, in the present.

The concept seems to me perfectly realised in the ending of *To Have and Have Not*. Earlier in the film, Cricket (Hoagy Carmichael) is composing a song at the piano while talking with Lauren Bacall about her relationship with Bogart; he has the melody but can't think of the words. His line to Bacall, 'Maybe it's better this way', is subsequently incorporated (with slight variation) in the song-text: the song, 'How Little We Know', later performed by Bacall in Bogart's presence, becomes a statement about their relationship. When, at the end of the film, Cricket asks Bacall whether she's still happy, her reply ('What do *you* think?') provokes him to a jazz version of the tune which accompanies her famous hip-wiggling walk out into the fog and the total uncertainty of the future. Any *generic* guarantee of permanence for the couple is decisively undercut: 'Maybe it's just for a day ...'

Hawks's Women

The characteristics of the Hawks woman have been thoroughly defined, and there is no need to recapitulate them here; no one, presumably, will now wish to enrol her in the Feminist cause. The women in Hawks's films, for all their vividness and idiosyncrasy, are clearly conceived from the male viewpoint: one would not wish to claim that women find a 'voice' in the films that is not male-determined. This is as true of the one Hawks film centred on women, *Gentlemen Prefer Blondes*, as of the rest: Marilyn Monroe and Jane Russell are there very clearly the embodiments of contrasted yet complementary male fantasies. The force of this generalisation is evident in the absence of female friendships or alliances in Hawks's work. Women, on the contrary, are conceived as rivals for the male, hence as his subordinates, their meaning given only in relation to him. One notes the instant antagonisms between Jean Arthur and Rita Hayworth in *Only Angels Have Wings*, Lauren Bacall and Dolores Moran in *To Have and Have Not*, Ginger Rogers and Marilyn Monroe in *Monkey Business*. The great exception, apart from *Gentlemen Prefer Blondes*, is *Red Line 7000*, with its Gail Hire/Charlene Holt partnership, their support of Laura Devon, and especially, the delightful scene in which Gail Hire and Marianna Hill discover an instant rapport *although* they are rivals for the same man, and exclude him from their conviviality of speaking French to each other. But the continuing delight of that film (my high estimate of which still stands, despite widespread opposition) is partly in its promise of entirely new developments in Hawks's thematic concerns, unfortunately not realised in his two subsequent films.

If Hawks's presentation of women certainly does not escape determination by the dominant sexist ideology, the Feminist tendency simply to dismiss it on those grounds seems somewhat hasty. The Feminist animus against Hawks comes out perhaps in the gross distortions of Laura

Mulvey's article in *Screen*, 'Narrative Form and Visual Pleasure', in which she offers the following remarkable account of *To Have and Have Not*:

> . . . the film opens with the woman as object of the combined gaze of spectator and all the male protagonists in the film. But as the narrative progresses she falls in love with the main male protagonist and becomes his property, losing her outward glamorous characteristics, her generalised sexuality, her show-girl connotations; her eroticism is subjected to the male star alone.

That Lauren Bacall does not appear in the film for the first ten minutes is perhaps a minor quibble. What is more important is that her 'show-girl' attributes only become prominent as the film progresses: though she sings casually and 'improvisationally' with Hoagy Carmichael earlier, her main number occurs about twenty minutes before the end, and her final exit very clearly emphasises the 'show-girl' characteristics. Her submission to the male has to be seen in the context of the Hawksian uncertainty: it is clearly provisional.

Despite the extreme freedom of the adaptation, it is instructive to compare *To Have and Have Not* with its source, the Hemingway novel. It is tempting to use the novel and the film to develop a thesis about the increasing richness of the popular cinema during the first half of the twentieth century and the corresponding impoverishment of 'serious' literature. Though such a thesis can scarcely stand on the comparison of one novel with one film, the juxtaposition beautifully exemplifies the differences, in our age, between solitary, alienated art and communal, integrated art. It is a matter of more than a simple distinction, the fact that just one person writes a novel while a number of people – director, screenwriter, actors, technicians – collaborate on a film. By its popular nature, the Hollywood film is subject to a complex network of social/cultural determinants beyond the analysable contributions of individuals, becoming, though not unequivocally, the expression of a culture.

This is not to suggest that Hemingway's book, because the work of a so-called 'serious' novelist, escapes ideological determination. Though ostensibly an outspoken anti-Establishment 'protest' work, it is more impoverished and constrained by ideological determination than Hawks's film – to be more precise, impoverished by the failure of its efforts to escape ideological determination. It seems to me an almost completely unprofitable work. On the one hand, its 'social protest' seriousness denies the reader what has traditionally been the most essential profit from art, if also the most dangerous: spontaneous delight, the kind of response Hawks's film evokes whenever it is shown. Such delight is itself complex: partly a satisfaction in being given what we want (which may be merely what we have been taught to want), but partly a delight in surprise, or a delight arising out of the tension between the familiar and the unexpected, the creative use of conventions; it is also, at its best, a delight in freely functioning creativity (another dangerous, but I still believe indispensable concept). Hemingway's creativity in his meagre (not just in length) novel doesn't seem to function very freely. While denying us delight, the book falls everywhere into the simplest ideological traps. An attack on the capitalist social set-up, it can envisage no systematic alternative, in fact negating the possibility of imagining one (see its treatment of Communists and revolutionaries), and celebrates an independent outsider whose admirableness depends on his remaining just that. As all rich people are decadent and miserable (i.e. either promiscuous or impotent), and Harry and Marie are so healthy (i.e. faithful and strongly sexed), the secret moral is clearly that poverty is better for you.

As for the presentation of women, Feminists may not be exactly falling over themselves to applaud Hawks's treatment of Lauren Bacall in the movie, but Hemingway's Marie must be one of the all-time sexist archetypes: a female character conceived exclusively as a medium for the worship of male potency, her attitude to Harry being one of simple adoration, apart from which she has no function in the book and no independent existence, even (or especially) after Harry's death. The book's morbid preoccupation with impotence on the one hand and the fantasies of super-sexuality embodied in Harry Morgan on the other goes with our sense of Hemingway's isolation and clearly determines the presentation of Marie (Altman caught the whole syndrome very well in the Sterling Hayden character of *The Long Goodbye*, confessedly based on Hemingway). It is the Hawksian context, similarly, that makes possible the Marie of the film (or 'Slim', as she quickly becomes), her comparative independence centred on what Mulvey calls her 'show-girl' attributes, which allow her a measure of self-assertion (albeit as entertainer for a male audience). Her relationship with Hoagy Carmichael (built, as so often with Hawks, on a shared song – see *The Big Sky*, *Rio Bravo*, *Red Line 7000*) is important here, a relationship of equality and creativity. Hemingway's Marie has no meaning after Harry's death; Hawks's is a woman who will always be able to take care of herself, whatever happens to her man.

With Hawks's women, the principle of ambiguity again operates. The clearest way to establish this is to extend the now standard comparison with women in the films of Ford. The Fordian world view provides Woman with an entirely logical and central role: she is wife and mother, at once the validation for the man's building of civilisation and the guarantee of its continuance; she is essential to the transmission of values from past to future. A sequence of scenes early in *Young Mr Lincoln* exemplifies this precisely. Lincoln, still a humble shopkeeper, encounters a family who want to trade with him: the image of the covered wagon led by the father, with the two sons inside presided over by the mother, is itself an archetypal Fordian image of order and family. The mother mentions an old barrel which 'might be worth fifty cents'; the father recalls that it's full of books, which belonged to his grandfather. From this Lincoln inherits the book of the Law (Blackstone's *Commentaries*) – the Law of patriarchy which the mother, significantly, is debarred from reading; *her* function has been to preserve the books in perfect condition, not to understand them. There follows the scene with Ann Rutledge, a scene rich in the myths of our culture. Before Ann appears, Lincoln, amid the multitudinous signifiers of natural fertility, has translated the legal rights and wrongs of Blackstone (the basis of Western capitalism, in effect) into universal Right and Wrong: a marvellously concise example of the naturalisation of ideological assumptions. It is Ann's function not to teach but to inspire: she exemplifies the myth of the 'great woman behind every great man', urging Lincoln (who alone possesses knowledge) to 'make something of himself'. Abruptly, Ann is dead, but ice is breaking up on the swift-flowing river and Lincoln brings the first spring flowers to her grave. It is her continuing influence that drives Lincoln on, his allegiance to her memory (as also to the memory of his mother, who is 'resurrected' in Mrs Clay) being crucially important.

Hawks's attitude to women, like Ford's, cannot be separated from his attitude to death, to society, to tradition. With the Fordian address to the grave (repeated in *My Darling Clementine* and *She Wore a Yellow Ribbon*) compare the famous steak scene of *Only Angels Have Wings* ('Who's Joe?'). With Ford's insistence on the future developing out of the past, a past which must always be revered, commemorated in transmitted ritual, compare the Hawksian insistence on life in the present. One might, I think, claim that Ford's work embodies the traditional concept of the woman's role under patriarchy at its noblest, finest, most respectable. In Hawks's world that role has no possible place: woman is unnecessary, either as a pretext for the building of civilisation or as its preserver and transmitter. Hawks's male groups are clearly patriarchal (the leader is actually addressed as 'Poppa' in, for example, *Only Angels Have Wings* and *Rio Bravo*), but they lack a crucial constituent of traditional (or Fordian) patriarchy, the notion of inheritance which gives woman her function. There lies the enormous interest of Hawks's women: they are anomalous and threatening, but *there*. The much-noted attempt to turn them into men never quite works: they remain, obstinately, men/women, demanding a recognition somewhat different from that exchanged between the males; they are a permanent problem, as they scarcely are in Ford.

Hawks's cinema, in other words, if it never offers any positive approach towards establishing a new female consciousness, raises the problem of the woman's role as it is raised nowhere else in classical cinema, by removing or rendering irrelevant the role which the woman traditionally fills. I think it is this, as much as the desire on Hawks's part to provide male fantasy-figures, which may account for the remarkable and (whatever ideological uneasiness one may feel) perpetually fresh aliveness of so many actresses' performances in his films: the assertion of life, the refusal to be confined in the traditional role, repeatedly undermines the generic patterns of resolution.

Male Relationships

The interest which Hawks's work can be argued to have for Feminism is exactly paralleled by its interest for Gay Liberation. Again, there is no question whatever of the films producing a clear-cut positive image of gay relationships that could be felt to have direct political force; again, the operative word must be 'ambiguity'; yet again, within the classical Hollywood context, the films raise questions, open up possibilities.

Many critics have sensed the presence of a gay subtext running right through Hawks's output. Its presence would, of course, have been vehemently denied by Hawks himself, though he was able to describe two of his films (*A Girl in Every Port*, *The Big Sky*) as 'a love story between two men'. A practice common to so many recent 'male bonding' films (e.g. *California Split*, *Midnight Cowboy*, *Scarecrow*) whereby the possible homosexual implications of the heroes' relationships are disowned by being projected on to an effeminate, ridiculous or vicious minor character, is fully anticipated in *Fig Leaves*. *A Girl in Every Port* stands out as the one film in which a close male relationship is finally confirmed, the girl (Louise Brooks) being dismissed from the film. Elsewhere, the progress is towards a heterosexual resolution (*The Big Sky*, *Red River*, *Rio Bravo*, *El Dorado*) or the death of one of the men (*Dawn Patrol*, Thomas Mitchell in *Only Angels Have Wings*). There are numerous striking examples of homosexual symbolism in Hawks's films, of which the most overt is perhaps the Montgomery Clift/John Ireland shooting contest in *Red River* (a scene unfortunately cut from the British release prints), for which the men exchange guns, with clear mutual admiration (Ireland subsequently gives as his reason for joining the cattle drive the hope that he may get Clift's gun some day). The way Hawks plays with, then rejects, homosexual attraction is neatly epitomised in a tiny, characteristic moment in *The Thing*, difficult to convey in words because it depends entirely on the way two men look at, and smile at, each other: the moment where the sergeant (Dewey Martin) manoeuvres the captain (Kenneth Tobey) into shortening the watches over the monster in the ice and says, 'I think you're right, Captain.' The looks exchanged and the smile of mutual affection are both intimate and held; then the captain looks across at the woman Nicky (who has a male name and wears trousers), and crosses the room to join her.

One also notes the procession of young men (particularly in Hawks's later work) who have the appearance of gay male icons and whose role invariably involves a close intimacy with the hero, carrying the constant (if constantly submerged) impression of being a potential alternative to the woman: Montgomery Clift in *Red River*, Dewey Martin in *The Big Sky* and *The Thing*, Ricky Nelson in *Rio Bravo*, James Caan in *El Dorado*.

Reversals

The sexual relationships in Hawks's work have finally to be seen in the context of its most curious and consistent phenomenon, the obsession with reversal-patterns. It is a commonplace of Hawks criticism that his entire work is structured on reversal: the opposition between the adventure films and the comedies, however one reads it. The opposition is not as neat or complete as is sometimes suggested: it is synthesised, for example, in *Rio Bravo*, the elements of Hawksian comedy (notably the scenes involving Angie Dickinson) being successfully integrated within the 'adventure' framework.

Further, certain films reverse the reversal, so to speak, their auteur structure relating them to their generic opposites: thus *Scarface* belongs with the comedies and *His Girl Friday* with the adventure films (the male group isolated from yet attached to society, the hero in control throughout). The opposition holds good in general, however; one way of defining it is to consider the notion of chaos that is everywhere near the surface of Hawks's world. In the adventure films, centred on the male group, chaos is *out there* (the Andes mountains, the jungles of the Pacific islands, the Arctic wastes); the master motif (literal or metaphoric) is the small circle of light amid the surrounding darkness. In the comedies, set inside established society, chaos erupts from within. It carries quite different connotations in the two situations: in the adventure films it is a threat held at bay by the values of the group (self-respect, loyalty, spontaneous affection and sharing); in the comedies what is threatened (the established social order) is not valued, and the eruption of chaos becomes liberating and positive.

It is in the comedies (or the lighter adventure films like *The Thing* and *Hatari!*) that reversal-patterns are most prominent and central (though not of course restricted to them). Children and adults are reversed in *The Ransom of Red Chief* (the child dominating the adults), *Gentlemen Prefer Blondes* (as Hawks himself put it, the child was the only adult on the ship) and, supremely, *Monkey Business*, where adults literally become children (in behaviour if not appearance). Primitive and civilised are reversed in *Monkey Business* (Cary Grant as Red Indian) and, intricately, in *Hatari!*, where Elsa Martinelli's initiation into the Warusha tribe, her skin blackened, is followed by the scene where she is covered in her 'civilised' warpaint, cold cream. *Hatari!* also reverses animals and humans, with Martinelli becoming the 'mother' of three baby elephants; the film opens with truck and jeep converging on a rhinoceros on the veld and ends (almost) with the elephants converging on the woman in a supermarket. Most curiously, *The Thing*, with its 'intellectual carrot', reverses human and vegetable. All these reversals are manifestations of the chaos that the civilised order suppresses; apart from the human/vegetable reversal in *The Thing*, all are regarded at least ambivalently, with good humour; most carry strong positive connotations. An alternative word for reversal here is 'interchangeability'.

The master reversal-pattern, and surely the key to this phenomenon in Hawks, is of course that of male and female. In *Fig Leaves* there is a mock-courtship scene in which one of the men plays the woman's role. Men wear women's clothes in *Bringing Up Baby*, *I Was a Male War Bride*, *Monkey Business*, *Gentlemen Prefer Blondes* and, almost, *Rio Bravo* (the red bloomers held up against John Wayne). In *The Big Sky* a huge Frenchman pretends to be a woman in a dance on the ship's deck. In *His Girl Friday* Rosalind Russell literally plays the 'man's role'. Women wear masculine clothes in *I Was a Male War Bride*, *The Thing* and *Hatari!*; according to Hawks (*Wide Angle*, Summer 1976), he gave Sternberg the idea of dressing Dietrich in men's clothes for her first stage appearance in *Morocco*, including, embryonically, the exchange with a woman in the audience – a scene rich in bisexual connotations. A distinction needs to be made here. Consistently in the films it is funny for men to dress as women, but attractive and enhancing for women to dress as men; the men are in drag, the women in work-clothes of uniform. Nevertheless, the implication of interchangeability or role reversal is clearly there.

One less obvious but highly suggestive example is worth registering in detail: the interchangeability of Angie Dickinson in *Rio Bravo* and James Caan in *El Dorado*. Both are travelling people, and gamblers; both are given the same little bit of business with a pack of cards; both are identified by idiosyncratic clothing (Caan's hat, Dickinson's feathers); both stay on (in the long-standing tradition of Hawks heroines – cf. *Only Angels Have Wings* and *To Have and Have Not*) after Wayne has dismissed them; both simultaneously attract and exasperate him; both have the same line, 'I always make you mad, don't I?' That Caan, rather than Charlene Holt, is the film's replacement for Dickinson and *almost* becomes the love-interest may help to account for the absence of the expected, really obligatory, John Wayne/Charlene Holt resolution at the end, especially as the Caan character's heterosexual relationship is also left unconfirmed. One has the sense that Hawks was simply unable to close the film; he pulls back on the 'safe' buddy-relationship of Wayne and Mitchum.

In Hawks's world everything is potentially reversible or interchangeable; that is the real meaning of the chaos so ambivalently viewed, through the dual perspective of the adventure films and the comedies. The central, though always suppressed or disguised, drive of his work overall is towards the ultimate in interchangeability, bisexuality – the final breakdown of the established social order, the release, at once terrifying and exhilarating, of what society most fundamentally represses.

Classicism and Containment
There is a brief sequence in *The Thing*, showing the flight back to base from the location where the flying saucer has been inadvertently destroyed and the monster dug out of the ice. A shot establishing the situation – a general view of the plane's interior – is followed by a sequence of five shots which is perfectly symmetrical in structure. Shots 1 and 5 show the captain and navigator in the cockpit, the camera filming them from the front; shots 2 and 4 are the reverse of these, looking from inside the plane into the cockpit, as the men discuss the nature and significance of the creature in the ice. The central, pivotal, shot shows the block of ice, the husky dogs uneasy around it. The sequence begins with light banter between the men, and ends with a joke involving the repetition of the long number of a bulletin. The banter and the joke *contain* the brief, central moment of terror, providing a means of either denying or distancing the threat of the unknown ('chaos').

The sequence can be taken as the epitome of Hawks's classicism, which is both the classicism of Hollywood (invisible technique, symmetry, orderly and logical narrative, economy of means) and an attitude to life. Classicism is Hawks's means of containing the chaos to which his work points, and which the comedies ambivalently celebrate.

172

The *Rio Bravo* song sequence can stand as the perfect enactment of the working of this classicism/containment in relation to male love or attraction in Hawks's work. The first song ('My rifle, my pony and me') opens with a close-up of Dean Martin, singing unaccompanied, as if he were alone; when the camera draws back to reveal the presence of the other men, the song develops into a 'love duet' for Martin and Ricky Nelson. The editing excludes both Walter Brennan and Wayne during this, concentrating attention on the intimate exchange of looks between the two – those looks of mutual admiration and affection that recur throughout Hawks's work. When the song ends, Stumpy/Brennan demands '. . . something I can join in', and we have the folk song 'Cindy' with its communal refrain: the potentially 'dangerous' love-relationship is contained, and redefined, by the integration of the couple in the group, the sequence moving to a final group shot that unites the three men and Wayne, paternally looking on.

What I have called 'containment' Andrew Britton calls 'repression': one's final attitude to Hawks may well depend on the distinction between the two terms. I don't think one has any right to demand that an artist's work reflect or reinforce one's own ideology; one wants rather to define the relationship between them. Hawks's work is *both* progressive and conservative, at once opening up possibilities of 'chaos' and formally containing them. It cannot be claimed that Hawks's work embodies a viable alternative to established Western culture, but it would be quite unreasonable to demand that it should: such a project has never been a necessary function of art. What it represents is an inexhaustibly fascinating and suggestive *intervention*, which raises the most fundamental questions about the nature of our culture and the ideological assumptions that structure it. Apparently safely contained within Hollywood Classicism and the 'entertainment' syndrome, its implications throw everything open, put everything into question.

(This essay owes much to the influence of Andrew Britton and Richard Dyer, though both would probably disagree with its conclusions.)

Sensibly, Robin Wood has resisted rewriting his earlier work, but at the same time he has been very open to looking back and reflecting upon it. In the case of Hawks, as Wood himself points out in this postscript to the original book, Wood's ideas have been modified by the centrality to 1970s and 1980s debates about the film of the concept of ideology, by the decisive role played in film writing since the 1970s by feminist film criticism, and by his own 'coming out' as gay in the 1970s. This gay perspective was first explored at length in a 1978 essay in *Film Comment*, 'Responsibilities of a Gay Film Critic', where Wood reconsiders his earlier views on Renoir, Bergman and Hawks, saying that his Hawks book is the one that would least embarrass him.

Wood's work with the concept of ideology has often been very productive (see for example, 'Ideology, Genre, Auteur: *Shadow of a Doubt*', reprinted in *Hitchcock's Films Revisited* (New York: Columbia University Press, 1989), and the later writing collected in *Hollywood from Vietnam to Reagan* (New York and Guildford, Surrey: Columbia University Press, 1986)). However, his engagement with feminist critiques of Hawks's representation of women is somewhat less satisfying. Having got the title of Laura Mulvey's ground-breaking essay wrong (it is titled 'Visual Pleasure and Narrative Cinema'), Wood also has an odd overall perspective. It is not clear what writing Wood has in mind, but it is certainly difficult to think of what Haskell and Wise have to say as 'animus against Hawks'. Probably, Wood has in mind the more theoretical writing of critics like Mulvey. Mulvey, clearly, is not being 'dismissive' of Hawks but her fascination with and enjoyment of Hawks – so evident in her essay on *Gentlemen Prefer Blondes* in this volume – does not prevent her from trying to discern the ideological mechanisms at work, just as Wood tries to do, albeit with a different agenda. Finally, though, Wood's stress here on 'ambiguity' and 'suggestive intervention' go a long way to explaining the continuing richness and fascination found by so many in Hawks's work.

How Howard Hawks Brought *Baby* Up: An Apologia for the Studio System

RICHARD B. JEWELL

From *Journal of Popular Film and Television*, vol. 11, no. 4, Winter 1984.

When the merging of studios, exchanges and theaters into a few large corporations, and the extravagances of the 'out-spending' era, had brought an end to the independent production, the inelastic methods of bureaucracy replaced the loose practices of democracy in picture making. Now a new idea, instead of having to win the 'OK' of one autocrat of a little kingdom, had to run the gauntlet of editorial boards, production committees, and conferences of various sorts. A multitude of alleged experts awaited the fellow with the new thought, and when his innovation had completed the circuit of the studio's intricate system there was seldom a trace of originality left in it. The sharp shears and heavy smoothing-irons of the experts had transformed the wild, crazy idea to one of the rigid patterns in favor, at the time, with the studio head and his yes-men and yes-women.

Benjamin B. Hampton, 1931[1]

Production methods under this rigid system became mechanized: the 'assembly line' appeared in Hollywood. The resulting standardization of pictures caused the downfall of the most important directors during the late twenties. The various branches of production were divided and specialized so specifically and minutely that directors had a lessening opportunity to contribute to the whole. Most directors became 'glorified foremen' under the producer-supervisors.

Lewis Jacobs, 1939[2]

Many books and articles dealing with the American cinema have been written since Benjamin Hampton and Lewis Jacobs completed their pioneering studies in the 1930s. Yet the basic descriptions which these two men applied to the studio system, and the general hostility which they expressed toward it, still predominate in contemporary scholarship. No fewer than six recent and major books utilize Jacobs's 'factory' and 'assembly-line' analogies in their discussions of Hollywood's major studios.[3] Although most qualify their assessments to some extent, the authors of these books tend to agree with Hampton and Jacobs that the studios were bureaucratic, impersonal, conservative, rigidly structured, and antagonistic to technical innovation and artistic achievement. Men and women of taste, intelligence, and imagination are often portrayed as being destroyed by this system – either squandering their talents by producing the formulaic, escapist entertainment demanded by the system, or rebelling against it, only to be crushed (e.g., von Stroheim) by its steamrolling, assembly-line operations.

The authors often find themselves with a major predicament when they move beyond these general evaluations of the studios to more specific discussions of the film-makers who worked for them. The writers admire the works of many of these directors, so they are faced with explaining how their favorites could make exemplary films within such a restrictive organizational structure. Here is one representative attempt to reconcile the contradiction:

> These Hollywood directors worked under studio rule, presumably as journeymen employees involved in the mass production of popular entertainment. They were assigned a script rather than choosing one. They were given a cast of performers and told by a producer to shoot the film in so many days. . . . Yet despite all these restrictions and enforced collaborations, somehow these directors, over the years, managed to make films which were stamped with their particular vision.[4]

This type of argument is wonderfully romantic. It conjures up visions of an elite cadre of auteur supermen bending an iron-clad system to their wills or, at the very least, of a slippery band of Houdinis able to wriggle out of their studio straitjackets and 'be free'. Unfortunately, the explanation does not provide a clue as to how the directors managed these feats of creative hocus-pocus.

The recent availability of studio records – dusty and unmagical though they may be – will help fill in many important gaps in Hollywood scholarship and provide some specific answers to the studio versus auteur dilemma. By studying the production histories of individual films, we gain a more complete understanding of how the studios actually functioned and how auteur directors managed to protect and project their styles and visions while employed by the studios.

My test case is *Bringing Up Baby*, the screwball comedy *par excellence*, directed by Howard Hawks and released by RKO Radio Pictures in 1938. The story of the making of *Baby* has been pieced together from files in RKO's West Coast archive.

In order to understand how this comedic treasure came to be produced, it is necessary to flash back to late 1935, when Samuel Briskin took charge of production at RKO. Briskin was brought from Columbia to RKO by Leo Spitz, the company's newly appointed corporate president. Although in receivership at the time, RKO was holding its own. *Roberta*, *Alice Adams*, *The Informer*, and *Top Hat* had been released in 1935, and each had received excellent critical notices and performed well at the box office. These films were the product of a unit production system overseen by B. B. Kahane and J. R. McDonough – two executives who allowed their staff producers to handle their pictures with minimal supervision or interference from the front office.

Despite the fine results generated by the system, Spitz followed a well-established principle of corporate management and brought in his 'own man' to superintend the studio's film-making activities. Sam Briskin had developed a reputation as a tough, stubborn, aggressive executive at Columbia. He was, in the words of Frank Capra, a 'hit-first type'.[5] Highly ambitious, Briskin must have been delighted to be the top man at RKO after laboring in Harry Cohn's shadow for many years. Briskin's initial move as production chief was to do precisely what Leo Spitz had done – recruit his own staff. By mid-1936, Edward Small, Jesse Lasky, and Howard Hawks were members of the Briskin team, developing projects which he hoped would become hits and strengthen his position at RKO.

Producer-director Hawks was given an exclusive two-year contract that called for a salary of $2,500 per week, plus a percentage of the profits from his pictures. The first project to interest him was *Gunga Din*. Staff producer Edward Small had brought the rights to the famous Kipling poem with him to RKO and, after some negotiations, agreed to turn the property over to Hawks for development. Hawks, in turn, interested one of the top writing teams in Hollywood, Ben Hecht and Charles MacArthur, in doing the script, and all three went to New York to work on it. There the writing proceeded at a very leisurely pace; this exasperated Briskin, who periodically informed the threesome of his impatience, but he was powerless to speed them along. Hawks did inform his employer that the story would require three virile male leads, so Briskin began putting out feelers to other studios, hoping to borrow the right stars since RKO had no suitable prospects under contract.

In April 1937, the Hecht-MacArthur script was ready, but Sam Briskin was not. He had failed to convince Louis B. Mayer to lend him Clark Gable, Spencer Tracy, and Franchot Tone, and Ronald Colman had also refused to do the picture. Briskin had no choice but to put *Gunga Din* on the shelf until an appropriate cast could be secured. He, therefore, instructed Hawks to develop something else.

By this time, Howard Hawks had been working for RKO for more than a year without shooting a single frame of film. This reflected negatively on Briskin; a production head's job was to turn out a steady stream of commercially successful pictures, not to pay big salaries to directors who were not making a contribution. Although Briskin might grumble about the length of time required to complete the *Gunga Din* script, he knew that Hawks was not to blame for its postponement. Still, he needed a Hawks film and he needed a good one, for his RKO tenure was not developing as he had hoped. The films made by Briskin's other handpicked producers had, by and large, been an undistinguished and unprofitable lot.

In addition, Sam Briskin had a crucial star problem to solve. Katharine Hepburn had been considered RKO's top female performer when Briskin

177

joined RKO. Beginning with *Sylvia Scarlett*, the studio's first release of 1936, Miss Hepburn had appeared in one flop after another, thereby tarnishing her box-office image and diminishing RKO's star roster. This was much more upsetting than the Hawks situation because, compared to its major competitors, RKO was sadly lacking in star power. Since a company sold its product blocks largely by promising to deliver a certain number of films featuring public favorites, it was considered imperative to boost Hepburn back to the lofty position she had once occupied in the show business hierarchy.

Miss Hepburn did not come to mind immediately when Hawks informed Briskin in May that he wished to make a film based on a *Collier's* magazine story entitled 'Bringing Up Baby'. The RKO story departments had recommended 'Baby' for purchase in April, and its head, Robert Sparks, had encouraged Briskin to hire the story's author, Hagar Wilde. Briskin, however, had shown no interest until Hawks made his decision.

Then everything changed. Dudley Nichols, one of RKO's top writers, went to work on the story with Hawks, Miss Wilde was brought out from the East to collaborate with the director and screenwriter, and, in short order, a decision was made to star Katharine Hepburn. The role of daffy socialite Susan Vance would be unlike any part she had played before; perhaps the public would embrace this new Hepburn persona.

The writing continued through the summer of 1937. While Nichols and Wilde developed the script, Briskin and Hawks hunted for the right male lead. Fredric March, Ray Milland, Fred MacMurray, and Leslie Howard were considered before Cary Grant won the job. Grant and Hepburn had worked together before in *Sylvia Scarlett*.

Budget was a matter of special concern to Sam Briskin. Realizing that public hostility to Katharine Hepburn was real enough, at least for the moment, he calculated that *Bringing Up Baby* had little chance of making a profit if it cost much more than a half-million dollars. He told Hawks that the script should be prepared so that $600,000 would be the absolute maximum expenditure. Despite this admonition, the director and his writers gave their imaginations free rein. The first estimating script weighed in at a hefty 242 pages, the revised draft at 194 pages, and the final shooting script at 202 pages. Given a certain amount of 'overwriting', this still represented a mammoth amount of material. By the time the film was ready to go before the cameras, the budget had been estimated at $767,000, for a fifty-one-day shooting schedule.

Briskin now had three apparent options. He could scrap the film altogether because of the excessive cost; postpone it until script and budget could be brought into line; or allow it to go forward, but instruct Hawks that he must prune the script so that the film would cost no more than $600,000. In reality, the latter was the only viable option. Briskin could not afford to cancel the project for several reasons, including the money that had already been invested in it (Hawks's salary, the writers' salaries, set construction costs, etc.) and the company's need to provide exhibitors with 'A' pictures. He could not postpone the film either, because of the nature of the studio commitment system, which, for example, gave RKO the services of Cary Grant for a limited period of time. If Grant were not used during that time, RKO lost him but had to pay his salary anyway.

Therefore, Briskin reluctantly gave Hawks the go-ahead, hoping the director would find a way to whittle down the script and budget. Briskin had become a truly beleaguered executive by this time. His major productions (*The Woman I Love, New Faces of 1937*, and *The Toast of New York*) had proved to be highly disappointing, and he had had more difficulty meeting release schedules than any previous RKO production head. When a company's distribution network promised a film to its most important customers on a certain date and then failed to deliver the picture as promised, it caused shock waves throughout the entire corporate system. Publicity and advertising were disrupted, a mad scramble ensued to find an adequate filler picture, and the film in question often entered the marketplace at a less-than-opportune release time. Most important, the situation damaged the credibility of the studio itself, making the exhibitors wary of buying blocks of films from the company in the future.

Briskin definitely needed a breakthrough film to release the pressure that was building up against him, and he must have felt that *Bringing Up Baby* could be that film. *Baby* did not even have to be a blockbuster; it would be enough if it returned Katharine Hepburn to public favor, thus breathing life into RKO's moribund star contingent.

Howard Hawks certainly understood all this. He realized that a great deal was riding on *Bringing Up Baby*, and he also realized that, politically speaking, he occupied the true position of power. About six weeks before the film went into production, Briskin's assistant Lou Lusty sent the following memo to his boss. It serves both to confirm the basic auteur contentions about Hawks and to reveal how a cagey director could manipulate the system.

I know, because the gentleman has said so in so many words that he's only concerned with making a picture that will be a personal credit to Mr Hawks regardless of its cost – and your [Briskin's] telling him the other day that it would be suicidal to make a Hepburn picture for seven or eight hundred thousand dollars I know made no impression on him at all. . . . Hawks is determined in his own quiet, reserved, soft-spoken manner to have his way about the making of this picture. . . . With the salary he's been getting he's almost indifferent to anything that might come to him on a percentage deal – that's why he doesn't give a damn about how much the picture will cost to make – and you know so well that you couldn't even break even if a Hepburn show cost eight hundred grand. All the directors in Hollywood are developing producer-director complexes and Hawks is going to be particularly difficult.[6]

Shooting commenced on 27 September 1937. In order to protect the studio's interests, Briskin assigned an associate producer to the film. The man chosen was Cliff Reid, a veteran who had worked in the same capacity

179

on John Ford's award-winning RKO film *The Informer*. Reid's job was to 'remind' Hawks that the script had to be cut and to make sure the production ran smoothly and efficiently. Reid, however, turned out to be something of a pushover. Disregarding the pressure from both Reid and Briskin, Hawks proceeded at a deliberate pace. Every day the dialogue would be rewritten on the set, causing the company to shoot less than the production department had estimated. Katharine Hepburn had some difficulty learning how to play screwball comedy, so Hawks introduced her to Walter Catlett, who tutored her throughout the rest of the production.[7] Hepburn also missed seven full days due to illness, and Hawks never got around to removing anything from the script. For these and other reasons, the picture quickly fell behind schedule. It soon became obvious that it would go beyond its projected date of completion and exceed its already excessive budget estimate.

These facts did not elude Leo Spitz or the RKO board of directors. A little over one month into the production, Briskin was forced to resign. Although certainly not the sole reason, the chronicle of *Bringing Up Baby* was a factor in Briskin's departure. Production reports indicate that the shooting pace slackened even more after Briskin left. The major question at this point is why RKO did not simply fire Hawks and turn the film over to someone else. One can only speculate, though the reasons seem obvious: the insertion of a new director, who was unfamiliar with both the story and its treatment, would have caused confusion and resentment on the part of cast and crew and, quite probably, have slowed things down even more. It might also have ruined the picture altogether.

Hawks went on working past the November date when the original schedule indicated completion, beyond the holidays and into the new year. Finally, on 8 January 1983, the shooting was completed. The original, fifty-one-day schedule had ballooned to ninety-three days, and the final budget amounted to $1,073,000.

The aftermath was fairly predictable. *Bringing Up Baby* was released to mixed critical notices and average box-office business. It did not seem to do much for Katharine Hepburn's career either. Briskin proved to be right in his prediction that a Hepburn film costing more than $700,000 could not make a profit. The final RKO loss on *Baby* amounted to $365,000. It also turned out to be Hepburn's last RKO picture. After a loan-out to Columbia for *Holiday*, she returned to her home studio, refused to appear in *Mother Carey's Chickens*, and was released from her contract. The RKO braintrust were convinced that she was washed up, but she would prove them wrong at MGM, beginning in 1940.

Likewise, Hawks found himself out of a job. *Gunga Din* had been reactivated while *Bringing Up Baby* was shooting. Knowing that it would be a much more ambitious and complicated picture than *Baby*, new executive producer Pandro Berman decided to turn it over to a more reliable director: George Stevens. (Ironically, Stevens developed his own perfectionist qualities on *Gunga Din*, which went $700,000 over budget.) Hawks's brother and agent, William, was called into the studio and informed that Howard would be terminated. The director was upset by this – not because he would be giving up his $2,500 weekly salary but because he would not have an opportunity to direct *Gunga Din*, which was precisely the type of male adventure saga he loved best. Nevertheless, his contract was canceled upon payment of $40,000 severance money.

It might seem that the system had prevailed over Hawks after all, since he was now branded as profligate and undependable and was out of a job. But, of course, the system was much larger than RKO Radio Pictures; within a short time, Hawks was back at work at Columbia on *Only Angels Have Wings*. It is important to note that that picture and Hawks's next effort, *His Girl Friday*, both starred Cary Grant. Hawks and Grant had obviously established a solid working relationship on *Bringing Up Baby*, which suggests that Hawks had actually increased his industry clout on *Baby*, rather than decreasing it. In addition to making memorable comedy, he had forged an alliance with a star whose career was rising rapidly. If Cary Grant wanted to work with Howard Hawks, Hawks's pictures would be made by one studio or another.

Now that we have surveyed the making of *Bringing Up Baby*, I would like to offer the following modest proposals:

The time has come to dispense with the assembly-line analogy for studio production. Although the moguls no doubt wished their operations could be as efficient and predictable as those of a Ford plant, their product militated against standardization.[8] It is true, of course, that the production of *Bringing Up Baby* is not typical; the film resulted from a special set of circumstances which enabled its director to control the picture more completely than would normally have been the case. Still, the departmental structures and operating methods of studios never turned film-making into a conveyor-belt business. Most pictures presented special problems which could not have been solved by inflexible, factory-inspired methods.

Leo Rosten, who studied the studio system when it was at its peak, has described it very well:

> Movie making is not a systematized process in which ordered routine can prevail, or in which costs can be absolute and controlled. Too many things can and do go awry, every day, every hour, during the manufacture of a movie. Movies are made by ideas and egos, not from blueprints and not with machines. Every story offers fresh and exasperating problems; every actor, director, writer carries with him curious preferences and needs; and the omnipresent hand of a mutable public throws sudden switches in the traffic of ideas through which the making of movies flows. The movie business moves with relentless speed, change is of the essence, and Hollywood must respond to change with short-spanned flexibility.[9]

Unfortunately, most scholars have preferred the depersonalized studio characterizations of Hampton and Jacobs to the somewhat nebulous, but more accurate, depiction of Rosten.

The power and influence of the movie industry's 'A'-level talent during the studio years have been seriously underestimated. The conception of the artist as corporate slave was fueled by periodic tirades against the moguls and their methods. One need only recall Frank Capra's 1939 letter to the *New York Times* in which he claimed that '80% of the directors today shoot scenes exactly as they are told to shoot them without any changes whatsoever, and . . . 90% of them have no voice in the story or in the editing',[10] or Bette Davis's well-publicized battles to prevent Jack Warner from forcing her to appear in mediocre pictures. Nevertheless, studio records contradict the impressions produced by these and other angry outbursts against the system. Most major actors and actresses could and did turn down parts they did not like (even at Warner Brothers), and it was normal for 'A' directors to have considerable freedom in their choice of material, to work with writers on the preparation of the script, to have the strongest voice in casting decisions, and to be left alone when they were directing the film. These basic conventions might be breached if a picture went widely over budget or if the studio executive felt the footage was no good. Still, as in the case of *Bringing Up Baby*, a studio rarely fired a director or halted production, even if the film did run over in both time and money.

The last proposal is for an open-minded reevaluation of the system itself and of each individual studio. There is more scholarly work to be done if we are to move beyond the one-sided generalizations that prevail in the current literature. We need, first of all, to recognize the complexity of these organizations. It is wrong to lump MGM, Paramount, Warner Brothers, Twentieth Century-Fox, RKO, and, oftentimes, Columbia, Universal, and United Artists together and treat them as if they were carbon copies of one another. Each of these companies had its own special characteristics, and each underwent significant changes during the studio system era. Each was a world unto itself with its own ways of making movies and making money. It is also time that we recognize the intrinsic genius of the system. There were both sound business sense and artistic advantage in the assembling of a diverse group of specialists under one umbrella structure. These talented individuals were able to grow and learn and work together in ways that enriched them all, as well as the capitalistic organizations they served.

A modern systems analyst studying the old Hollywood studios would certainly find them grossly inefficient and honeycombed with flaws. Ironically, these very weaknesses enabled the studios' more imaginative employees to make pictures that are still studied and appreciated today. The studios have taken enough punishment; we should give them a second look, recognizing that they may represent the best system for commercial filmmaking thus far developed in world cinema.

1. Benjamin B. Hampton, *History of the American Film Industry*, new edn (New York: Dover Publications, 1970), pp. 416–17.
2. Lewis Jacobs, *The Rise of the American Film*, new edn (New York: Teachers College Press, 1967), p. 296.
3. Thomas W. Bohn and Richard L. Stromgren, *Light and Shadows*, 2nd edn (Sherman Oaks, Calif.: Alfred Publishing, 1978), p. 199, 204–5; David Bordwell and Kristin Thompson, *Film Art: An Introduction* (Reading, Mass.: Addison-Wesley, 1979), pp. 8–9; David A. Cook, *A History of Narrative Film* (New York: W. W. Norton, 1981), pp.

265–9; Louis Giannietti, *Masters of the American Cinema* (Englewood Cliffs, NJ: Prentice-Hall, 1981), pp. 9–13; Gerald Mast, *A Short History of the Movies*, 2nd edn (Indianapolis: Bobbs-Merrill, 1976), p. 265; David Thomson, *American in the Dark* (New York: William Morrow, 1977), pp. 69–70.

4. Thomas Sobchack and Vivian C. Sobchack, *An Introduction to Film* (Boston, Mass: Little, Brown, 1980), p. 299.

5. Frank Capra, *The Name above the Title* (New York: Macmillan, 1971), p. 90.

6. Lou Lusty, memo to Sam Briskin, 10 August 1937, 'Howard Hawks' file, RKO West Coast Archives, Los Angeles, California.

7. Joseph McBride, *Hawks on Hawks* (Berkeley and Los Angeles: University of California Press, 1981), p. 72.

8. Even at the 'B' level, where production elements were more strictly controlled than the 'A' level, the 'assembly-line' conception is inaccurate. The creative team that worked on the Val Lewton films at RKO, for example, had ample leeway to develop a new strain of psychologically penetrating horror films. Their budgets were limited, but, otherwise, their innovative efforts were unencumbered by studio policies and procedures.

9. Leo C. Rosten, *Hollywood, the Movie Colony, the Movie Makers* (New York: Harcourt, Brace, 1941), p. 255.

10. Frank Capra, letter to *New York Times*, 2 April 1939, quoted in Louis Giannetti, *Masters of the American Cinema*, p. 19.

One of the effects of the critique to which early auteur studies were subjected was a greater interest in researching the way the movie industry, or 'Hollywood', actually worked. Jewell's essay is an example of such work, seeking to address questions about the degrees of latitude which existed in the studio system. Was it the rigid, production-line system it was often imagined to be? What kind of work was it possible to achieve within it, and within what constraints? Thomas Schatz, borrowing his title from André Bazin, addresses such issues in *The Genius of the System: Hollywood Film-Making in the Studio Era* (New York: Pantheon Books, 1988) and these issues are also a major focus in Janet Staiger (ed.), *The Studio System* (New Brunswick, NJ: Rutgers University Press, 1995), which reprinted Jewell's essay.

John Wayne, Howard Hawks and Joanne Dru shooting *Red River*

Borden Chase, Howard Hawks and *Red River*

RICHARD CORLISS

From Richard Corliss, *Talking Pictures* (Woodstock, NY: The Overlook Press, 1985).

Borden Chase's story, repeated throughout a decade of films that stretched from *Red River* (1948) to *Night Passage* (1957), was that of the civilizing of the American West. His films were miniature epics of westward movement and colonization, with the forces of Good and Evil in an embryonic age often battling within the same person, whether hero or villain. The stalwart figures of Montgomery Clift (*Red River*), Gregory Peck (*The World in His Arms*), Burt Lancaster (*His Majesty O'Keefe*), and especially James Stewart (*Winchester '73, Bend of the River, The Far Country*) were ideal repositories for the precarious values of civilization that Chase tested relentlessly as his cattle drives, wagon trains, and traveling vendettas headed into the wilderness. His Stewart–Anthony Mann films epitomize the social (but antisocialist) Westerns of the fifties, with each step toward an uncharted land revealing more of the characters' equally uncharted psychologies. Chase's 'message' was that only under the pressure of savagery, at a far remove from the trappings of culture, can we ever really know if a man is truly civilized, or if he is only a beast in a ruffled shirt.

Red River (1948)

The influence of the *New Yorker* school on Hollywood films of the thirties and forties was established, and possibly exaggerated, by Pauline Kael in her long essay on *Citizen Kane*. But the *New Yorker* wasn't the only magazine to send its writers and their stories out West. The *Saturday Evening Post* may not have been able to provide its contributors with an Independence Square equivalent of the Algonquin (Bookbinders?), but it nevertheless sired a school of fiction which, in its exaltation of rural virtues and the American historical legend, may have had a more pervasive influence on Hollywood – if only because it carried the already outmoded ideals of silent movies credibly, and creditably, into the fast-talking, amoral talkie era.

Whatever the reason, the *Post*'s Clarence Buddington Kelland (*Mr Deeds Goes to Town*), David Goodis (*Dark Passage*), Paul Gallico (*The Clock*), Norman Reilly Raine (*Tugboat Annie*), C. S. Forrester (*The African Queen*), Robert Carson (*A Star Is Born*), Dorothy M. Johnson (*The Man*

185

Who Shot Liberty Valance), Ernest Haycox (*Stagecoach*), James Street (*Nothing Sacred*), and A. B. Guthrie, Jr (*The Big Sky*) – all *Post* regulars in the late forties – stamped the magazine's moral and craftsmanlike imprint onto virtually every movie genre. As is evident from the preceding list, the *Post*'s influence on the Western was especially great. James Warner Bellah's stories of the American Cavalry ('Massacre', 'The Big Hunt', 'War Party', and 'Mission with No Record') were developed with surprising fidelity by John Ford and his screenwriters into the 'cavalry trilogy' of *Fort Apache*, *She Wore a Yellow Ribbon*, and *Rio Grande*; when Bellah came to Hollywood, Ford teamed him with Willis Goldbeck to script *Sergeant Rutledge* and *Liberty Valance*. The other major postwar graduate of the *Post* school was Borden Chase, whose serial, *The Chisholm Trail*, became the grandest of forties Westerns, *Red River* – and who reworked the theme of 'The Chisholm Trail' in a dozen important Westerns over the next decade.

Chase's films were mostly concerned (as Chase himself was largely obsessed) with the building of the West. In recreating a 'Western' civilization, he was in effect creating an American fantasy of how the more general Western Civilization should have been built. From the early lines in *The Chisholm Trail* – a vision of Conestoga wagons 'crawling snakelike across the face of a continent. Heading west. Always west' – to his final, unrealized project about the first wagons heading over the Sierra Trail to California, Chase eulogized westward movement, expansion, colonization. In a word, Civilisation.

Interwoven with this theme was that of a love-hate relationship between two strong men: 'That I believe is the greatest love story in all the world,' Chase told Jim Kitses in an interview just before his death. 'I have always believed that a man can love and respect another man more so than he can a woman.' In the same interview Chase recalls competing with another screenwriter on *This Man's Navy* in 1945: 'I said . . . "I'm trying to write you off this thing, aren't you trying to write me off it? If you're not, you're stupid!" ' This raw mixture of camaraderie and combat marked Chase's films as well as his life, and distinguishes his signature from those of other writers in a genre often thought to be sole property of the director.

Most of Chase's films trace a journey westward, with a benign dictator imposing rudimentary civilization at gunpoint. *Red River* is different: the trek is north by northeast, from the wild plains of Texas to the streets and shops of Abilene, Kansas, and the hero's role is transferred from Thomas Dunson, the intransigent, reactionary loner, to Matthew Garth, a more liberal social being – 'an image [of Dunson] that had grown taller and straighter and equally strong'. The climax of *The Chisholm Trail* had Matthew defeat Dunson not by outdrawing him, but by *not* drawing on him. Dunson, already mortally wounded, keeps firing away at Matthew, and with every missed shot Matthew establishes his own moral supremacy and that of the civilization Dunson had rejected. In this aspect and in others, *Red River* is a particularly satisfying 'late' film that comes, perversely, early in Chase's Hollywood career.

As they fight, Dunson thinks of Matthew as a traitor to the unwritten code of savage nobility the older man had instilled in him; afterward, Dunson realizes that his own primitive justice and Matthew's civilized mercy are complementary tools needed if the West is to be built and not merely claimed. Dunson had implicitly understood this interdependence when he first met the boy, a generation earlier, wandering orphaned through Texas with only his pet calf. 'My bull and your calf,' Dunson had proclaimed. 'My gun and you at my back. We'll build an empire, Matthew! We'll build an empire!' Dunson's bull (animal force) and Matthew's calf (human reason) drive thousands of cattle and scores of men from Texas to Kansas. The same parlay will 'win the West' (subdue the Indian nations) and construct a society on fertile new ground. Dunson remembers first seeing Matthew 'dragging a cow across a continent. God knows where he expected to go. California, I suppose.' And just as Dunson epitomizes Texas frontier pride, Matthew prefigures the eclectic resilience of the Golden State.

(Today, we can see in the film a spectacularly bizarre prefigurement of the political relationship between Lyndon Johnson and Robert Kennedy. Bobby was no adopted son of Johnson's, and there was never any shred of reconciliation between the two. But Johnson's foray into the Big Muddy of South Vietnam, and Kennedy's role in diverting that tragic cattle drive toward the civilized path of withdrawal, bear such striking metaphorical similarity to the plot and character of the Chase story that, had the film been made in 1968 instead of 1948, a title like *Red River* would have seemed too baldly, politically pointed. John Wayne's uncanny resemblance in the forties to Johnson – even more evident in *She Wore a Yellow Ribbon*, when he dons a pair of LBJ rimless spectacles – and Clift's to the Kennedy clan make this comparison iconographically as well as thematically apt.)

Howard Hawks made a characteristically tense, uncharacteristically handsome film from Chase's script, by sticking close to the author's master plan; a lot of dialogue from *The Chisholm Trail* survives intact in the film. But Hawks made two major changes which even Robin Wood identifies as 'weaknesses in the construction of *Red River* as we now have it: one, that the intriguing relationship between Montgomery Clift [Matthew] and John Ireland [Cherry Valance] is so little developed. . . . The second, more important, is inherent in the conception of the film: Tess Millay (Joanne Dru) is introduced so late that the development of her relationships with the two men (Wayne and Clift) seems contrived' – and that, because of this, 'the ending of *Red River* has been much criticized'. An investigation of the film's history may uncover the reasons for these weaknesses, and indicate besides some of the difficulties inherent in attributing thematic cohesion to works of art based on collaboration and compromise.

In *The Chisholm Trail*, Cherry Valance is a likable gunman and cynical middleman between Dunson, the obsolescent idealist, and Matthew, the new-and-improved idealist. Cherry and Matthew personify the alternatives available to the young West: anarchy with a smile, or clear-eyed order. Their introduction is shot portentously, with sparks of anticipated dramatic conflict careening off them into the audience; and Chase increases the tension between the two by suggesting a personal, reciprocal attraction. In the serial, Chase had Cherry break off from the cattle drive once Matthew assumed control, the better to raid it and take the spoils for himself – which is exactly what the revenge-crazed Dunson planned to do. But Cherry's and Dunson's interests have merged so completely that one of them is now superfluous, and must be eliminated: in a showdown, Dunson kills Cherry, but sustains a bullet wound that will ultimately prevent him from killing Matthew.

In the film, Cherry's crucial role 'was chopped completely', according to Chase. 'Duke called me one day and he said . . . "We're dumping Cherry Valance." I said, "What do you mean?" "Well," he said, "He's fooling around with Howard's girl." I can't remember her name, she's married now. I said, "What the hell has that got to do with making a picture? I don't care if he's fooling around with the Virgin Mary, you've got a picture to make and the guy is good." "Well," he said, "look, he's out. That's it." . . . Talk about a crucifixion, that was it.' The guy was John Ireland; the girl was Joanne Dru, who played Tess Millay. They were married a year later.

Chase's Tess Millay is not only a pivotal character; she is a central character, appearing throughout the serial, beginning before Matthew returns to Texas from the Civil War. Dunson notes a change in Matthew, a truculent independence from his foster father's iron rule, and the difference is Tess: his love for this New Orleans saloon siren forces him to consider, for the first time, a West that a woman can live in. Tess's movement toward Abilene – first with Cherry, then with Matthew, and finally with Dunson – lends formal as well as narrative excitement to Chase's plot, and it is appropriate that she is regenerated by the composite Western spirit of Matthew and Dunson even as she saves both the pride of the man she admires (Dunson, the stern patriarch) and the life of the man she loves (Matthew, her eventual spouse).

Hawks's Tess enters only in the final third of *Red River*. Instead of allowing her to help Dunson complete a moral progression from savagery to civility, Hawks created an *Ur*-Tess in the person of Fen, Dunson's young fiancée whom he had abandoned early in the film to the same Indian massacre that left Matthew an orphan. Dunson is thus an *homme maudit* throughout *Red River*, and Tess's affectionate words comprise an incantation that breaks the spell of his loneliness. All this makes sense, but the viewer's interest has been focused for so long on the Dunson–Matthew conflict that Tess's sudden appearance comes as an unwelcome intrusion – the *dea ex machina* whose clumsy contrivances will tidy up a more complex dilemma.

Once Hawks got hold of Tess (or Miss Dru), he refused to let go. Chase's original epilogue – with the fatally wounded Dunson being taken back to Texas by Tess and Matthew, and standing up to die on Texas soil just after they cross the Red River – had already been thrown out. (According to Chase, Hawks simply said, 'Look, Wayne isn't going to die.') But Hawks also rewrote Chase's version of the Dunson–Matthew gunfight, so that Tess's intervention – with the words, 'Now you two boys stop fighting!' –

turns a showdown between two kinds of nobility into the melodramatic setup for a comic punchline worthy of *Bringing Up Baby*. No wonder Chase calls the film's climax 'garbage'! With a few scribbles on his famous yellow lined pad, Hawks nearly ruined *Red River*; for surely, if the protagonists' conflicts can be resolved with one schoolmarmish scolding, they can hardly have had much dramatic stature to begin with.

It takes a strong effort of will to ignore this resolution, or at least to see it as one flawed piece in the ambitious and serene mosaic Chase and Hawks had created up to then – a vision most vibrantly expressed in Chase's description, in *The Chisholm Trail*, of the building of Abilene and, by extension, the West itself:

> And so a town was born. It wasn't planned. No dreamers in Congress sketched its streets. Men built it! Hard men. Americans! Built it with gall and guts and sweat. Built it for profit and built it for fun. It was good to build. Good to spread their country across a continent. They made mistakes. Hundreds of mistakes. Thousands of mistakes. But they set out to build a country, and they got the job done.

Richard Corliss has devoted much of his critical writing to arguing the case for the importance of considering the influence of screenwriters on Hollywood movies in a critical world where, since the 1960s, the director as auteur has been king. Hawks's debt to his regular screenwriters is no longer in doubt and Corliss's brief examination of the relationship of Borden Chase's script for *Red River* to the finished film allows us to see both what a writer could bring to a project and the kinds of ways in which writers' contributions were handled during production. Corliss's piece is extracted from his book *Talking Pictures*, which also includes discussions of Ben Hecht and *Scarface*, Jules Furthman and *Only Angels Have Wings* and Charles Lederer and *His Girl Friday* and *Gentlemen Prefer Blondes*. See also Richard Corliss (ed.), *The Hollywood Screenwriters*, which has essays by Richard Koszarski on Jules Furthman and Corliss on Ben Hecht. Also in this book is an interview with Borden Chase, by Jim Kitses, which Corliss draws upon in his discussion of Chase, Hawks and *Red River*. It is worth noting that in Joseph McBride's interview book *Hawks on Hawks* Hawks rejects Chase's version of events in no uncertain terms: 'He must have been drinking when he said that, because he's so full of shit.'

Classic Hollywood's Holding Pattern: The Combat Films of World War II

ROBERT B. RAY

From Robert B. Ray, *A Certain Tendency of the Hollywood Cinema 1930–1980* (Princeton, NJ: Princeton University Press, 1985).

Casablanca's immense lasting popularity has obscured the film's decidedly topical origins. Indeed, the most neglected fact about *Casablanca* is that it was a war movie, one of a cycle of American films made between 1941 and 1945 with a definite propagandistic intent. Nevertheless, *Casablanca*'s simultaneous status as an explicit allegory of US military intervention and as the culmination of Classic Hollywood's reconciliatory pattern indicates how little World War II affected the American Cinema. In fact, even the combat features made during the war adhered to the model of choice avoidance established as the norm for the commercial movie. If anything, this model merely became more obvious, rendered less subtle by the simplification procedures that Basil Wright has seen as typical of the wartime film:

> To the artist war brings – at least to begin with – instant simplification. Issues are no longer in doubt, or at any rate are not seen to be so. One knows what to do. Wartime films are therefore ideologically and emotionally very simple. Their value in later times tends to be historical rather than aesthetic.[1]

Far from prompting a new kind of popular film, therefore, World War II merely provided the American film industry and its audience with an occasion for reaffirming the traditional forms. For despite their reliance on realistic *mise en scènes*, the combat pictures were essentially romances that magically resolved the tensions created by contradictory needs.

The continuity between Hollywood's Classic movies and the wartime films derived at least partially from the influence of Howard Hawks's pre-war *Only Angels Have Wings* (1939). As a model for the simplification process undertaken by the war movies, Hawks was the inevitable choice, for of the great Hollywood directors, he had most consistently reduced the reconciliatory pattern to its basic elements, producing broadly drawn optimistic films that sometimes resembled cartoons.

Hawks's movies, like the combat films, are often misunderstood as being simply about groups. In fact, his groups were very special, capable of accommodating individualism without devouring it, relying as much on

190

personal acts of heroism as on teamwork. The members of these groups were carefully particularized: Hawks's ideal world was a melting pot full of distinctly different individuals. Thus, his films represented a mythic solution to the individual–community opposition central to American culture, and as such, were the inevitable model for the combat films whose propagandistic project was to reaffirm the American myth that, even in wartime, essential choices could be avoided.

Although *Only Angels Have Wings* was not a war film *per se*, it contained almost all the motifs that became the basis of Hollywood's portrayal of World War II combat: the male group directed by a strong leader, the outsider who must prove himself by courageous individual action, the necessity for stoicism in the face of danger and death, the premium placed on professionalism, and the threat posed by women. So broad was *Angels'* use of these motifs that the movie functioned as an archetypal source for the World War II films that followed.

No one has ever topped Manny Farber's plot summary of *Only Angels Have Wings*:

This movie about a Zeta Beta Tau fraternity of fliers in a South American jungle is a ridiculous film of improbability and coincidence, the major one being that Bat McPherson, the blackest name in aviation, the man who betrayed Thomas Mitchell's kid brother and married Grant's old flame, should show up years later broke and in need of a job in Barranca, where buddies Grant and Mitchell are busting up planes on the strangest stalactite mountains. . . . *Only Angels*, a White Cargo melodrama that is often intricately silly, has a family unit living at the Dutchman's, a combination bar, restaurant, rooming house, and airport run by a benevolent Santa Claus (some airline: the planes take off right next to the kitchen, and some kitchen: a plane crashes, the wreck is cleared and the pilot buried in the time it takes them to cook a steak; and the chief control is a crazy mascot who lives with a pet donkey and serves as a lookout atop a buzzard-and-blizzard-infested mountain as sharp as a shark's tooth).[2]

Farber does neglect to mention some specifics: the reason given for the film's action (the men – some pilots, some investors – had signed a contract to deliver the mail to towns across a dangerous mountain range), the complications (the arrival of Bat, a woman, and chronic bad weather), and the solution (acts of individual heroism by Bat – Richard Barthelmess – and the group's leader, Jeff – Cary Grant). This fantastic, clichéd plot, full of hokey coincidences and stylized melodrama ('frankly terrible', Peter John Dyer called it[3]) was not nearly so important as what Hawks managed to do with it: on this story, he hung all the motifs that would dominate the wartime films.

1. The Isolated Male Group Involved in a Life-and-Death Task
The group of flyers in *Angels* became the model for the patrols or platoons of the wartime movies – patrols cut off from the main body of the army

(*Flying Tigers, Air Force, Wake Island, Guadalcanal Diary*) or assigned to a particularly dangerous mission behind enemy lines (*Destination Tokyo; Thirty Seconds over Tokyo; Objective, Burma!*). The war movies employed these small, isolated groups as a device for viewing a world war that, without this focusing, would have seemed only an enormous, impersonal machine. The point of view of the single platoon was the movies' equivalent of Henry James's narrative consciousness – an organizing principle.

2. The Group, Composed of Distinct Types, That Relies on Both Teamwork and Individual Exploits

The men in *Angels* were friends (especially Jeff and 'The Kid', played by Thomas Mitchell), but more importantly, they worked as a team. In the opening scene, Jeff and 'The Kid' operated together to 'talk down' a pilot lost in the fog over the runway. As Robin Wood has noticed, the sequence showed 'Mitchell using his ears and Grant his voice as if they were two aspects of the same human being'.[4] The point was that the lost pilot, Grant, and Mitchell were a team of three – it took all three to save the plane. When the same pilot subsequently ignored the orders of his 'teammate' Grant (hurrying to land despite orders, in order to keep a date), he crashed. The moral: you can't do it alone.

The men evinced their mutual dependency in other ways as well. The cook, Dutchy (Sig Ruman), did not fly but had financed the entire operation, buying the planes and paying the pilots' salaries. But his investment depended in turn on the flyers' willingness and ability to keep the mail moving, despite crackups and bad weather.

Although *Angels* overtly emphasized the values of the group, its detailed characterizations implicitly affirmed the American ideological insistence on the compatibility of individual and communitarian values. Each member of the *Angels* team embodied a distinct type: Dutchy, the comic butt with the heavy foreign accent; 'The Kid', the aging flyer losing his eyesight; Jeff, the glamorous leader matter-of-factly executing the duties of command. Ultimately, too, the group's success depended on individual acts, especially on Jeff's final mission, undertaken in the worst possible weather.

3. Professionalism and Stoicism in the Face of Danger and Death

Faced with a task that required them to risk their lives on a daily basis, the flyers in *Angels* built up protective mechanisms either to deny the possibility of death or to deal with it, if it came, in a ritualized manner. Crucial was the belief in professionalism with its faith that death did not come by chance but as a result of someone's failure to do his job properly. By allowing the flyers to feel some control over their fates, this belief encouraged a respect for discipline, care, and skill. Thus Grant's blaming Joe's death on the fact that 'he wasn't good enough' comforted the remaining flyers, each certain of his own ability.

The stoic, stiff-upper-lip response to disaster played an integral part in this code. By eating the steak prepared for the dead pilot, Grant asserted that life had to go on – and also that their situation was too precarious to stop and mourn the dead. Because he had died for a foolish reason (to keep a date on time), Joe had become a debilitating threat to the rest of the pilots' ability to perform. Therefore, he had to be dismissed. 'That's Joe's steak you're eating,' Jean Arthur said to Grant, shocked by his callousness. 'Who's Joe?' Grant replied.

As a part of this stoic attitude toward danger, Hawks's characters spoke in oblique Hemingwayesque language, which Hawks himself called 'three-cushion'. ('In order to say something, you bounce around from one cushion to another and then you've said it and it doesn't become a rash state-ment.' [5]) Part of this language was, in fact, nonverbal, particularly the Hawksian routines with cigarettes and matches. In *Angels*, Grant never had a match, and by having to ask others for one, particularly Mitchell, he suggested his dependence on them. As Mitchell was dying, Grant at least re-turned the favor by giving him a cigarette. Together, they used the ritual as a way of not talking about death: Joe crashed and Grant turned to Mitchell, asking 'Got a match?' Women resisting this kind of refusal to express emo-tion openly could win acceptance only by playing the game – Arthur finally achieved entry into Grant's world by recognizing the proposal hidden in his offer, 'Stay if it's heads, you leave if it's tails', made with a two-headed coin.

The combat films repeatedly used another basic element of the stoicism motif, the inventory of the dead pilot's belongings. Almost always, these men left little behind but a handful of loose change and a few pictures of someone back home. Nevertheless, serious inventory of even the meager possessions implied the community behind the individual, at once support-ing and depending upon him.

Angels also confronted the possibility that stoicism could break down at the last: the dying Mitchell asked Grant to leave the room because he was not sure of his own courage. The war movies, borrowing this idea, contin-ually stressed that really brave men admitted to fear (see especially the cave scene in *Guadalcanal Diary* and William Bendix's soliloquy about fear).

4. Outsiders Enter the Group and Become Threats to It

While *Angels*' outsiders did in fact come from remote, external sources, the war films' outsiders were typically malcontents within the group itself (e.g., the Garfield character in *Air Force*). The first outsider in *Angels* was Bonnie Lee (Jean Arthur), a wandering showgirl stranded in Barranca ('I quit a show at Valparaiso'). She disrupted the carefully established rituals and teamwork of the group: Joe's date was with her. Further, her grief for him was too explicit. By refusing to adopt the stoic, oblique-language game, by nagging at Grant and the men to pay attention to Joe's death, she threat-ened to break down the protective barriers enabling them to avoid paralyz-ing fear. Bat's wife (Rita Hayworth) posed a different kind of threat: voluptuous, seductive, she not only prevented the men from concentrating on their work, but also stirred up jealousy that eroded group teamwork. Bat himself, however, proved the greater threat, for as the pilot who had let another man down, he sowed the seeds of doubt and fear in the others.

5. The Outsiders Must Win Admission into the Group

The women in *Angels* could gain admission into the group only by accepting the male world on its own terms. While Bat's wife made her peace by tacitly supporting her husband, Bonnie Lee gained entrance by engaging Jeff in his own tongue-in-cheek banter. As a male, however, Bat's route back to the group was arduous, requiring a suicide mission over mountains in zero-visibility weather and an aerial version of a no-man's-land rescue, his refusal to bail out of a damaged plane and leave a wounded Mitchell behind. (This motif reappeared in *Air Force*, where the 'person' to be rescued was the plane itself, the *Mary Ann*.)

Although it was nominally an action/adventure picture, *Only Angels Have Wings* had very few real action sequences – and they were the worst thing in the movie, at times using weird, obviously fake mountains, giant condors, and recognizably miniature planes. In fact, like most of the combat films that copied it, *Angels* was less about adventure itself than men's reactions to it. Influential, too, was Hawks's simple, even stark, technique based on invisible editing, simple sets, and a sparing use of close-ups, a style whose reductiveness matched the broadness of the film's reconciliatory pattern. (A convoluted technique would have commented ironically on that pattern.) Invariably, the combat movies employed similar techniques, emphasizing what appeared to be a casual, semi-documentary look that attempted to portray war not as a strange distortion of the normal world, but as something solvable by 'business as usual'.

But despite the superficial realism of the combat films, they were in fact as stylized as *Only Angels Have Wings*. Even with a self-effacing technique, Hawks made little effort toward verisimilitude, preferring instead a melodramatic quality fueled by the hothouse atmosphere of a frankly artificial staging. The dramatic opening sequence, the best few minutes in *Angels*, was typical. Working in the dark, Grant and Mitchell tried to 'talk down' Joe, lost overhead in the fog. No background music accompanied this scene, only the drone of the invisible plane's props. The darkness and obvious artificiality of the studio set actually worked to increase the tension – without light, without vistas of any kind, the *mise en scène* invoked an oppressive heat and a jungle world where pilots and ground crews lived on top of each other, growing irritable with the weather, the constant danger, and their own fear. The closed-in atmosphere of the set furthered the idea of the men's absolute mutual dependence, but also glamorized the individual leader. Against the black background of Dutchy's bar and the night, Grant stood out in his white suit.

Clearly, *Only Angels Have Wings* came from the world of the romance. As Farber put it, the film 'isn't dated so much as removed from reality, like the land of Tolkien's Hobbits'.[6] By using *Angels*' reductive version of the Classic Hollywood pattern as the model for its combat films, therefore, the industry proposed to its audience that reality be ignored for the duration of World War II. What was seen on the screen, as a result, was less a true image of combat than a special genre using the traditional Hollywood pattern. Made only a few weeks after Pearl Harbor, and released in early 1942, *Flying Tigers* established the trend. The movie was actually a remake of *Only Angels Have Wings*, with no credit given to Hawks. The plot was identical: Hawks's male group of South American mail pilots became General Chennault's volunteer irregulars, fighting the Japanese in China before American entry into the war. Although the men were adventurers of the *Angels* breed (they did not *have* to be there), the Japanese threat reduced the gratuitousness of their flying. As the group leader, John Wayne assumed Cary Grant's *Angels* role, even to the extent of being called 'Pappy' (as Grant had been) by obviously older men. Like Grant, he stressed teamwork: a pilot who had foolhardily taken up an unarmed plane and been forced to crash-land received a lecture. 'You're not the first ball carrier who didn't appreciate his blockers.' The others joined in: 'A few more flights like this and he'll qualify as a Jap ace.'

Into this cozy setup came a pilot who had been a coward. Wayne turned him away, but as Rita Hayworth had done for her husband Barthelmess in *Angels*, the outcast's wife pleaded for another chance. Again, the film, for all of its talk about teamwork, stressed the importance of individual acts: to gain readmittance into the privileged group, the pariah had to prove himself by hiding on board a plane and subsequently saving an injured Wayne on a suicide mission. In the meantime, Wayne's own girlfriend began to cause trouble by taking up with a reckless flyer. When a date with her made the pilot too late for a mission, Wayne's best friend, grounded for bad vision like Mitchell in *Angels*, took his place and was killed – presumably, it was the woman's fault. New recruits were lectured on the policy of teamwork ('Don't try to win the war by yourself') while Wayne struggled to hold the men together. Hawks should have sued for plagiarism.

Flying Tigers was a sign of things to come. All of the major combat films were, in effect, remakes of *Only Angels Have Wings*. All sought in specific to reconcile the individual–group conflict by demonstrating that even the effort required by the war did not undermine the essential American myth that all such oppositions were ultimately resolvable. The symbolic affirmation of this myth, seized upon by the movies, was the Doolittle Raid on Tokyo in April 1942, a mission whose military purpose was subordinate to its possibilities as a moral-building gesture. 'Of all the military operations in the first two years of the war,' war-movie historian Lawrence H. Suid writes, 'probably nothing so stimulated the imagination of the American people as Doolittle's mission against Japan.'[7] At the time, the raid seemed important only as a demonstration of the American capability to strike at the Japanese mainland. In fact, it was the special character of the carefully staged event that established its appeal. In an enormously complicated, potentially abstract conflict, the Doolittle Raid was a simple, direct, understandable action, a Western-style tactic easily dramatized. More important, with its reliance on interservice teamwork (the navy took the army pilots to within striking distance of the Japanese coastline) and individual heroism (of the men who flew the mission), the raid yielded an ideal image of America at war. It was inevitable that the Doolittle Mission would become a subject for the movies, and, indeed, three wartime combat pictures told the story: *Destination Tokyo* (1943) concerned itself with a US submarine stealing into Tokyo Bay to gather information for the raid; *Thirty Seconds over Tokyo* (1944) recounted the preparations, the raid itself, and the subsequent rescue of the downed flyers; and *The Purple Heart* (1944) focused on the problems of those pilots shot down and captured by the Japanese. Because of its concentration and obvious capacity for romance, the Doolittle Raid, in thinly disguised form, provided the basis for the overtly unrealistic Errol Flynn movies *Desperate Journey* (1942) (RAF pilots shot down over Germany) and *Objective, Burma!* (1945) (paratroopers operating behind Japanese lines).

In addition to these movies' particular reliance on the Doolittle Raid as an image of American-style combat, almost all the major war movies developed around the motifs established by *Only Angels Have Wings* that I discussed above.

1. The Isolated Male Group Involved in a Dangerous Situation

Each of the wartime movies focused on a limited group as a vantage point for the wider theaters of war. Hawks's own *Air Force* (1943) centered on the crew of one B-17, en route to Pearl Harbor on 7 December 1941, and subsequently appearing at all of the principal battlegrounds of the Pacific War's first week – Wake Island, the Philippines, and the Coral Sea. The heroes of *Wake Island* (1942) were the few hundred marines and civilians who managed to hold off the vastly superior attacking Japanese for over a week before being overrun. *Guadalcanal Diary* (1943) portrayed the war for that island from the point of view of one of the first marine platoons to land there. *Thirty Seconds over Tokyo* used the captain of one of Doolittle's planes as the narrative center of consciousness for an account of the Tokyo mission. In *Destination Tokyo*, the same story was told from the perspective of a submarine crew doing reconnaissance work for the flyers. *Objective, Burma!*, the most fanciful of the films, followed the adventures of one patrol parachuted behind enemy lines fighting its way back to safety. All of these groups were the combat equivalent of *Angels*' mail pilots.

2. The Group, Composed of Distinct Types, That Relies on Both Teamwork and Individual Exploits

All of the war films followed *Angels*' model of the Hawksian group composed of distinct types working together under an idealized leader. The racially mixed platoon or flight crew (foreshadowed by Hawks's Dutchy-Jeff-Kid team) became a stock device of these films: *Air Force* had a Winocki and a Weinberg; *Destination Tokyo*, a Greek (known as Tin Can because of his unpronounceable name) and a New Yorker; *Guadalcanal Diary*, a Brooklyn cab driver and an Indian; *Objective, Burma!*, an entire melting pot (except for a black) – a Hogan, a Nebraska Hooper, a Miggleori, a Hennessey, a Negulesco, a Brophy, a Higgins, and even a helpful Burmese.

In stressing the importance of cooperation, Hawks's own *Air Force* was unusually realistic. While most flight movies focused on the pilots, *Air*

Force eagerly demonstrated the importance of each crew member. Even the navigator's success in locating Wake Island, 'a tiny speck in this ocean', came to seem heroic. Similar sequences suggested how much the success or failure of a mission could depend on a tail gunner (John Garfield) or a bombardier. And, in the film's climactic scene, each member of the crew, supervised by the chief sergeant, worked feverishly to repair the plane as the Japanese approached. On this job, the normally glamorous pilots contributed the least: the mechanics (especially Harry Carey) were the heroes.

Thirty Seconds over Tokyo portrayed an even broader kind of teamwork. Cooperation between crew members was, of course, still crucial: the navigator located Tokyo, the bombardier timed and released the weapons, the mechanics kept the plane running, and the pilots flew it. At another level, the movie showed the cooperation among the crews of the different planes, training together, learning from each other's mistakes as they adapted to the short takeoffs needed on a carrier, and the hedge-hopping flight patterns used over Tokyo. At a still higher level, the movie placed great emphasis on the army–navy teamwork necessary to produce the Doolittle Raid. On first boarding the carrier *Hornet*, the planes' crews displayed routine distrust for the navy – a distrust furthered by the sailors' ability at poker. But with the goal of the mission revealed, the mutual chauvinisms and distrust fell away, the new-found teamwork clinched by the symbolic gesture of giving the pilots the best beds. After the flyers crash-landed in China, *Thirty Seconds* took a new tack, celebrating cooperation between the Chinese and the Americans, as an underground network of Chinese villagers passed the wounded Americans from hand to hand, keeping them from being captured by the Japanese.

Destination Tokyo's portrayal of submariners' mutual dependence depended on a compendium of submarine picture clichés: the fresh recruit, who saved the ship by deactivating a live but unexploded torpedo, was subsequently operated on for appendicitis by the pharmacist's mate, tended to in turn by the cook. More important, the sub's task, gathering information for the Tokyo Raid, demanded systematic intraservice cooperation.

Even though the combat films overtly celebrated teamwork, they continued to glamorize the individual heroes on whom a mission's success utterly depended. 'I'd go through hell for that man,' a crew member said of submarine captain Grant in *Destination Tokyo*, and clearly Doolittle (Spencer Tracy) in *Thirty Seconds over Tokyo*, Brian Donlevy in *Wake Island*, and Errol Flynn in *Objective, Burma!* were equally important to their platoons. Inevitably, these films turned on individual feats: Garfield's miraculous landing in *Air Force*, Grant's daring tactics that managed to sink a threatening Japanese destroyer, the courageous last stands of *Wake Island* and *Guadalcanal Diary*. The pattern was the traditional Hollywood reconciliation of contradictory values. Even in combat, these movies proposed, there was no need to choose between individual and group.

3. Professionalism and Stoicism in the Face of Danger and Death
All of the combat features followed *Angels*' model in suggesting stoicism as

the proper way for dealing with danger and death. *Air Force* repeated *Angels'* inventory of a dead pilot's meager collection of belongings with the same litany, 'Not much to show for twenty years.' Again as in *Angels*, the film allowed no time for grieving: the crew of the *Mary Ann* had to ready her for take-off.

In *Guadalcanal Diary* and *Wake Island*, the stoic, professional attitude revealed itself through humor (William Bendix's jokes and worries about the Dodgers and his girlfriend back home) and the willingness to admit fear (Bendix asking the chaplain to pray). Both films portrayed the maturation of green platoons, who moved from naïve overconfidence to a grudging respect for the Japanese as an enemy.

The combat films often stressed that the inevitable dehumanization accompanying the assumed stoic attitude constituted only a temporary departure from the natural and proper pattern of civilian life. None of these movies followed the earlier, bleak suggestion of *All Quiet on the Western Front* (1930) that the emotional stunting occasioned by war had permanently debilitating effects. Instead, normal lifestyles were easily resumed. Submarine captain Grant's home-pier reunion with his wife proved typically uncomplicated. Less blithe homecomings (in *Thirty Seconds over Tokyo* and *Pride of the Marines*) were explained away as special cases, resulting from crippling injuries that required radical readjustments.

4 and 5 Outsiders Who Are threats to the Group But Finally Win Admission into It

Almost all of the combat pictures had versions of *Angels'* Bat McPherson, a malcontented, disruptive outsider required to perform an individual act of heroism to be admitted into the group. *Air Force*, in fact, contained two such figures: tail-gunner Winocki, angry at not making pilot and eager to quit the service, and Lieutenant Raider, a flashy, devil-may-care fighter pilot who made fun of the slower, less maneuverable bombers. The assimilation of these two derived partially from the declaration of war. As Winocki saw what the Japanese had done to the Americans at Pearl Harbor, Wake, and the Philippines, his complaints vanished. Similarly, fighter-pilot Raider, at first only a hitchhiker on the B-17 (which was to fly him to a new assignment), eventually assumed the pilot's role after the regular captain's death. Winocki's peace, however, was less natural. Like Bat in *Angels*, he had to perform special tasks to prove himself: refusing to bail out and leave the wounded pilot behind (a sequence repeated exactly from *Angels*), and hurrying to rescue a parachuting flyer being attacked by Japanese planes.

Both *Objective, Burma!* and *Wake Island* depicted the outsider as a civilian (*Burma*'s war correspondent, *Wake*'s contractor). But the war correspondent's latent pacifism was only slightly threatening and easily corrected. More troubling was contractor McClosky's initial refusal to obey air raid warnings, his disdain for the American servicemen on the island ('Just once, I'd like to see a marine do a good day's work'), and his general insubordination ('I've got my government contract, and there's not one word in it about taking orders from brass hats'). Inevitably, however, he

198

changed his tune when the Japanese attacked, sharing a foxhole to the last with the island's marine commander, swapping football stories between grenade throws.

Hollywood's combat films, therefore, were merely a new and radically simplified version of the classic pattern of reconciliation established by the prewar commercial cinema. Above all, they reaffirmed the myth that proposed the compatibility of individual and community values. Only after the war, when the need for morale-boosting disappeared, did the real image of World War II and its effects on American culture begin to appear. The movies made between Pearl Harbor and VJ Day, then, were merely the last products of the Classic Hollywood whose enormous power could convert even a world war into another occasion for its exercise.

1. Basil Wright, *The Long View* (New York: Knopf, 1974), p. 153.
2. Manny Farber, *Negative Space* (New York: Praeger, 1971), pp. 26–7.
3. Peter John Dyer, 'Sling the Lamps Low', in *Focus on Howard Hawks*, ed. Joseph McBride (Englewood Cliffs, NJ: Prentice-Hall, 1972), p. 85.
4. '*Rio Bravo*', in *Focus on Howard Hawks*, ed. McBride, p. 129.
5. Richard Schickel, *The Men Who Made the Movies* (New York: Atheneum, 1975), p. 105.
6. *Negative Space*, p. 27.
7. Lawrence H. Suid, *Guts and Glory: Great American War Movies* (Reading, Mass.: Addison-Wesley, 1978), p. 53.

Robert B. Ray's *A Certain Tendency of the Hollywood Cinema, 1930–1980* (Princeton, NJ, and Guildford, Surrey: Princeton University Press, 1985), from which this essay is a chapter, was a hugely ambitious attempt to make sense of the ideological and formal strategies of Hollywood in changing industrial and historical circumstances. Ray's convincing argument here is that the classic structure of *Only Angels Have Wings*, though itself not a war film, set the model for the combat films made during World War II. Ray's work combines the increasing acceptance of the need for ideological analysis of movies (see, for example, Sklar's essay on *Red River*, in this volume) with the growing interest at this time in identifying and understanding the narrative and visual conventions of 'classical Hollywood', represented notably by David Bordwell, Janet Staiger and Kristin Thompson, *The Classical Hollywood Cinema: Film Style and Mode of Production to 1960* (New York: Columbia University Press and London: Routledge & Kegan Paul, 1985). The title of Ray's book reworks the title of a famous, polemical 1954 essay on French cinema by François Truffaut.

Howard the Dreamer

SLIM KEITH

From Slim Keith, *Slim* (New York: Simon & Schuster, 1990).

For all of Howard's coldness, he always wanted me with him. He appreciated my style, and the comfort I provided his guests and the little things I did to make our home special; but mostly, I think he liked the way I looked. For him, I was a fabulous armpiece, the ultimate decoration, the embodiment of the Hawks woman. It wasn't about the woman herself, it was about a look. Howard liked a no-nonsense femininity. His woman could be chic, she could be sexy, but you'd better believe she could also make a ham and hoe a row of beans.

That was pretty much how I looked when I met Howard. He took it a step further by supplying me with gear – sporty things, always in beige. He liked me in well-cut, man-tailored styles. If you can compare this look to anything today, it's the Ralph Lauren image of a woman.

In film history, this clean-cut, frank female has come to be known as the Hawksian woman. She's unusual in the Hollywood movies of the thirties and forties because, although she's quite direct about wanting to be with a man, she's not passive, clinging, or dependent. On the contrary, she's an equal. She can hold her own against any man in verbal ping-pong, as Katharine Hepburn did in *Bringing Up Baby*. She can work on the same professional level as a man, like Rosalind Russell in *His Girl Friday*. And although Carole Lombard regresses at the end of *Twentieth Century*, we remember her mostly for her strong-minded refusal to be duped after years of being strung along.

There were many flavors of this Hawks woman. Physically, though, I think there were only two: Lauren Bacall and me. The former was created by Howard Hawks to be a screen image of his wife. I'm not saying that I was the inspiration for the Hawks woman – Howard had been working out this formula woman for years in his films. Rather, it was that, until he met me, the woman of his dreams was only in his head. And until Howard got to Betty Bacall, there hadn't been an actress to make that dream come alive on screen.

I want to be clear here. In *To Have and Have Not*, Howard wasn't exploiting me, not in the least. I knew he was having trouble casting the role of Marie – the character Bogart always calls 'Slim'. And I knew that the 'natural look', which is what Howard wanted, wasn't to be found in the actresses then popular in Hollywood. There were tough women, there were outdoorsy women, and there were sleek women; but you couldn't name one actress who, in one movie, could be all of those women. And *To Have and Have Not*, as Howard envisioned it, required an actress with a knack for sultry, insolent delivery but who could maintain a thoroughbred look.

Betty Bacall would have surfaced sooner or later. Thanks to Diana Vreeland, she was often on the cover of *Harper's Bazaar*. And she deserved to be; in those shots, Betty was just outstanding. So, when I saw her picture on the cover of *Bazaar*, I knew that she was the unknown Howard had been searching for. She was certainly my taste in beauty – scrubbed clean, healthy, shining, and golden. And there was definitely a bit of the panther about her.

I showed Howard the magazine. He immediately had Charlie Feldman, his agent and then partner, call to find out about this girl. They flew her out to Hollywood, gave her a screen test, then had her hang around for six months until the movie came together.

Though I'm often credited with 'discovering' Betty, what was more significant was the way Howard used me as the model for her character in *To Have and Have Not* – he used my clothes, my name, and my speech. Once he hired Betty, he suddenly became very interested in everything I had to say. Now he listened to me as if I were speaking lines created by the screenwriters Jules Furthman and William Faulkner. In his eagerness, Howard would sometimes show his cards and directly ask me what I'd say in a certain situation. Dutifully, I'd answer the question. The next thing I knew, Furthman and Faulkner were running it through their typewriters.

At the end of this process, Jules Furthman told me, 'You know, Slim, you should also get screen credit on this film, because so much of the material is yours. The character certainly is.' All those memorable lines like, 'You know how to whistle, don't you? – just put your lips together and blow,' or, 'No matter how bad it is, don't apologize for it; there it is, take it or leave it,' were certainly not Hemingway's words. Nor were they Faulkner's or Furthman's.

Howard was no ingrate about my contribution. I didn't get a writing credit, but he did acknowledge me for discovering Lauren Bacall. When he signed her for the film, he put her under contract – and gave me half ownership. Later, we 'sold' Bacall. This was my first – and last – lucrative business deal, similar to selling a very fine racehorse. It sounds crass and absurd to talk about contractual ownership of a person in this way. But that was how it was done then. The important thing is that Betty Bacall understood my interest in her extended far beyond a business deal. We were friends then. Forty years later, we still are.

Slim Keith was Hawks's wife at the time of some of his finest films. Molly Haskell suggests that the 'Hawksian woman', which Naomi Wise and

Leigh Brackett discuss in their entries in this volume, was not fully formed until the 1940s, and this certainly fits in with Keith's claim here that she was an important influence in the emergence of this figure, or type. Certainly, it is useful to put her comments alongside those of James Agee and Lauren Bacall's own account in *By Myself*. Keith's book also tells a lot of tales of Hawks's personal life, and such revelations will have fed into, for example, David Thomson's 1994 postscript to his 1970 Hawks entry in *A Biographical Dictionary of Film* (published as *A Biographical Dictionary of the Cinema* (London: Secker & Warburg, 1970, revised 1975; revised and enlarged edition, London: Andre Deutsch and New York: Knopf, 1994)): 'The more one learns of his life, the clearer it is that he was a chronic liar and compartmentalizer, a secretive rogue, a stealthy dandy, and a ruinous womanizer', pointing to 'the mess of his life beside the heroic grace of the films'.

Fig Leaves in Hollywood: Female Representation and Consumer Culture

JEANNE THOMAS ALLEN

From Jane Gaines and Charlotte Herzog (eds), *Fabrications* (New York and London: Routledge, 1990).

A narrative, theorists tell us, requires a motivating enigma or problem. The de-stabilized or unresolved situation moves toward a new configuration or returns to the status quo. Making a woman's 'lack' (she 'hasn't a thing to wear') the propelling engine of an entire feature-length film may seem at first a *thin* plot structure and then a remarkably *transparent* ideological project. To harness 'natural' female acquisitiveness to capitalist market imperatives! Containing this engine of propulsion within patriarchal prerogatives becomes the 'driving force' within Howard Hawks's film of 1926, *Fig Leaves*.[1]

The film's narrative precludes the possibility of woman's economic and sexual self-reliance by casting her rebellion against her husband's control as a flight into near-prostitution (the familiar film noir dichotomy revived in *Klute* (1971) and *Fatal Attraction* (1987)). Within that narrative dynamic, women's clothing becomes the ground of a struggle, both literal and figurative, for control of women's bodies. The disclosure of a sexual double standard in the film's dramatic climax, which drops the mantle of parody and satire in an exclusively serious moment, discloses the tension which also contains the film's project – the machinery of male competitive individualism and female manipulative sexuality for economic advantage. Tensions can propel but they can also burst in the text with the possibility of alternatives. But in the case of *Fig Leaves* such a rupture depends upon the viewer and the context; the text contains the tension. This analysis of the conjuncture of text and context will explore the resources for containment and rupture in this moment of Hollywood film representation by exemplifying some of the ways in which film and social practices are related in the representation of female sexuality and identity.

Hollywood and film glamour. It is difficult to see one apart from the other. Glamour unites Hollywood production technique to consumer values, particularly around the image of woman as the ultimate product for consumption and mark of social class distinction. The conjunction of film stars with consumer products in luxurious surroundings which Charles Eckert explicates in his history of pressbook promotion,[2] and the placement of this representation in a viewing context of similar splendor as Ben Hall and Charlotte Herzog describe in their histories of the movie palace,[3] reveal some of the ways in which consumerist social philosophy in urban America coincided with the building of a motion picture audience. Motion pictures offered the American population the image of an opulent lifestyle and the chance to rent it for a couple of hours.

Stuart Ewen has outlined consumerist social philosophy (the construction of social identity and behavior through buying) in his history of American advertising in the 1920s,[4] published only a few years before Lary May's social history of the motion picture traced the relation between movies and consumer culture, a conjuncture reminiscent of American's national birth and industrialization.[5] May describes Hollywood as a national symbol and trend-setter for the modern consumer lifestyle. A year later Richard Griffith similarly points to the films of Cecil B. DeMille as an index to a shift in social mores from Victorian thrift, hard work, and asceticism to consumerist sensuality and opulence.[6] Although Griffith cites more specific elements of *mise en scène* than May, he stops short of an explication of a single film.[7]

'The Film Viewer as Consumer', in which I consider both direct and indirect uses of film to advertise and promote consumer products, indicates a recognition of the promotional value of motion pictures in the industry's exhibition practices. In this earlier article I discuss the influence of promotion on thematic and stylistic elements in my analysis of the 1935 RKO Astaire-Rogers vehicle *Roberta*. Rather than arguing as May does that this conjuncture was a phenomenon of the 1920s, however, my study points instead to early motion picture history and an inherited legacy within the legitimate theater and other 'picturing' media which bound together spectatorial entertainment, possession, and class position. Motion pictures, as I show here, would extend this alliance in the era of national chain store marketing and motion picture theater chains.[8]

Raymond Williams's discussion of 'realism' in the European theater (1870–1920) acknowledges the importance of luxuriously appointed and richly detailed surroundings in establishing the material and class-inflected context of psychological realism;[9] John Berger's examination of Western European oil paintings as celebrations of the ownership of private property and its tactile qualities takes this thread of ideologically motivated representation even further back to 1500.[10] The American version of this representational tradition is seen in the last decades of the nineteenth century in the commercial trade-off which produced opulent interiors for Boston theaters: businesses donated lobby and stage ornamentation in return for credits on the program.[11]

Although May does not discuss these practices which specify the late nineteenth-century consumer/spectator's relation to props and property, he sees motion pictures as extending the spectatorial relations of the theater (incorporating the tactile aesthetic of realism described by Berger and Williams) to a mass public.[12] With the enhancement of an increasingly sophisticated set of codes which constitute Hollywood glamour, film fashions in dress became one of the codes of opulent realism that dominated the *mise en scène*. Film fashions were also inextricably tied to the bodies of women and to the representation of the female form. This was the same link that had sold theater tickets just as earlier fashion lithographs and prints had sold thousands of women's mass circulation magazines in the nineteenth century. It is this relation between representational, social, and economic practices as well as the relation between fashion and narrative that is crystallized and disclosed in the instance of *Fig Leaves*.

In *Fig Leaves*, consumerist values are cast in terms of Original Sin: forbidden, guilt-inducing, titillating, and alluring. The story alternates between a Biblical/pre-historic setting and a modern day household. In both periods, the same newly married couple argues about domestic purchases until the wife, on the sly, oversteps the bonds of matrimony to earn money for her new clothes. Original Sin is traditionally linked to a curiosity which results in a knowledge of good and evil and of sexual shame. Eve's case of the 'gimmes' (Adam says, 'Ever since you ate that apple, you've had the gimmes – first twin beds and now clothes'), as good a slang term for consumerism as any, indicates her knowledge of consumer products and her desire for new clothes. In this pre-Production Code film, Adam and Eve as honeymooners display their twin beds and argue about a sale on fig leaves, blending notions of sex, sin, and consumer indulgence. After the prehistoric Adam leaves for work, Eve's friend, represented by a puppet in the form of a snake, enters her house. The subtitle tells us: 'The serpent in Eden was in all likelihood a Woman who lived across the hall and sympathized with Eve.' The serpent tells Eve that 'men don't realize women must have pretty things'.

But by the 1920s men were not only 'realizing that women must have pretty things', they were telling them that they must. A 1927 article in *Theatre Management*[13] stressed the importance of women as the primary motivators of film attendance and argued that both the appeal of the film and the allure of the theater must be geared to pleasing women's sensibilities. Art works in the lobbies and attractive interior design appealed to women's tastes for opulence and spaciousness. Music rooms and comfortable lounges for reading simulated domestic intimacy. Another dimension of exhibition practice associated film viewing with shopping as early as 1910, projecting consumer products available for sale at department stores. This practice would culminate after World War II with the pre-television 16mm Sonovision (film in a screened cabinet), and plans to make film exhibition a magnet at suburban shopping centers and recreational complexes.[14] In the 1920s the motion picture palace's aristocratic decor matched the proximity of film viewing to shopping areas as invitations to merge on-screen and off-screen surroundings.

The knowledge that trade, both domestic and international, 'follows the film' was evident in the United States during the second decade of the twentieth century. A seminar at the Harvard Business School acknowledged the business community's indebtedness to film as a means of showcasing products and thereby stimulating exports.[15] The Webb-Pomerene Act of 1918 had legislated Hollywood's ability to act as a cartel, internationally

205

advancing America's trade balance strength with an attractive product and a vehicle for the promotion of American consumer lifestyles.[16] One aspect of this was featured in *Paramount's Picture Progress*, an in-house promotional magazine which in 1916 offered articles explicitly arguing the potential of motion picture to shape consumer habits: a forecast of spring fashions designed exclusively for Paramount Pictographs and a description of the way in which fashionable women derive ideas for interior decorations by copying film sets.[17]

Initially set in a 'cave man' quasi-Biblical era, *Fig Leaves* would seem an unlikely showcase for fashionable interiors. Indeed, in comparison with the exquisite clothing and lighting of the fashion show sequence, the *mise en scène* of *Fig Leaves* is low budget and drab. Although in a later interview director Howard Hawks cites the fact that only the fashion show segments appeared in color, he gives us no real explanation for this aesthetic choice. Color processes at this point were highly unusual for technical and economic reasons, but Hawks makes no reference to that element of *mise en scène* over which he had little control and which provides the *raison d'être* for color – the costumes.[18] Designed by leading Hollywood fashion designer Gilbert Adrian, the costuming is such a major 'character' that Adrian competes with Hawks (perhaps as 'principal source of enunciation'), a competition made more apparent by the rivalry between the Hawksian situation of comradely working men, the humor of sexual stereotypes, and the world of *haute couture*.

Given what we know from auteurist studies of Howard Hawks, his second feature seems an anomaly. But there is an affinity between the director's 'screwball comedies' (*Bringing Up Baby*, 1938, and *His Girl Friday*, 1940) and this film's comedic play with gender difference. *Fig Leaves* balances the visual glamour and narrative centrality of fashion against the effete villainy and final renunciation of the couturier (if not the clothes) – a very Hawksian gesture. In *Fig Leaves*, the auteur director meets the auteur designer. Adrian was one of a handful of Hollywood fashion designers whose screen costumes had a direct influence on retail fashion marketing, although MGM never merchandized copies of his gowns as Warner Brothers marketed their designer Orry-Kelly's clothes. Adrian's entrepreneurship, however, is clear in his authorial signature and in his conscious attempt to affect consumption trends.[19] While on first consideration Hawks doesn't seem to be an ideal collaborator, one might recall that his first job in the film industry was as prop man for Cecil B. DeMille, the one director whom Griffith and May both identify as the key proponent of Hollywood's consumerist lifestyle. After an apprenticeship with DeMille, Hawks scripted, directed, and financed two comic shorts at Paramount and then MGM. But his first feature as a director, *The Road to Glory* (1926), was a melodrama which failed both financially and critically. Hawks quickly recouped his losses with *Fig Leaves* which he claimed he wrote in one night. The film made its costs at a single theater.[20]

Fig Leaves's comedy is based on gender stereotypes and the threat of role reversal. The 'Adam and Eve' setting naturalizes the 'battle of the sexes' into a universal, positing female greed exceeding patriarchal loyalty. Having introduced Adam and Eve in their primitive surroundings which parody and yet universalize modern lifestyles, the film reverts to a contemporary setting after Adam's departure for work on the dinosaur-drawn commuter wagon. Left to mend the very clothes which the narrative sets up as her 'problem', Eve is visited by the neighborly and talkative snake. In a dissolve, the snake becomes a modern woman advising her female friend to get herself the clothes she wants by getting a job.

After Eve delivers Adam's lunch to him and charms five dollars from him for a hat, she accidentally is hit by a car carrying Joseph Andre, a famous couturier. He whisks her off to his house of fashion design to replace her damaged clothes and to woo her with charm and an offer to model his designs. Eve seeks to win Adam over to the idea but fails and decides to work for Andre without telling Adam. The neighbor who has advised Eve to get a job so that she can buy her own clothes meanwhile tries to seduce Adam, implying that she is untrustworthy and perhaps motivated in her advice by the desire to lure Eve's husband away from her. Unbeknownst to Eve, Adam has succumbed to her pleas for fancy clothes. He goes to Andre's to choose a dress for her, and instead finds his wife modeling the fanciest and skimpiest dress in the show. He denounces what he sees as her preference for clothes over her husband, although he *pays for them*, and leaves without her. Eve wins Adam back by confronting her neighbor and championing her husband who overhears her and returns. At the end, the film reverts to the 'cave man' setting, and Adam suggests that they go to a party whereupon Eve complains that she hasn't 'a thing to wear'.

The comedy of the film rests in the incompatibility of the stereotypical man and woman whose gender is defined oppositionally and who manipulate each other's dependency rather than act on mutual self-reliance with compromise, the same incompatibility which is interpolated as tragic contradiction in melodrama. In *Fig Leaves*, gender incompatibility is explained as female acquisitiveness threatening to subvert male dominance and control, although the market imperative for acquisitiveness or the ideological imperative for patriarchal dominance is not disclosed. Instead, acquisitiveness is naturalized and mystified into a feminine essence responsible for a disturbance in the status quo, rather than the very maintenance of the status quo.

The film's solution is the comedic presentation of an endless chain of buying to reassure social class position after the struggle over ownership – the woman's possession of clothes, the man's possession of the woman. The film's denouement implies that one struggle can be resolved by another: if men continue to buy clothing to please women, they can prevent women from working and gaining economic self-sufficiency. When Adam visits the House of Andre to select a gown for his wife, suspense builds during the fashion show because of the audience's knowledge that Eve will shortly appear as a model and that she has kept the fact of her employment a secret from him. The fashion show sequences then rivet audience attention on several levels: that of the *mise en scène* because these are the only scenes in color and are lavishly lit and staged, and that of the narrative because it is constructed as building dramatic tension through suspense. In this sense, the eight-minute fashion show is not a point of narrative stasis but rather a climactic crescendo. Cut-aways to and reaction shots of Adam's work partner flirting with the models as they pass the fashion show audience and another observer's question, 'Which one did you like best, father? I mean the clothes', support the way the film positions the House of Andre as an expensive brothel and prepare for Adam's explosion of horror and indignation as he sees his wife modeling an especially dramatic dress, cut in a revealing manner.

The dialogue confrontation between husband and wife shortly after the modeling scene consists of this exchange:

'What a fine wife you turned out to be.'
'But I only wanted clothes.'
'More clothes? A fig leaf would be an overcoat for you.'
'You didn't get them for me so I went out to earn them – that's every woman's right.'
'– and every man's right is to respect his wife and not have her parade around half naked. You cared more for clothes than you did for me. Keep the clothes.'

This verbal exchange, marked by a lack of parody or humor, is significant for the way it intertwines positions about women's marital, sexual, and economic dependence. *Woman's right* to economic self-reliance is conflated with sexual indecency, confirming Julie Matthaei's observation that nineteenth-century Victorian patriarchal ideology constructed male potency as marked by the ability to keep a woman as a non-paid domestic servant.[21] In *Fig Leaves*, the 'shop floor' is only a step away from the theatrical stage of high-class burlesque. Clothing design is featured as a male activity, evidenced by the subtitle of the fashion show program which reads: 'Joseph Andre's gifts to glorious womanhood'. As Jane Gaines's introduction points out, 'extravagant costuming, justified as history, confirms a woman's concerns and interests by elevating them from ordinariness to the status of exquisite object. The elegant gown is an homage to woman's "preoccupations".' No factories staffed by women, no female operators of textile machinery nor any sales women in clothing stores are represented. The film, however, contextualizes women's work as theatrical performance which is self-indulgent, disloyal, sexually indecent, and even adulterous. The narrative climax and resolution make it clear that for Eve, the appropriate avenue for realizing her goals is the manipulation of her husband.

Although forty to fifty percent of single women were in the labor force at any one time in the 1920s, they differed from men in that their participation was regarded as a temporary stage to be superseded after marriage by the labor of homemaking.[22] Since the whole motive in working was to serve the family, these women compromised the benefits of self-improvement. By contrast, the competitive ethic became the predominant masculine ethic, harnessing masculine competition to capital expansion. The presence of white married women in the home conferred upon their husbands the position of family provider as the essence of emerging manhood. In 1924 statistics on married women working in industrial jobs indicate that the only purpose for married women to be gainfully employed was 'to provide necessities for their families or raise their standard of living'.[23] Married women at work were less often pioneering new roles for women than fulfilling – in times of economic crisis – essentially domestic obligations.

Yet after World War I, Alice Kessler-Harris reports, a new generation of female wage workers emerged who hoped for more than economic survival, partly as a result of non-traditional employment opportunities during the War, the beginning of the Federal Civil Service, and the expanding need for telephone and telegraph operators as well as clerks and bookkeepers.[24] 'To significant numbers of women, marriage and work no longer seemed like mutually exclusive alternatives . . . the proportion of married women (from 1920 to 1930) had jumped from 22.8 percent to 28.8 percent of the female work force – an increase of more than 25 percent.'[25] Yet the earnings gap widened until at the end of the decade women's wages averaged only 57 percent of men's.[26] At the same time, advertising, seeking to locate the markets created by newly electrified and relatively prosperous households, targeted women. Eighty percent of sales decisions were made by women: 82 percent of department store purchases, 81 percent of grocery stores, 75 percent of piano purchases and men's socks, 90 percent of jewelry, 80 percent of electrical supplies, 40 percent of automobiles. Women spent more on clothes than any other member of the family.[27]

Women's rights are referred to twice in the *Fig Leaves* dialogue, once in the exchange previously quoted as the right to earn money for clothes if her husband refuses to buy them and earlier when Adam commutes to work and pushes a woman from her seat so that he can sit and read. At this point the woman turns to another standing next to her and says, 'Mark my words, dearie – some day we'll get our rights.' Women's rights here are neither economic nor political independence and suffrage but the right to Victorian paternalism. But the definition of husbands' and wives' rights – the husband's right to contain his wife's sexuality and the wife's rights to earn money if the husband doesn't buy her what she wants, the rights which propel the engine of capitalist patriarchy – is less apparent in the dialogue's display of a double standard in *Fig Leaves* than in the parallel construction of scenes organized around romantic jealousy.

Eve's seductive attempts to persuade Adam to allow her to work for pay outside the home are unsuccessful and then interrupted by the woman neighbor's request for assistance. Adam leaves their apartment to help although the request is revealed as a pretense for her to flirt and ply him with alcohol. Adam returns after a prolonged absence, disheveled and smeared with lipstick. Berated by his wife, he mocks and laughs at her ('You're so cute when you're mad' is his familiar trivializing line). He is neither responsible for disloyalty nor does he feel remorse for his actions. Yet the scene in which he discovers his wife's deceitful behavior – modeling clothes behind his back – borrows the narrative conventions of a husband's discovery of adultery. The scene is free from any marking of parody or satire, although there is no suggestion of intimacy between the couturier and Eve analogous to the sexual 'dallying' between Adam and his neighbor. Eve has betrayed Adam with her attraction for clothes; the film situates women's work outside the home as virtual adultery.

The fashion show provides the vehicle of suspense building to Adam's outraged confrontation of Eve with the evidence of her 'infidelity' and the outcome of the dramatic crisis. The spectator simultaneously experiences the greatest sensual pleasure the film offers and the anxiety of anticipating the discovery of deceit: forbidden fruit and Original Sin. The fact that numerous films of previous years presented extra-marital sexual dalliance for the majority of the narrative only to satisfy conventional morality with a swift and correct resolution helps us to understand the fashion show as the representative stand-in for illicit sex. Further, the show functions as a condensed version of the language of conventional female wiles much as the gangster ballet in the musical *The Band Wagon* (1954) condenses and formalizes the gangster genre conventions. The pose of the fashion show model is a kind of parody of the manipulative behavior Eve uses with her husband. Thus in the demure, coy, alternately exhibitionistic and submissive gestures of the models we see an extrapolation of the codes of wifely conduct. The seeming contradiction in Adam's denunciation of this behavior is suppressed by the fact that the fashion show is public, and that the models are 'performing' for other men. The striking contrast between this sequence and the rest of the film, which is flat in lighting and design, is stylistically emphasized by cutting between the stunning depth and gloss of the models on the dais backed by draperies of silver and the reactions of the spectators. The contrast recalls the discrepancy in production costs and values between television advertisements and prime-time programs.

The sexually manipulative spectacle/object nature of fashion show modeling carries over into the models' offstage behavior in the House of Andre. They are approached consecutively by a Svengali type who offers to make them a star: 'Be my inspiration for creative genius.' One of the chief models indicates that she is not jealous of Eve because she is well provided for and reveals an expensive jeweled bracelet. The line between 'true love' and economically motivated or 'purchased' love in the film is a fine one, opening a web of contradiction almost endlessly imitated on American prime-time soaps. The devious woman neighbor conveys the implication that Andre bestows clothing in return for sexual favors, making ambiguous the basis of earning a wage yet holding the worker responsible. In this context, the fashion show comes to resemble the parade or 'stable' for customer selection of sexual favors rather than the selection of clothes.

The rarely acknowledged parallels between the socially required behavior of wives and the socially outlawed behavior of 'kept women' surface only occasionally in the American film. One recalls Julie Christie's madame in *McCabe and Mrs Miller* (1971) instructing a prospective prostitute: 'You get to keep the money – and you don't have to do any dishes.' Also Eve's fashion show self-presentation – wearing a cut-away skin-tight dress with breasts thrust forward, back arched, and arms extended behind her for maximal vulnerability – is exactly the pose imitated endlessly in pornography. However, Eve's renunciation of Andre with the line, 'It would take a dozen Joseph Andre's to make one Adam Smith', not only suggests a pun on the name of the early leading capitalist theorist and proponent of the division of labor, but an explicit indication that she has chosen the couturier over her husband and now regrets that choice. Working women do not gain financial independence so much as they substitute the prerogatives of a male employer for those of a husband in a situation where the employer is presumably shared among women and the women are less valued than they would be in marriage.

Woman working as fashion model has been collapsed into near-prostitution through recourse to the dramatic conventions employed in the narrative exposure of illicit, adulterous sexuality: deception, anticipation, confrontation, the sight of the transgression, and the look of horror. And in this melodramatic scenario, Andre figures as a manipulative and villainous 'Don Juan'. The technical and melodramatic conventions which present the fashion show and which make clothes the primary motivator of narrative action also give them the status of romance or sexual desire which are all the more alluring for their forbidden quality. Hollywood's consciousness of fans' desire to imitate the stars lends a double entendre quality to the line, 'It would take a dozen Joseph Andre's to make one Adam Smith.' Indeed a dozen capitalist entrepreneurs governing a female labor force might generate an economic theorist who would invent the cornerstone of mass production to generate the mass consumption which *Fig Leaves* so excellently models and showcases.

This analysis has traced the intersection of American social history (women's labor history in particular), film exhibition practices, film style and narrative structure, and the ideological contradictions surrounding women's social role in patriarchal capitalism. However, the comedic tone of the film suggests the possibility that the double standard of male and female behavior might be a subject for parody, might break out of the fissures of the narrative and its *mise en scène*. Indeed, a feminist 'reading against the grain' of *Fig Leaves* might find the structural parallel between unmarried women working outside the home and married women working within it as a condition revealing signs of strain. But the melodramatic seriousness of Adam's renunciation of Eve's 'wrong-doing' and her penitent return to him suggest the 'rescued from a life of sin' tradition of nineteenth-century melodrama as seen in *Way Down East* (1920). I suspect that this pattern was strong enough in 1926 to override an oppositional reading. The moment of dramatic climax, when the film's ideological project synthesizes the gaze of patriarchal condemnation with the theatrical convention of adultery exposed, is unambiguously serious. Were there women in that era of strained expectations – married women entering the labor force when the gap was widening between men's and women's salaries, but advertising was increasingly pitched at women consumers – for whom the contradictions

211

may have reached the breaking point? We have no way of knowing for certain.

The attractions of consumer culture via fashion are showcased but held out of women's reach – unless, of course, they gain them within the bounds of patriarchal respectability as wife or courtesan, the parallel which lurks here but is largely denied. The goals of subservience, dependency, and female sexual modesty are best served, *Fig Leaves* overwhelmingly maintains, within the channels of patriarchal proprietary dominance. The post-apology implication of repetition ('Let's go to a party'/'But Adam, I haven't a thing to wear') implies the continuation of the engine of capitalism – female acquisitiveness contained by male competitive individualism and patriarchal prerogative – more than the rupture of the contradictions.

1. *Fig Leaves* (1926). Produced by Fox Film Corp. Directed by Howard Hawks. Written by Hope Loring and Louis D. Lighton. Story by Howard Hawks. Photographed by Joseph August (two sequences in Technicolor). Costumes by Adrian. Cast: George O'Brien, Olive Borden, Andre de Beranger, Phyllis Haver, Heine Conklin, and William Austin.
2. Charles Eckert, 'The Carole Lombard in Macy's Window', *Quarterly Review of Film Studies*, vol. 3 no. 1 (Winter 1978), pp. 1–23.
3. Ben Hall, *The Best Remaining Seats* (New York: Bramball House, 1961), p. 136; see also Charlotte Herzog, 'Movie Palaces and Exhibition', *Film Reader* 2 (January 1977), pp. 185–97.
4. Stuart Ewen, *Captains of Consciousness: Advertising and the Social Roots of the Consumer Culture* (New York: McGraw-Hill, 1976).
5. Lary May, *Screening Out the Past: The Birth of Mass Culture and the Motion Picture Industry* (Chicago: University of Chicago Press, 1980).
6. Richard Griffith, Arthur Mayer and Eileen Bowser, *The Movies* (New York: Simon & Schuster, 1981), pp. 123–33.
7. Griffith, Mayer, and Bowser, *The Movies*, pp. 130–3.
8. Jeanne Thomas Allen, 'The Film Viewer as Consumer', *Quarterly Review of Film Studies*, vol 5 no 4 (Fall 1980), pp. 481–99.
9. Raymond Williams, 'A Lecture on Realism', *Screen*, vol. 18 no. 1 (Spring 1977), pp. 66–7.
10. John Berger, *Ways of Seeing* (New York: The Viking Press, 1972), pp. 83–112.
11. Schubert Theatre handbill, Boston, Massachusetts, 4 August 1908 (Theatre Collection, University of Iowa Library, Iowa City, Iowa).
12. May, *Screening Out the Past*, p. 36.
13. Peggy Goldberg, 'You've Got to Sell the Ladies – the Buyers of Amusement', *Theatre Management* (November 1927), pp. 43–4; Larry S. Harris, 'Large Enough for a Community with the Comforts of Home', *Theatre Management* (January 1928), p. 71.
14. Peggy Goldberg, 'A Motion Picture Theatre in a Department Store', *Edison Kinetogram*, vol. 1 no. 11 (1 January 1910), p. 12; *Business Screen*, vol. 6 no. 6 (1945), p. 6; J. Harry Toler, 'Motion Picture Theaters, a $300,000,000 Market for Industrial Products', *Industrial Marketing*, vol. 30 no. 6 (June 1945), pp. 45ff.
15. Sidney R. Kent, 'Distributing the Product', *The Story of the Films*, ed. Joseph P. Kennedy (New York: A. W. Shaw Co., 1927), pp. 202–32.
16. Thomas Guback, 'Hollywood's International Market', *The American Film Industry*, ed. Tino Balio (Madison: The University of Wisconsin Press, 1976), pp. 387–409.
17. S. Zalud, 'Forecast of Spring Fashion', *Picture Progress* (March 1916), pp. 13, 20; Dorothy Nutting, 'Home Making', *Picture Progress* (January 1917), pp. 16–17.
18. Joseph McBride (ed.), *Hawks on Hawks* (Berkeley: University of California Press, (1982), p. 4.
19. Maureen Turim, 'Fashion Shapes', *Socialist Review*, no. 71 (September/October 1983), p. 83. The author offers no source for this information. See also Charlotte Cornelia Herzog and Jane Marie Gaines, ' "Puffed Sleeves Before Teatime": Joan Crawford, Adrian and Women Audiences', *Wide Angle*, vol. 6 no. 4 (1985), p. 25.
20. McBride, *Hawks on Hawks*, pp. 21–2.

21. Julie Matthaei, *An Economic History of Women in America* (New York: Schocken Books, 1982), p. 121.
22. Matthaei, *Economic History of Women*, pp. 155–6.
23. Leslie Woodcock Tentler, *Wage-Earning Women* (New York: Oxford University Press, 1979), p. 142.
24. Alice Kessler-Harris, *Out to Work: A History of Wage-Earning Women in the United States* (New York: Oxford University Press, 1982), p. 226.
25. Kessler-Harris, *Out To Work*, p. 229.
26. Kessler-Harris, *Out To Work*.
27. Alice Kessler-Harris, *Women Have Always Worked: A Historical Overview* (Old Westbury, NY: The Feminist Press, 1982), p. 133.

In her essay which concludes this volume, Laura Mulvey refers to the important discoveries being made in current research into the history of the Hollywood film industry. Jeanne Thomas Allen's essay on *Fig Leaves*, one of Hawks's first films, is a good example of such work, combining as it does a broad feminist framework and a consciousness of Hawks as auteur with a range of historical perspectives relating to women in the labour force, consumer society and film exhibition practices. It is at this point that film criticism and theory blurs into the wider discipline of cultural studies.

Gentlemen Prefer Blondes: Anita Loos/Howard Hawks/Marilyn Monroe

LAURA MULVEY

Although *Gentlemen Prefer Blondes* must be Howard Hawks's biggest hit and his best-known film today, it has not had an easy time finding its place in the Hawksian *œuvre*. André Bazin even uses it to disavow auteurist extremism, saying: 'I don't have to like *Gentlemen Prefer Blondes*' in order to argue that all of a serious director's films need not be valued equally. Rather, the film lives on in popular imagination because it seems essential Hollywood in its gaudy Technicolor brashness, its flamboyant musical numbers and its unabashed flaunting of female sexual spectacle. And, as it launched the emblematic Marilyn Monroe look and style that came to stand for 50s Hollywood, its place in Hawks's works has been overshadowed by its own monumental reputation.

Two women have written 'seriously' about *Gentlemen Prefer Blondes* from an auteurist feminist and a feminist theoretical angle respectively. Molly Haskell describes it as 'a musical that is as close to satire as a Hawks film ever gets on the nature (and perversions) of sexual relations in America, especially the mammary-mad 50s'.[1] Maureen Turim draws attention to its relation to Anita Loos's 20s novel and to its apparent celebration of 50s consumerist values. She points out that 'the excesses of the film create a terrain of ambiguity fertile enough to support the perfect mass entertainment – a film whose ideological foundations are at once so evident and so hidden as to escape analysis'.[2] It is as though, like the perfect fetish, the film's shiny surface holds the gaze with a fascination that blocks out all inquiry and is rendered anathema to traditional and male auteurist critics. Although it is tempting, in this day and age, to break with this tradition and evaluate *Gentlemen Prefer Blondes* in terms of history, ideology and symptomology, without reference to the Hawks *œuvre*, the film does, in fact, need to be understood within an auteurist perspective. It thus raises significant issues for contemporary film theory. How can a film which so epitomizes the ideological overdeterminations of its historical moment be restored to the work of its director? And how can the collected works of a director be restored to historical context without infringing their coherence? Taking a feminist perspective may provide a starting point which can cross critical divides. *Gentlemen Prefer Blondes* is of interest on several immediate counts: it il-

214

luminates the central and perverse place of gender in Hawks's comedies, it belongs to the tradition of the desiring and daring Hawksian woman, while also encapsulating, like a symptom, American ambivalence about female sexuality, its ideological uses and its anxiety-provoking excesses.

Robin Wood, in his pioneering Hawks monograph published in 1968, had an appendix section called 'Failures and Marginal Films'. Here he describes *Gentlemen Prefer Blondes* as 'distinctive without being particularly distinguished' and ends: 'Of all Hawks's films, *Gentlemen Prefer Blondes* is the one most flawed by discrepancies between Hawks's daring originality and the "safe" conventions of a commercially orientated industry. It contains striking things but it disintegrates under analysis.' Wood identifies two main sources of failure. First of all, 'The brittle, petty humour of Anita Loos's book is incompatible with Hawks's robust and generous comic sense.' And then, 'Malone seems little more virile than Lorelei's helpless victim. . . . The characteristic humiliations imposed on Malone at the hands of the two women . . . quite overshadow any innate dignity he possesses'.[3]

Robin Wood's sense of the film's weaknesses coincides quite closely with my sense of its strengths. Not only is there more of Hawks than he allows but it is the Hawksian negotiation of the seemingly incongruous encounter between Anita Loos (essentially a figure of the 20s) and Marilyn Monroe (essentially a figure of the 50s) that makes the film, in the last resort, greater than a great auteur movie. Wood does, of course, point out the persistent significance of gender in Hawks's films, his uninhibited 'male love stories' in the action movies, his recurring headstrong women and the way he uses them to make fun of men in the comedies. Peter Wollen also pointed out the importance for Hawks's comedies of 'sex-reversal and role-reversal'.[4] In the 60s, arguments about the status of the director and consistency of themes in the aesthetics of popular cinema were crucial. Now, in the 90s, the film theory agenda has moved on. The struggle to establish auteur consistency tended to take a director's career and his films out of their historical context. *Gentlemen Prefer Blondes* demands to be understood both in the context of the 20s and the 50s; and Hawks as an auteur director, with his idiosyncratic attitude to women and to comedy, was able to preserve something of the liberated 20s into the repressive 50s. The result is, perhaps, more interesting than an absolutely pure Hawksian film.

1. *Gentlemen Prefer Blondes*: from Anita Loos to Howard Hawks

Gentlemen Prefer Blondes went through a number of transitions from medium to medium between 1926, when Anita Loos first came up with the story of Lorelei and her best friend Dorothy, and 1953, when the cycle closed with Hawks's film starring Marilyn Monroe and Jane Russell. In 1926 Anita Loos was working as a screenwriter in Hollywood and the original story starts in her beloved New York, travels across Europe and is resolved in Hollywood with Lorelei's apotheosis as movie star and mogul. The blonde ends up, appropriately, on the screen. While the film substitutes marriage for Hollywood, the 'history' of *Gentlemen Prefer Blondes* also connects chronologically with the history of Hawks's own Hollywood career, drawing attention to the director's own origins in pre-synch sound cinema and 20s Hollywood. He directed his first two films in 1926, after working his way up in the industry for about ten years. From then he directed continuously, producing films almost every year, and very often more than one a year, until 1953. Soon after *Gentlemen Prefer Blondes* the Hollywood industry went into crisis and Hawks's career went into a new, and for him disconcerting, phase.

If there is something timely about the place of *Gentlemen Prefer Blondes* in Hawks's career, there is also something symptomatic about its representation of contemporary relations between the United States and Europe. Just as Lorelei and Dorothy were sailing across the Atlantic to Paris in the early 50s, the *Cahiers du Cinéma* critics were reassessing Hollywood cinema in the name of 'Hitchcocko-Hawksianism'. American–European relations were also being remodelled politically and economically by the Marshall Plan and the Cold War. US industry and the federal government saw in unison that American commodities had a sexiness that could counter the colourless asexuality of communism. If America was to export the democracy of glamour into post-war, impoverished Europe, the movies could be its shop window. The Hollywood industry, depending more than ever on the European box office for profits, eagerly joined in the export effort. So the US economy as a whole looked to Hollywood to promote a desire for 'American-ness' in these newly emerging markets that the industry itself needed to conquer. Marilyn Monroe, with her all-American attributes and streamlined sexuality, came to epitomize in a single image this complex interface of the economic, the political and the erotic. By the mid-50s, she stood for a brand of classless glamour, available to anyone using American cosmetics, nylons and peroxide. Later, of course, Marilyn was twice to play an American showgirl seducing the old world, in the form of Laurence Olivier in *The Prince and the Showgirl* (Warner Bros., 1957) and Yves Montand in *Let's Make Love* (20th Century-Fox, 1960).

There are certain parallels between this period and the mid-20s of the original *Gentlemen Prefer Blondes* novel. Then, too, America was making inroads into Europe economically and culturally. Hollywood had more or less established total domination of the international film industry and was also a successful shop window for American consumer goods. As William Fox said in 1926, 'I have tried to bring government officials to realise that trade follows the American motion picture, not the flag.'[5] Hollywood's power abroad was economic, built on its industrially organized, vertically integrated system of production, distribution and exhibition. But economics alone cannot account for its popularity. It was the projected image of America as a modern, affluent, free-thinking and progressive society that drew international audiences into the cinema. And this image was encapsulated above all else by the fashionable, liberated women who appeared on the screen. The women who wrote so many of these scenarios were as fashionable and liberated as the fictional characters they created and the stars who played them. Anita Loos herself worked hard, shopped hard and worked hard at fun with her close female friends, particularly Constance

'Dutch' Talmadge, for whom she wrote a series of comedy vehicles. By the 50s, the atmosphere in Hollywood was no longer so favourable to women professionals or to the kinds of stars or stories that had flourished in the 20s. For instance, Hawks's early films often have women credited as writers, whereas, later in his career, his use of Leigh Brackett is considered unusual. And the significance of Lorelei and Dorothy's relative autonomy and their same-sex friendship is rather overshadowed by the film's 50s look.

Anita Loos's *Gentlemen Prefer Blondes* is both a satire and a celebration. It celebrates the flapper, particularly Dorothy with her carefree promiscuity, her indifference to money and her down-to-earth, wise-cracking humour. It satirizes the blonde gold-digger, her insatiable appetite for shopping and the men who pay her bills. This is the social comment side of the story. From a personal point of view, Anita Loos has described the twofold origin of her observation of the blonde phenomenon. She was travelling by train from New York to Hollywood with her director husband John Emerson and Douglas Fairbanks and his entourage, which included his new leading lady, Mabel Minnow. Her effect on all the 'gentlemen' present caught Loos's attention and it also dented her usual confidence in her own powers of attraction: 'Could her strength possibly be rooted (like Samson) in her hair? She was a natural blonde and I was a brunette.' Later, she wrote up her blonde story as a revenge on her friend H. L. Mencken: 'Menck liked me very much indeed; but in the matter of sentiment, he preferred a witless blonde.'[6] Mencken suggested she should send the story to *Harper's Bazaar*, but the *Harper's* editor suggested she should turn it into a serial and, before long, this satire on men's taste in women was attracting a huge male readership. (James Joyce, who was losing his eyesight, saved his reading for Lorelei Lee.) The book was then such an astounding success that Florenz Ziegfeld immediately wanted to turn it into a musical. But, due to a prior commitment, Anita Loos dramatized it into an almost equally successful Broadway play and, after a lot of competition between studios, Paramount made it into a movie in 1928 (directed by Malcolm St. Clair and now lost).

Gentlemen Prefer Blondes finally became a musical in 1949, in another era. Now nostalgic rather than up-to-the-minute modern, it appeared on Broadway as a 20s costume piece; Anita Loos wrote the dialogue and was closely involved in all stages of the production. At the time, Hollywood was picking up successful Broadway musicals to tide over financial difficulties which were early intimations of crises to come. These high production values could compete with television and were less risky when based on famous Broadway successes only previously seen in major cities. By the early 50s, 20th Century-Fox was investing all its resources into the development of CinemaScope, which would be launched the same year as the release of *Gentlemen Prefer Blondes*. It was Hawks's only musical (apart from the almost disowned *A Song Is Born*) and his first colour film, leaving aside, that is, the Technicolor sequences incorporated into the fashion show in *Fig Leaves* (1926). Although he emphatically denied involvement with the production numbers, which were directed by the veteran choreographer

Jack Cole, they are integrated into the film's overall themes. The original relation of these themes to the 20s is disguised by updating the situation, which introduces its essential 50s style and includes the topical appearance of the Olympic team, on their way to the 1952 Helsinki Games.[7] Hawks also brought in his old collaborator Hoagy Carmichael, who had appeared as Cricket in *To Have and Have Not*, to compose the Olympic team number and also 'When Love Goes Wrong'. It is probably this song to which Hawks is referring when he says 'I did the little numbers that were part of the story . . . we did a quiet little song that Marilyn sang.'[8]

2. *Gentlemen Prefer Blondes*: the Hawksian Comic Tradition

Hawks was always cavalier with other people's original stories and made the most of his scriptwriters. Jules Furthman completely transformed *To Have and Have Not* (Warner Bros., 1945, with William Faulkner) and *The Big Sleep* (Warner Bros., 1946, with Leigh Brackett and William Faulkner) to accommodate the kind of dialogue Hawks considered 'fun' and to construct the essential framework for a Bacall/Bogart vehicle (which meant a proper love story). A Furthman/Brackett type of script has its own significance within Hawks's collected works. So, indeed, does a Charles Lederer script. Lederer's remodelling of *Gentlemen Prefer Blondes* also conforms to a completely different tradition of Hawks film. This is not to resurrect the old scriptwriter versus director debate but to point out that a director such as Hawks, who was very often his own producer, had the freedom and the finances to build up strands of auteur themes by calling on specific scriptwriters who had specific skills. Lederer was close to Ben Hecht and Charles MacArthur and has the main script credit on *His Girl Friday* (Columbia, 1940), which they adapted collaboratively from Hecht and MacArthur's original Broadway play *The Front Page*. The script collaborations on Hawks's crazy comedies vary but Lederer emerges at a certain point and remains a constant presence. It is almost as though he could be trusted to come up with the Hecht/MacArthur factor – that is, a fast-paced, hectic farce with a slightly sinister undertone.[9]

Hawks's talkie comedies developed their particular style by degrees, but immediately picked up on the comic potential of speech. Dialogue delivered at breakneck speed sets a new rhythm for the films and language becomes the means to deceive, lie, perform and ultimately entrap a victim who doubles as love object. Hawks, in keeping with industry practice at the time, turned to Broadway for material and he used the Hecht/MacArthur partnership to turn the stage play into a screen play. *Twentieth Century* (Columbia, 1934) marks the beginning of the screwball genre, with John Barrymore's performance as Oscar Jaffé. Critics have tended to over-streamline male and female oppositions in Hawks's comedies, leading Molly Haskell to compare Carole Lombard (in *Twentieth Century*) and Katharine Hepburn (in *Bringing Up Baby*). In fact it is the Barrymore performance that foreshadows Hepburn's. Hawks says he cast Barrymore as 'the greatest ham of all time' to play an actor-manager who turns Carole Lombard into a star as she learns how to ham the melodramas of everyday life from him. Their exhibitionist histrionics may be naturalized by the theatrical milieu, but it feminizes Barrymore, who furthermore spends most of the movie in a dressing-gown. His hysteria and histrionics foreshadow Cary Grant's in *His Girl Friday*, the next Hecht/MacArthur adaptation, made six years later. Cary Grant in *His Girl Friday* is just as willing to go to any lengths to win back Rosalind Russell from domesticity, for himself, and for the newspaper, as Barrymore is to win back Carole Lombard from Hollywood, for himself, and for Broadway. However, Walter Burns is not an exhibitionist actor but an unscrupulous newspaperman and consequently the ethical implications of the story are rather different.

In between these two productions, Hawks read a short story which became *Bringing Up Baby* (RKO, 1938) and got the writer, Hagar Wilde, to co-script the screen adaptation with Dudley Nichols. She was then brought back to co-write *I Was a Male War Bride* (20th Century-Fox, 1949) with Lederer. Many of the Hecht/MacArthur themes persist. Katharine Hepburn, in her first great comedy role, continues the fast-talking, reality-evading prototype. By the end of both stories, Cary Grant is forced to capitulate to the heroine's way of seeing the world – that is, the way she wants it rather than the way it rationally is. The gags expose the hero to public humiliation, often involving crossdressing, particularly, of course, in *I Was a Male War Bride*. All Hawks's comic characters of this type, male or female, lie, cheat and go to any lengths to gain their ends. They deliver their line, and their lines, at breakneck speed, talking across rational protest, recklessly regardless of reality. In *The Big Sleep*, Bogart and Bacall suddenly slip out of genre and deliver Hecht/MacArthur-style dialogue at a bewildered policeman on the other end of the telephone. In *Gentlemen Prefer Blondes* (for which Lederer has solo script credit) traces of these comedy themes persist. Although Marilyn Monroe has her own, very particular pace, Lorelei is characteristically histrionic and obsessive, 'hamming' just as Oscar Jaffé 'hams', single-minded like Susan, and as unencumbered by ethics as Walter Burns. But her single-mindedness is directed not so much at a human love object but at diamonds, most particularly, of course, a diamond tiara. And the fictional character's duplicitousness condenses with the ambivalence of Monroe's own image which is, in turn, heightened by her ironic performance of 50s femininity.

The transition from the main body of Hawks comedies to *Gentlemen Prefer Blondes* revolves around *Monkey Business* (20th Century-Fox, 1952), which immediately preceded it, scripted by Hecht and Lederer (with I. A. L. Diamond also credited). Here, both male and female leads (Cary Grant and Ginger Rogers) get to play the part of the reality-rejecting ham. But as the state is induced by taking a youth drug, the element of infantilism, simultaneously evil and innocent, that had always hovered over this character type becomes explicit. The immoral egoism of 'His Majesty the Baby' (Freud's term) combines, in Hawks's comedies, with an insistently anti-adult kind of fun. Earlier that year (1952) Hawks had made the 'Ransom of Red Chief' episode of Fox's *O. Henry's Full House* about a tyrannical child who turns the tables on his kidnappers.[10] In *Monkey*

Business the generational mix-up goes considerably further and meets the male humiliation ritual when Ginger Rogers, in her regressed state, locks Cary Grant (once again the absent-minded professor) out in his pyjamas. In the morning, adult and maternal once more, she wraps him in her very feminine coat, echoing the dressing-gown scene in *Bringing Up Baby*. In *Gentlemen Prefer Blondes*, Lorelei and Dorothy bundle Malone, trouserless, out of their cabin in Dorothy's frilly dressing gown.

The generational cross-overs in the Hawks/Lederer *Gentlemen Prefer Blondes* shift the tone of Anita Loos's original story. Sir Francis Beekman starts off as a parsimonious young man about London. He ages in the intervening versions, but becomes the extremely elderly owner of a South African diamond mine (Charles Coburn) only in the 1953 film. This persona – diamond miner – neatly balances Lorelei's – gold-digger. Mr Henry Spofford III starts off as a puritanical Presbyterian millionaire whom Lorelei ultimately marries, becomes Dorothy's love interest on the stage and ends up as the child (George Winslow) in the film. Earlier Hawksian versions of these two characters have already been established in *Monkey Business*. Charles Coburn had played the elderly business tycoon in search of a youth drug and George Winslow was the serious, husky-voiced child in Cary Grant's 'Red Indian' gang. These two *Monkey Business* veterans might well have inspired Lederer and Hawks to carry the generational cross-over theme to fuse with the demasculinization theme that is so central to their version of *Gentlemen Prefer Blondes*.

3.   Updating Lorelei and Dorothy

Marilyn Monroe herself creates a continuity with *Monkey Business*, in which she gives a witty performance as Charles Coburn's dumb blonde secretary who is not allowed to type. (Watching her walk out of his office, he says thoughtfully: 'Anyone can type.') On the screen, she acts out pure pin-up fantasy for the spectator and, in the story, for Charles Coburn. With hindsight, she exists, even then, on the edge between *acting* a part and *being* the living sex symbol. In her autobiography, Marilyn tells the story of her audition for the Marx Brothers' *Love Happy*. As she walked up and down in front of them, Groucho exclaimed: 'She's Theda Bara, Tallulah Bankhead and Little Bo Peep rolled into one. And don't walk around like that outside the studio.' Just like in the song, Marilyn had worked at her image 'all around the clock'; she knew exactly what she was doing and how to do it. During her years in the Hollywood wilderness, she had taught herself her walk, her voice and her facial expressions, taking acting, dancing and singing lessons. She groomed her dumb blonde look and, adding an almost imperceptible grain of salt to the icon, gave it a certain degree of indecipherability. Although he could see Marilyn's point, neither the look nor the persona that went with it were to Hawks's own taste. The fashions of the 50s were in complete contrast to flapper fashion, which had thrown away Victorian corseting. As Anita Loos says, 'we find in the 20s, a young lady full of grain alcohol had no corset to confine her, her skirt was above her knees normally, her stockings rolled down, and her hair Wind Blown, so that she was at all times in complete Harmony with the natural activities of the Period'.[11]

Marilyn Monroe's career took off after *Gentlemen Prefer Blondes*, which established her fabulous sex symbol status. After *Monkey Business*, Fox had cast her unsuitably in *Niagara* (Henry Hathaway, 1952). Hawks, always a raconteur but not necessarily one with a strict regard for historical accuracy, has given the following account of his discussion with Zanuck about the failure of Monroe's Fox films:

> 'You did real pictures and she isn't real. She's just a complete fantasy, there isn't one real thing in her. She ought to do a musical comedy.' He said, 'She can't sing.' I said 'Yes she can.' 'How do you know?' 'She goes to cocktail parties in Palm Springs, and nobody'll take her home so she comes around and asks if I will. And then she doesn't talk. One time I said "If you can't talk, can you sing?" and she said yes. We turned on the radio and she sang along – so I know she can sing.'

Zanuck said 'OK, you make the picture.' Hawks also told Zanuck he could 'get' Jane Russell. According to his story, her loyalty to him dated back to the time when he had 'found' her working as a dentist's assistant and had suggested her to Howard Hughes for the female lead in *The Outlaw*. Production on *The Outlaw* rambled on for years, with Hawks at some point involved with its direction and script. By the time of *Gentlemen Prefer Blondes*, Russell was a major star, Hollywood sex symbol *par excellence*, and big enough box office to carry the relative newcomer, Marilyn Monroe. Jane Russell, with her tough, wise-cracking persona and straightforward, assured sexuality, has a lot in common with the type of 20s new woman that Anita Loos liked and used as a basis for Dorothy's character. And both of them, Jane Russell and Dorothy Shaw, have a lot in common with the independent, sexually assertive women who appear in so many different Hawks films that they have condensed into the 'Hawksian woman' – tough, smart and sexually experienced.

Naomi Wise saw the connection between the Hawksian woman and the fact that Howard Hawks began his career 'when the flapper age was at its height'.[13] She implies that his taste for female characters who can look after themselves ('that's the kind of girl I like') and initiate romance ('let the girl do the chasing') could well have been formed by a 20s attitude to femininity.

Hawks was thirty in 1926 when he got the chance to direct, and the scripts he developed were very much in tune with fashionable Hollywood productions of the time. While his very first film was a heavy melodrama, out of its failure he learnt the importance of 'fun'. His next three films can be roughly grouped as husband-and-wife comedies, in which questions of sex and money have to be negotiated across comic and quite risky pitfalls to a happy and more conservative end. How to reconcile modernity and marriage was an enduringly popular topic of the time and was a speciality of Cecil B. DeMille, for whom Hawks had briefly worked. These were the last days before the mass conversion to synch sound, before censorship

221

really hit Hollywood, and before the 1929 crash. Both Anita Loos and Howard Hawks would have been addressing a largely female, sexually sophisticated, audience that also wanted 'fun'. Only, perhaps, in Anita Loos's reminiscences of the 20s does this word appear as often as in Hawks's reminiscences of his movie-making career.

Hollywood in the 20s had taken on board the 'new woman' phenomenon, responding to gradual but remarkable changes in women's social and economic status. As the number of women in the workforce escalated, so did the market in female-oriented consumer goods. In the nineteenth-century, department stores and advertisers had pioneered the elision of femininity, commodity and desirability. But as the film industry consolidated in the post-World War I United States, newly emerging 'Hollywood' became the shop window of America. And the shop window offered itself to young women with spending power; since they also accounted for the majority of box-office returns, 'photoplays' had to take them into account. Lary May summarizes Hollywood's response to this phenomenon:

> Films that featured a new woman were usually written by female scenarists and played by one of the large number of actresses under twenty-five who worked in the Hollywood industry. The female heroine was generally found in contemporary urban society and whether she was an emancipated wife or a flapper played by Clara Bow, Mae Murray, Joan Crawford, Gloria Swanson or Norma or Constance Talmadge, she portrayed a restless young woman eager to escape from an ascetic home.[14]

Off screen, the Talmadge sisters and their mother Peg were close friends of Anita Loos, who was particularly fond of Constance. It was her wit, zest for life and not-so-innocent sexuality that Loos has cited as the main source for Dorothy's character. But although the new woman's sexual freedom was reflected on the screen, too much liberation also provoked social anxiety. During the 20s, the United States was engulfed in a moral panic with battles over film censorship at the centre. Anita Loos parodies American puritanism in different ways throughout *Gentlemen Prefer Blondes*. Mr Spofford specializes in 'senshuring' films in Philadelphia, and after their move to Hollywood Lorelei bribes all the girl extras to tell him how wicked they've been so he can save them. Pre-Hays Code Hollywood movies did have to acknowledge and address the 'new woman' but also find ways to defuse and contain her potential for social disruption. In the flapper movies this compromise is achieved through a condensation between femininity and consumption. Female sexuality, once it had become linked to modern fashionableness, could be channelled into commodification and negotiated through male relation to money and power. Anita Loos's characterizations of Lorelei and Dorothy reflect this doubling process of emancipation and commodification. Dorothy is interested in sex and not money; Lorelei is interested in money and not sex. The question of gender relations becomes satirically tied to questions of value and exchange. The free exchange of sexual value is juxtaposed with the quantifiable exchange of commodity value.

Howard Hawks's second film, *Fig Leaves* (William Fox, 1926), for which he also wrote the original story, exemplifies the Lorelei side of the double woman. Eve feels that she never has 'anything to wear' and as Adam won't or can't provide her with 'pretty things' she rebels and starts a modelling career. This makes it possible to show-case Adrian's fashions but it can bring the couple back together in the end with Adam in command of the family finances. Jeanne Thomas Allen has analysed the film in the context of contemporary consumer culture:

> The film's solution is the comedic presentation of an endless chain of buying to reassure social class position after the struggle over ownership – the woman's possession of clothes, the man's possession of the woman. The film's denouement implies that one struggle can be resolved by another: if men continue to buy clothing to please women, they can prevent women from working and gaining economic self-sufficiency . . . the narrative climax and resolution make it clear that for Eve, the appropriate realisation of her goal is the manipulation of her husband.[15]

And she comments: 'The line between "true love" and economically motivated or "purchased" love in the film is a fine one.' This point leads directly across the decades to Hawks's streamlining of Lorelei's character in *Gentlemen Prefer Blondes*.

Hawks's *A Girl in Every Port* (William Fox, 1928) was the film that Hawks was planning to remake just before his death. It has generally been discussed in terms of the male friendship theme and Louise Brooks has been described as undervalued in the part of a *femme fatale*. In fact, she is a gold-digger nursing a broken heart with a luminous transparency that is characteristic of the Hawksian woman and inconceivable in a *femme fatale*. She seduces Victor MacLaglen (title: 'I've got most of his dough and I'm about through'). But she is still in love with his friend, played by Robert Armstrong. She could perhaps have said: 'There was a man once . . .'. When she goes to appeal to Armstrong, she finds him in bed and immediately takes his clothes. The scene foreshadows future Hawksian scenes of female desire and male anxiety, as Armstrong, dressed in his nightshirt, wrapping himself in a blanket, shouts: (title) 'Gimme back my pants!' Louise Brooks stands between the 20s Lorelei-type gold-digger and the later Hawksian woman who, like Susan in *Bringing Up Baby*, Edwina in *Monkey Business* and Dorothy in *Gentlemen Prefer Blondes*, will have no hesitation in stealing the trousers of the man they love. A travelling showgirl, like many of Hawks's future heroines, she was once Tessie from Coney Island and has become 'Mam'zelle Godiva', diving fearlessly from a high wire into a tank of water. She wears a costume which is quite plain apart from an outrageously bejewelled crotch. This slight gesture towards the fetishistic interface between sex and money is central to *Gentlemen Prefer Blondes*, returning in Lorelei's glittering costumes and extended to her understanding of her erotic exchange value (in diamonds).

More obviously *A Girl in Every Port* is about a woman's threat to male friendship, a theme that recurs over and over again in Hawks's action pictures. Friendship between women is hard to find in Hollywood. In *Gentlemen Prefer Blondes*, however, Hawks takes the theme of female friendship straight from the Loos original and maintains its place firmly in the emotional centre of the story. In *The Crowd Roars* (Warner Bros., 1932), he had already demonstrated that he could find space for relationships between women. He gives Ann Dvorak and Joan Blondell enough screen time and dialogue together to establish a real friendship which only later, as the story spirals out of control, becomes overtaken by plot points. But this was still 'before the Code' – before, that is, the gradual ghettoizing of women's problems and preoccupations to 'women's pictures'. Anita Loos claims, in typical style, that the end of Prohibition killed the flapper. There was, of course, also the economic aftermath of the 1929 Wall Street crash and, on the screen, the flapper was hit hard by the increasingly strict censorship that followed the arrival of the talkies. Many directors of the sophisticated sex-and-marriage comedies of the 20s (for instance, both Malcolm St. Clair, director of the 1928 *Gentlemen Prefer Blondes*, and Marshall Neilan,[16] Hawks's dissolute and glamorous early mentor) failed to make it in the changed atmosphere, first of the talkies and then the Hays Code. The 'modern' discourse of sexuality and the female desire it articulated were distorted by the Code, and for the next twenty or so years overt sexuality was invested rather in the image of certain highly erotic female stars.

When Marilyn Monroe, perhaps the apotheosis of this trend, came to superstardom a new, more explicit discourse of sexuality was emerging in the United States in its Korean-war-fuelled affluence. *Gentlemen Prefer Blondes* was released in 1953. The same year saw the publication of the Kinsey Report on female sexuality and the first issue of *Playboy*, with Marilyn on the front cover and her notorious nude calendar pin-up photograph 'Golden Dreams' reissued as the centre spread.[17] While the Kinsey Report focused attention on the 'problem' of female sexuality and women's difficulties in achieving sexual pleasure, *Playboy* represented sexuality as an exclusive male preserve and tailored its images accordingly. Its airbrushed, cosmeticized pin-ups found a consumer acceptability that had evaded previous sex publications, and that was perfectly in keeping with the ethos of the time. This kind of sexual iconography unequivocally addressed a male consumer without any of the ambivalence that had characterized the 20s. The dominant consumer address to women was concentrated on marriage, the home and the values of new suburban prosperity. Sexuality, economics and politics weave together into a capitalist whole, which Marilyn and her persona in *Gentlemen Prefer Blondes* both epitomize and ironize.

4. *Gentlemen Prefer Blondes* as a Hawks comedy
One of Hawks and Lederer's most significant contributions to the film rewrite of *Gentlemen Prefer Blondes* was to give back to Dorothy some of the characteristics that had been discarded in the intervening versions. She had lost her free-wheeling promiscuity and had been married off to the

millionaire Mr Spofford, thus losing her other crucial quality of indifference, verging on aversion, to men with money. Although the film does give Dorothy the private detective as the love interest, he is, at least, poor while Mr Spofford, of course, is turned into a child. This streamlining of Dorothy's character and situation restores the binary opposition between the two women and thus a trace of the 20s antinomy between emancipation and commodification. The theme of infantilism and male impotence that runs through certain Hawks comedies is diffused across the whole of *Gentlemen Prefer Blondes*, affecting its cinematic and comic aesthetic. The erotics of the male gaze, which so often act as a basis for a representation of masculinity on the Hollywood screen, become a central focus for comic role reversal. As the male characters are all drained of erotic allure, the male gaze itself becomes a site of impotence, as Hawks reverses the usual erotic economy of the Hollywood screen and its organization of male and female relations. 'Two Little Girls from Little Rock', the production number which opens the movie, frames the two stars closely enough to crate a spectacle directly for the audience. The image on the screen is literally glittering, organized around a red, white and blue colour coding, and there is no mediation between Jane Russell's and Marilyn Monroe's spectacular, eroticized performance and the spectator. This 'communion' is suddenly interrupted. As Marilyn, in her most characteristic close-up, gazes out of the screen there is a cut to Mr Esmond, who immediately takes the place of the spectator in the exchange of looks. But his image is quite at odds with conventional screen representation of masculinity and, rather than providing a relay for the spectator's gaze, he distances it. His thick glasses underline the weakness of his look and his timid wave is comic and certainly not experienced as an appropriate surrogate that can carry the spectator's look into the screen story.

Then there is the fate of the Olympic team. They first appear, apparently reversing the Mr Esmond effect, in an exaggerated display of conventional masculine voyeurism. Lorelei and Dorothy arrive at the dock as Coach calls the roll and the athletes gradually fall silent before breaking into whistles. (Dorothy and Gus respond respectively: Dorothy: 'The Olympic team! Just for me . . . wasn't that nice of someone?' Gus: 'Dorothy Shaw, I trust you'll keep those athletes to yourself!') But, in an even more dramatic switch in convention than the introduction of Mr Esmond, the Olympic team are promptly deheterosexualized. In the 'Ain't There Anyone Here for Love' number, they perform a chorus dance of physical fitness that is more a homoerotic display than a heterosexual celebration.[18] Gerald Mast struggles with it in the following way:

It is Busby Berkeley in sexual reverse. Given Hawks's deliberate sexual reversals in this film and elsewhere, the parody of Berkeley's sexlessly smiling faces and sexlessly geometicised female limbs may even be intentional. But there is something disturbingly 'Hollywood sterile' about these male bodies, this plethora of well-muscled flesh which is also completely (and repulsively) inhuman.[19]

Once the Olympic team has been dispatched, Dorothy's interest is transferred too Malone, who, at first glance, seems at least within the conventional mould of Hollywood masculinity. But his erotic look is undercut by the fact that he is masquerading as a rich man, while actually spying on Lorelei. As he snaps Lorelei and Piggy through the porthole, his snooping is staged to give him the perverse connotations of a peeping Tom. He is then subjected to one of 'Hawks's deliberate role reversals'. Dorothy and Lorelei make him drunk, drug him, undress him and send him off in a dressing-gown. Malone appears for the first time in the 1953 film, as though Hawks were giving a comic twist to the private eye's serious covert snooping, hinted at in Humphrey Bogart's gay impersonation in *The Big Sleep*.

But the key moments, which provide a clue to the significance of this erasure of masculinity, involve Lorelei's relation to diamonds. She replaces desire as sex/love with money/diamonds. And, the film implies, she understands her erotic value in terms of economic exchange value, and her position as woman as that of ultimate consumer. She can negotiate within the terms offered by the logic of capitalism rather than the logic of romantic love. The close-up of Mr Esmond in the opening sequence is closely followed by Lorelei's extrasensory perception that he has a diamond for her. Piggy is almost literally awestruck when he first sees Lorelei and her X-ray eyes turn his elderly, asexual face into a large and sparkling desirable diamond. The mutual attraction is instantaneous.

5. Final Reflections

The film exaggerates the uncertainty associated with feminine masquerade, not through the film-noir motif of the *femme fatale*, but through its comic extension, the 'dumb blonde'. Jane Russell plays, as it were, the 'straight man' to Marilyn's wild divergence from common sense. Lorelei's attitude to life zigzags between calculation and naivety, so that, combined with her intensely spectacular sexuality, the instability of her persona becomes inscribed into the comedy. But this kind of comic performance involves another level of instability, in which the audience has difficulty separating the performance from the performer. Surely, it takes the most consummate actor to construct a foolish persona? But, on the other hand, Marilyn's public image was of the dumb blonde personified. . . . In this way, the spectator's oscillation between belief in the image and knowledge of its construction is doubly layered, through the genre of comedy, and through the iconography of female sexuality. As Hawks noted, Marilyn's appearance is supremely cosmetic. Her features came to life through the application of make-up. But the more perfect the mask, the more it suggests that something is concealed, which adds a hidden threat to the appearance of beauty. Of course, many stories, legends and folk-tales tell the story of a woman whose beauty is only an appearance which conceals a body that is in fact decaying and disgusting.

Marilyn seemed to have some sense that the artificiality of cosmetics is a protection from the body itself and its inevitable slide into decay. Whitey Snyder, her make-up man who was also a close friend, has told the following anecdote. Once, when Marilyn was about to leave hospital after a minor operation, she sent for Whitey, seeing that fans and press had assembled outside. She said, 'Whitey, if anything should really happen to me – you know what I mean – do you promise you'll do this for me one last time?' He said, 'If I get you while you're warm.' She had a dollar bill clip made for him inscribed 'Whitey, dear, while I'm warm. Love Marilyn.' When she died, Joe Di Maggio reminded Whitey of his promise and he went to the morgue and made up her face – even though she was no longer warm.[20] This connection between cosmetics and death and decay is also implicit in Andy Warhol's Marilyns, especially when the paint drips and smears, leaving her face disintegrating into skeletal shapes.

Hawks's favourite actress was Frances Farmer, who was not only highly professional on the set, but 'real' off it: 'The cleanest, simplest, hardest-working person I ever knew. She came a couple of times to my boat wearing her sweatshirt and her dungarees and carrying a toothbrush in her pocket.'[21] Marilyn, on the other hand, was not 'a professional' but a frightened little girl. Hawks's comment, which could come from one of his own scripts, was: 'She didn't think she was good enough.' In the character of Lorelei Lee, however, are traces of the 20s preoccupations that had marked Hawks's own early movies. The theme of the woman who commodifies herself through her desire to accumulate commodities was worked through in *Fig Leaves* and resurfaces quite appropriately in the consumer-obsessed 50s. On the other hand, whatever Marilyn might have been 'really', her performance belongs to the genre of irrational histrionics that was Hawks's preferred comic raw material. Hawks, despite his own carefully fostered self-image as a gentleman, retained an affection for 'gold-diggers', but emphatically did not prefer blondes, let alone unprofessional ones. Hence the conflicting signals that run through a film which is both auteurist and against the Hawksian grain.

1. Molly Haskell, 'Howard Hawks. Masculine Feminine', *Film Comment*, March–April 1974, p. 34.
2. Maureen Turim, 'Gentlemen Consume Blondes', in Bill Nicholls (ed.), *Movies and Methods*, Vol. 2 (Berkeley: University of California Press, 1985), p. 370.
3. Robin Wood, *Howard Hawks* (London: Secker & Warburg, 1968), p. 171.
4. Peter Wollen, *Signs and Meaning in the Cinema* (London: Secker & Warburg, 1969), p. 91.
5. Charles Eckert, 'The Carole Lombard in Macy's Window', in Gaines and Herzog (eds), *Fabrications* (London: Routledge, 1991), p. 104.
6. Anita Loos, *Fate Keeps on Happening* (New York: Dodd Mead, 1984), p. 54. In *A Girl Like I*, Loos amalgamates the two stories and names Mencken's blonde as Mae Davis. She is more forthright about being 'in love with Menck' and using herself as a model for Dorothy.
7. The Olympic team make a minor appearance in the 1949 musical, perhaps in honour of the 1948 (London) Olympics, which are backdated in the story to 1924 when the Olympics were actually held in Paris. The original novel has no Olympic team. I would like to thank Jerry Delamater for his very kind help in distinguishing between the Broadway and Hollywood versions of the story.
8. Joseph McBride, *Hawks on Hawks* (London: Faber & Faber, 1996), p. 160.
9. Quite coincidentally, Anita Loos knew both Lederer and MacArthur extremely well. Of Lederer she says: 'Charlie Lederer's script for *GPB* was better than I could have done myself' – *A Cast of Thousands* (New York: Crossett and Dunlap, 1977), p. 105. In describing the origins of her friendship with Helen Hayes (who was turned down for the

stage *Gentlemen Prefer Blondes*) she notes, 'I was addicted to a zany young humorist called Charlie MacArthur, who had fallen in love with her' – ibid., p. 148.

10. Peter Wollen draws attention to the theme of regression to childhood in Hawks's crazy comedies, witness the repeated scene of the adult about to be scalped by painted children in *Monkey Business* and 'The Ransom of Red Chief'. In *Monkey Business*, of course, the 'painted children' are led by Cary Grant in his regressed state – *Signs and Meanings*, p. 91.
11. Anita Loos, *Fate Keeps on Happening*, p. 17.
12. Interview with Hawks, *Take One*, vol. 3 no. 8, 1983.
13. Naomi Wise, 'The Hawksian Woman', reprinted in this volume. Tina Olsen Lent's comment: 'In three significant areas, the screwball women protagonists perpetuated the attributes of the flapper . . .' This suggests that the 30s comedy heroines could act as a link between Hawks's origins in the 20s and the emergence of the later 'Hawksian woman' in the 40s – 'Gender Relations in the Screwball Comedy', in Kristine Brunovska Karnick and Henry Jenkins (eds), *Classical Hollywood Comedy* (London: Routledge, 1995), p. 317. See also Peter Wollen's point in the introduction to this book.
14. Lary May, *Screening Out the Past* (Oxford: Oxford University Press, 1980), p. 218.
15. Jeanne Allen, '*Fig Leaves* in Hollywood: Female Representation and Consumer Culture', reprinted in this volume.
16. It is interesting to speculate on the influence that Neilan may have had on Hawks. Adele St John Davies has given the following description of him: 'Mickey was an extremely attractive imp. Everybody was crazy about him. He was as witty a man as I ever knew and if you're as good looking as Mickey was and as charming . . . everybody fell for him. And Pickford wanted him and got him as a director for a while.' It was while Neilan was missing from the set that Mary Pickford gave Hawks his first chance to direct.
17. Richard Dyer's excellent essay 'Monroe and Sexuality' is the source of this point – *Heavenly Bodies: Film Stars and Society* (London and New York: British Film Institute/Macmillan, 1986).
18. Alex Dhoty first pointed out to me that this sequence had longstanding gay cult status. It has since been included in *The Celluloid Closet* (where it appears next to a sequence from *Red River*).
19. Gerald Mast, *Howard Hawks Storyteller* (New York/Oxford: Oxford University Press, 1982), pp. 357–8.
20. See Lawrence Crown, *Marilyn at Twentieth-Century Fox* (London: Zachary Kwintner Books, 1987).
21. *Hawks on Hawks*, p. 117.

Laura Mulvey – teacher, theorist and film-maker – has been probably the most influential voice in British feminist film theory and criticism. Her essay 'Visual Pleasure and Narrative Cinema' (*Screen*, Autumn 1975, reprinted in many anthologies of film theory and criticism and also in Mulvey's own collection of writings, *Visual and Other Pleasures* (London: Macmillan, 1989)) set in train (along with work such as Pam Cook and Claire Johnston's essay on 'The Place of Woman in the Cinema of Raoul Walsh', in Phil Hardy (ed.), *Raoul Walsh* (Edinburgh Film Festival, 1974)) much feminist theoretical work, within a psychoanalytic framework, on voyeurism and the look in cinema (though it was also a sort of scorched-earth manifesto for feminist avant-garde film-making, in which, in association with Peter Wollen, Mulvey was very active in the 1970s and 1980s, with films like *Riddles of the Sphinx* (1977). Clearly, these same concerns inform her essay on *Gentlemen Prefer Blondes* although, apparently paradoxically, Mulvey gives considerable importance to Hawks's authorial vision and his almost conscious address to 'theoretical' issues about looking. At the same time, Mulvey acknowledges a clear debt to the kind of work represented by Jeanne Thomas Allen's essay on *Fig*

Leaves. Mulvey's essay also draws on her more recently focused interest in fetishism, very clear in her most recent collection of writings, *Fetishism and Curiosity* (London: British Film Institute and Bloomington: Indiana University Press, 1996).

Hawks with Carole Lombard and John Barrymore while making *Twentieth Century*

Filmography

While studying at Cornell University, Hawks spent vacations in 1916 and 1917 working in the property department of Famous Players-Lasky Studio. In 1917 he directed several scenes in *The Little Princess* (directed by Marshal Neilan, with Mary Pickford and ZaSu Pitts). After returning from World War I and working as a racing car driver, aviator and aeroplane builder, Hawks independently produced a number of films for directors such as Neilan and Allan Dwan. In 1922, Hawks joined the story department at Paramount, working on the scripts of some forty pictures. In the hope of being able to direct, he moved to MGM in 1924 and spent a year in their story department, leaving to sign a contract with William Fox. Hawks received writing credits on at least four films before directing his first films: *Quicksands* (directed by Jack Conway, 1923, also produced by Hawks), *Tiger Love* (directed by George Melford, 1924), *The Dressmaker from Paris* (directed by Paul Bern, 1925), and *Honesty – The Best Policy* (directed by Chester Bennett, 1926).

Films as Director
Silent Films
1926
The Road to Glory (Fox Film Corp.)
dir: Hawks; *prod:* William Fox; *scr:* L. G. Rigby, from a story by Hawks; *ph:* Joseph August; *cast:* May McAvoy, Leslie Fenton, Ford Sterling, Rockliffe Fellowes.
Premiere: 7 February 1926.

Fig Leaves (Fox Film Corp.)
dir: Hawks; *prod:* Hawks; *scr:* Hope Loring, Louis D. Lighton, from a story by Hawks; *ph:* Joseph August (with two sequences in Technicolor); *ed:* Rose Smith; *cast:* George O'Brien, Olive Borden, Phyllis Haver, Andre de Beranger, Heinie Conklin.
Premiere: 22 August 1926.

231

1927

The Cradle Snatchers (Fox Film Corp.)
dir: Hawks; *prod:* Hawks; *scr:* Sarah Y. Mason, from the play by Russell Medcraft and Norma Mitchell; *ph:* L. William O'Connell; *ed:* Ralph Dixon; *cast:* Louise Fazenda, Ethel Wales, Dorothy Phillips, J. Farrell MacDonald, Franklin Pangborn.
Premiere: 28 May 1927.

Paid to Love (Fox Film Corp.)
dir: Hawks; *prod:* Hawks; *scr:* William M. Conselman, Seton I. Miller, Benjamin Glazer, from a story by Harry Carr; *ph:* L. William O'Connell; *ed:* Ralph Dixon; *cast:* George O'Brien, Virginia Valli, J. Farrell MacDonald, Thomas Jefferson, William Powell.
Premiere: 23 July 1927.

1928

A Girl in Every Port (Fox Film Corp.)
dir: Hawks; *prod:* Hawks; *scr:* Seton I. Miller, Reginald Morris, James Kevin McGuinness, from a story by Hawks; *ph:* L. William O'Connell, Rudolph Berquist; *ed:* Ralph Dixon; *cast:* Victor McLaglen, Robert Armstrong, Louise Brooks, Myrna Loy, William Demarest.
Premiere: 26 February 1928.

Fazil (Fox Film Corp.)
dir: Hawks; *prod:* William Fox; *scr:* Seton I. Miller, Philip Klein, from the play *L'Insoumise* by Pierre Frondaie, and its English adaptation, *Prince Fazil*; *ph:* L. William O'Connell; *ed:* Ralph Dixon; *cast:* Charles Farrell, Greta Nissen, Mae Busch, John Boles, Tyler Brooke, Vadim Uraneff. (Released in both silent and sound effects with music versions).
Premiere: 4 June 1928.

The Air Circus (Fox Film Corp.)
dir: Hawks (dialogue scenes *dir:* Lewis R. Seiler); *prod:* William Fox; *scr:* Seton I. Miller, Norman Z. McLeod, Hugh Herbert, from a story by Graham Baker, Andrew Bennison; *ph:* Dan Clark; *ed:* Ralph Dixon; *cast:* Arthur Lake, David Rollins, Sue Carol, Louise Dresser, Charles Delaney. (A part-talking picture, released with music and synchronised sound effects, as well as dialogue scenes.)
Premiere: 30 September 1928.

1929

Trent's Last Case (Fox Film Corp.)
dir: Hawks; *prod:* Hawks; *scr:* Scott Darling, Beulah Marie Dix, from the novel by E. C. Bentley; *ph:* Hal Rosson; *cast:* Donald Crisp, Raymond Griffith, Raymond Hatton, Marceline Day, Lawrence Gray, Anita Garvin, Edgar Kennedy. (Released in both silent and sound effects with music versions.)

Premiere: 31 March 1929.

Sound Films
1930
The Dawn Patrol (First National-Warner Bros.)
dir: Hawks; *prod:* Hal B. Wallis; *scr:* Hawks, Dan Totheroh, Seton I. Miller, from the story 'The Flight Commander' by John Monk Saunders; *ph:* Ernest Haller; *ed:* Ray Curtiss; *mus:* Leo F. Forbstein; *cast:* Richard Barthelmess, Douglas Fairbanks Jr, Neil Hamilton, William Janney, James Finalyson, Frank McHugh, Gardner James.
Premiere: 10 July 1930.

1931
The Criminal Code (Columbia)
dir: Hawks; *prod:* Hawks, Harry Cohn; *scr:* Seton I. Miller, Fred Niblo Jr, from the play by Martin Flavin; *ph:* Teddy Tetzlaff, James Wong Howe; *ed:* Edward Curtiss; *cast:* Walter Huston, Phillips Holmes, Constance Cummings, Mary Doran, Boris Karloff, Clark Marshall, Andy Devine.
Premiere: 15 January 1931.

1932
Scarface (Scarface, Shame of a Nation) (Atlantic Pictures/United Artists)
dir: Hawks; *prod:* Hawks, Howard Hughes; *scr:* Ben Hecht, Seton I. Miller, John Lee Mahin, W. R. Burnett, Fred Pasley, from the novel by Armitage Trail; *ph:* Lee Garmes, L. William O'Connell; *ed:* Edward Curtiss, Douglas Biggs; *mus:* Adolph Tandler, Gus Arnhcim; *cast:* Paul Muni, Ann Dvorak, Karen Morley, George Raft, Osgood Perkins, Boris Karloff, Vince Barnett, C. Henry Gordon, Inez Palange, Edwin Maxwell. (Produced in 1930, but not released until 1932.)
Premiere: 9 April 1932.

The Crowd Roars (Warner Bros.)
dir: Hawks; *prod:* Hawks, Bryan Foy; *scr:* Kubec Glasmon, John Bright, Seton I. Miller, Niven Busch, from a story by Hawks; *ph:* Sid Hickox, John Stumar; *ed:* Thomas Pratt; *mus:* Leo F. Forstein; *cast:* James Cagney, Joan Blondell, Ann Dvorak, Eric Linden, Guy Kibbee, Frank McHugh, Charlotte Merriam.
Premiere: 16 April 1932.

Tiger Shark (First National-Warner Bros.)
dir: Hawks; *prod:* Hawks, Bryan Foy; *scr:* Wells Root, from the story 'Tuna' by Houston Branch; *ph:* Tony Gaudio; *ed:* Thomas Pratt; *mus:* Leo F. Forbstein; *cast:* Edward G. Robinson, Richard Arlen, Zita Johann, Vince Barnett, J. Carrol Naish, William Ricciardi.
Premiere: 24 September 1932.

1933
Today We Live (MGM)

dir: Hawks; *prod:* Hawks; *scr:* Edith Fitzgerald, Dwight Taylor, William Faulkner, from the story 'Turnabout' by Faulkner; *ph:* Oliver T. Marsh; *ed:* Edward Curtiss; *cast:* Joan Crawford, Gary Cooper, Robert Young, Franchot Tone, Roscoe Karns.
Premiere: 3 March 1933.

1934

Viva Villa! (MGM)
dir: [Hawks], Jack Conway; *prod:* David O. Selznick; *scr:* Ben Hecht, Hawks (uncredited), from the story by Edgcumb Pinchon, O. B. Stade; *ph:* James Wong Howe, Charles G. Clarke; *ed:* Robert J. Kern; *mus:* Herbert Stothart, Juan Aguilar; *cast:* Wallace Beery, Leo Carrillo, Fay Wray, Stuart Erwin, Donald Cook, Henry B. Walthall, Joseph Schildkraut.
Premiere: 27 April 1934.

Twentieth Century (Columbia)
dir: Hawks; *prod:* Hawks; *scr:* Ben Hecht, Charles MacArthur, from their play adapted from the play *Napoleon on Broadway* by Charles Bruce Mulholland; *ph:* Joseph August; *ed:* Gene Havlick; *cast:* John Barrymore, Carole Lombard, Walter Connolly, Roscoe Karns, Charles Levison, Edgar Kennedy, Etienne Girardot.
Premiere: 11 May 1934.

1935

Barbary Coast (Goldwyn Productions/United Artists)
dir: Hawks; *prod:* Samuel Goldwyn; *scr:* Ben Hecht, Charles MacArthur (and Edward Chodorov); *ph:* Ray June; *ed:* Edward Curtiss; *mus:* Alfred Newman; *cast:* Miriam Hopkins, Edward G. Robinson, Joel McCrea, Walter Brennan, Frank Craven, Brian Donlevy, Harry Carey, Donald Meek.
Premiere: 27 September 1935.

1936

Ceiling Zero (Cosmopolitan Productions/First National-Warner Bros.)
dir: Hawks; *prod:* Hawks, Harry Joe Brown; *scr:* Frank Wead, from his play; *ph:* Arthur Edeson; *ed:* William Holmes; *mus:* Leo F. Forbstein; *cast:* James Cagney, Pat O'Brien, June Travis, Stuart Erwin, Barton McLane, Isabel Jewell, Henry Wadsworth.
Premiere: 25 January 1936.

The Road to Glory (20th Century-Fox)
dir: Hawks; *prod:* Darryl F. Zanuck; *scr:* Joel Sayre, William Faulkner, from the film *Les Croix de bois* by Raymond Bernard and the novel by Roland Dorgèles; *ph:* Gregg Toland; *ed:* Edward Curtiss; *mus:* Louis Silvers; *cast:* Fredric March, Warner Baxter, Lionel Barrymore, June Lang, Gregory Ratoff, Victor Kilian.
Premiere: 2 June 1936.

Come and Get It (Goldwyn Productions/United Artists)
dir: Hawks, William Wyler (disclaimed); *prod:* Samuel Goldwyn, Merritt Hulburd; *scr:* Jane Murfin, Jules Furthman, from the novel by Edna Ferber; *ph:* Gregg Toland, Rudolph Maté; *ed:* Edward Curtiss; *mus:* Alfred Newman; *cast:* Edward Arnold, Frances Farmer, Joel McCrea, Walter Brennan, Frank Shields, Andrea Leeds, Mary Nash. (Reissued as *Roaring Timber*).
Premiere: 29 October 1936.

1938
Bringing Up Baby (RKO)
dir: Hawks; *prod:* Hawks; *scr:* Dudley Nichols, Hagar Wilde, from a story by Wilde; *ph:* Russell Metty; *ed:* George Hively; *mus:* Roy Webb; *cast:* Cary Grant, Katharine Hepburn, Charles Ruggles, Walter Catlett, Barry Fitzgerald, May Robson, Fritz Feld, Virginia Walker, George Irving, Leona Roberts, Tala Birell.
Premiere: 18 February 1938.

1939
Only Angels Have Wings (Columbia)
dir: Hawks; *prod:* Hawks; *scr:* Jules Furthman, from a story by Hawks; *ph:* Joseph Walker, Elmer Dyer; *ed:* Viola Lawrence; *mus:* Dimitri Tiomkin; *cast:* Cary Grant, Jean Arthur, Thomas Mitchell, Richard Barthelmess, Sig Ruman, Rita Hayworth, Victor Kilian, John Carroll, Allyn Joslin, Noah Beery Jr, Melissa Sierra.
Premiere: 25 May 1939.

1940
His Girl Friday (Columbia)
dir: Hawks; *prod:* Hawks; *scr:* Charles Lederer, from the play *The Front Page* by Ben Hecht, Charles MacArthur; *ph:* Joseph Walker; *ed:* Gene Havlick; *mus:* Morris Stoloff; *cast:* Cary Grant, Rosalind Russell, Ralph Bellamy, Gene Lockhart, Abner Biberman, Porter Hall, Ernest Truex, Clarence Kolb, Roscoe Karns, Frank Orth, John Qualen, Helen Mack, Alma Kruger, Billy Gilbert, Edwin Maxwell.
Premiere: 18 January 1940.

1941
Sergeant York (Warner Bros.)
dir: Hawks; *prod:* Jesse L. Lasky, Hal B. Wallis; *scr:* Abem Finkel, Harry Chandlee, Howard Koch, John Huston, from *The War Diary of Sergeant York*, edited by Sam Cowan, *Sergeant York and His People*, by Sam Cowan, and *Sergeant York, Last of the Long Hunters*, by Tom Skeyhill; *ph:* Sol Polito; *ed:* William Holmes; *mus:* Max Steiner; *cast:* Gary Cooper, Walter Brennan, Joan Leslie, George Tobias, Stanley Ridges, Margaret Wycherley, Ward Bond, Noah Beery Jr, June Lockhart, Dickie Moore.
Premiere: 9 September 1941.

Ball of Fire (Goldwyn Productions/RKO)
dir: Hawks; *prod:* Samuel Goldwyn; *scr:* Billy Wilder, Charles Brackett, from the story 'From A to Z' by Wilder, Thomas Monroe; *ph:* Gregg Toland; *ed:* Daniel Mandell; *mus:* Alfred Newman; *cast:* Gary Cooper, Barbara Stanwyck, Richard Haydn, Oscar Homolka, Dana Andrews, Dan Duryea, Henry Travers, S. Z. Sakall, Tully Marshall, Leonid Kinskey, Aubrey Mather, Mary Field, Kathleen Howard.
Premiere: 9 January 1942.

1943
Air Force (Warner Bros.)
dir: Hawks; *prod:* Hawks, Hal B. Wallis; *scr:* Dudley Nichols, William Faulkner; *ph:* James Wong Howe; *ed:* George Amy; *mus:* Franz Waxman; *cast:* John Garfield, John Ridgely, George Tobias, Harry Carey, Gig Young, Arthur Kennedy, Charles Drake, James Brown.
Premiere: 20 March 1943.

To Have and Have Not (Warner Bros.)
dir: Hawks; *prod:* Hawks; *scr:* Jules Furthman, William Faulkner, from the novel by Ernest Hemingway; *ph:* Sidney Hickox; *ed:* Christian Nyby; *mus:* Leo F. Forbstein (song 'How Little We Know' by Hoagy Carmichael, Johnny Mercer); *cast:* Humphrey Bogart, Walter Brennan, Lauren Bacall, Hoagy Carmichael, Marcel Dalio, Walter Sande, Dan Seymour, Walter Molnar, Dolores Moran, Sheldon Leonard, Aldo Nadi, Paul Marion.
Premiere: 20 January 1944.

1946
The Big Sleep (Warner Bros.)
dir: Hawks; *prod:* Hawks; *scr:* William Faulkner, Leigh Brackett, Jules Furthman, from the novel by Raymond Chandler; *ph:* Sidney Hickox; *ed:* Christian Nyby; *mus:* Max Steiner; *cast:* Humphrey Bogart, Lauren Bacall, John Ridgely, Louis Jean Heydt, Elisha Cook Jr, Regis Toomey, Sonia Darrin, Bob Steele, Martha Vickers, Tom Rafferty, `Dorothy Malone, Charles Waldron, Charles D. Brown, Tom Fadden.
Premiere: 31 August 1946.

1948
Red River (Monterey Productions/United Artists)
dir: Hawks; *prod:* Hawks; *scr:* Borden Chase, Charles Schnee, from the se-rialised novel *The Chisholm Trail* by Chase, later published as *The Blazing Guns on the Chisholm Trail*; *ph:* Russell Harlan; *ed:* Christian Nyby; *mus:* Dimitri Tiomkin; *cast:* John Wayne, Montgomery Clift, Walter Brennan, John Ireland, Joanne Dru, Noah Beery Jr, Chief Yowlachie, Paul Fix, Hank Worden, Harry Carey Sr, Harry Carey Jr, Ivan Parry, Colleen Gray, Mickey Kuhn, Shelley Winters.
Premiere: 20 August 1948.

A Song Is Born (RKO)
dir: Hawks; *prod:* Samuel Goldwyn; *scr:* Harry Tugend, based on the film
Ball of Fire (Hawks, 1941); *ph:* Gregg Toland (Technicolor); *ed:* Daniel
Mandell; *mus:* Emil Newman, Hugo Friedhofer (songs by Don Raye, Gene
DePaul); *cast:* Danny Kaye, Virginia Mayo, Benny Goodman, Hugh
Herbert, Steve Cochran, J. Edward Bromberg, Felix Bressart, Ludwig
Stossel, O. Z. Whitehead, Esther Dale, Mary Field.
Premiere: 6 November 1948.

1949
I Was a Male War Bride (a.k.a. *You Can't Sleep Here*) (20th Century-Fox)
dir: Hawks; *prod:* Sol C. Siegel; *scr:* Charles Lederer, Leonard Spigelgass,
Hagar Wilde, from a story by Henri Rochard; *ph:* Norbert Brodine,
Osmond H. Borrodaile; *ed:* James B. Clark; *mus:* Cyril Mockridge; *cast:*
Cary Grant, Ann Sheridan, William Neff, Eugene Gericke, Marion
Marshall, Randy Stuart, Kenneth Tobey.
Premiere: September 1949.

1951
The Thing (original title *The Thing from Another World*) (Winchester
Productions/RKO)
dir: Christian Nyby and (uncredited) Hawks; *prod:* Hawks; *scr:* Charles
Lederer, Hawks, from the story 'Who Goes There?' by John W. Campbell
Jr; *ph:* Russell Harlan; *ed:* Roland Cross; *mus:* Dimitri Tiomkin; *cast:*
Kenneth Tobey, Margaret Sheridan, Douglas Spencer, Dewey Martin,
Robert Cornthwaite, James Young, Robert Nichols, John Dierkes, James
Arness, William Self.
Premiere: April 1951.

1952
The Big Sky (Winchester Productions/RKO)
dir: Hawks; *prod:* Hawks; *scr:* Dudley Nichols, from the novel by A. B.
Guthrie Jr; *ph:* Russell Harlan; *ed:* Christian Nyby; *mus:* Dimitri Tiomkin;
cast: Kirk Douglas, Dewey Martin, Arthur Hunnicutt, Elizabeth Threatt,
Hank Worden, Jim Davis, Buddy Baer, Steven Geray, Henri Letondal, Paul
Frees, Barbara Hawks.
Premiere: August 1952.

O. Henry's Full House (episode 'The Ransom of Red Chief') (20th Century-
Fox)
dir: Hawks; *prod:* Andre Hakim; *scr:* Nunnally Johnson, from the short
story by O. Henry; *ph:* Milton Krasner; *ed:* William B. Murphey; *mus:*
Alfred Newman; *cast:* Fred Allen, Oscar Levant, Lee Aaker, Kathleen
Freeman, Alfred Mizner, Robert Easton.
Premiere: September 1952.

Monkey Business (20th Century-Fox)
dir: Hawks; *prod:* Sol C. Siegel; *scr:* Ben Hecht, I. A. L. Diamond, Charles Lederer, from a story by Harry Segall; *ph:* Milton Krasner; *ed:* William B. Murphy; *mus:* Leigh Harline; *cast:* Cary Grant, Ginger Rogers, Charles Coburn, Marilyn Monroe, Hugh Marlowe, Robert Cornthwaite, Esther Dale, George Winslow, Harry Carey Jr, Heinie Conklin.
Premiere: September 1952.

1953
Gentlemen Prefer Blondes (20th Century-Fox)
dir: Hawks; *prod:* Sol C. Siegel; *scr:* Charles Lederer, from the musical comedy by Anita Loos and Joseph Fields, based on the novel by Loos; *ph:* Harry J. Wild (Technicolor); *ed:* Hugh S. Fowler; *mus:* Jule Styne, Leo Robin, Hoagy Carmichael, Harold Adamson; *cast:* Marilyn Monroe, Jane Russell, Charles Coburn, Elliott Reid, Tommy Noonan, George Winslow, Marcel Dalio, Harry Carey Jr.
Premiere: August 1953.

1955
Land of the Pharaohs (Continental Productions/Warner Bros.)
dir: Hawks; *prod:* Hawks; *scr:* William Faulkner, Harry Kurnitz, Harold Jack Bloom; *ph:* Lee Garmes (interiors), Russell Harlan (exteriors) (CinemaScope, Warnercolor); *ed:* Rudi Fehr, V. Sagovsky; *mus:* Dimitri Tiomkin; *cast:* Jack Hawkins, Joan Collins, Dewey Martin, Alexis Minotis, James Robertson Justice, Luisa Boni, Sydney Chaplin, Kerima.
Premiere: 2 July 1955.

1959
Rio Bravo (Armada Productions/Warner Bros.)
dir: Hawks; *prod:* Hawks; *scr:* Jules Furthman, Leigh Brackett, from a story by Barabara Hawks McCampbell; *ph:* Russell Harlan (Technicolor); *ed:* Folmar Blangsted; *mus:* Dimitri Tiomkin; *cast:* John Wayne, Dean Martin, Walter Brennan, Angie Dickinson, Ricky Nelson, Ward Bond, John Russell, Pedro Gonzalez-Gonzalez, Estelita Rodriguez, Claude Akins, Harry Carey Jr, Bob Terhune.
Premiere: 4 April 1959.

1962
Hatari! (Malabar Productions/Paramount)
dir: Hawks; *prod:* Hawks; *scr:* Leigh Brackett, from a story by Harry Kurnitz; *ph:* Russell Harlan, Joseph Brun (Technicolor); *ed:* Stuart Gilmore; *mus:* Henry Mancini; *cast:* John Wayne, Elsa Martinelli, Hardy Kruger, Gérard Blain, Red Buttons, Michèle Girardon, Bruce Cabot, Valentin de Vargas.
Premiere: 31 December 1961.

1964

Man's Favorite Sport? (Gibraltar & Laurel Productions/Universal)
dir: Hawks; *prod:* Hawks; *scr:* John Fenton Murray, Steve McNeil, from
the story 'The Girl Who Almost Got Away' by Pat Franklin; *ph:* Russell
Harlan (Technicolor); *ed:* Stuart Gilmore; *mus:* Henry Mancini; *cast:* Rock
Hudson, Paula Prentiss, Maria Perschy, John McGiver, Charlene Holt,
Roscoe Karns, Norman Alden, Forrest Lewis, Regis Toomey.
Premiere: 29 January 1964.

1965

Red Line 7000 (Laurel Productions/Paramount)
dir: Hawks; *prod:* Hawks; *scr:* Hawks, George Kirgo; *ph:* Milton Krasner
(Technicolor); *ed:* Stuart Gilmore, Bill Brame; *mus:* Nelson Riddle; *cast:*
James Caan, Laura Devon, Gail Hire, Charlene Holt, John Robert
Crawford, Marianna Hill, James Ward, Norman Alden, George Takei.
Premiere: 10 November 1965.

1967

El Dorado (Laurel Productions/Paramount)
dir: Hawks; *prod:* Hawks; *scr:* Leigh Brackett, from the novel *The Stars in
their Courses* by Harry Brown; *ph:* Harold Rosson (Technicolor); *ed:* John
Woodcock; *mus:* Nelson Riddle; *cast:* John Wayne, Robert Mitchum, James
Caan, Charlene Holt, Michele Carey, Arthur Hunnicutt, Christopher
George, R. G. Armstrong, Edward Asner, Paul Fix, Robert Donner, Jim
Davis, Johnny Crawford, Olaf Wieghorst.
Premiere: 31 December 1966.

1970

Rio Lobo (Malabar Productions/Cinema Center)
dir: Hawks; *prod:* Hawks; *scr:* Leigh Brackett, Burton Wohl, from a story
by Wohl; *ph:* William Clothier (Technicolor); *ed:* John Woodcock; *mus:*
Jerry Goldsmith; *cast:* John Wayne, Jorge Rivero, Chris Mitchum, Jack
Elam, Jennifer O'Neill, Susana Dosamantes, Sherry Lansing, Victor French,
David Huddleston, Mike Henry, Bill Williams, Jim Davis, Robert Donner,
George Plimpton, Edward Faulkner, Hank Worden.
Premiere: 6 November 1970.

Other Credits

As well as producing many of his own films, listed above, Hawks also produced *Corvette K-225*, directed by Richard Rosson, 1943, produced by
Universal, with Randolph Scott, Ella Raines, Barry Fitzgerald. Rosson had
been Hawks's assistant on *Scarface* and *Tiger Shark*, and Hawks played a
major role in scripting and production, so much so that the film is often
included in his major credits (as is usually the case also with *The Thing*,
directed by Christian Nyby, who had been Hawks's editor on *The Big Sleep*
and *Red River*).

Hawks also directed, uncredited, parts of several other films before being replaced by other directors: *The Prizefighter and the Lady* (directed by W. S. Van Dyke, 1933); *The Outlaw* (directed by Howard Hughes, 1943). See also *Viva Villa!*, above.

As well as contributing to the screenplays of all his productions, though rarely credited, Hawks also prepared the scripts for, and planned to direct, *Sutter's Gold* (directed by James Cruze, 1936) and *Gunga Din* (directed by George Stevens, 1939).

Hawks also contributed to numerous unrealised scripts (listed in Gerald Mast, *Howard Hawks, Storyteller*) as well as, uncredited, to the screenplays of pictures directed by others, including: *Underworld* (directed by Josef von Sternberg, 1927); *Morocco* (directed by Josef von Sternberg, 1930); *Red Dust* (directed by Victor Fleming, 1932); *Shanghai Express* (directed by Josef von Sternberg, 1932); *Captains Courageous* (directed by Victor Fleming, 1937); *Test Pilot* (directed by Victor Fleming, 1938); *Gone With the Wind* (directed by Victor Fleming, 1939); *Indianapolis Speedway* (directed by Lloyd Bacon, 1939, based on a Hawks story and a remake of *The Crowd Roars*); *For Whom the Bell Tolls* (directed by Sam Wood, 1943); *Murder in the Air* (directed by Lewis Seiler, 1940); *Scandal Sheet* (directed by Phil Karlson, 1946); *Moss Rose* (directed by Gregory Ratoff, 1947); *The Left Hand of God* (directed by Edward Dmytryk, 1955); *The Sun Also Rises* (directed by Henry King, 1957); *Casino Royale* (produced by Charles K. Feldman, 1967).

Bibliography

Astruc, Alexandre, 'Sheriff: Alexandre Astruc Does Justice to Howard Hawks', *Paris-Match*, no. 1108, 1 August 1970, translated in *Wide Angle*, vol. 1 no. 2, Summer 1976.

——, 'A Massacre in Sequence: *Rio Lobo* by Howard Hawks', *Paris-Match*, no. 1139, 6 March 1971, translated in *Wide Angle*, vol. 1 no. 2, Summer 1976.

Bacall, Lauren, *By Myself* (New York: Knopf, 1978; London: Jonathan Cape, 1979).

Becker, Jacques, Rivette, Jacques, and Truffaut, François, 'Interview with Howard Hawks', *Cahiers du Cinéma*, no. 56, February 1956, translated in Andrew Sarris (ed.), *Interviews with Film Directors* (New York: Bobbs-Merrill, 1967).

Bellour, Raymond, 'The Obvious and the Code', *Screen*, vol. 15 no. 4, Winter 1974/5 (close analysis of twelve shots from *The Big Sleep* as an example of classical film form).

Belton, John, '*Monkey Business*', *Film Heritage*, no. 6, Winter 1970/1.

——, 'Hawks and Co.', *Cinema* (UK), no. 9, 1971, reprinted in Joseph McBride (ed.), *Focus on Howard Hawks* (section on *Only Angels Have Wings* reprinted in Belton, *The Hollywood Professionals*, Vol. 3).

——, '*I Was a Male War Bride*', *The Velvet Light Trap*, no. 3, Winter 1971/2 (reprinted in this volume).

——, 'John Wayne: As Sure as the Turning o' the Earth', *The Velvet Light Trap*, no. 7, Winter 1972/3 (on the Wayne 'persona' in *Red River* and *She Wore a Yellow Ribbon*).

——, *The Hollywood Professionals*, Vol. 3, *Howard Hawks, Frank Borzage, Edgar G. Ulmer* (New York: Barnes & Co., 1974).

——, '*Scarface*', *Bright Lights*, vol. 1 no. 4, Summer 1976.

——, Letter on *Red River*, *Movietone News*, no 52, October 1976.

Bernstein, Judith, 'The Valley of the Shadow', *Focus!*, no. 8, Autumn 1972 (on the *Rio Bravo/El Dorado/Rio Lobo* trilogy).

Bogdanovich, Peter, *The Cinema of Howard Hawks* (New York: Museum of Modern Art, 1962) (interview reprinted in *Movie*, no. 5, December 1962, and reprinted in this volume).

——, '*Hatari!*', *Film Culture*, no. 25, Summer 1962.

——, '*El Dorado*', in Joseph McBride (ed.), *Focus on Howard Hawks*.

Bordwell, David, and Thompson, Kristin, *Film Art* (Reading, Mass., and London: Addison-Wesley, 1979; second and third editions New York: Knopf, 1986, 1989; fourth edition New York: McGraw-Hill, 1993) (offers an analysis of the narrative structure of *His Girl Friday* as an example of classical narrative).

Brackett, Leigh, 'A Comment on The Hawksian Woman', *Take One*, July–August 1971.

241

Britton, Andrew, *Katharine Hepburn: Star as Feminist* (London: Studio Vista; New York: Continuum, 1995) (revised edition of Britton, *Katharine Hepburn: The Thirties and After* (Newcastle-upon-Tyne: Tyneside Cinema, 1984) (chapter 7, on Hepburn and Tracy, includes a discussion of *Bringing Up Baby* and *To Have and Have Not*).

Byron, Stuart, '*Auteurism*, Hawks, *Hatari!* and Me', in Philip Nobile (ed.), *Favorite Movies* (New York: Macmillan, 1973).

Campbell, Marilyn, '*His Girl Friday*: Production for Use', *Wide Angle*, vol. 1 no. 2, Summer 1976.

Cavell, Stanley, 'Leopards in Connecticut', *The Georgia Review*, vol. 30 no. 2, Summer 1976 (on *Bringing Up Baby*), reprinted in revised form in Cavell, *Pursuits of Happiness*, reprinted in this volume.

——, *Pursuits of Happiness: The Hollywood Comedy of Remarriage* (Cambridge, Mass., and London: Harvard University Press, 1981) (chapters on *Bringing Up Baby* and *His Girl Friday*).

Clarens, Carlos, *Crime Movies* (London: Secker & Warburg, 1980) (includes a discussion of *Scarface*).

Cohen, Mitchell, 'Hawks in the 30s', *Take One*, vol. 4 no. 12, 1975.

Comolli, Jean-Louis, 'The Ironical Howard Hawks', *Cahiers du Cinéma*, no. 160, November 1964, translated in Jim Hillier (ed.), *Cahiers du Cinéma* Vol. 2 (London: Routledge & Kegan Paul; Cambridge, Mass.: Harvard University Press, 1986).

Corliss, Richard, *Talking Pictures: Screenwriters in the American Cinema* (Woodstock, NY: The Overlook Press, 1974) (see sections on Ben Hecht and *Scarface*, Borden Chase and *Red River* (reprinted in this volume), Billy Wilder and *Ball of Fire*, Charles Lederer and *His Girl Friday* and *Gentlemen Prefer Blondes*).

—— (ed.), *The Hollywood Screenwriters* (New York: Avon Books, 1962) (see Corliss on Ben Hecht, Richard Koszarski on Jules Furthman and interview with Borden Chase by Jim Kitses).

D'Arc, James V., 'Howard Hawks and the Great Paper Chase: Memoirs of a Desert Encounter', in Boorman, John, and Donohue, Walter, *Projections 6* (London: Faber & Faber, 1996).

Durgnat, Raymond, 'Hawks Isn't Good Enough', *Film Comment*, vol. 13 no. 4, July–August 1977 (see William Paul, below).

——, 'Durgnat vs. Paul', *Film Comment*, vol. 14 no. 2, March–April 1978.

Dyer, Peter John, 'Sling the Lamps Low', *Sight and Sound*, vol. 31 no. 3, Summer 1962.

Farber, Manny, 'Underground Films', *Commentary*, November 1957 (reprinted in Farber, *Negative Space* (New York: Praeger; London: Studio Vista, 1971); and in this volume).

——, 'Howard Hawks', *Artforum*, April 1969 (reprinted in Farber, *Negative Space*, and in Joseph McBride (ed.), *Focus on Howard Hawks*.

Ford, Greg, 'Mostly on *Rio Lobo*', *Film Heritage*, Fall 1971 (reprinted in Joseph McBride (ed.), *Focus on Howard Hawks*.

Goodwin, Michael, and Wise, Naomi, 'An Interview with Howard Hawks', *Take One*, vol. 3 no. 8, July–August 1971.

Gregory, Charles, 'Knight Without Meaning?', *Sight and Sound*, vol. 42 no. 3, Summer 1973 (on Hollywood representations of Raymond Chandler's Philip Marlowe, including *The Big Sleep*).

Haskell, Molly, 'The Cinema of Howard Hawks', *Intellectual Digest*, April 1972.

——, 'Man's Favorite Sport? (Revisited)', originally published in *The Village Voice*, 21 January 1971; revised version reprinted in Joseph McBride (ed.), *Focus on Howard Hawks*, and in this volume.

——, *From Reverence to Rape: The Treatment of Women in the Movies* (New York: Holt, Rinehart & Winston, 1973, 1974; London: New English Library, 1974 (see chapters on 'The Thirties' and 'The Forties').

——, 'Howard Hawks: Masculine Feminine', *Film Comment*, vol. 10 no. 2, March–April 1974.

——, 'Howard Hawks', in Richard Roud (ed.), *Cinema: A Critical Dictionary* (London: Secker & Warburg; New York: Viking Press, 1980).

Hogue, Peter, 'Hawks and Faulkner: *Today We Live*', *Literature/Film Quarterly*, vol. 9 no. 1, January 1981.

Jameson, Richard T., 'Talking and Doing in *Rio Bravo*', *The Velvet Light Trap*, no. 12, Spring 1974.

——, 'People Who Need People', *Movietone News*, no. 40, April 1975 (on *To Have and Have Not*).

Kawin, Bruce, *Faulkner and Film* (New York: Frederick Ungar, 1977) (chapter 4 discusses Faulkner's work on a number of Hawks films, part of which is reprinted in this volume).

—— (ed.), *To Have and Have Not* (Madison: University of Wisconsin Press, 1980) (the screenplay, with a long introduction by Kawin).

Keith, Slim, with Tapert, Annette, *Slim* (New York: Simon & Schuster, 1990), extract pubished in this volume.

Langlois, Henri, 'The Modernity of Howard Hawks', *Cahiers du Cinéma*, no. 139, January 1963, translated in Joseph McBride (ed.), *The Films of Howard Hawks* (reprinted in this volume).

Lehman, Peter (*et al.*), 'Howard Hawks: A Private Interview', *Wide Angle*, vol. 1 no. 2, Summer 1976.

Luhr, William, 'Howard Hawks: Hawksthief: Patterns of Continuity in *Rio Bravo*, *El Dorado*, and *Rio Lobo*', *Wide Angle*, vol. 1 no. 2, Summer 1976.

McBride, Joseph (ed.), *Focus on Howard Hawks* (Englewood Cliffs, NJ: Prentice-Hall, 1972) (essays entered separately by author in this bibliography).

——, 'Hawks', *Film Comment*, vol. 14 no 2, March–April 1978.

——, *Hawks on Hawks* (Berkeley, Los Angeles and London: University of California Press, 1982; London: Faber and Faber, 1996).

——, 'Working with Writers', in Boorman, John, and Donohue, Walter, *Projections* 6 (London: Faber & Faber, 1996); extracted from McBride, *Hawks on Hawks*.

——, 'Do I Get to Play the Drunk This Time? An Encounter with Howard Hawks', *Sight and Sound*, vol. 40 no. 2, Spring 1971.

McBride, Joseph, and Peary, Gerald, 'Hawks Talks', *Film Comment*, vol. 10 no. 3, May–June 1974.

McBride, Joseph, and Wilmington, Michael, 'A Discussion with the Audience of the 1970 Chicago Film Festival', in Joseph McBride (ed.), *Focus on Howard Hawks*.

McNiven, Roger, 'Howard Hawks, *Monkey Business*', *Bright Lights*, vol. 1 no. 3, Spring 1975.

Mast, Gerald, *Howard Hawks, Storyteller* (New York and Oxford: Oxford University Press, 1982).

Monaco, James, 'Notes on *The Big Sleep*/Thirty Years After', *Sight and Sound*, vol. 44 no. 1, Winter 1974/5.

Murphy, Kathleen, 'Of Babies, Bones and Butterflies', *Moveietone News*, no. 54, June 1977 (on *Bringing Up Baby*, an excerpt from Murphy's PhD dissertation,

'Howard Hawks: An American Auteur in the Hemingway Tradition', University of Washington, 1977).

Narboni, Jean, 'Against the Clock: *Red Line 7000*', *Cahiers du Cinéma*, no. 180, July 1966, translated in Jim Hillier (ed.), *Cahiers du Cinéma* Vol. 2 (London: Routledge & Kegan Paul; Cambridge, Mass.: Harvard University Press, 1986).

Paul, William, 'Hawks vs. Durgnat', *Film Comment*, vol. 14 no. 1, January/February 1978.

Peary, Gerald, and Groark, Stephen, 'Hawks at Warner Brothers: 1932', *The Velvet Light Trap*, no. 1, June 1971 (discussions of *The Crowd Roars* and *Tiger Shark*; Peary on *The Crowd Roars* is reprinted as 'Fast Cars and Women' in Joseph McBride (ed.), *Focus on Howard Hawks*).

Perkins, V. F., 'Comedies', *Movie*, no. 5, December 1962 (reprinted in Ian Cameron (ed.), *Movie Reader* (London: November Books; New York: Praeger, 1972) and in this volume).

——, '*Hatari!*' *Movie*, no. 5, December 1962 (reprinted in Ian Cameron (ed.), *Movie Reader* (London: November Books; New York: Praeger, 1972)).

Poague, Leland A., *Howard Hawks* (Boston, Mass.: Twayne Publishers, 1982).

Powers, Tom, '*His Girl Friday*: Screwball Liberation', *Jump Cut*, no. 17, 1978.

Ray, Robert B., *A Certain Tendency of the Hollywood Cinema 1930–1980* (Princeton, NJ: Princeton University Press, 1985) (Chapter 4, 'Classic Hollywood's Holding Pattern', is reprinted in this volume).

Richards, Jeffrey, 'The Silent Films of Howard Hawks', *Focus on Film*, no. 25, 1976.

Rivette, Jacques, 'Génie de Howard Hawks', *Cahiers du Cinéma*, no. 23, May 1953 (reprinted as 'Rivette on Hawks' in *Movie*, no. 5, December 1962, and as 'The Genius of Howard Hawks' in Joseph McBride (ed.), *Focus on Howard Hawks*, and in Jim Hillier (ed.), *Cahiers du Cinéma* (London: Routledge & Kegan Paul; Cambridge, Mass.: Harvard University Press, 1985), Vol. 1 (also reprinted in this volume)).

Rohmer, Eric, 'Howard Hawks: *The Big Sky*', *Cahiers du Cinéma*, no. 23, May 1953, translated in Eric Rohmer, *The Taste for Beauty* (Cambridge and New York: Cambridge University Press, 1989).

Rothman, William, 'To Have and Have Not Adapted a Film from a Novel', in Gerald Peary and Roger Shatzkin (eds), *The Modern American Novel and the Movies* (New York: Frederick Ungar, 1978); reprinted in William Rothman, *The 'I' of the Camera* (Cambridge and New York: Cambridge University Press, 1988).

——, 'Howard Hawks and *Bringing Up Baby*', in Rothman, *The 'I' of the Camera* (Cambridge and New York: Cambridge University Press, 1988).

Russell, Lee, 'Howard Hawks', *New Left Review*, no. 24, March–April 1964 (reprinted in this volume).

Sarris, Andrew, 'The World of Howard Hawks', *Films and Filming*, July 1962 and August 1962 (reprinted in Joseph McBride (ed.), *Focus on Howard Hawks*).

——, 'Howard Hawks', in Sarris, *The American Cinema* (New York: E. P. Dutton, 1968) (reprinted in this volume).

——, Review of *El Dorado*, *The Village Voice*, 27 July 1967; reprinted in Sarris, *Confessions of a Cultist* (New York: Simon & Schuster, 1971).

Shatzkin, Roger, 'Who Cares Who Killed Owen Taylor?', in Gerald Peary and Roger Shatzkin, *The Modern American Novel and the Movies* (New York: Frederick Ungar, 1978) (comparison of Chandler's novel and the Hawks film of *The Big Sleep*).

Shivas, Mark, 'Blondes', *Movie*, no. 5, December 1962 (reprinted in Ian Cameron (ed.), *Movie Reader* (London: November Books; New York: Praeger, 1972)) (on *Gentlemen Prefer Blondes*).

Suid, Lawrence Howard (ed.), *Air Force* (Madison: University of Wisconsin Press, 1983) (the screenplay, with a long introduction by Suid).

Thomas, Deborah, 'John Wayne's Body', in Ian Cameron and Douglas Pye (eds), *The Movie Book of the Western* (London: Studio Vista, 1966; published as *The Book of Westerns*, New York: Continuum, 1996) (discussion of Wayne as star with case studies of Ford's *Rio Grande* and Hawks's *Rio Bravo*).

Thompson, Richard, 'Hawks at Seventy', *December*, Winter 1966 (reprinted in Joseph McBride (ed.), *Persistence of Vision* (Madison: Wisconsin Film Society Press, 1968), and in McBride (ed.), *Focus on Howard Hawks*) (on *Red Line 7000*).

Thomson, David, *Movie Man* (London: Secker & Warburg, 1967) (several references to Hawks, as well as a section on Hawks – 'Behaviourist: Hawks' – in chapter 6, 'Narrative Personality').

——, 'All Along the River', *Sight and Sound*, vol. 46 no. 1, Winter 1976/7 (on *Red River*).

——, *A Biographical Dictionary of Film* (London: André Deutsch; New York: Knopf, 1994); originally published as *A Biographical Dictionary of the Cinema* (London: Secker & Warburg, 1970, revised 1975) (entry on Hawks).

——, *The Big Sleep* (London: British Film Institute Film Classics, forthcoming 1996).

Turim, Maureen, 'Gentlemen Consume Blondes', *Wide Angle*, vol. 1 no. 1 (revised and expanded, 1979) (on *Gentlemen Prefer Blondes*).

Walker, Michael, '*The Big Sleep*: Howard Hawks and Film Noir', in Ian Cameron (ed.), *The Movie Book of Film* (London: Studio Vista; New York: Continuum, 1992).

Wellman, William, Jr, 'Howard Hawks: The Distance Runner', *Action*, November–December 1970 (reprinted in McBride (ed.), *Focus on Howard Hawks*).

Williams, Alan, 'Narrative Patterns in *Only Angels Have Wings*', *Quarterly Review of Film Studies*, vol. 1 no. 4, November 1976.

Willis, Donald C., *The Films of Howard Hawks* (Metuchen, NJ: The Scarecrow Press, 1975).

Wise, Naomi, 'The Hawksian Woman', *Take One*, vol. 3 no. 3, April 1972 (reprinted in this volume).

Wollen, Peter, *Signs and Meaning in the Cinema* (London: Secker & Warburg; Bloomington: Indiana University Press, 1969; second edition, 1972) (chapter on 'The Auteur Theory').

Wood, Robin, 'Rio Bravo', *Movie*, no. 5, December 1962.

——, 'Who the Hell is Howard Hawks?', *Focus!*, no. 1, February 1967, and no. 2, March 1967.

——, *Howard Hawks* (London: Secker & Warburg; Garden City, NY: Doubleday, 1968; reprinted with a 'Retrospect', London: British Film Institute, 1981) (the section on *Rio Bravo* from chapter 2 and the 1981 'Retrospect' are both reprinted in this volume).

——, 'To Have (Written) and Have Not (Directed)', *Film Comment*, vol. 9 no. 3, May–June 1973 (on authorship and *To Have and Have Not*).

——, 'Acting Up', *Film Comment*, vol. 12 no. 2, March–April 1976 (about film acting, including a discussion of the opening scene of *The Big Sleep*).

——, *Personal Views* (London: Gordon Fraser, 1976) (the chapters 'Reflections on the Auteur Theory' and 'Hawks De-Wollenized' both relate to Hawks and criticism).

——, 'Responsibilities of a Gay Film Critic', *Film Comment*, vol. 14 no. 1, January–February 1978 (includes a discussion of the way in which Wood's view of Hawks – as well as of Renoir and Bergman – has changed since his 1968 study in the context of his acknowledgment of his gayness).

Index